MURDER, Inc.

MURDER, Inc.

THE CIA UNDER JOHN F. KENNEDY

JAMES H. JOHNSTON

Potomac Books

AN IMPRINT OF THE UNIVERSITY OF NEBRASKA PRESS

All rights reserved. Potomac Books is an imprint of
the University of Nebraska Press.
Manufactured in the United States of America.

Library of Congress Cataloging-in-Publication Data
Names: Johnston, James H., 1944– author.
Title: Murder, Inc.: the CIA under John F. Kennedy
/ James H. Johnston. Other titles: Murder,
Incorporated
Description: [Lincoln, Nebraska]: Potomac Books, an
imprint of the University of Nebraska Press, [2019] |
Includes bibliographical references and index.
Identifiers: LCCN 2018055529
ISBN 9781640121553 (cloth: alk. paper)
ISBN 9781640122147 (epub)
ISBN 9781640122154 (mobi)
ISBN 9781640122161 (pdf)
Subjects: LCSH: United States. Central Intelligence
Agency—History—20th century. | United States.
Central Intelligence Agency—Corrupt practices. |
Intelligence service—United States—History—20th
century. | Assassination—United States—History.
| Kennedy, John F. (John Fitzgerald), 1917–1963. |
United States—Foreign relations—1961–1963.
Classification: LCC JK468.16 J628 2019 | DDC
327.1273009/046—dc23 LC record available at
https://lccn.loc.gov/2018055529

Set in Questa by E. Cuddy.

To my sister, Joan Mulkern, for encouraging me to write and to my brother, Mike Johnston, for encouraging me to write this particular book.

CONTENTS

Introduction . . ix

1. Castro, Oswald, and Kennedy . . 1
2. The Bay of Pigs . . 14
3. Mongoose . . 27
4. Missile Crisis . . 38
5. The Brigade . . 53
6. Fidel and Hidell . . 73
7. Oswald in New Orleans . . 84
8. Assassins and Spies . . 94
9. AMLASH . . 101
10. Mexico City . . 111
11. Hubris . . 121
12. Carpe Diem . . 130
13. The Plot Accelerates . . 137
14. The Last Weekend . . 143
15. A Barrier Once Removed . . 148
16. John Kennedy and the Rogue Elephant . . 152
17. Washington, Paris, and Dallas . . 159
18. November 22, 1963, in Dallas . . 163
19. November 22, 1963, in Other Cities . . 170
20. The Days After . . 176
21. An Investigation Hobbled from the Start . . 181
22. The Investigation Sputters On . . 192
23. Regime Change . . 197
24. The Warren Report . . 211
25. The Never-Ending Investigations . . 225
26. John Kennedy and the CIA . . 237
27. Lyndon Johnson and the CIA . . 245

Acknowledgments . . 253
Appendix A: Where It Might Have Led . . 255
Appendix B: Richard Helms's Testimony on
  the Assassination Investigation . . 267
Appendix C: Sources and Secret Files . . 271
Notes . . 273
Bibliography . . 331
Index . . 335

INTRODUCTION

Late in life, former president Lyndon Johnson told a reporter that he didn't believe the Warren Commission's finding that Lee Harvey Oswald acted alone in killing President John Kennedy. Johnson felt that Cuban president Fidel Castro was behind it. After all, Johnson continued, Kennedy was running "a damned Murder, Inc. in the Caribbean," giving Castro reason to retaliate.[1] A later Senate investigation reported on the CIA's assassination operations but was skimpy with details. However, since then the secret files on the CIA's Cuban operations have been made public, allowing this more complete and troubling story about the operations and their effect on the Warren Commission investigation of Kennedy's death.

Kennedy's animosity toward Castro is well known. He ordered an invasion of Cuba at the Bay of Pigs in 1961 and moved to the brink of World War III in the Cuban Missile Crisis in 1962. Hidden by secrecy, however, is the fact that the assassination operations were a continuing part of the CIA's bag of tricks and played a role in both events.

When the CIA entered the assassination business, it turned to organized crime to do the dirty work of killing Castro. This began in the last few months of the Eisenhower administration. But after an assassination plan went awry, the CIA's Bay of Pigs invasion was the only other option for getting rid of Castro as quickly as the new president, Kennedy, wanted. The underworld plots didn't end though. The CIA continued trying for eighteen more months. Apparently, it even had an assassination team in Cuba during the missile crisis. The CIA's long-term relationship with the mob proved sordid. When mobster Sam Giancana was caught illegally wiretapping one of his girlfriends, he essentially black-mailed the agency into blocking the FBI investigation. The CIA's relationship with the mob became even more problematic after FBI director J. Edgar Hoover discovered Kennedy was having an affair with another of Giancana's girlfriends.

The underworld operations ended with the missile crisis in October 1962. By the next April, the CIA had a new head of Cuban operations, Desmond FitzGerald. He proposed a coup in Cuba. Orchestrating a coup was a conventional way to bring about regime change, FitzGerald argued. Given a green light by the president, the CIA recruited Castro's friend Rolando Cubela, who felt Castro had to be "eliminated" at the start of the coup. He wanted the CIA to give him assassination weapons. Having a direct hand in mur-der gave the agency pause, but after off-the-record meetings with Attorney General Robert Kennedy and the president on Novem-ber 19, 1963, the CIA made the decision to give Cubela the weap-ons. It was working out the details with him at the very moment the president was murdered three days later.

The obvious question at the time should have been whether Cas-tro had retaliated. In September 1963 he had said that U.S. leaders would not be safe if the CIA plotting against him continued, and it had. The CIA also knew that Oswald met with Cuban intelligence officers in Mexico soon afterward. But it never mentioned its plots to the Warren Commission, and there is no evidence it investi-gated retaliation on its own. When questioned in a later congres-sional investigation, a CIA officer blandly said, "I don't believe the thought [of retaliation] ever occurred to me at the time."[2]

The denial is ludicrous of course. But why hide the Cubela oper-ation? If Kennedy knew of and approved it, then the CIA may have thought itself a kind of Praetorian Guard, protecting his memory and legacy from word of the dirty business becoming public. If he did not approve, though, then the CIA was protecting only itself. The public would probably have demanded the CIA be abolished at the mere hint its operation had backfired and resulted in the death of the president regardless of whether Castro was responsible.

But suppose the CIA told the new president, Lyndon Johnson. If he authorized a cover-up, the CIA would be exonerated by history although it could still be faulted for being a Praetorian Guard beholden to presidents rather than the public. This would explain Johnson's Murder, Inc., comment.

I was introduced to the subject as a lawyer for the 1975–76 Senate Intelligence Committee investigations of CIA assassination plots and of links between those and Kennedy's death and questioned some of the witnesses quoted in this book. Committee chairman Senator Frank Church (D-ID), for whom the committee was named, coined the phrase "rogue elephant" to ask if presidents had approved assassination efforts or if the CIA had charged off on its own. The committee chose rogue elephant but did not seem particularly alarmed at the implication that, if this were true, the CIA was dangerously out of control.

No one could challenge the conclusion because the underlying documents and testimony were classified. However, in 1992 Congress passed a law to make public the secret files on Kennedy's assassination. As a result a huge trove of material not only on the assassination but also on Kennedy's and Johnson's Cuban policies was turned over to the National Archives. This included a great deal of material that had not been made available to the Senate investigation. Thus this book is sourced from formerly classified national security documents and testimony. It includes not only the high-level deliberations on the operations but also the spycraft of assassination.

This is largely a chronological narrative. Chapter 1 sets the background, telling who Fidel Castro, Lee Harvey Oswald, and John Kennedy were. The next six chapters summarize the early years of the Kennedy administration's approach to Cuba, including the attempt to invade the island at the Bay of Pigs, underworld plots to assassinate Castro, the pointless Operation Mongoose to harass the Cuban regime, and the Cuban Missile Crisis. Chapter 8 breaks from the chronological approach to provide a primer on the bloody subject of assassination.

The chronological narrative picks up again in chapters 9 through 18 and details how the highest levels of the national security establishment of the United States were won over to a CIA plan to oust Castro in a coup in the fall of 1963, a coup to be triggered by his assassination, and how the assassination aspect came to the fore in the last, fatal week of Kennedy's life.

Chapters 19 through 25 deal with the investigation of Kennedy's murder, Lyndon Johnson's succession to the presidency, his quick dismantling of Kennedy's plan to oust Castro, and investigations by the Warren Commission, the Rockefeller Commission, the Church Committee (Senate Select Committee on Intelligence), and the House Assassinations Committee. Chapter 26 is a summary of events during the Kennedy administration, while the final chapter, 27, summarizes what happened under Lyndon Johnson and examines the claims of senior CIA officers that they never made a connection between the plot to kill Castro and the assassination of the president.

There are three appendices. The first considers the implications of all this for the Warren Commission's conclusion that Oswald acted alone and details how the commission failed to follow leads of foreign involvement. The second consists of the testimony before the Rockefeller Commission and the Church Committee by Richard Helms, the CIA's deputy director in 1963, as he cleverly avoided answering questions of whether President Kennedy had known about the CIA's assassination efforts. The third explains what the so-called secret files are and what is missing from them.

In his inaugural address, John Kennedy said: "Let every nation know, whether it wishes us well or ill, that we shall pay any price, bear any burden, meet any hardship, support any friend, oppose any foe to assure the survival and the success of liberty." Did his pursuit of freedom for Cubans lead to his paying the ultimate price?

MURDER, Inc.

1

Castro, Oswald, and Kennedy

Fidel Castro was born in Cuba on August 13, 1926.[1] His father was born in Spain and immigrated to Cuba. Young Fidel was raised Roman Catholic and attended Catholic boarding schools, but he fell away from the church before adulthood. In 1945 he began the study of law at the University of Havana, where he took an interest in a movement that advocated ousting dictators throughout Latin America. He also had personal political ambitions. In 1952 he ran for a seat in Cuba's House of Representatives. His plans were stymied when General Fulgencio Batista, who had been living in the United States, returned to Cuba to lead a coup. Batista took over the government, canceled the election, and put himself in power. Castro decided his only recourse was to overthrow the dictator running his own country.

Initially, Castro used peaceful means. When these failed, he commanded an armed attack on a Cuban army base, the Moncada Barracks, on July 26, 1953. Many of his followers were killed; the rest, including Fidel and his brother Raul, were captured, tried, and convicted. Castro received a fifteen-year sentence but was released after two years. He then moved to Mexico and organized what he called the Twenty-Sixth of July Movement with the aim of returning to Cuba with a guerilla force and driving out Batista.

On December 2, 1956, Castro and his small paramilitary contingent landed on a beach in Cuba. Author Tad Szulc opens his biography of the Cuban leader with Castro crawling through the sand with his favorite weapon in hand, a Belgian-made light automatic rifle known by the abbreviation FAL. The weapon, equipped with a telescopic sight, allowed Castro to kill from a distance. Inexperienced and poorly equipped, Castro's forces were nearly wiped out by Batista's army, but Fidel, Raul, and the Argentinean Ernesto Guevara escaped to the countryside, where they launched a guerilla war. Guevara has gone down in history as Che, which is slang in South America for an Argentinean.

Castro's Twenty-Sixth of July Movement gained popular support in Cuba and began to grow. The United States attempted to be neutral, striving to help neither Batista nor Castro. A later study prepared by the Department of the Army was highly critical of this neutrality. It noted that someone had said, sarcastically, that U.S. policy toward Cuba was "so inept and ineffectual that it was pro-Batista to Castro and pro-Castro to Batista." The study concluded: "On balance, it seems that Batista was favored as long as he was capable of benefiting from favors . . . but, primarily because United States 'non-intervention' generally favored the status quo."[2]

The administration of President Dwight Eisenhower held stubbornly to this policy to the very end, rejecting requests to meet with emissaries both from Castro and from the Cuban military, which wanted to offer an alternative to Batista.[3] The result was that barely two years after Castro's landing, Batista gave up power and fled the country on January 1, 1959. Castro had won. In February he made himself premier.[4] At first his victory was well received in the United States. When he went to Washington DC in March 1959, he was a guest on the popular television show *Meet the Press*.[5]

The U.S. government, on the other hand, continued its policy of neutrality, and the policy continued to be a failure. Claiming it was not taking sides, the United States did nothing as the new Cuban government nationalized industry, seized American-owned enterprises, and instituted farm collectives. Cuban government appropriation of private land holdings began in June 1959. It was a mammoth undertaking. For example, all told, Atlantica del Golfo Sugar Company lost more than four hundred thousand acres of land.[6]

In January 1960, a year after Castro's takeover, President Eisenhower reiterated that the United States would not intervene in the domestic affairs of any country, including Cuba, although he mildly complained about certain actions of the Cuban government that were contrary to international law and the rights of American citizens.[7] When a plane sent by Cuban exiles bombed Cuba and crashed, killing its American pilot, Eisenhower insisted on maintaining neutrality and ordered the U.S. government to stop any more such air attacks on Cuba.[8]

But with its eyes on the upcoming presidential election in November 1960, the Eisenhower administration soon took a harder line toward Cuba and began verbal sparring with the Soviet Union about the island country. In February the administration rejected a Cuban offer to negotiate differences, while the Soviets took the friendly approach of sending Deputy Premier Anastas Mikoyan to Cuba to work out a trade deal and to announce that the Soviets would send "technicians" to the island.[9]

In May the Eisenhower administration said it would end military aid to Cuba within a month and end all economic aid by the end of the year. The administration upped the ante in July by using new legislative authority to cut Cuban sugar sales to the United States by 95 percent. This action alone cost Cuba an estimated $92.5 million in revenue. Soviet Premier Nikita Khrushchev taunted the U.S. military cutoff by saying, "Soviet artillerymen can support the Cuban people with their rocket fire if the aggressive forces in the Pentagon dare to launch an intervention against Cuba." When Eisenhower responded that the United States would not be deterred by Soviet threats, Che Guevara fired back, "We are defended by one of the most powerful military forces in history" and added that the Monroe Doctrine, which warned European countries not to get involved in Latin America, was dead.[10]

The verbal fight between the United States and the Soviet Union escalated. Khrushchev suggested he might put Russian missiles on the island, forcing Eisenhower to respond that he would not "permit the establishment of a regime dominated by international Communism in the Western Hemisphere." But in August Eisenhower confused his message by warning simultaneously that he would take "definite action" if Cuba fell under the control of the Communists and then contradicting himself by adding that he did not see "how the United States could properly object or intervene" if the Cuban people freely chose Communism. The same month, under prodding from the United States, Latin American foreign ministers to the Organization of American States warned the Soviet Union not to "export its doctrine or otherwise intervene in the Western Hemisphere through the gateway of Cuba."[11]

In September Fidel Castro thumbed his nose at the United States by going to New York and speaking at the United Nations. He interjected himself into the American presidential campaign as well. Though no fan of Eisenhower or his vice president, Richard Nixon, who was locked in a close presidential race against John Kennedy, Castro took a swipe at Kennedy, calling him "an illiterate and ignorant millionaire."[12]

In October Nixon said the United States should impose economic sanctions against Cuba. The next day the United States embargoed all exports to Cuba except medical supplies and food. On November 1, less than a week before the presidential election, President Eisenhower restated that the United States would defend its naval base at Guantanamo, Cuba.

Cuba was naturally an issue in the presidential campaign. When a moderator at one of the famous debates between Nixon and Kennedy asked Nixon, "Mr. Vice-president, Senator Kennedy said last night that the Administration must take responsibility for the loss of Cuba," Nixon answered that the country wasn't lost. Kennedy continued to hammer away on the issue. In campaign stops in Florida, he said variously, Cuba had been "lost to the Communists," "in Cuba the Communists have gained a satellite," and "I wasn't the Vice President who presided over the Communization of Cuba." Realizing the damage this was doing to his campaign, in the last debate with Kennedy, Nixon called for one more debate limited solely to Cuba.[13]

On December 2, after the election, the United States officially declared Cuba a "Communist-controlled" country. On January 3, 1961, two years after Castro's takeover, the outgoing Eisenhower administration finally severed diplomatic relations with Cuba.[14]

Castro had more than enough enemies in America. First among these were Batista supporters who had fled to the United States, particularly southern Florida where they could easily return to Cuba if things should change. Thus Castro's most bitter enemies were alive and well and in the United States. This exile community would swell over the years from a steady flow of Cubans that fled for a variety of reasons. Second were the American businesses whose properties had been nationalized. Third were conservatives to whom any man who called himself a Communist was anathema. And last was the matter of Castro's ties to the Soviet Union. For almost 140 years, the United States had followed the Monroe Doctrine to prevent meddling by European nations in the Western Hemisphere, yet now the United States' most dangerous adversary, the Soviet Union, had a toehold on an island only ninety miles offshore. The long and short of it was that regardless of the effect Castro's policies had in Cuba, they gave him many enemies and few friends in his giant neighbor to the north. He was not in an enviable position. Things would get worse once John Kennedy became president.

. . .

Lee Harvey Oswald was born in New Orleans, Louisiana, on October 18, 1939. His parents, Robert Edward Lee Oswald and Marguerite Claverie Oswald, were married in the Lutheran church. It was the second marriage for both. Oswald's father died of a heart attack two months before his son was born.

Marguerite remarried, but this third marriage was not a happy one. She and Oswald's stepfather fought repeatedly. In January 1947 they moved to Fort Worth, Texas, but the fighting continued, and the marriage finally ended in divorce with a jury placing the blame on Marguerite.

In August 1952 she moved with Oswald to New York City to be close to another of her sons and his wife, who had an apartment there. By the time he was fourteen, Lee Oswald was running into trouble with authorities. Repeatedly truant from public school, he was placed in the Youth House for psychiatric study. According to the Warren Commission Report of President Kennedy's assassination, social workers at the Youth House found that Oswald "was a withdrawn, socially maladjusted boy, whose mother did not interest herself sufficiently in his welfare and had failed to establish a close relationship with him."[15]

In January 1954, Marguerite and Lee Oswald returned to New Orleans. She apparently moved to get out of the jurisdiction of the

New York court, which was bent on ordering her difficult son into custody. Lee stayed out of trouble once he was back in Louisiana but dropped out of high school in his sophomore year and went to work as a clerk and messenger for several companies.

In August 1956 Marguerite moved again to Fort Worth, and Oswald went with her. He reentered high school but only for a few weeks. Paradoxically, he wrote the Socialist Workers Party in New York, announcing that he was a Marxist and asking for more information on its youth league, and a few weeks later, when he turned seventeen, he enlisted in the Marine Corps. On the corps's aptitude tests, his overall score was two points below average but "significantly above average in reading and vocabulary and significantly below average in arithmetic and pattern analysis."[16] He qualified on the M1 rifle as a sharpshooter, which, despite the impressive name, meant his aim was average for a marine.

Oswald spent his first few months in the corps in training at bases in San Diego, California; Jacksonville, Florida; and Biloxi, Mississippi. In July 1957 he shipped off for Japan, where he was assigned to air controller duties. This meant that in combat he would help direct marine pilots to enemy aircraft or ground targets. It was a tactically but not strategically important job. During his service in Asia, he was court-martialed twice. The first occasion was when he was struck by a bullet from his own pistol that fell from his locker onto the floor and discharged. He was court-martialed a second time for getting drunk and insulting a non-commissioned officer.

Throughout his time in the Marine Corps, Oswald continued his interest in Communism. He studied Russian, listened to Russian music, and subscribed to Russian newspapers. He also took an interest in Castro and the revolution that was under way in Cuba. Nelson Delgado, a fellow marine who knew Oswald when they were both stationed in Santa Ana, California, in 1959, testified that Oswald talked to him about going to Cuba to help Castro and about how to get there. Delgado said Oswald knew a little Spanish. He thought someone from the Cuban consulate in Los Angeles came to see Oswald once and spent about an hour and a half with him one night.[17] In short in the Marine Corps, Oswald's disaffection with the U.S. government and his interest in Communism grew, although he may have done this at least in part to draw attention to himself and prove he was different from, and superior to, his peers.

On September 11, 1959, Oswald was discharged from the Marine Corps three months early on the basis of his claim that he needed to take care of his mother. In fact within a week he was on board the freighter the ss *Marion Lykes*, sailing from New Orleans to France. From there he wound his way through England and Finland bound for Moscow.

Oswald arrived in Moscow on October 16. Almost immediately he set about trying to defect to the Soviet Union, but it did not prove easy. Arguably despondent over the possibility that he would not be allowed to stay, Oswald slashed his wrist, an action that the Warren Commission referred to as "an apparent suicide attempt." This is an overstatement, however. Oswald slit a vein in his arm.[18] A Russian doctor who treated Oswald later told the writer Norman Mailer that the wound was superficial. It was an inch long and required only four stitches.[19] Oswald's mood at this time is reflected in a letter he wrote to his brother in America, saying, "I will never return to the United States which is a country I hate."[20]

The Russians were suspicious. Oswald not only wanted to live in the Soviet Union; he also wanted citizenship. According to Russian documents turned over to the United States many years later, two other foreigners had previously been given citizenship and later left the country. The embarrassing incidents were not something the Russians wanted to repeat. Besides, they didn't know enough about Oswald.[21]

Finally, on January 4, 1960, the Soviet government notified Oswald that he would be allowed to stay in the country but that his request for citizenship was denied. He was sent to Minsk, 450 miles southwest of Moscow, and told to report to work in a radio factory. Oswald was paid a salary, which was doubled by a special supplement, and given an unusually nice apartment at a low rent.[22]

Oswald had higher aspirations. Sometime during this period, he applied for admission to the Patrice Lumumba Friendship University in Moscow.[23] The university had been established by Nikita

Khrushchev in 1960 for the stated purpose of educating "students from underdeveloped countries so they [could] return to their homelands to become the nucleus for pro-Soviet activities." In fact, as John Barron points out in his book KGB, the university was created as a front for educating students from Third World countries who might be useful to the Soviet intelligence agency, the KGB. The vice rector and many on the faculty were KGB officers.[24] Academically promising students from Third World countries were typically not placed at Patrice Lumumba but rather at one of the many legitimate universities in the Soviet Union. Soviet experts at the CIA jokingly referred to Patrice Lumumba University as "TU" or Terrorist University because of the KGB sponsorship.[25] In May 1961 Oswald was notified that his application was turned down because he was not from an underdeveloped country.[26] But the fact that he knew of the university raises the possibility that he had met students from Third World countries such as Cuba who were attending.

About this time Oswald discovered he didn't like the Soviet Union any better than he liked the United States. On the first anniversary of his being told he could stay, he wrote in what he grandiosely called his "historic diary" that he was starting to reconsider his decision: "The work is drab. The money I get has nowhere to be spent. No nightclubs or bowling allys [sic] no places of recreation acept [sic] the trade union dances. I have had enough."[27] In point of fact, the Central Committee had stipulated that the question of Oswald's receiving citizenship would be resolved after a year. Thus, while there is no record that such a decision was made, conceivably Oswald was told he would not be made a citizen, and his sudden unhappiness with the Soviet Union stemmed from this.[28]

In March 1961 Oswald met a nineteen-year-old Russian girl named Marina Prusakova at a dance in Minsk. They married within a month. She later told the Warren Commission that Oswald had expressed admiration for Castro even while they still lived in Russia.[29]

. . .

John "Jack" Fitzgerald Kennedy was born May 29, 1917. His twenty-eight-year-old Harvard-educated father had already made money and a mark in Boston banking. His mother was the daughter of John F. Fitzgerald. "Honey Fitz," as he was known because of his sweet talk, was a legendary Boston politician, congressman, and mayor. Looks, charm, and politics were in Jack Kennedy's genes, and money was in his pocket. However, it was older brother, Joe, who Honey Fitz predicted would be president of the United States.[30]

Jack Kennedy was blessed with an ingratiating personality and a powerful family. Although he scored only a high average on intelligence tests, he was admitted to the best schools, where he was an average student.[31] He also suffered from constant health problems that limited his activities and interfered with normal life. For example, his father arranged for him to be admitted to Princeton University, but young Kennedy's poor health forced him to drop out after two months. Some suggest that these health problems were colitis, which in his case might really have been an autoimmune disease of the intestines. The cortisone injections that were used to treat his condition would lead to skeletal problems later in life.[32]

When his health improved, Kennedy applied to Harvard for fall term 1936. His application was accepted three days later. He made Bs and Cs in his first year, but that was understandable for he put most of his energy into sports—football, swimming, golf, yachting—and social activities. To his pleasant surprise, he found himself a lady's man. He also began to travel, and his father sent him on a summer tour of Europe.

In 1938 the elder Kennedy became ambassador to Great Britain, so Jack went there in the spring of 1939 to take full advantage of the celebrity and privileges. Back at Harvard that fall, his grades improved. He used his European experience and his father's connections to diplomats to research and write a senior thesis about events in Europe titled "Appeasement at Munich," criticizing England's appeasement of Adolph Hitler's ambitions. Despite technical faults the paper was considered impressive and allowed Jack Kennedy to graduate magna cum laude. He fixed those faults with the help of a *New York Times* columnist and turned his thesis into the book *Why England Slept*, which received favorable reviews.[33]

Kennedy graduated from Harvard in the spring of 1940 and enrolled in graduate school at Stanford for the fall. But his heart was not in it, so he followed in the footsteps of his older brother, Joe, by going into the military. Kennedy was commissioned an officer in the navy and commanded a patrol torpedo, or PT, boat in the Pacific theater. It was there that Kennedy's exploits first came to national attention. While attacking a Japanese convoy, his PT-109 was sunk. Through Kennedy's leadership all but two members of the crew were rescued after a harrowing seven days on a deserted island. "[Ambassador] Kennedy's Son Is Hero in Pacific as Destroyer Splits His PT Boat" headlined the *New York Times* when it got the story.[34] Thus Kennedy added war hero to his already-impressive political résumé. This was tempered by the death of his brother Joe when the bomber he was flying in an experiment exploded in the air and by Jack's continuing serious health problems.

Still, with Joe's death, Jack was next in line to fulfill Honey Fitz's prediction of a president named Kennedy, so he ran for a seat in Congress from Boston. He transformed his aristocratic charm into a retail political persona, and that, with plenty of his father's money, won him the Democratic primary with 40 percent of the vote and the November general election with 72 percent.[35]

Kennedy had already set his sights on higher office and began thinking about the issues that might propel him there. He settled on foreign policy. Perhaps this choice reflected what he considered his own expertise given his travels, the experience with his father in Great Britain, his Harvard thesis and book, and his war record. Yet he could not campaign on a résumé. He needed a popular issue, so he settled on anti-Communism. Kennedy biographer Robert Dallek points out that even as a freshman congressman, Kennedy was a hawk on defense issues: "The common thread running through these pronouncements was the defense of the West against a communist advance."[36] Kennedy began criticizing Democratic president Harry Truman, blaming him for allowing Communists to take over China, for inadequate civil defense planning in case of nuclear war, and for initial military defeats in the Korean War. He voted for the McCarran Act, which would have required the registration of Communists and which Truman vetoed. Kennedy even once remarked about Wisconsin Republican senator Joseph McCarthy, who was forever looking for Communists, "He may have something." Of course, this was about the only nice thing Kennedy said about McCarthy.[37]

Kennedy's next step up the political ladder came in 1952, when he ran for U.S. senator from Massachusetts. His Republican opponent was the Boston Brahmin Henry Cabot Lodge. Kennedy's younger brother Robert served as his campaign manager and put together a formidable organization that was independent of the Democratic Party in the state. Indeed, while the Republican presidential candidate, Dwight Eisenhower, beat Democrat Adlai Stevenson in Massachusetts with a margin of almost 9 percent, Kennedy won against the tide, defeating Lodge by 2 percent. Despite Kennedy's focus on the issues, most observers agree that he won on personality.[38] He was charming!

As senator, Kennedy continued to see foreign policy as his forte. His was an interesting political calculus. Though a legitimate war hero, he had been but a lowly navy lieutenant in World War II, whereas President Eisenhower had been a four-star general commanding the greatest amphibious invasion in the history of warfare at Normandy. The public thought of Eisenhower as the man who defeated Nazi Germany. Nonetheless, Kennedy challenged Eisenhower on his proposal for cuts in the defense budget. In a May 1953 speech, Kennedy articulated a theme that would guide him through his own presidency, "There is, of course, good reason to believe that the ultimate reliance of the Soviet Union will be on the weapons of subversion, economic disintegration, and guerilla warfare to accomplish our destruction, rather than upon the direct assault of an all-out war."[39] He began to advocate a military buildup that would allow for a flexible response, a tit-for-tat rather than a nuclear holocaust, to Soviet attempts to subvert other countries' governments.

In 1956 Adlai Stevenson ran again for president against Eisenhower and passed over Kennedy as his vice presidential choice in favor of Tennessean Estes Kefauver. The favor may have been Kennedy's, a fact he later recognized. Robert Kennedy spent time with Stevenson's campaign and called it "disastrous." Jack Kennedy used it as a chance to get national exposure; he campaigned in twenty-four states for the Stevenson-Kefauver ticket. And he honed his winning political persona and self-deprecating humor. After riding in an open car in a motorcade in Idaho in freezing weather, he told his audience: "There were more of us in the motorcade than there were on the streets to greet us."[40]

Kennedy benefited by having an excellent senate staff. Perhaps most notable was the young Nebraska lawyer Ted Sorensen, who served as speechwriter and ghostwriter. In the latter capacity, Sorensen penned articles for his boss that appeared in such prestigious publications as *Vogue, Life, Look,* and the *New York Times* magazines. In addition to his senate salary, Sorensen received half the fee the magazines paid Kennedy. Together the two men wrote a second book that was published under Kennedy's name alone, *Profiles in Courage.* This one not only got good reviews; it also won a Pulitzer Prize in 1957.[41] Kennedy was living a charmed life, at least politically.

Kennedy's campaign for president was much the same as the campaign he had run for senate in 1952. Brother Robert was campaign manager and assembled a huge organization to win the primaries. In the general election against Richard Nixon, who was Eisenhower's vice president, Kennedy ran on the issues, but it was his good looks and winning personality, his "charisma" as it was called at the time, that were the deciding factors. Sorensen, who saw Kennedy almost daily for ten years, described the appeal: "John F. Kennedy was a natural leader. When he walked into a room, he became its center. When he spoke, people stopped and listened. When he grinned, even on television, viewers smiled back at him. He was much the same man in private as he was in public. It was no act—the secret of his magic appeal was that he had no magic at all. But he did have charisma."[42]

Kennedy's choice for vice president was Senator Lyndon B. Johnson of Texas, the majority leader of the Senate. Nixon chose Henry Cabot Lodge, the man Kennedy had beaten for the Senate seat in 1952. It was an odd choice. In the end Kennedy proved to be considerably more likable than Nixon although his victory was a narrow one.

Kennedy continued to run on anti-Communism. As a senator he had criticized the Eisenhower administration for allowing the United States to fall behind the Soviets in intercontinental missiles. There was, he claimed, a "missile gap" that favored the Russians. It wasn't true, although Kennedy didn't know this. He resurrected the issue in the 1960 election, arguing that Nixon was part of an administration that was letting America fall behind militarily. And since Castro had taken over Cuba on Eisenhower's watch, Kennedy could lay the blame for that on Nixon too. The issue was especially important in Florida, where voters were as close as ninety miles to a Communist country.[43]

On January 20, 1961, John Fitzgerald Kennedy stood at the Capitol in Washington DC and took the oath of office as president. While not explicitly mentioning Cuba, Castro, or the Soviet Union, he was referring to them in his famous inaugural speech, which Sorensen helped write, with the warning: "Let all our neighbors know that we shall join with them to oppose aggression or subversion anywhere in the Americas. And let every other power know that this Hemisphere intends to remain the master of its own house."[44] On that same January 20, 1961, Fidel Castro was premier in Cuba, and Lee Harvey Oswald was in Minsk.

2

The Bay of Pigs

John Kennedy began the transition from campaign to governance faster than many of his successors. Two days after winning, he announced his first appointments. Allen Dulles, the brother of Dwight Eisenhower's secretary of state John Foster Dulles, would stay on as the director of the Central Intelligence Agency (CIA). J. Edgar Hoover would continue to lead the Federal Bureau of Investigation (FBI).[1] Hoover had held the job since 1924, when the agency was much smaller and known as the Bureau of Investigation. Kennedy was careful to pick both Republicans and Democrats to fill the other major posts in his administration but reserved the most important in his mind, attorney general, for his brother and campaign manager Robert.

Kennedy wanted the transition to be as smooth as possible. He scheduled two meetings with the outgoing president. Cuba and Berlin were on the agenda for both. With respect to Cuba, Eisenhower made the point that Castro would not be allowed to continue. He did not tell the president-elect that the CIA was working on a plan to invade the island, but Kennedy had already heard from others that something like this was going on.[2] However, a short time later, on November 18, the CIA's Dulles and Richard Bissell, deputy director for plans, briefed Kennedy on the plan.

Eisenhower also failed to mention an evaluation of the CIA that was under way and would be finished before Kennedy took office. Eisenhower had the completed report in hand when he sat down with CIA director Dulles on January 5, 1961. The report concluded that the CIA had strayed from its primary mission of intelligence gathering, which had been given it in its enabling act in 1947. Instead, it was spending too much time and too many resources on what was called "covert action," meaning that it was engaging in secret activities with foreign policy objectives in mind, for example, countering Communist subversion in Third World countries and overthrowing unfriendly governments. "Regime change" is the phrase now used for some of these activities. The report said that the CIA's covert-action programs subverted its intelligence-gathering function. Eisenhower phrased it in more emotional terms. He told Dulles that he, Eisenhower, was leaving "a legacy of ashes" for succeeding presidents.[3]

Inheriting this legacy didn't bother Kennedy. As biographer Richard Reeves writes: "He had little ideology beyond anti-Communism and faith in active, pragmatic government."[4] Indeed, rather than try to sweep up Dulles's ashes, Kennedy had asked the director to stay on. He was absolutely enthralled with covert action, the fifty undercover CIA stations, and the $100 million in unvouchered funds that came with it.[5] The CIA offered precisely what the new president meant by a flexible response to Communism and how he might change things in Cuba without nuclear war. John McCone, who would serve Kennedy as CIA director after Dulles, testified in the 1975 investigations into CIA abuses: "Well, certainly right from the very start of the Kennedy Administration there was pressure to do something about Cuba, something about Castro. After all, a bitter political campaign had been waged, and one of the themes of it was that the Eisenhower Administration was soft on Communism, soft on Castro and all of the rest of it. And it was natural when they came in, why they wanted some action."[6]

With the thinly veiled promise in his inaugural address to do something about Cuba, Kennedy should theoretically have been pleased with CIA plans to fund the invasion of the island by an exile group. Brigade 2506, a 1,300-man paramilitary force, was training in Guatemala for this purpose. In addition the CIA was working with organized-crime figures to kill Castro.[7]

These operations fell within Richard Bissell's bailiwick at the agency. As author Evan Thomas notes, Bissell was sometimes called "the smartest man in Washington."[8] This may have been an exaggeration, but Bissell was an intellectual and an organizational talent. He had been educated at Groton, Yale, and the

London School of Economics. He finished his doctoral thesis for the London School after returning to Yale to teach. His students included two future national security advisors, McGeorge Bundy and Walt Rostow. During World War II, he moved to Washington, where he systematized ocean shipping to support the war effort. At war's end he taught at the Massachusetts Institute of Technology. He returned to Washington in 1947 to organize and implement the Marshall Plan for rebuilding Europe.[9]

In 1953 the CIA recruited Bissell to look into ways to roll back the Iron Curtain. A year later he was given the assignment of developing a new, high-flying spy plane, the U-2. It proved a huge technological and intelligence success. It could fly over the Soviet Union unmolested and snap photographs to give early warning of any Soviet military buildup in advance of an attack on Europe and to reveal such things as missile testing. In 1958 Bissell was rewarded with promotion to deputy director for plans.[10] The DDP was in charge of covert action as opposed to intelligence collection. Next to the director, the DDP was the most important job at the CIA

Kennedy was by no means conducting foreign policy exclusively through the agency, but his thinking still had an anti-Communist slant. For instance, on March 13, 1961, he announced the Alliance for Progress, a ten-year plan to boost the standard of living in Latin America via economic cooperation among the countries there and with the United States. Still, cynics called it the "Fidel Castro Plan" because it was striking at the economic appeal of Communism in Latin American countries.[11]

Nonetheless, it was the CIA that Kennedy depended on most for foreign policy guidance. He once told a reporter friend: "I don't care what it is, but if I need material fast or an idea fast, CIA is the place I have to go. The State Department takes four or five days to answer a simple yes or no." On another occasion, Kennedy said about the CIA, "You can't beat the brains."[12] In an oral history recorded in 1964, Robert Kennedy seemed to share his late brother's preferences, saying, "The State Department wouldn't really have done their homework and wouldn't have positions on major matters."[13]

When Bissell first conceived the idea for overthrowing Castro in early 1960, the plan was simpler and more straightforward than what eventually happened. The idea was to recruit about twenty Cubans to be trainers. They would in turn bring in perhaps sixty more and train them as the core of a paramilitary force that would build a true underground in Cuba. As late as the summer of 1960, the CIA naively believed there was so much dissatisfaction with Castro that this small underground movement could overthrow him. By November, however, CIA calculations increased the needed core to several hundred, and it continued to grow to more than one thousand in the planning.[14]

When Kennedy became president, he told the CIA that he didn't like parts of the plan. Among other things, it was too "noisy." It should be more secret, meaning at a remote place less accessible to the press. Moreover, the CIA was planning on using too many aircraft to bomb the landing site in advance of the invasion. The number was eventually cut from forty sorties to eight. Nonetheless, Dulles and Bissell gave assurances that the plan would work, and after all, they were the professionals.[15]

Kennedy wasn't a reluctant warrior though; he embraced Bissell's plan. He had thirteen informal meetings with the CIA man in the months leading up to the invasion. Author Lars Schoultz argues in his book *That Infernal Little Cuban Republic* that the Kennedy administration was not "merely the victim of Eisenhower-era momentum, and the upcoming failure was not simply the result of misleading reports from Bissell's CIA. The documents suggest that President Kennedy and most of his key advisers exuded the same can-do attitude as Bissell."[16]

Invasion wasn't the only method the CIA had for bringing about regime change in Cuba. In the late summer of 1960, before Kennedy was elected, Richard Bissell was thinking about what he euphemistically called "a capability to eliminate Castro."[17] He asked Sheffield Edwards, who was director of the Office of Security at CIA, to see what he could do. Edwards was an unusual choice since his job was to protect the CIA from penetration by foreign intelligence services. He did not normally engage in covert action. Edwards gave the assignment to his chief of operational support, James O'Connell. According to O'Connell, Edwards said that CIA director Allen Dulles approved the idea. O'Connell was a former FBI agent, and he turned for help to Robert Maheu, who was also a former FBI agent and who, after leaving the bureau, did consulting work for the CIA.[18]

O'Connell and Maheu felt that the gambling syndicate, which operated in both the United States and Cuba, could do what was needed. In their minds the syndicate had men who were "tough enough," apparently meaning they weren't bothered by murder. Maheu offered to get in touch with the underworld figure Johnny Roselli as a way into the syndicate. Maheu broached the subject with Roselli at the Brown Derby Restaurant in Beverly Hills. Roselli was hesitant; he wanted to meet the CIA officer personally. So Maheu arranged a get-together with O'Connell at the Plaza Hotel in New York around the time of Castro's visit to the United Nations in September 1960.[19] A few weeks later, Roselli brought into the operation Momo Salvatore Giancana from the Chicago underworld, and Giancana in turn brought in Santos Trafficante, head of the Cosa Nostra in Cuba. Trafficante was still traveling to Cuba, trying to get Castro to reopen the casinos that he had closed after the revolution.[20] Trafficante had the added talent that he, unlike the others, spoke Spanish.

A CIA partnership with the underworld through a former FBI agent gave rise to scenes that seemed out of a Hollywood gangster movie. O'Connell remembered when he and Roselli were in Miami with nothing to do.

> [Roselli] suggested we go to a Haberdashery [sic] store. For one reason or another he took a dislike to my shirt that I was wearing and suggested he buy me a real fancy shirt. I wasn't particularly keen on his choice of it but to humor him I went along and he bought a very fancy silk shirt for me. While we were in there it became obvious he knew quite a few of the employees. It ended up by our going to the back of the store where instead of being a stockroom as I envisioned it would be, it was rather a lavish layout which looked like a club of some sort. There were several individuals there and he introduced me to these people. . . . Then after we left the store when we were walking away he said, "Remember the fellow who was sitting at such and such a location in the

backroom?" He said, "That's Joe. He's our courier." Now I wasn't really focusing on this individual there were just a lot of faces but there I guess I did meet Trafficante.[21]

Despite the fact that the operation was being run by the CIA's Office of Security, the security was terrible. The FBI learned about it within a month. In a memorandum of October 18, 1960, Hoover wrote Bissell: "During recent conversations with several friends, Giancana stated that Fidel Castro was to be done away with shortly."[22] Giancana predicted the assassination would take place within a month, Hoover added. The FBI director probably knew that Bissell was involved with Giancana and may have sent the memorandum as a warning to the CIA that its operation was insecure.

To make things worse, at Giancana's request Maheu had a wiretap installed in an apartment in Las Vegas about this time. The purpose of the wiretap seemed to be to learn if Giancana's girlfriend was cheating on him.[23] The device was discovered by accident and reported to the local sheriff. Since wiretapping was a federal crime, the FBI was notified, and the CIA had to intercede with the bureau on Maheu's behalf to protect the assassination operation.[24] Little wonder that Castro was alive and well as the year 1960 drew to a close.

The fact that Castro stayed in good health was not for a lack of trying by the CIA. Sidney Gottlieb of the Technical Services Division was tasked with providing technical support to the assassination efforts. Poisons were the preferred method. While the CIA had chosen to do business with the underworld because it apparently had visions of hit men machine-gunning Castro down like they did in gangster movies, Giancana said that he wouldn't be able to get anyone to do that in Cuba because the gunmen would never escape. It would be a suicide mission, for which not even the mob could recruit. Giancana asked the CIA to develop a poison pill that could be dropped in Castro's food or drink to take effect slowly and give the killer time to get away before Castro showed symptoms. In August 1960 Gottlieb was given a box of Castro's favorite cigars and asked to coat them with botulinum toxin. They would kill Castro if he merely put one in his mouth.

Gottlieb accomplished the task by early October and put the poison cigars in storage until needed. They were never used, however, and were eventually destroyed.[25]

On January 25, 1961, only five days after Kennedy was sworn in as president, Bissell tapped William Harvey to create an "executive action" capability within the CIA. Executive action is a euphemism for political assassination. The idea was for the CIA to develop a stable of trained assassins. The project was later given the code name ZRRIFLE. CIA code names typically had a designator, such as ZR, followed by a descriptive term, such as "rifle," to serve as mnemonic devices.

Harvey, like Maheu, had been an FBI agent before joining the CIA, and he enjoyed a reputation for being a very good operative. He didn't look the part. Author Evan Thomas describes him as "short, fat and hideous looking with bulging eyes from a thyroid condition and with a froglike voice. His nickname was 'the Pear.'"[26] But, Thomas said, he had "street smarts." For example, he outed British intelligence officer Kim Philby as working for the KGB while others at CIA were still taking Philby to lunch at their clubs in Washington.[27] He lived such a dangerous life that he reportedly kept a revolver tucked between the rather ample cheeks of his posterior.[28]

Once given the job, Harvey didn't waste time. In early February 1961, he touched base with Gottlieb to see what poisons and weapons he had available.[29]

For Gottlieb business was booming. In addition to the cigars, he concocted a batch of botulinum toxin pills that dissolved when dropped into a glass of water. He tested them on monkeys and determined that they would kill. On February 13, 1961, Gottlieb gave the poison pills, said to be packaged in a pencil, perhaps a mechanical one, to O'Connell. They would soon end up in Roselli's hands. Roselli said he received six pills since the Cubans he was working with wanted enough to poison Fidel Castro, Che Guevara, Raul Castro, and others in the Cuban leadership.[30]

At about this time, Senator George Smathers of Florida talked with President Kennedy on the White House lawn. According to Smathers the president mentioned Castro's assassination because

Kennedy "had apparently discussed this and other possibilities with respect to Cuba" with someone. Kennedy was certain it could be accomplished. Smathers told Kennedy he disapproved of the idea. In his testimony to the Church Committee, Smathers recalled the president saying that he completely disapproved. However, in an earlier oral history attached to Smathers's testimony, the senator's recollection was different: that Kennedy did not, in fact, indicate his own views.[31]

Any such disapproval by the president failed to reach the CIA, however. In fact precisely the opposite happened. Harvey testified that Bissell told him the idea for developing the executive action capability had come from the White House in late January 1961, shortly after Kennedy took office.[32] Within a month Johnny Roselli was at the Fontainebleau Hotel in Miami with Gottlieb's poison pills and a briefcase with $10,000 in cash for Castro's assassination. Maheu was there too. He reportedly told one of Roselli's friends: "Johnny's going to handle everything, this is Johnny's contract."[33] Ultimately, Roselli said, the pills got to Cuba, but the agent didn't carry out the plan because he never received a "go-signal." The CIA inspector general's report, however, concluded that the operation failed because the agent lost his access to Castro.[34]

President Kennedy had a different kind of problem with signals. He was boxing himself in with words. At a press conference on April 12, he said the U.S. military would not intervene in Cuba "under any conditions," and no Americans would become involved in military operations in Cuba.[35] The CIA was on the verge of sending Brigade 2506 to invade Cuba, and Kennedy had publicly ruled out giving any support from the navy or air force in the event of difficulties. Robert Kennedy recalled that after the landing and the brigade got in trouble "Secretary Rusk was strongly against sending any airplanes in, that the president had made a public announcement that no military forces of the United States would be used, and therefore, he'd be going back on his word if American forces were in fact used in order to save it." Moreover, given that Bissell and the CIA were running the operation, Kennedy was splitting hairs by saying that Americans were not involved in military operations in Cuba.[36]

In any event, since assassination had not worked, the CIA gave the green light to the invasion. The original plan was for the brigade to land in a populated region around the city of Trinidad near the Escambray Mountains, from which it could wage guerilla warfare. But since the president thought this location was noisy, a remote site that was less favorable militarily had been chosen.[37] Still, both the CIA and the Defense Department thought the invasion would work, whereas the State Department had serious reservations, worrying about diplomatic consequences at the United Nations and in Latin America.[38]

Landings began at the Bay of Pigs on April 17. The location lived up to its name; the operation was a disaster. Castro took personal charge of the defense and assembled an overwhelming force that included both Russian-provided tanks and tanks the United States had provided the Batista regime.[39] In the planning Kennedy had decided to scale back the air support available to the brigade, but more air support might have made the difference. Although an investigation concluded that the operation never had a chance, John McCone, the next CIA director, thought Kennedy's decision not to provide more air support was one of two mistakes that doomed the invasion.[40]

Robert Kennedy later claimed to have been told that Fidel Castro himself flew over the landing in his helicopter, shooting members of the brigade who tried to escape through the swamps along the beach.[41] Whether true or not, the image stuck in his head and contributed to Robert Kennedy's emotional demands to get rid of Castro.

Publicly, President Kennedy accepted the blame. Privately, he and almost everyone else blamed Dulles and Bissell at the CIA. He told Bissell: "In a parliamentary system I would resign. In our system the President can't and doesn't. So you and Allen [Dulles] must go."[42] In an oral history in 1964, Robert Kennedy said about the fallout from the Bay of Pigs invasion: "Allen Dulles handled himself awfully well, with a great deal of dignity, and never attempted to shift the blame. The president was very fond of him, as I was." As for Bissell Robert Kennedy said he deserved credit for developing the U-2 and "this new plane," which may have been the SR71 spy plane, but "he did make a bad mistake" in planning the Bay of Pigs invasion.[43]

Still, John Kennedy bore some of the blame, particularly because he listened to advice that he doubted and because his public statement before the invasion that Americans wouldn't be involved in Cuba had boxed him in when, a week later, he was told that navy and air force support was the only way to save the brigade.

Two weeks later Kennedy reversed himself completely. "The highest levels of government [a euphemism for the president]," a Department of the Army study said, "decided that the possibility of a military invasion of Cuba in the future should not be foreclosed."[44]

Kennedy aide and speechwriter Sorensen wrote in retrospect: "[Kennedy] should never have permitted his own deep feeling against Castro (unusual for him) and considerations of public opinion—specifically, his concern that he would be assailed for calling off a plan to get rid of Castro—to overcome his innate suspicions."[45] Kennedy's national security advisor and former student of Bissell, McGeorge Bundy, was blunter. He wrote a memorandum to the president saying: "Cuba was a bad mistake. . . . We do have a problem of management; centrally it is a problem of your use of time. . . . We can't get you to sit still. . . . Calling three meetings in five days is foolish—and putting them off for six weeks at a time is just as bad."[46]

Secretary of State Rusk talked about Kennedy's management quirks in his memoir *As I Saw It*, complaining that the president made no distinction between cabinet officers and junior officers in meetings at this time. He remembered one at the State Department: "There were seven or eight people around the table, some of them very junior, and yet he [the president] went right around the table, asking each one to give his views on the operation. . . . I never again took part in that kind of session."[47]

The chaos continued for months after the Bay of Pigs invasion. According to a memorandum for the record at CIA, the day after the surrender, the president, the secretary of defense, and the chairman of the Joint Chiefs of Staff met with members of the Cuban groups that had backed the invasion. No one told the dignitaries that one of the Cubans at the meeting had helped get the poison pills to Cuba for the assassination of Castro. The president and other top officials were meeting personally with those involved in the CIA-supported assassination operation with organized crime.[48] This would not be an isolated occurrence.

The confusion continued into the late fall of 1961. To solve the CIA's problems, the president wanted to move his brother from the Justice Department to the CIA, but this notion ran afoul of an intelligence principle known as "plausible denial." Plausible denial means that the U.S. government should have a plausible cover story to prevent anyone from tracing the action back to the United States, for example, preventing someone from proving that the Bay of Pigs invaders were funded by the CIA. A corollary to the doctrine was that even if it should be proved the CIA was behind an action, the president should have plausible denial. He, at least, should be able to say, plausibly, that he didn't know. Plausible denial is one of several principles of American intelligence invented and followed by the agency without any legal basis. So when John Kennedy offered the CIA job to him, Robert pointed out that John would never have this latter form of plausible denial.[49] Everyone assumed that John knew whatever Robert did, and this was generally true. Robert turned the job down.

Nonetheless, even though Robert Kennedy refused to take the title of CIA director, the president insisted that he be de facto director at least with regard to Cuba. In his history of the CIA, *Legacy of Ashes*, Tim Weiner calls it "one of the least wise decisions of his presidency."[50] Years later Secretary of State Rusk described the president as "emotional" about Castro. Secretary of Defense Robert McNamara once used the word "hysterical" to describe the Kennedys' attitude.[51] When in 1967 the CIA's inspector general prepared a report on the agency's assassination efforts, he began it with the warning: "We cannot overemphasize the extent to which responsible Agency officers felt themselves subject to the Kennedy administration's severe pressures to do something about Castro and his regime."[52]

Robert Kennedy's oversight of Cuban operations was achieved organizationally by creation of the Special Group (Augmented) of the National Security Council to deal with the Cuban situation.

The parenthetical "Augmented" meant that the attorney general and retired general Maxwell Taylor, a special presidential advisor, were members.

The president called Taylor out of retirement to look into failure of the Bay of Pigs invasion and, together with the attorney general and CIA director Dulles, prepare a report on what went wrong. But until that was done, the management chaos continued. Appearing before the so-called Taylor Committee on May 18 were several Cuban exile leaders who had been involved in the poison plot against Castro.[53]

Maxwell Taylor had extraordinary military credentials. He commanded the 101st Airborne Division in World War II and jumped with them at Normandy, making him the first U.S. general in France during the war. He went on to become chief of staff of the army. He came to John Kennedy's attention after he retired from the army in 1959 and wrote a book titled *The Uncertain Trumpet*, which criticized the Eisenhower administration's defense policy of relying entirely on nuclear weapons to deter Soviet aggression. Taylor argued for having a "flexible response." This approach fit in nicely with Kennedy's thinking.

The Taylor Committee handed its report to the president on June 13.[54] Dulles resigned at the end of the month, and Bissell became acting CIA director.[55] However, John Kennedy didn't get around to naming the new, permanent CIA director, John McCone, for another two months, and McCone did not take over until November because he was touring CIA stations in the Far East with Bissell and in Europe with Dulles.[56] Thus Bissell, one of the architects of the Bay of Pigs disaster, which had been the reason for the personnel changes, was acting CIA director from July until November 1961. He finally retired from the CIA in February 1962.[57]

The new director, McCone, was a Republican like his predecessor Allen Dulles. An engineer by training, he had gone on to be a highly successful businessman. Eisenhower had appointed him to the Atomic Energy Commission in 1958, a position that gave him a background in national security since the AEC not only oversaw nuclear power plants but also bore responsibility for production of nuclear weapons. Kennedy thought of him as a manager who could straighten out the CIA and as someone skilled in the ways of Capitol Hill.

Although neither John nor Robert Kennedy knew McCone personally before he was appointed, McCone became friends with Robert Kennedy and especially his wife, Ethel. Soon after taking over as CIA director, McCone's wife died, and Ethel helped him through his grief.[58]

During the Church Committee investigation of the CIA, Senator Frank Church famously asked if the CIA was a "rogue elephant" in plotting the assassination of foreign leaders. The senator was suggesting that the agency was not responsive to the president. This question prompted a resentful CIA officer to explode and tell the author that he had watched Ethel Kennedy pull up to CIA headquarters on a motor scooter. A suited John McCone climbed on behind her, and they puttered off for lunch at Hickory Hill, Robert and Ethel's house in Langley, Virginia, that was a few blocks away. To the CIA officer, this illustrated the cozy relationship between the CIA and the Kennedys during McCone's tenure.[59] The new director was a dapper man whose physical appearance reinforced his image as a no-nonsense manager.[60] And Hickory Hill was so close to CIA headquarters that the attorney general could stop there in the morning to see McCone before going on to work at the Justice Department in downtown Washington.[61]

In his review of McCone's tenure, CIA historian David Robarge concludes that while McCone and Robert Kennedy were close personal friends, senior CIA officers differed on whether the attorney general visited agency headquarters on his way to or from work. CIA inspector general Lyman Kirkpatrick said that he did, but DDP Helms could not recall "frequent, unscheduled drop-ins."[62]

Thus six months after the debacle at the Bay of Pigs, Kennedy had reorganized the bureaucratic structure for dealing with Cuba and put a new man in charge. John McCone was CIA director, but the attorney general was really in charge on Cuban matters, exerting his influence officially as a member of the Special Group (Augmented) and unofficially through his friendship with McCone. The personnel changes, however, didn't help.

3

Mongoose

The reorganization after the Bay of Pigs invasion was notable mainly for making a change for the worse in Cuban policy. Stasis and more confusion set in. Almost a year would be wasted as the Kennedys kept trying to make do with the ad hoc, rickety structure they had created.

In part the problem continued to be management. The Taylor Committee was looking into what went wrong at the Bay of Pigs, and investigations are never good management tools. In testifying before the Church Committee in 1975, Richard Bissell called the committee a "court of inquiry."[1] He of course was a principal suspect, and it was hardly a morale booster for him or the CIA.

Also, having the attorney general involved in Cuban policy in both official and unofficial capacities blurred the nice, clear lines of authority that had characterized the Eisenhower administration. The Kennedys were free-wheeling, caring about results rather than process. But bureaucracies tend to be about process. In the 1975 Church Committee investigation, Senator Gary Hart of Colorado and Richard Helms had this exchange about the Kennedys' breezy management style:

SENATOR HART OF COLORADO. We had a prior witness who suggested that the Attorney General [Robert Kennedy] in the early 1960's routinely if not cavalierly . . . picked up the phone and called people at not only the middle levels, but also the lower levels at the Central Intelligence Agency. Do you have any reason to believe that happened?

MR. HELMS. Yes, I do. I want to be fair about the level, but let's say at the case officer level.[2]

Robert Kennedy's talking to case officers meant he knew not only the general thrust of Cuban policy but also the details of specific CIA operations against Castro. CIA historian Robarge concludes that McCone could have learned about CIA assassination plots from Robert Kennedy, suggesting the attorney general knew more about what was going on at the CIA with respect to Cuba than the director did.[3]

The turmoil at the top of the CIA had not helped matters either with Dulles hanging on for months after the Bay of Pigs fiasco only to be succeeded by Bissell. And although John McCone became director in September, he left Bissell in charge while he visited the CIA's far-flung overseas stations until early November.[4] Leaving the CIA without a leader who enjoyed the confidence of the president for more than six months was a prescription for inaction. Although the new Special Group (Augmented) had declared in July 1961 that Castro's overthrow remained the basic objective of U.S. policy toward Cuba, a strategy for doing this was missing, and there was little activity.[5]

The first inkling that the administration was thinking beyond the Bay of Pigs invasion came in the fall of 1961. On October 6 the Special Group was told that a covert-operations plan for Cuba was in the works and that it would be complemented with a contingency plan for what to do if Castro were removed. The CIA's Board of National Estimates—a group charged with analyzing intelligence for long-range planning purposes—was also preparing a study, "The Situation and Prospects in Cuba."[6]

This tentative step forward suffered a setback when the study came in. It concluded that the death of Castro would trigger a power struggle in Cuba and result in an increase in the Communist Party's influence.[7] This was precisely the opposite of what the Kennedys wanted to hear. The study mentioned assassination as one of the ways Castro might die but did not explain how this might come about.[8]

Exasperated, the president looked for someone who could come up with new ideas. He found that man, he thought, in air force general Edward Lansdale. Lansdale was a legend. Kennedy was still a senator when he first read of someone like Lansdale in the novel

The Ugly American. The fictional Colonel Hillandale was able to combat the spread of Communism in an underdeveloped country by improving the economic situation and lives of the poor. Senator Kennedy was so impressed that in 1960 he joined others in taking out an ad in the *New York Times* about the book. He even sent copies of *The Ugly American* to all his fellow senators.[9] At the time he didn't know that the fictional Hillandale was based on the real-life Lansdale—with a great deal of literary license.

By the fall of 1961, however, Kennedy had heard of the real Lansdale and his exploits. He was credited with blocking Communist subversion in the Philippines. More recently he had begun applying his special techniques in Vietnam.

Thus with the situation in Cuba unacceptable and seemingly intractable, the president recommended to his brother Robert that Lansdale be put in charge of Cuban policy. John Kennedy was grasping at straws. Whatever Lansdale's strengths and expertise were, his success had come in dealing with Communist insurgents in Asia, not with an established and entrenched Communist regime in Latin America.

Lansdale was at the White House on November 3 when the president made his move. The general was there to join Maxwell Taylor in reporting to the president on their recent trip to Vietnam. Both generals were advising on that country too. The president asked Lansdale to stay after the meeting and, instead of talking to him about Vietnam, asked if he would work on Cuba.

The next day Lansdale attended a meeting of the Special Group where, according to Richard Reeves's biography of the president, the attorney general yelled at the committee, including Defense Secretary McNamara, Alexis Johnson of the State Department, and Bissell of the CIA: "Get off your ass about Cuba! The Cuban problem carries top priority in the U.S. Government. No time, money, effort, or manpower is to be spared." Robert Kennedy's notes of the meeting record that "Ed Lansdale (the Ugly American)" was there. The notes continue: "McNamara said he would make latter available for me—I assigned him to make survey of situation in Cuba—the problems and our assets. My idea is to stir things up on island with espionage, sabotage, general disorder, run & operated by the Cubans themselves. . . . Do not know if we will be successful in overthrowing Castro but we have nothing to lose in my estimate."[10] Lansdale had no experience in such things, and Robert Kennedy overlooked the fact that the Kennedys might have a great deal to lose by taking on Castro.

Initially, Lansdale was successful, at least in currying favor with Robert Kennedy. After reading the Board of National Estimates' conclusion that the Communists in Cuba would be strengthened if something happened to Castro, Lansdale wrote the attorney general criticizing the board for saying that a popular uprising was improbable and adding, the estimate "seems to be the major evidence to be used to oppose your program."[11]

Lansdale and Taylor were spending their time on Cuba and Vietnam because those were the places where President Kennedy hoped to roll back Communism. But even to John Kennedy there were limits on what he would do, particularly in committing American servicemen to faraway Vietnam. When McNamara argued for sending as many as two hundred thousand troops there, the president bluntly told him at a November 11 meeting, "Troops are a last resort." Robert Kennedy was more absolute: "We are not sending combat troops. [We are] not committing ourselves to combat troops." This was reinforced at a National Security Council meeting four days later.[12]

No one was suggesting that the United States should use troops to solve the problem in Cuba at this time. There were other ways to deal with Castro. On November 9, at Robert Kennedy's suggestion, the president met with reporter Tad Szulc, who covered Cuba for the *New York Times* and who knew Castro. In the course of the meeting, the president asked, "What would you think if I ordered Castro to be assassinated?" Szulc said it was morally wrong and added it wouldn't change things in Cuba. The latter assessment was the same as the National Board of Estimates. The president responded to Szulc: "I agree with you completely."[13] Kennedy's approach to Szulc was similar to the one he had used with Senator Smathers earlier in the year when he floated the idea of Castro's assassination and said it came from unnamed advisors.

A week after the president's meeting with Szulc, Bill Harvey, who was developing the executive action capability called ZRRI-FLE for the CIA, was asked to take over contact with the organized crime figures that Sheffield Edwards had used in his plots to poison Castro earlier in the year, Maheu, Giancana, and Roselli. Harvey wouldn't personally meet with any of them until the next spring, however. Harvey remembered that he also had discussions in the fall of 1961 about using his ZRRIFLE assets, that is, trained assassins, to kill Castro.[14] The president may have told Szulc that he wasn't going to assassinate Castro, but the CIA was continuing to plan for exactly that.

On November 20 the president sent a memo to Secretary of State Rusk, who was chairman of the Special Group (Augmented), ordering him to make every effort to overthrow the Communist regime in Cuba. The president added that General Lansdale would be the group's new executive director.[15] Lansdale's star was rising.

Lansdale adopted the moniker "Operation Mongoose" for the effort against Castro. A mongoose is a ferret-like animal that kills snakes. No one could mistake what Lansdale had in mind, but exactly how this action would be done remained a mystery.

The CIA designated Bill Harvey as its point man for Mongoose and gave him an organization called Task Force W.[16] This was in addition to his ZRRIFLE responsibilities and his handling of the underworld plots. He had perhaps 225 people on staff at CIA headquarters.[17] Harvey had another 400 CIA employees at the agency's station in Florida, code-named JMWAVE, which had as many as 2,000 Cuban agents and a budget of $50 million a year.[18]

Robert Kennedy was still not happy with the scale of the effort. In January 1962 he again told Harvey's boss, Richard Bissell, to "get off his ass" on Cuba, saying again that Castro was the administration's "top priority," adding, "No time, money, effort—or manpower is to be spared. Yesterday Pres indicated final chapter has not been written—got to be done and will be done."[19] Yet the CIA already had time, money, effort, and manpower in abundance. What it lacked was a realistic plan.

Rusk chaired the Special Group (Augmented) if he was there. Otherwise Maxwell Taylor did. Robert Kennedy frequently attended.[20] In a meeting in early 1962, Rusk articulated an idea that would become almost an obsession for the president a year and a half later: "If it should be possible to prove Castro's involvement in efforts to subvert other Latin American countries then this might present an excuse to intervene."[21] By "intervene" he meant an invasion by American forces. Castro's attempts to subvert other countries would later be called "exporting the revolution."

In February 1962 Richard Helms replaced Bissell as DDP. He, Director McCone, and Harvey were the CIA representatives to the Special Group. Richard Helms was in many ways a clone of McCone. He was called one of the "prudent professionals" by columnist Stewart Alsop. These were CIA men who were known for a cool, rational approach to the spy business rather than the glamorous, reckless, swashbuckling, political activists in the agency who preferred performing feats of derring-do. A prudent professional was as much bureaucrat as spy. The young Dick Helms had gone to boarding school in Switzerland and to college at the small, liberal arts Williams College in Massachusetts. He spent a short time working as a reporter in Europe, where by pure luck he landed a one-on-one interview with German chancellor Adolph Hitler in the years leading up to World War II. Helms got his start in the spy business during the war with the Office of Strategic Services (OSS), the precursor to the CIA. The fact that he had personally met Hitler got him noticed within the OSS, and he stayed on after the war. Writer Evan Thomas characterizes Helms as extremely well organized and one of the "clean desk" men at the CIA, a bureaucratic survivor with good judgment. As deputy to the DDP then, Frank Wisner, Helms earned a reputation for being the steady hand when Wisner developed severe psychiatric problems. According to Thomas, Helms was not comfortable with those at the CIA who were considered part of the wealthy, preppy "Georgetown crowd."[22] On the other hand, Helms could get along with almost everyone whether he was comfortable with them or not.

Bill Harvey couldn't. Indeed, he proved to be the wrong man to represent the agency when the Special Group was augmented because he didn't get along with the only person who mattered, Robert Kennedy. One CIA official said that the attorney general wanted accomplishments, whereas Harvey was slow and plodding and "did not have fast actions or fast answers."[23] The tension between the two men would eventually explode, but until then they had to work together as the CIA's use of underworld figures to assassinate Castro came back to haunt them.

When Maheu, Giancana, and Roselli had run into trouble with the FBI for installation of the wiretap in Las Vegas, they had used their connection to the CIA as a defense. The FBI had questioned Maheu, himself a former FBI agent. He too said it was a CIA operation, and the CIA backed him up.[24] But this didn't end the matter.

Unaware of these details, Attorney General Robert Kennedy began pressing the FBI to investigate Giancana as part of his campaign against organized crime. An FBI memorandum of June 1961 noted Kennedy's interest in the case and reported on what was being done: "We are conducting a full investigation in this wiretap case requested by the Department [of Justice] and the field has been instructed to press this investigation vigorously. Accordingly, the Attorney General will be orally assured that we are following up vigorously."[25] Kennedy wasn't told that the mobster had been involved in the CIA plots to kill Castro. But in August 1961, the federal prosecutor in Las Vegas dropped the prosecution in part because of the CIA's opposition.

The matter was resurrected in January 1962, when the Justice Department, still clueless about the messy details, asked if the CIA still objected. The CIA said yes it still objected. But then things took a strange new twist.

By this time FBI director Hoover had learned that John Kennedy was having a relationship with a different girlfriend of Giancana. A review of the woman's telephone records showed that she was calling the White House. Hoover also knew that Giancana was involved with the CIA in plotting Castro's assassination. So on March 22, he sat down to a private lunch with the president. No record of the conversation survives, but suffice it to say the last phone call between the president and the woman took place later that afternoon.[26]

The results of the flap were several. First, Hoover forced the CIA to make a formal request that Maheu and the others not be prosecuted because it might expose a secret agency action connected to the Bay of Pigs invasion. This of course was a cover story. The underworld assassination plot had nothing to do with the Bay of Pigs.[27] However, Hoover's move had the dual purposes of making the august CIA kowtow and of providing him with a paper record for protection if someone should ask why there had been no investigation. Second, the CIA had to brief the attorney general on its use of the underworld in an assassination plot, and Kennedy in turn had to write a memorandum for the record for Hoover about the briefing. Given the attorney general's interest in the prosecution of Giancana, this made abundantly good sense, providing Hoover additional protection for not investigating. Third, at the CIA to protect Sheffield Edwards, whose project this had been, Bill Harvey told him for the record that he, Harvey, had terminated the relationship with the mob. Fourth, bizarrely, Harvey then gave Roselli more poison pills for Castro's assassination as well as explosives, rifles, handguns, radios, and radar for a boat.[28] The operation wasn't terminated at all. Harvey later testified that this was simply the kind of internal cover story the CIA used when responsibility shifted.[29] There is no evidence that Robert Kennedy was told the operation was continuing.[30]

Thus even before the dust settled from the flap over the CIA's involvement with the mob, Harvey was reestablishing contact with Roselli. He cut Maheu and Giancana out of the operation, though, because he thought too many people were involved. He also may have known of the attorney general's desire to investigate Giancana. That he also knew the president was having a relationship with the mobster's girlfriend is possible since Roselli probably knew and might have told him. And while Harvey had doubts about all aspects of the assassination operation, he slogged on. He liked Roselli personally and said of him later: "After I assessed him, and came up quite frankly, with a very high estimate and regardless of how he may have made his living [in organized crime] in the past, of his integrity as far as I was concerned in his dealings with me, of his loyalty to me, and of his basic dependability in continuing this thing at all."[31]

Operation Mongoose too lurched on. Lansdale originally predicted that he could oust the Castro government by October 1962.

The CIA was skeptical to say the least. It thought Lansdale's plans to foment discontent and revolt in Cuba through sabotage were unrealistic and unprofessional. One plan that never made it out of the laboratory of the CIA's Technical Services Division was to dust the inside of Fidel Castro's diving suit with a fungus that would produce a chronic skin disease.[32] In testifying later about this period, Richard Helms said many of the plans were "cockeyed."[33] He compared them to a plan he heard about during World War II. Someone discovered a place on the border between Switzerland and Germany where dairy cows wandered back and forth. The idea was to insert suppositories filled with propaganda leaflets in the cows when they were in Switzerland, and then when they grazed their way into Germany, they would deposit the leaflets to be blown away by the wind.[34] In other words nutty as the schemes may seem, they were not necessarily unusual in the spy business.

Bill Harvey was a constant naysayer. In April 1962 he wrote Director McCone, arguing that the United States had to be prepared to send the military into Cuba to destroy the Castro government and "the decision to use military force must be made *now*." Harvey also complained about micromanagement by the Special Group that was in his words "stultifying."[35]

Plagued with dissension and delays, Mongoose did not begin putting agents in Cuba until late August 1962, when they fired on a hotel from boats in Havana Bay, killing ten Russians and Cubans. Another group of agents successfully tainted a shipment of sugar with a chemical that would sicken whoever ate it, but the White House got cold feet and ordered the CIA to buy and destroy the tainted sugar.[36]

In addition to CIA-sponsored efforts, various Cuban exile groups hatched their own plans for raids into Cuba and assassination. Some of these groups were highly motivated. However, they didn't have the money and resources that the CIA did. Besides, the president, worried that uncoordinated operations by poorly trained exiles would result in needless loss of life, ordered the CIA to use its influence to stop them.[37] In short although Mongoose and exile raids were harassing, they didn't jeopardize Castro's hold on Cuba.

...

While these bureaucratic shufflings were taking place in Washington, Lee Harvey Oswald was having his own troubles with bureaucracy in the Soviet Union as he started the long process of getting the Soviet and American governments to let him return to the United States. He proposed to Marina on April 20, 1961, the same day Brigade 2506 surrendered, and the couple married ten days later. Oswald wrote the American embassy in Moscow to say that he was married and might return to the United States. In early July he traveled to Moscow to talk personally with embassy personnel. Securing all the permissions would take another eleven months, by which time the Oswalds were parents.

In the early summer of 1962, Oswald, his wife, Marina, and their infant daughter, June Lee, finally got permission to leave the Soviet Union. They left Russia on June 2 and arrived by ship in Hoboken, New Jersey, on June 13. They spent a day there before flying to Fort Worth to stay with Oswald's brother. Within two weeks FBI agents had tracked Oswald down and interviewed him, telling him to report any attempts by Soviet agents to contact him. The FBI interviewed him again in mid-August. He didn't tell the FBI that he had already begun corresponding with Communist and socialist organizations in New York.

In Fort Worth Oswald found a job and rented an apartment. He and Marina made friends in the small Russian community in the city. In early October Oswald moved to nearby Dallas and got a job with the Jaggars-Chiles-Stovall Company, which did graphic arts. Oswald did photoprint work, making advertising copy ready for printing. It was a relatively low-skilled job. He soon rented an apartment and had Marina and June Lee move in with him. Their marriage seemed no happier than his mother's marriage to his stepfather had been. Indeed, there were suggestions that he physically abused Marina. Their Russian friends liked Marina but not him.[38]

...

In Washington McGeorge Bundy was frustrated by how little Lansdale had accomplished. The only covert operation that seemed to have any chance of getting rid of Castro was Harvey's assassination work with the underworld. Therefore, on August 23, 1962, Bundy wrote National Security Action Memorandum NASM-181 ordering Maxwell Taylor to develop a plan to inspire a revolt in Cuba.[39] The stasis on Cuba was almost over, but in a way that no one expected.

4

Missile Crisis

John and Robert Kennedy and the Special Group weren't the only ones thinking about Cuba in the summer of 1962. Five thousand miles away in Moscow, Nikita Khrushchev and his advisors were doing the same. Historian Michael Beschloss writes that Khrushchev thought Kennedy planned to invade Cuba that fall. If so the suspicion was based on bad intelligence by the Soviets. Operation Mongoose was limping along, and the president had not considered invasion. National security advisor Bundy didn't even order the Special Group to begin thinking about inspiring a revolt until August 23.[1]

Khrushchev decided to act on his concerns by placing surface-to-air missiles (SAMs) and medium-range and intermediate-range ballistic missiles (MRBMs and IRBMs) in Cuba. Beschloss gives two reasons for Khrushchev's decision. First, the presence of the missiles would deter the United States from invading. The SAMs could shoot down attacking American aircraft, and the MRBMs and IRBMs could retaliate and hit the United States with nuclear warheads. Cuba could not be invaded with impunity. Second, putting the weapons there would close the worldwide atomic weapons gap that heavily favored the United States. When campaigning for president, John Kennedy had been terribly wrong in claiming the existence of a "missile gap." The United States had a vast advantage in jet bombers, long-range ballistic missiles, and medium-range missiles on submarines that would devastate the Soviet Union in the event of war. According to Kennedy biographer Richard Reeves, the advantage was five thousand warheads versus three hundred.[2] MRBMs and IRBMs in Cuba, though small in numbers, would narrow the gap ever so slightly. Medium-range missiles launched from Cuba could strike in an arc from Dallas, Texas, to Washington DC. The intermediate-range missiles could hit anywhere in the continental United States except the Pacific Northwest.[3]

Soviet Deputy Premier Anastas Mikoyan disagreed with Khrushchev about putting the missiles in Cuba. He presciently argued that Kennedy would never accept Soviet, nuclear-tipped missiles ninety miles off the coast of Florida.[4] In the waning days of his administration, President Eisenhower had warned Khrushchev that Soviet missiles in Cuba were unacceptable.

Khrushchev's miscalculation was made more dangerous because precisely at this moment the United States suffered its own intelligence failure and didn't detect what the Russians were doing. For one thing the Special Group, which was supposed to pay attention to Cuba, was distracted by another flap over assassination. At an August 10 meeting, Defense Secretary McNamara suggested the Special Group take up the matter of Castro's assassination.[5] This was an especially unfortunate meeting in which to utter the forbidden word because more people than the usual members were there. Edward R. Murrow, director of the United States Information Agency and a highly regarded newsman, was in attendance as was Secretary of State Rusk. Bill Harvey, who was running the assassination operation for the CIA, was also there, and he realized instantly it was a mistake to bring up the subject in front of such people. General Lansdale didn't. Three days later he circulated a memorandum to several members of the Special Group assigning to Harvey the job of preparing a paper on "Intelligence, Political, *including liquidation of leaders*, Economic, (sabotage, limited deception), and paramilitary." After a flurry of follow-up meetings, phone calls, and memoranda, all references to assassination and liquidation were deleted from the record, but the fuss had consumed almost a week.[6] Meanwhile, the Soviets were shipping their offensive missiles to Cuba.

CIA director McCone was the first to sound the alarm. Photographs from U-2 flights over the island showed SAMs were being installed. McCone felt that because the SAMs could shoot down a U-2, the missiles were in Cuba to hide something from aerial reconnaissance, and he guessed the something might be offensive missiles.[7]

The U-2 was the aircraft that former DDP Richard Bissell had developed for the CIA. The Soviets had been helpless to prevent its flying over their country until 1960, when they finally developed a SAM that could fly high enough to hit it. As soon as they had such a missile, they shot down a U-2. Khrushchev used the occasion to embarrass President Eisenhower by exhibiting to the press the wreckage and a needle tipped with lethal shellfish toxin. The pilot was supposed to commit suicide by stabbing himself with the needle rather than be captured. Khrushchev also had the pilot, who had elected not to die for a CIA that was infatuated with poisons.

Despite his objections to McNamara's talking about assassination at a Special Group meeting, Harvey continued working with underworld figures for that very purpose. On September 7 and 11, 1962, he met Johnny Roselli in Miami to see what could be done. Roselli told Harvey that the poison pills were still safe in Cuba, so he would send in another team to do the job. According to the 1967 *IG Report*, Roselli's second team never went to Cuba.[8]

However, as will be seen later in this chapter, the CIA's version may be incorrect because even internally it falsifies the record. Just like Harvey's telling Edwards that the underworld plots had ended in May of that year, when the exact opposite was true, the claim that Roselli did not send a team of assassins to Cuba at this time appears a cover story and in any event doesn't seem to be what happened.

The CIA not only missed detecting the ballistic missile buildup but also failed to count correctly the size of the armed forces on the island. In the early fall of 1962, the CIA estimated that about 10,000 Soviet troops were in Cuba and judged the Castro forces to be around 100,000. After the crisis was over, the estimates were revised upward to 43,000 and 275,000, respectively.[9] In other words the combined Soviet and Cuban military might was three times larger than estimated in the early fall of 1962. Presumably the Pentagon relied on the lower figures in updating its contingency plan for invading Cuba. The plan called for, if need be, moving 100,000 troops to bases on the East Coast, from North Carolina to Key West, in eight days in preparation for a full-scale invasion.[10] While this force might have been enough to handle the combined Soviet and Cuban forces in the first CIA estimate, it would have been woefully inadequate to take on the forces in the revised estimate. On the other hand, since the United States tends to feel that American soldiers are better than foreign troops, the higher numbers might not have fazed Pentagon planners.

On October 1, 1962, President Kennedy elevated General Maxwell Taylor from presidential advisor on Cuba to chairman of the Joint Chiefs of Staff, replacing Lyman Lemnitzer.[11] The President was slowly bending the entire national security apparatus in the direction of ousting Castro. Nikita Khrushchev was wrong to believe that the United States would invade Cuba in the fall of 1962, but the administration certainly hoped to get rid of Castro somehow. In any event the Soviets were acting faster than the United States was.

At about this time, the CIA finally detected the missile buildup in Cuba. Secretary of State Rusk advised the president "that Khrushchev may have intended his buildup in Cuba as a diversion from a new Soviet move against Berlin."[12] Rusk's view wasn't new. The defense of Europe was still the highest U.S. priority, so a Soviet move in some other part of the world was frequently viewed as a feint to distract the United States from the real objective, Berlin, or as a bargaining chip to be used to secure greater control over the city.

On October 14 a U-2 flying over Cuba came back with photographs that showed MRBMs and IRBMs were being installed there. What is more there appeared to be storage places nearby for nuclear warheads. McCone had been right, although it had taken almost two months to prove it.[13] The national security establishment scrambled to decide what to do.

Early in the afternoon of October 16, the CIA's Richard Helms attended a meeting on Mongoose with Robert Kennedy, General Lansdale, and others. The attorney general, who obviously had been told about the missiles in Cuba, exploded. According to Helms's memorandum for the record, Robert Kennedy "opened the meeting by expressing the 'general dissatisfaction of the President' with

Operation Mongoose." The strong language was a blunt reminder that talking to the attorney general was the same as talking to the president. The Kennedys wanted more "push," particularly with regard to sabotage by the CIA. Rather surprisingly, at least according to his memorandum, Helms stood up to the attorney general. He diplomatically pointed out that the ultimate objective of Mongoose had never been defined. The Cubans working for the CIA, said Helms, were unwilling to risk their lives for an operation that aimed for anything less than an invasion of Cuba by U.S. troops. Yet the Cubans had never been told that the United States would do this.

Within hours the Cuban Missile Crisis, as it would be called, pushed Mongoose into the background. Helms notes from the meeting say: "In passing, he [Robert Kennedy] made reference to the change in atmosphere in the United States Government during the last twenty-four hours, and asked some questions about the percentage of Cubans whom we thought would fight for the regime if the country were invaded."[14]

Once the crisis he had predicted came to pass, CIA director McCone's advice became less sagacious. At a White House meeting on October 17, according to author Richard Reeves, he bellicosely suggested: "Take Cuba away from Castro." McCone wasn't alone. The recommended courses of action for dealing with the crisis all leaned toward war. The four alternatives listed in the minutes were political moves followed by a military strike; military strike without warning; political moves followed by naval blockage and declaration of war; and full-scale invasion to take Cuba away from Castro.

John Kennedy was, for a change, the one at the meeting with the cool head. When air force general Curtis LeMay was asked what the Russians would do if the United States bombed the missile sites in Cuba, he said they would do nothing. Frustrated by being given only military options, the president later quipped that if the sites were bombed, thus starting World War III, there might not be anyone around to tell the generals they were wrong.[15] Robert Kennedy wavered back and forth, leading Dean Acheson, who had been secretary of state under President Harry Truman and who was invited to sit in on some of the meetings in the role of elder statesman, to call the attorney general an "inexperienced fool" behind his back.[16]

In the early days of the crisis, before the public knew, John Kennedy took time to speak to a conference at the State Department. He gave not a hint of what was happening in the secret meetings except to quote several lines written by the Spanish bullfighter Domingo Ortega. They seemed to capture the president's feelings about the pressure he was under:

Bullfight critics row on row
Fill the enormous plaza full
But only one is there who knows
And he is the one who fights the bull.[17]

As the crisis continued, Rusk expounded again at a meeting on October 18 on his belief that Khrushchev was trying to get Berlin: "I'm beginning really to wonder whether Mr. Khrushchev is entirely rational about Berlin. They may be thinking that they can either bargain Berlin and Cuba against each other, or that they could provoke us into a kind of action in Cuba which would give an umbrella for them to take action with respect to Berlin."[18]

The president convened a final meeting on October 20. Most of the older, Cold War warriors favored preemptive air strikes on the missile sites. But Soviet troops were there, and some would be killed in air strikes. Moreover, unless all the sites were destroyed, which the military said was virtually impossible, the Soviets would be able to retaliate with nuclear-tipped missiles, likely starting World War III. Elder statesman Acheson, General Taylor, McGeorge Bundy, John McCone, and Paul Nitze, the Defense Department's architect of Cold War strategy, all counseled for a preemptive attack. The alternative was a naval blockade, which was called a "quarantine" to avoid problems under international law. A majority at the meeting opted for the quarantine. So did the president. Of course, as his quote from the bullfighter poem makes clear, Kennedy knew that his was the only vote that counted. The minutes of the meeting say that since the choice was between limited action and unlimited action, meaning a blockade versus nuclear war, most attendees agreed it was best to start with limited action.[19] It is hard to see why there was disagreement.

The president went on national television to announce his decision on the night of October 22. Fifty-six U.S. warships were steaming into the Atlantic Ocean to impose a naval blockade to stop all ships trying to enter Cuban waters, thus preventing the Soviets from sending in any more troops, missiles, or warheads. Kennedy was also redeploying ninety thousand marines and airborne troops to bases along the East Coast. If needed they could invade Cuba in eight days.[20] Operating on the bad intelligence in the CIA's estimate of Russian and Cuban forces, Kennedy didn't realize that the force wasn't nearly large enough.

Kennedy's show of force worked though. The next morning the navy reported that Soviets ships headed for Cuba had stopped or turned around. It wasn't completely over, but as Rusk said when he heard the news: "We are eyeball to eyeball, and I think the other guy just blinked." It would take six days of deft negotiations with Khrushchev before the crisis was settled on October 28. In exchange for the Soviets removing the nuclear missiles from Cuba, the United States secretly agreed to remove from Turkey obsolete and unneeded Jupiter missiles aimed at the Soviet Union. Kennedy also gave a conditional promise not to invade Cuba, although the conditions he imposed and the vagaries of the language provided a great deal of leeway.[21] John Kennedy proved a much cooler and wiser head than his myriad national security advisers. He had stopped the Soviets from pursuing a military course in the Western Hemisphere without triggering nuclear war.[22]

One of the few U.S. casualties was the U-2 pilot who flew the October 14 mission that uncovered the missiles. On a later flight during the crisis, his plane was shot down by a SAM, and he was killed.

The CIA's Bill Harvey was also a casualty but not fatally. His fault lay in his handling of agents sent into Cuba. There are numerous versions of Harvey's run-in with the attorney general. They conflict not only about what happened but also about when it happened. Some date the incident to September 1962, which was before the missile crisis. Others date it to October 1962 during the missile crisis. Harvey himself implies it was after the missile crisis. These agents sent into Cuba were supposedly saboteurs, but they were possibly assassination agents. As explained later mobster Johnny Roselli was sending assassins to Cuba at this time and would claim they were captured and talked. According to Roselli this led Castro to make a decision to retaliate.

When Robert Kennedy was first introduced to the corpulent CIA officer with the bulging eyes, he asked incredulously, "Are you our James Bond?" Harvey was the antithesis of everything the Kennedys represented. He always carried a gun, even to the White House. Those around Kennedy found him appalling. Thomas Parrott of the CIA once explained: "They didn't realize he was just drunk." McGeorge Bundy told Parrott: "Your Mr. Harvey does not inspire great confidence." The feeling was mutual. Harvey didn't like General Lansdale, the man the Kennedys had chosen to run Mongoose. Harvey's staff at CIA referred to Lansdale as "FM" for field marshal. Harvey spoke less kindly of John and Robert Kennedy, once referring to them as "fags" and "those fuckers."[23]

In his memoir, *A Look over My Shoulder*, Helms characterizes Harvey's feelings with gentle humor: "If one were to cast about for someone positively to rub against every grain of Bill Harvey's being, the chance of finding anyone who might fit the measure more closely than Robert Kennedy would have been zero. . . . In office, Bob spoke with the full backing of his brother. Harvey had the DCI's [McCone's] confidence and mine, but when he spoke with Bob it was as a lieutenant dealing with a general. Harvey was never to see it that way."[24] Helms was charitable to Harvey. CIA historian Robarge suggests McCone came to the realization that Harvey "was personally and professionally unsuited for the job" well before his career-ending confrontation with Robert Kennedy.[25]

Helms dates the confrontation to before the missile crisis.[26] Author Evan Thomas in *The Very Best Men* says that it was in October at the end of the missile crisis: "Anticipating that the United States might want to invade Cuba, the Pentagon instructed Harvey to infiltrate advance intelligence teams onto the island at the peak of the crisis. Robert Kennedy was furious when he learned that the men could not be recalled. At a White House meeting at the end of October, Harvey aggravated the wound by suggesting that the missile crisis was the Kennedys' fault. Kennedy stormed from the room. 'Harvey has destroyed himself today,' CIA Director John McCone remarked to an aide. 'His usefulness has ended.'"[27]

Thomas includes the same version in his biography of Robert Kennedy, *RFK*, changing it slightly by saying Kennedy was angry because Harvey should have gotten approval before sending "reconnaissance teams" into Cuba." Thomas cites interviews with third parties.[28]

Walt Elder, who was McCone's executive officer, remembered the confrontation differently in sworn testimony to the Church Committee in 1975. He didn't recall the date but said there was a meeting at which Kennedy said to Harvey: "I have ten minutes to hear your plan, and Mr. Harvey set his chin on his chest and proceeded. After ten minutes the Attorney General left. Harvey droned on. After a couple of phone calls between McCone and the Attorney General it was clear that Mr. Harvey would have to be replaced." Elder also remembered a confrontation between Lansdale and Harvey in McCone's office where Lansdale complained that Harvey had sent teams into Cuba without his knowledge. McCone ordered the teams recalled, and they were.[29]

Army major general Charles E. Johnson III also remembered a confrontation between Robert Kennedy and Bill Harvey. He dates it to mid-September 1962, although it sounds like the October 26 meeting, which will be discussed later. But if it took place in mid-September, it was at about the same time that Harvey and Roselli met in Miami to send another assassination team to Cuba and would be consistent with Helms's version. According to Johnson, Kennedy and Harvey were at a Special Group (Augmented) meeting at the Pentagon along with McCone, Bundy, Lansdale, and others. It was near the end of the meeting. According to notes by congressional interviewers of what the general told them, Kennedy turned to Harvey and launched into a tirade.

It was the "damndest tyrade [sic]," a "shocking thing" [General Johnson said]. It apparently stemmed from a failure of a series of operations by the CIA. Mr. McCone was there and did not say one word in defense of Harvey. The incident "lasted quite a while, 8 to 10 minutes." It was directed personally at Harvey of that he [Johnson] was sure. He noted that Harvey might have been dozing just before RFK yelled at him. He remembered that the AG raised his voice. When the AG finished, "we adjourned or went on to something else." Harvey said little if anything in response. "I [Johnson] was surprised at the vehemence of this thing." "It couldn't have been a tyrade for just a failure to make Mongoose succeed. I don't thing [think]. It seemed to be something beyond that—a failure beyond that."[30]

Robert Kennedy was forthcoming and precise about an incident in his oral history. He referred to Harvey not by name but as the fellow who put the tunnel under the Berlin wall, an act for which Harvey was highly praised: "We'd been working with him [Harvey] for a year and no accomplishment. And then, then we had General Lansdale who I got to take this on. . . . He started developing some programs, but then he came to cross purposes with CIA, and they didn't like his interference, and then the military got upset, and . . . so that thing, that collapsed."

Kennedy gave details that jibe with General Johnson's recollection and dates it to the end of the missile crisis.

> I mean we had a terrible experience with the ones that were handling it at the time of the missile crisis. They [Harvey] were going to send sixty people into Cuba right during the missile crisis. Nobody knew what they were doing; they never told, explained. . . . I just heard about it because one of the fellows who was going to go wrote me—or got in touch with me—and said, "I, we don't mind going but we want to make sure we're going because you think it's worthwhile." And I checked into it, and nobody knew about it. . . . We had a meeting at the Pentagon on it. And I never saw, I've never seen him [Harvey] since.[31]

CIA historian Robarge details several confrontations. One occurred early in 1962 at the JMWAVE station in Florida, where Harvey stopped the attorney general from walking out of the room with a classified CIA cable. A second was when Kennedy learned a team that was supposed to be infiltrated into Cuba was still in training. Kennedy sarcastically said he would train them at his house in Virginia, Hickory Hill. Harvey replied with equal sarcasm by asking Kennedy if he was going to teach them babysitting.[32]

The last straw, according to Robarge, came at a Special Group (Augmented) meeting on October 26, 1962, two days before Khrushchev agreed to pull the ballistic missiles from Cuba. The meeting was to discuss Mongoose sabotage operations, which, surprisingly, continued during the missile crisis. Indeed, at the October 16 meeting referred to earlier, Helms had presented a list of eight sabotage operations that the CIA would undertake "as soon as possible," and Robert Kennedy had approved.[33] But in addition to these, Harvey sent a six-man team into Cuba on the night of October 19 to sabotage the Matahambre copper mine. This operation was not listed among those Kennedy had approved three days earlier. Four men made it out, but two did not. Harvey was then grilled about this operation at the October 26 meeting, but he didn't know if it had succeeded or failed or what happened to the two agents. McCone asked if Harvey had canceled, as McCone had suggested, the insertion of three additional teams into Cuba. Harvey said the teams had been dispatched and couldn't be recalled. Lansdale criticized Harvey and the CIA for planning to send ten teams of five men each into Cuba by submarine to collect information that might be needed by the military for an invasion because this was diverting resources from Mongoose. McCone defended Harvey by pointing out that the CIA had an independent mission to support the military. Kennedy, perhaps under the stress of the unresolved missile crisis, exploded at Harvey, who replied by saying something like "We wouldn't be in such trouble now if you guys had had some balls in the Bay of Pigs."[34] In his oral history, Kennedy seems to conflate Lansdale's complaint about the submarine teams with McCone's criticism of Harvey for not being able to recall three different teams. In any event Harvey's career was ended. A few weeks later, Radio Havana announced that the two unaccounted-for agents sent to sabotage the Matahambre copper mine had been captured.[35]

These weren't the only teams being sent to Cuba though. Mobster Johnny Roselli had gone to Florida to send another assassination team to Cuba just before the missile crisis and returned during the crisis to see if his underworld connections had intelligence about the missiles.[36] He testified to the Church Committee: "We were trying to find out—Mr. Harvey asked me to see if they had any intelligence on [for] us, on the missiles."[37] In this second visit, Roselli learned that the Cuban he was working with to kill Castro was training frogmen to blow up ships in Havana harbor. Roselli's attorney, Thomas Wadden, interrupted the questioning of his client to explain: "During the Cuban Missile Crisis they [Roselli's Florida contacts] were planning on going in and trying to blow up some of the ships."[38] To further confuse the history, at the October 16 meeting Robert Kennedy had approved "an underwater demolition attack by two Cuban frogmen against shipping and port facilities at the port of La Isabella, Las villas Province," and this conceivably was part of the same frogmen operation that Roselli was talking about.[39]

In any event it seems that when Harvey sent Roselli to Florida to collect intelligence during the missile crisis, Roselli discovered that the man he was working with to assassinate Castro also planned to blow up Russian ships docked in Havana. Asked how Harvey reacted, Roselli answered: "He said, go ahead and talk [to] him about that, we are not going to give him any help on that."[40] Thus Harvey sent Roselli to Florida in September with more poison to kill Castro and in mid-October sent him back to collect intelligence from the same men.

Roselli's version is reinforced—and the waters muddied—by the rather startling, elliptical account of these events that Harvey gave to the Church Committee. He was asked whether CIA director McCone made certain that the underworld plots against Castro were terminated after McNamara suggested Castro's assassination in August 1962. "No," Harvey answered. However, he continued, once the CIA learned that surface-to-air missiles were being deployed in Cuba in late August 1962, "a tentative decision had been made at that point that the only sensible thing to do with this particular operation [the Roselli effort to assassinate Castro] was to terminate it as rapidly and cleanly as it could be done."[41]

Harvey went on:

I am sure that I had discussed with Roselli, at least on a tentative basis, by August [1962], the probable necessity of terminating this. . . . I do not remember the exact date, or the exact specifics of that discussion.

As the Missile Crisis developed . . . and the informal commitment was made not to attempt to overthrow the Castro government by American force of arms as part of the general solution to the missile crisis [in late October], I may have deferred for a period of a few weeks giving an actual order to terminate this as soon as possible, because very frankly at that stage, and with the deep concern that we had at that point over what rightly or wrongly I think all of us then felt was a very vital matter of the security of this nation, I was not about to terminate any possible asset.[42]

That Harvey had an assassination team in Cuba during the missile crisis gains further support from his testimony to the Church Committee about the circumstances in which assassination was justifiable: "I can conceive of it being perfectly within the province of an intelligence service . . . to eliminate a threat to security of this country by any means whatever whether it's a nuclear strike or a rifle bullet if I may be that blunt. . . . There was good reason to believe in the summer and fall of 1962 that we were faced with exactly that kind of a threat." When asked what he meant, Harvey immediately answered: "I am referring to the placement of missiles in Cuba." Rather than talking about a hypothetical, Harvey may have been trying to justify what he had done. Harvey was not asked to clarify his meaning by the committee.[43]

Thus, although there were multiple confrontations between Harvey and Kennedy, the last straw was the one that Kennedy, General Johnson, and author Thomas talk about. It may have occurred at the Pentagon during the missile crisis. Contrary to the rather innocuous accounts that several CIA officers gave, Kennedy wasn't angry because Harvey gave long-winded and ambiguous answers to questions. He surely committed that offense. Nor did Kennedy blow up because of Harvey's sarcastic reference to teaching babysitting at Hickory Hill.

But Kennedy was infuriated by Harvey at the October 26 meeting, in part because the CIA was sending teams into Cuba without Lansdale's knowledge and because of Harvey's inability to answer McCone's questions. However, it is possible that Kennedy also knew Harvey was involved with the underworld and had an assassination team in Cuba during the missile crisis. Maybe General Johnson was right. Robert Kennedy wasn't angry about Harvey's failure to make Mongoose work. It was "a failure beyond that." Because of Harvey, Fidel Castro might be assassinated in the middle of the missile crisis.

This confrontation between Robert Kennedy and Bill Harvey during the missile crisis is important because Roselli would later claim that Cuban intelligence captured one or more of his agents, got them to talk, learned their mission was to assassinate the Cuban leader, and retaliated. Why Robert Kennedy blew up at Harvey may not be entirely clear, but one thing is certain: the most dangerous, secret, and controversial plan for getting rid of Castro had been entrusted to William Harvey, a man in whom no one except perhaps Richard Helms had confidence by October 26, 1962.

...

While John Kennedy spent a good part of the fall of 1962 fighting Communism, Lee Harvey Oswald was showing renewed interest in the opposite direction. His unhappy experiences under Communism in Russia did not diminish his enthusiasm for the doctrine. So within a few months of returning to the United States, Oswald, who was living with Marina in Dallas, began corresponding with Communist and socialist organizations in New York.

He may have run into these organizations when he was a teenager in the Bronx. He wrote that his first awareness of Communism was when he was fifteen years old and read the *Communist Manifesto* and the first volume of Karl Marx's *Das Kapital*. In those, his teenage, years, Oswald was in trouble for being truant from school. There is no evidence of what he did with his truancy—because the Warren Commission didn't bother to investigate—but he may have been going to Greenwich Village.[44] It was only a forty-five-minute subway ride and held the offices of the leftist groups with which he would later correspond. The Communist Party of the United States (CPUSA) was located at 23 West Twenty-Sixth Street. The Socialist Workers Party (SWP) was ten blocks south with headquarters at 116 University Place. The SWP was Leon

Trotsky's branch of Communism, whereas the CPUSA aligned itself with the government of the Soviet Union. That Oswald ran into leftists while he lived in New York could explain why, after his return to Texas, he contacted these two organizations, although, of course, he may have just read about them.

In August 1962 he wrote the Socialist Workers Party asking for information. The SWP sent him a catalog of its publications. He ordered a book on Leon Trotsky from the party's publishing arm, Pioneer Press.[45] Oswald was at least smart enough to be aware of the differences between the SWP and the CPUSA. He observed correctly in his notes that the CPUSA was the tool of Stalin and the Soviet Union.[46]

In November 1962, after the end of the missile crisis, Oswald's correspondence with the New York organizations became bolder. He wrote the Gus Hall—Benjamin J. Davis Defense Committee offering to do photo work without charge and enclosed samples.[47] This was odd. Oswald had called the CPSUA a tool of the Soviet Union, but the Gus Hall Committee was a creation of the CPUSA. Thus even though he disliked the organization because of its ties to the Soviets, he was offering to work for its affiliate.

In the same month, he made a similar offer to the Socialist Workers Party. The Warren Report says that Oswald's offers "were not accepted."[48] This isn't correct. James Tormey of the Gus Hall Committee answered Oswald diplomatically to say that his offer of help would be kept on file.[49] Bob Chester of the SWP, however, was encouraging. He wrote, "There might very well be occasion on which we could utilize your skill for some printing project."[50] Oswald must have been pleased with Chester's letter because a few days later he began subscribing to the SWP's publication, the *Militant*.[51]

...

The missile crisis of 1962 showed John Kennedy at his best, and as the year was coming to a close, Lee Harvey Oswald was living in Dallas and corresponding with both the Communist Party and the Socialist Workers Party.[52]

5

The Brigade

The men of Brigade 2506, captured at the Bay of Pigs and rotting in a Cuban prison, were never out of the Kennedys' minds. John Kennedy had made the decision that put them there, and he would get them out of their predicament just like he did the men of PT-109. By the time the missile crisis was over, Brigade 2506 had been in prison eighteen months. As Robert Kennedy poignantly expressed it in his oral history: "The one thing that really hung over from the Bay of Pigs was the fact that those eleven hundred and fifty or so prisoners remained in jail, and that they were going to die, and not only did we have the responsibility for carrying out the Bay of Pigs in an ineffective way, but also costing the lives of all these men. So we wanted to do whatever was necessary, whatever we could to get them out. I felt strongly about it, and the president felt strongly about it."[1]

In September 1962, before the missile crisis, Robert Kennedy had raised the subject of ransoming the prisoners in a meeting with Bundy, Rusk, and others. Bundy cautioned against paying a ransom to Communists with a presidential campaign starting in a little over a year. Kennedy fired back: "I don't care if we lose every election until Kingdom come. We put those guys in there and we are going to get them out." Kennedy stormed out of the meeting.[2]

Once the missile crisis was settled, the attorney general turned to New York lawyer James Donovan for help. Although Kennedy didn't know Donovan personally, he knew of him. Donovan had negotiated with the Russians for the release of the U-2 pilot the Soviets had shot down in 1960, Francis Gary Powers, the man who had refused to commit suicide with CIA poison. After hearing that the prisoners in Cuba were dying, Kennedy told aides to get them out by Christmas.[3]

Donovan was a persuasive negotiator, and Castro was willing. Donovan reportedly said to Castro about the prisoners, "If you want to get rid of them, if you are going to sell them, you've got to sell them to me. There's no world market for prisoners."[4] Ultimately, they struck a deal: the prisoners in exchange for $53 million in medical supplies and $3 million in cash. All of it was raised from private donors. On Christmas Day 1962, most of the surviving members of Brigade 2506—1,113 men—walked off planes at Miami airport to be greeted by loved ones. The rest returned by boat. Robert Kennedy had met his self-imposed deadline. He celebrated with vodka, perhaps an intentionally ironic choice after staring down the Russians in the missile crisis.[5]

The president spoke to the returned prisoners at the Orange Bowl in Miami on December 29. On stage with him and Mrs. Kennedy were two of the brigade's leaders, Manuel Artime and Jose Perez "Pepe" San Román.[6] Artime had been in the Twenty-Sixth of July Movement and fought with Castro against Batista. When Castro won, Artime joined the Castro government, but when Castro embraced Communism, Artime fled. He was one of the first men the CIA recruited for the invasion of Cuba. He landed at the Bay of Pigs and evaded Castro's forces for about a month before capture.[7] San Román was commander of the brigade.[8] Robert Kennedy would become personally close to both men and several other members of the brigade.

When the returnees presented Jack Kennedy with the brigade flag at the Orange Bowl event, the president let himself be carried away by the emotion of the moment and promised to return the flag to a free Havana. The crowd felt the emotion too and chanted, "Guerra, Guerra," "war, war."[9]

The promise was never kept, but the planning for a return had already begun.[10] Bill Harvey could not, of course, continue to run the CIA's Cuban operations, Task Force W. He was eventually reassigned to the CIA's Rome station. But before he left, he drafted a memorandum on continuing operations against Cuba and discussed it with Helms and McCone on November 27, 1962. In light of Harvey's confrontation with Robert Kennedy, the memo seems both prescient and bitter. It begins by saying that the president's no-invasion pledge at the end of the missile crisis "will preclude any meaningful CIA action . . . to provoke a revolt in Cuba, since . . . such a revolt . . . would be totally destroyed by Cuban counteraction . . . unless supported by a major United States Military commitment." Paramilitary operations, including commando operations, which, the memo says, have a "high noise level," would "be unacceptable as a matter of policy." So, Harvey thought, Castro would only get stronger.[11]

The memo continued with a slap at the Kennedys' vacillation: "Despite the above factors, Higher Authority probably will continue heavy pressure on the CIA for a maximum effort against Cuba and may even continue to contend that the ultimate objective is the overthrow of the Castro-communist regime."[12]

Bill Harvey wasn't the only one at CIA to commit to writing his bitterness toward Mongoose, Lansdale, and the Kennedys. George McManus, Richard Helms's deputy for Cuba, began a November 5, 1962, memorandum by saying, with obvious pleasure, that Mongoose died with the president's no-invasion pledge. He cynically observed: "Looking back at the origins for Mongoose one finds the Attorney General and Mr. McNamara seeking primarily to remove the political stain left on the President by the Bay of Pigs failure." And he criticized the entire national security structure, except for General Taylor, for wanting to destabilize the Castro government while at the same time shying away from the logical outcome of that policy, military intervention.[13]

McManus felt that Mongoose had effectively given Lansdale control of Harvey's Task Force W. Therefore, the CIA officer wrote, its death gave the agency a chance to normalize things with respect to Cuban operations. Task Force W should not go through "bankruptcy," he wrote, but rather submit to "an unpublicized receivership and reorganization" and should be reabsorbed into the standard agency structure. He warned that the CIA shouldn't try to orchestrate Lansdale's departure. Referencing the bad feelings between Bill Harvey and Robert Kennedy, McManus wrote, "Remember that the Attorney General was fighting Lansdale's battle as recently as two weeks ago." Besides, McManus said, McNamara still looked on Lansdale "as something of a mystic." McManus felt Lansdale suffered from being too close to power, writing, "Lansdale's reaction to any reassignment is apt to be a violent one. He undoubtedly realizes the he never again will be in the position of a special advisor to the two most powerful men in the country."[14]

Neither Harvey nor McManus painted a very enticing picture of the structure for Cuban policy for Harvey's successor. Harvey's predictions about where the Kennedys would go next with the policy proved to be fairly accurate, and McManus's proposal that the CIA normalize its Cuban operations was implemented in a way. The CIA got rid of Lansdale and his Mongoose, but Robert Kennedy still called the shots on Cuban affairs.

Harvey and McManus weren't the only ones who were less than enamored with the Kennedy administration's performance during the missile crisis. Secretary of State Rusk implies in his memoirs that the president had exaggerated the likelihood of nuclear Armageddon during the missile crisis, writing, "Fortunately we never saw nuclear warheads on Soviet missiles or launchers ready to fire. We thought their warheads were on ships coming through the Strait of Gibraltar when we imposed the quarantine because those ships were the first to turn back."[15]

Truman's secretary of state Dean Acheson, whose advice for air strikes against the missile sites in Cuba was ignored by John Kennedy, dismissed Kennedy's success, telling Rusk later, "It was just plain dumb luck." Rusk fired back, "Of course it was dumb luck. We were lucky; the Russians were lucky; the whole world was lucky. But I would hasten to add, you can give yourself a chance to be lucky."[16]

One of Rusk's security agents, Bert Bennington, had a simpler view. Bennington and another agent were riding in an elevator with Rusk, Acheson, and George Ball during the crisis when Rusk pointed toward the agents and said to Acheson and Ball, "You know, the only decent advice I have had this past week has come from these two fellows." Bennington, a plain-spoken, former professional football lineman, replied: "The reason for that, Mr. Secretary, is that you have surrounded yourself with nothing but dumb fucks!"[17]

Fidel Castro was reportedly furious at the way Khrushchev settled the missile crisis, calling the Soviet leader, "Son of a bitch! Bastard! Asshole!" Castro felt abandoned without even the courtesy of advance notice of the decision. Soviet deputy premier Anastas Mikoyan was dispatched to Cuba to smooth Castro's ruffled feelings.[18] Mikoyan had correctly warned Khrushchev that Kennedy wouldn't allow the Russians to put missiles in Cuba. According to Rusk, Mikoyan told him about the Cuban visit later: "You know, that fellow Castro is crazy. He kept me, Mikoyan, waiting for ten days without seeing me. I finally told him that if he didn't see me the next morning, I was going home and he would be sorry. He finally saw me. That Castro is crazy."[19] Rusk, like Khrushchev, ignored Mikoyan, and seemed not to worry about angering Castro.

Meanwhile, at the CIA Richard Helms chose Harvey's successor within a month of the end of the missile crisis. His primary aim was to find a man who could get along with the attorney general. To that end the choice was Desmond FitzGerald. He shared the same last name as the president's grandfather, Honey Fitz, but he was not family. In fact, unlike the Kennedys, who were Irish Catholic, FitzGerald was descended from a Protestant English family that had settled in Ireland. He was New England Yankee to the core, not Boston Irish Catholic.[20]

FitzGerald, unlike Bill Harvey, who got his degree from a state school, Indiana University, was a Harvard man like John and Robert Kennedy. He had been a lawyer in New York City before enlisting in the army at age thirty to fight in World War II. He served as liaison officer to a Chinese regiment in the Pacific theater. He rejoined his New York law firm after the war, but then DDP Frank Wisner persuaded him to move to Washington and work for the CIA. FitzGerald was part of the so-called Georgetown crowd, young, brainy men who were interested in foreign affairs and working at places like the CIA and the Defense and State Departments. Senator John Kennedy and his new wife had briefly rented a house only a block away from the FitzGeralds' in Georgetown. During the Korean War, FitzGerald worked with a Chinese Nationalist military unit in southern China, adjacent to Laos and Vietnam, to force the Chinese to divert some of their military forces there rather than to the fight in Korea.[21]

Immediately prior to moving into Harvey's job, FitzGerald had been in charge of the CIA's Far East operations, focusing on counterinsurgency in Laos and Vietnam. He was the CIA's best covert-action leader.[22] If the selection seems to be déjà vu of the president's thinking in the selection of General Lansdale a year earlier, so be it. This nuance may have been a factor in Helms's choosing Fitz-Gerald. In any event the name Task Force W, which had been used for the staff William Harvey led, was changed to Special Affairs Staff, or SAS for short.

Helms picked William Colby, one of FitzGerald's underlings, as the new head of the CIA's Far East efforts. Colby would gain unwanted infamy for being in charge of that section of the CIA during the Vietnam War. Later he was director of CIA during the Church Committee's investigation of CIA assassination efforts before being replaced by George H. W. Bush.

FitzGerald was a handsome doer, just the opposite of the frog-like, plodding Harvey. In fact he was Harvey's opposite in almost every way imaginable. Colby remembered: "With a lovely George-town house and a country residence in Virginia, he was well connected throughout Washington, where his romantic activism produced great dinner talk."[23] A relative described FitzGerald, who would suffer an early death in 1967 from a heart attack after a game of tennis, as extremely genial and always a gentleman. He had a smile on his face all the time and loved to laugh. He was also extremely motivated. He was a generous man for whom money was not important.[24]

The FitzGeralds were fixtures in Georgetown society. The Thanksgiving-time house tour there in 1960 was chaired by the CIA's Thomas Parrott, and included the FitzGeralds' home as well as those of Supreme Court justice John Harlan and National Gallery of Art director John Walker II.[25] The *Washington Post* reported that the theme at the FitzGeralds' would be oriental with Steuben glass goblets, Japanese porcelain plates, and a centerpiece with an ivory moon goddess.[26] The next year the *Post* reported that FitzGerald's wife was the chairperson of the annual Washington Debutante Ball. In addition to the FitzGeralds' daughter, the debutantes included the daughters of *Washington Post* owners Phillip and Katherine Graham, of *Washington Post* editor Fred Friendly, of banker Paul Mellon, and of Nancy Mackall, a descendant of one of the oldest and wealthiest families in Georgetown.[27] A year later FitzGerald's wife landed on page 1 of the society section of the *Washington Post* for raising $349,000 for a charity for aphasic children. The paper carried a photograph of her right below a half-page spread and photograph of Robert Kennedy's wife, Ethel, and her children. Mrs. FitzGerald was described as "the wife of a Washington government official."[28] And in January 1963, Mrs. FitzGerald posed for a photograph with Mrs. Hugh Auchincloss, Jackie Kennedy's mother, for another *Washington Post* story on the charity.[29]

Decades later Sam Halpern, FitzGerald's executive officer, told Brian Latell for the book *Castro's Secrets* that FitzGerald socialized with the attorney general on weekends in the horse country around Middleburg, Virginia. Halpern recalled FitzGerald would come into the office on Monday morning "all charged up" and would say things like: "I saw Bobby in Middleburg. Here's what we've got to crank up for next month." But like Lansdale, FitzGerald may have suffered from being too close to power. According to Latell, "Halpern concluded that Bobby was a bad influence on Des [FitzGerald], reinforcing his worst instincts."[30] Robert Kennedy described FitzGerald concisely in his oral history: "Then they [CIA] put Des FitzGerald on [the Cuban problem]. Des FitzGerald was much better [than Bill Harvey]."[31]

FitzGerald realized what Harvey had not, that President Kennedy had wiggle room on his no-invasion pledge. Historian Michael Beschloss notes: "Many critics have complained about what they consider to be the Kennedy's pledge not to invade Cuba. Close study of the settlement suggests that the President may have deliberately avoided such an unambiguous commitment." Beschloss points out that in a November 20, 1962, press conference, Kennedy put three conditions on his pledge: no more offensive weapons in Cuba; no export of the revolution from Cuba; and Cuba should not violate certain international agreements.[32] In the end

Beschloss says, "One must therefore conclude that the President deliberately booby-trapped his no-invasion pledge in order not to rule out further American efforts to topple the Castro regime, including invasion."[33]

John Kennedy had no intention of taking the option of an invasion of Cuba off the table. At a meeting of the Executive Committee of the National Security Council in late November 1962, attended by the president, the attorney general, Joint Chiefs chairman Taylor, Rusk, and McNamara, the discussion turned to the Soviet ground troops that were still in Cuba. The minutes of the meeting record: "The President commented that the Russians won't take out their ground forces until we give a no-invasion assurance. *It is better for us to have the Soviet units in Cuba than to give a formal no-invasion assurance.*"[34]

The president began the new year of 1963 by vacationing for a week in Palm Beach, Florida. He took in a football game at the Orange Bowl, dined with friends, went for long cruises with actor and in-law Peter Lawford on board the family boat, *Honey Fitz*, and attended to official business. Vice President Johnson flew down for a cruise on the last day of the vacation.

After he returned to the White House on January 8, the president met with his national security team, Rusk, McNamara, and McCone, in the afternoon and with congressional leaders in late afternoon. That evening he and Mrs. Kennedy dined at large party at the French embassy. They then went to the National Gallery of Art, where its director, John Walker—one of Desmond Fitzgerald's Georgetown friends—hosted a ceremony to unveil the Mona Lisa portrait, which was on loan from the Louvre in Paris.[35]

Earlier that day McGeorge Bundy had signed and released a national security memorandum creating the Interdepartmental Coordinating Committee for Cuban Affairs, answering to the secretary of state. Even its acronym, ICCCA, was long and awkward. Representatives of the Departments of Defense and Health, Education, and Welfare would be regular members as would the attorney general and officials of the CIA and the United States Information Agency. One of the ICCCA's principal functions was to deal with Cuban refugees. The secretary of state would chair the committee and designate a coordinator. The coordinator would be responsible for both overt and covert operations but report to the Special Group, rather than to the secretary of state, on covert matters. The White House wanted to integrate the government's overt programs to help Cuban refugees, including the returned members of Brigade 2506, with covert operations aimed at overthrowing Castro.[36]

On the plus side, the new structure facilitated the recruitment of returnees and refugees for covert operations. But on the minus side, it added new layers of bureaucracy between the president and operations. For example, the Defense Department named Secretary of the Army Cyrus Vance as its representative to the ICCCA, and he named his special assistant Joseph Califano as his representative. Califano in turn designated James Patchell to be his assistant.[37] This development not only made action more cumbersome; it also widened the number of people who knew what was going on with respect to covert actions against Cuba.

At the giant Defense Department, the wheels of the bureaucracy began to spin with new missions in mind. Memoranda such as "Future Policy toward Cuba" were drafted and revised time and time again. Even General Lansdale, who had been removed from his role as coordinator of the Special Group because the Kennedys lost faith in him, participated in the planning. A consensus quickly developed on two options. The first was to "actively and boldly pursue . . . the overthrow of the Castro/Communist regime." The second was to "adopt a substantially less active policy." If the first was chosen, the planners visualized a phased approach, beginning with propaganda and workers' strikes and building up to sabotage, air strikes, sabotage of shipping, and "ultimately, the use of U.S. military forces." The second alternative called for passive isolation of Cuba.[38] In other words the Department of Defense thought the choices were between war and diplomacy.

By January 19 the Defense Department analysis reached Gordon Chase, who was an assistant to McGeorge Bundy. It also reached the State Department, showing how difficult it was to keep secrets in Washington. In a memo to Bundy, Chase rejected both Defense Department options. The passive approach was too limiting. As for the active approach, Chase in his memorandum agreed with the State Department: "At best, [the Defense Department plan is] a useless exercise and waste of time and, at worst . . . an insidious attempt by DOD dreamers to bring to life a policy which will earn battlefield promotions at the expense of U.S. national interest."[39]

The president was insulated from the bureaucratic infighting. On the same day that Chase wrote his memo for Bundy, the CIA reported to Kennedy that as many as 1,500 individuals from other Latin American countries had passed through Cuba the previous year for indoctrination or guerilla training. A small number of them went on to Sino-Soviet bloc countries for further training. In other words Castro was doing his best to export the revolution to the rest of Latin America. After reading the CIA report, the president ordered the ICCCA to take up the matter and get back to him.[40]

The State Department's official memorandum on Cuba was up for consideration at the January 25 meeting of the National Security Council Executive Committee. The paper ignored the Defense Department's active option and chose the completely passive approach of economic sanctions, intelligence collection, support of exile groups, and disbanding Brigade 2506.[41]

Meanwhile, at the very bottom of the huge national security effort directed at Cuba, Bill Harvey met with Johnny Roselli sometime in January. He paid Roselli $2,700 to defray the expenses the Cubans had incurred in trying to assassinate Castro. A few weeks later, Harvey told Roselli the operation was terminated. Roselli never bothered to tell the Cubans.[42]

In February 1963 Kennedy was asked at a press conference about the chances of eliminating Communism in Cuba before his term ended. One way, the president said, was through an internal revolt, but that would be difficult because of the security forces of the Cuban government. "The other way would be by external action. But that is war," he said. He concluded a very long answer by leaning ambiguously toward the passive approach: "But when they start talking about how, and when, they start talking about Americans invading Cuba and killing thousands of Cubans and Americans, with the hazard around the world, that is a very serious decision, and I noticed that that is not approached directly by a good many who have discussed the problem."[43]

Behind the scenes the president was anything but passive. On February 15 he wrote Rusk, McNamara, and McCone, referencing his remarks at the press conference and the flow of students, labor leaders, and others to Cuba for training and indoctrination, and concluded: "I would appreciate it if CIA would assign a leading official to this." To underscore the fact that this was not an idle request on his part, he asked for weekly progress reports from the ICCCA.[44] Kennedy may not have wanted to go to war over Cuba, but he wouldn't put up with export of the revolution to other countries in Latin America.

The giant intelligence bureaucracy aimed at Cuba presented its own management problems, ones that were aggravated by past mistakes and edicts from the top. For example, the confrontation between Bill Harvey and Robert Kennedy and General Lansdale over Harvey's putting agents into Cuba without clearing it with Lansdale apparently led the Defense Department to require that all agent activity in Cuba be cleared with the CIA. (This was the opposite of what Lansdale had wanted, that the CIA report to him.) On February 19 the army asked the CIA for permission to infiltrate a trained radio operator into Cuba to service an existing clandestine network of agents the army had there. The CIA had objections, but those were resolved in two days. Next the army had to get approval from the Special Group, but in the meantime, the CIA raised additional objections. A month later the infiltration was still being held in abeyance. There is no indication that clearance was ever given. The Special Group was micromanaging Cuban operations at the agent level.[45]

Completely outside this governmental structure, the attorney general was maintaining his own personal ties with Brigade 2506 leaders, especially commander Manuel Artime, deputy commander Erneido Oliva, Roberto San Román, Pepe San Román, and Enrique Ruiz-Williams.[46] He had the CIA pay for a house in Maryland for Manuel Artime and a house for Pepe San Román in Virginia not far from Kennedy's Hickory Hill. He went horseback riding with the latter. Kennedy was deeply affected by what had happened to

San Román during the Bay of Pigs invasion, recalling in his oral history: "I was getting the reports in as quickly as possible from the beach and the cries and calls for more ammunition and the last report that I received from Pepe San Roman [on the beach] saying that 'we fired our last shell—we're all taking to the swamp.' It was a very sad, difficult period of time."[47]

The attorney general began to harbor the notion that the exiles themselves might do what the CIA seemed unable to do and bring about regime change in Cuba.[48] In an oral history, he was asked, "Do you, did you have high peop [sic]—any Cubans that you used particularly? I remember meeting one at your birthday party who kept in touch with me." Kennedy answered, "Enrico Williams," and the interviewer continued, "Yeah. What was he supposed to be. . . . He wanted to go to the Dominican Republic and do something from there."[49] Kennedy didn't respond, seeming not to want to talk about what Williams was doing.

One reason for creation of the ICCCA group in January 1963 had been to use returned brigade members in covert action against Cuba. It proved not to be very covert. In early February Artime held a press conference to announce that interested returnees would soon be training with the U.S. military at bases across the country.[50] Oliva would later say that about this time he "was commissioned as a second lieutenant in the U.S. Army and began work on the secret operations as a liaison to then-Secretary of the Army Cyrus Vance and his aide, Lt. Col. Alexander Haig."[51] In all about 108 of the returnees went into the U.S. Army and trained at Fort Benning, Georgia.[52]

President Kennedy seemed inspired by the Cubans and began thinking there might be a rebellion in Cuba. On February 28 he met with the Joint Chiefs of Staff. According to a Defense Department memorandum of the meeting, the president wanted to know how long it would take to put American troops in Cuba in the event of an uprising. The generals said that existing plans assumed there would be a period of tension prior to the insertion of troops. They could deploy an armed force within eighteen days of notification. Kennedy said he wanted to be able to put troops in Cuba "at a much earlier date than 18 days." The memo went on to say that the Joint

Chiefs were revising their plans, hoping to be able to put at least airborne forces in Cuba more quickly, and were separately studying how best to react to an uprising. The memo noted that the State Department was also studying how to react to an uprising from its perspective. Thus it seemed perfectly clear by late February that the no-invasion pledge did not apply if there was an uprising in Cuba. Left open was the question of how widespread such an uprising needed to be.[53]

At the CIA Desmond FitzGerald's thinking was well ahead of the president's and the rest of the national security establishment. In a draft of a memorandum for McCone in March 1963, Fitzgerald dismissed as "unrealistic" the possibility of a popular revolt in Cuba. Even if there were one, FitzGerald wrote, the United States would then face the dilemma of either sending in military forces or doing nothing. FitzGerald was thinking about what had happened in Russian-occupied Hungary. When the Hungarians revolted against the Russians in 1956, the Eisenhower administration took no action, and the Russian army crushed the revolt.

FitzGerald felt the best option was for the United States to employ a "pincers strategy of economic strangulation to weaken and undermine the [Communist] regime" and combine this with a military coup. If McCone agreed, then FitzGerald would proceed to identify and recruit dissidents in the Cuban military and other high-level officials in the Castro government who could lead the coup. The main effort would be among key officers in the military. To get these men to risk a coup, FitzGerald argued, the CIA would, among other things, have to convince them that the American military would intervene in the event of stalemate or in the event the Soviets tried to protect Castro. He meant the United States should not let the Russians put down any revolt in Cuba as they had done in Hungary. FitzGerald added that after the coup, the United States would support "the free will of the Cuban people in [sic] as expressed [in] free elections when feasible." Despite implying that he would accept a Communist government if freely elected, FitzGerald wrote elsewhere in the draft that the Communists would, of course, have to be excluded from any new regime.[54]

The State Department competed for the president's attention

by offering its passive approach. On March 11 Bundy circulated to the National Security Council two State Department talking papers. One was on U.S. policy in Europe. The other was for Cuba. The State Department's view contrasted sharply with what Fitz-Gerald had envisioned in his secret recommendation to McCone. State's position was essentially one of containment. That is, the United States should fight the spread of Communism to other Latin American countries and should advocate free elections in Cuba. However, the only action directed at Cuba itself would be "to tighten the noose around the Cuban economy" and to take political action to make the Castro regime "a complete pariah." One specific program mentioned was to curtail free world shipping with Cuba, which had dropped from 128 ships in January 1962 to 12 in January 1963.[55] Of course the naval blockade of Cuba during the Cuban Missile Crisis three months earlier had blocked all ships from Cuba while it was operating and may have continued to scare away ships of free-world countries.

Another threat to shipping came from naval attacks by Cuban exile groups. On March 18 one such group, Alpha 66, attacked a Soviet ship and Soviet installations in Cuba. For the president this was completely unacceptable. He wanted to get rid of Castro, but he didn't want to confront the Soviets again. At his press conference four days later, he expressed concern and said the United States might want to stop such raids. The Justice and State Departments got together and quickly concluded that exile raids violated neutrality laws and that the perpetrators should be prosecuted.[56]

The exile raids seemed to bother the president more than they bothered Castro and with good reason. An unsigned and undated memorandum from this period in army files said that only four to six exile groups in the past year had raided Cuba. Alpha 66 was the most visible and perhaps the most effective. Still, the total strength of all these groups never exceeded 250 men. They had limited and poor-quality equipment and ten to twelve boats armed with .50 caliber machine guns and antiquated recoilless rifles. They had no more than ten bases in the Florida and Bahamas Keys.[57] Militarily, they were no threat to the Castro government.

Kennedy's prohibition against exile raids on Cuba did not apply to raids sponsored by the intelligence agencies, but it was difficult to distinguish which groups had government support and which did not. For example, although the CIA was the principal agency aimed at Cuba, army intelligence was also involved. It had 120 Cuban agents, more than half of whom were on the island.[58] They were gathering the kind of intelligence that the army would need in the event of an invasion. In military parlance this is called "order of battle" information, which is designed to identify opposing military units and their leaders.

Alpha 66 was another example of how the line between government-sponsored and private groups could be blurred. As late as February 1963, army intelligence officers in Puerto Rico and Miami had been in contact with Alpha 66 because Lansdale had been interested in the group. The army had not made operational use of Alpha 66 since February, but this might have changed if Alpha 66 hadn't drawn the president's displeasure by shooting up the Soviet ship. Army files contain a letter drafted for Secretary of the Army Vance at the end of February asking permission to work with Alpha 66. However, the document is lined through and marked "Not Used," presumably because of the president's ire at what Alpha 66 had done.[59]

The president's policy on these raids became clear by the end of March when the State and Justice Departments issued a joint statement saying that every effort would be made to prevent such raids being "launched, manned, or equipped from Untied States territory."[60] The wording contained a huge loophole though. Exile groups could continue to fund raids on Cuba provided the boats did not depart from U.S. soil, and the CIA could do whatever it wanted.

The CIA still wasn't doing much. At the ICCCA meeting of April 1, the agency outlined its plans for the traditional Communist holiday of May Day. The CIA would float balloons over Havana, where they would burst and release hundreds of thousands of leaflets belittling Castro and with "cartoons illustrating sabotage techniques." The idea harkened back to the one from World War II that Richard Helms remembered about inserting suppositories filled with leaflets in cows that grazed from Switzerland to Germany. Some attendees argued that the CIA should take advantage of the loophole in the prohibition against exile-group raids and have them launched from outside the United States. Helms pointed out that it was impossible to control exile groups and that they still might attack Soviet ships. Others suggested that American propaganda programs should encourage Cubans to attack Soviet troops on the island. Army Secretary Vance wisely counseled that this might lead to major fighting between Cuban civilians and Soviet troops, presenting the United States with the dilemma of intervening in Cuba militarily or sitting on its hands.[61]

Such was the dismal state of thinking when the president scheduled a meeting on the morning of April 3 at the White House. In attendance were the attorney general, Vance, Bundy, Helms, Fitz-Gerald, and others, and the topic was Cuba. The documents suggest that the Kennedys intended to test the CIA's mettle. Two CIA participants, FitzGerald and his Georgetown neighbor Thomas Parrott, wrote memoranda for the record of the meeting.

The president opened by saying he wanted to review the CIA's program for Cuba. In fact he focused mainly on pushing the CIA to resume sabotage operations. Perhaps he or his brother had read of the meeting on April 1 at which the CIA's approach to sabotage consisted of dropping leaflets with cartoons showing Cubans how to commit sabotage. More likely the attorney general had been hearing complaints from his friends in the Cuban exile community about how little was being done.

FitzGerald began his presentation at the meeting by describing the environment in which the CIA operated in Cuba. Castro's capabilities in counterinsurgency, for example, nabbing raiders and putting down uprisings, were good. The Cubans weren't so good in counter-espionage, that is, catching spies. In the past year, FitzGerald explained, the CIA had run seven "black [clandestine] operations," but only one had been sabotage.[62]

The president focused on sabotage. He wanted to know what the CIA had in mind. FitzGerald responded by saying that sabotage operations had not been in favor since the Cuban Missile Crisis. He added that while such raids might bolster the morale of exiles, they were counterproductive to the extent that Cubans didn't like them. His implication was the Cubans didn't like them because innocent civilians on the island were killed and their property destroyed in the raids. Bundy explained to the president that the Special Group had indeed insisted on low-key operations. Kennedy volunteered that he himself had no objection to raids if they hit worthwhile targets. He also didn't object to seaborne raids as long as they didn't attack Soviet ships. He did object to the "froth" that went along with the raids and to exile groups holding press conferences to gloat about them afterward.

FitzGerald switched to talking about the CIA's failures in mounting its own sabotage operations in Cuba. He said the Cuban government was very good at uncovering internal resistance groups. It used the classic "block system," introduced by the KGB. Presumably, he meant appointing block captains whose job it was to know everyone in a neighborhood and therefore could quickly identify strangers as possible CIA agents.

The attorney general asked about future plans. FitzGerald responded by identifying what he considered the most important question—"whether time is on our side or on Castro's"—and the Board of National Estimates was working on that very question. The attorney general might not have been too pleased to hear this. His push to get rid of Castro in the fall of 1961 had been undercut when the Board of National Estimates reported that the Communists might become stronger if Castro were removed. Lansdale had chimed in on that occasion to support the attorney general, but no one did this time. In fact the president observed that if the board concluded Castro would only get stronger, then it might be necessary to find a way to live with him. In any event, FitzGerald said, Cuban security forces were too good to allow a popular uprising, and he explained his idea for a military coup.

Robert Kennedy asked whether it was useful to consider large-scale commando raids with hundreds of men. FitzGerald answered that big raids were out of the question given how good Castro's security forces were. Castro tended to respond to incursions by sending in military forces that outnumbered the invaders by a one hundred to one ratio. Bundy provided a veiled reminder of the president's unhappy decision in Bay of Pigs invasion by saying that the question of American military support would come up if a large-scale raid got into trouble. Nonetheless, the attorney general insisted that all possibilities for aggressive action over the next six months needed to be considered.

At the end of the meeting, the president said he wanted the Board of National Estimates to complete its work and a sabotage plan to be submitted to the Special Group the next week. The Kennedys, it seemed, liked sabotage regardless of the fact that no one else did.

The president concluded by asking FitzGerald to suggest a plan of action on the assumption he would be "given unlimited policy and funds." FitzGerald seemed stunned, writing in his memorandum of the meeting: "No specific time was indicated for the submission of such a plan and I stated that we did not presently have such a plan in hand." But the president had told FitzGerald to think big, and this was something he loved to do.

These must have been maddening times for FitzGerald. Later in the day, hours after the president had told him to think big, the CIA man went to a bizarre meeting of the mid-level ICCCA chaired by the State Department representative. According to a memorandum of the meeting, FitzGerald, Vance, and those State Department officials present discussed whether it was wise to urge Cubans to attack Soviet troops. Divorced from reality the committee bickered, split hairs, and concluded, according to the minutes, that it was "O.K. for individual Cubans to attack Soviet troops or installations but that it was undesirable for groups of Cubans to organize attacks against the Russians." The convoluted reasoning was that Castro's forces were good at ferreting out organizations and that there might be widespread reprisals. The memorandum took pains to state the obvious: widespread reprisals were "not generally considered a good thing."[63]

Finally, the topic of sabotage came up. FitzGerald had spent the morning being roasted by the president and the attorney general on the CIA's failures in this regard. One suggestion at this ICCCA meeting was to affix limpets, magnet explosives, to Cuban ships in Havana harbor. This idea was rejected on the grounds that the limpets might sink a ship, which of course is the very purpose of a limpet. As a subsequent memo notes, FitzGerald "went on to say that he came away from [the] meeting with the President with the feeling that the President would like some noise level in our sabotage program for morale purposes." Army Secretary Vance cautioned that the limpet plan should be submitted to the Special Group the next day. Whether because of bureaucracy or of wiser heads prevailing, the Kennedys' pressure on the CIA for sabotage operations was being vitiated.[64]

The Special Group met the next week, and its micromanagement of operations was again in evidence. Sabotage was the main topic for discussion. FitzGerald had several such operations planned for upcoming weeks, but there were objections. Negotiator James Donovan was working with the government anew to get several Americans released from Castro's prisons. The Special Group didn't want any raids to take place during negotiations.

Once this discussion concluded, FitzGerald briefed the group on recent agent infiltrations and future plans. But like the ICCCA, the Special Group bridled at the Kennedys' push for sabotage. It agreed unanimously that more study into the likelihood of success and the benefits of sabotage was needed before changing the existing policy against sabotage. It was easy enough for the Special Group to buck the president; only Bundy and FitzGerald had felt the heat at the meeting with him the previous week. CIA director McCone had not been in that meeting, so he felt free to express "great skepticism" about resuming sabotage operations without a larger objective in mind. Therefore, the Special Group agreed to talk again with "higher authority," meaning John Kennedy.[65]

Four days later McCone met privately with the president in Palm Beach. McCone's notes reveal that they talked in detail about Donovan's efforts to negotiate the release of Americans in Cuba. The president raised the question of Miro Cardona, the leader of the exile group Cuban Revolutionary Council. Cardona had appeared onstage with President and Mrs. Kennedy, Manuel Artime, and Pepe San Román at the Orange Bowl event on December 29, 1962, to honor the return of Brigade 2506. Cardona was threatening to step down from his leadership position unless the president presented a plan to liberate Cuba. FitzGerald had sent McCone a memorandum two days earlier saying Cardona's usefulness to the U.S. government was at an end. Presumably because of FitzGerald's memo, McCone advised Kennedy not to engage in a public argument with the exile leader.

Naturally, the topic of sabotage came up. Kennedy had not given up on the idea. McCone pointed out the political dangers of the United States saying, on the one hand, that it was cracking down on sabotage by exile groups and, on the other, letting the CIA engage in it. Kennedy thought perhaps the sabotage should come from within Cuba. McCone did not respond.

He turned instead to talk about an overall plan for Cuba. McCone recommended either that the United States try to work with Castro or that it pressure Khrushchev to withdraw Soviet troops. The latter option would give the United States more freedom of action in bringing about Castro's downfall. The president opined that the two different approaches could be pursued simultaneously.[66]

As April drew to a close, the United States had yet to come up with any new idea for ousting Castro. No one could persuade the Kennedys that sabotage was not a strategy. But then a better solution had yet to be agreed upon. McCone advised either negotiations with Castro to get the Soviets out or negotiations with Khrushchev to the same end, while FitzGerald advocated a military coup.

6

Fidel and Hidell

ee Harvey Oswald was still working at the Jaggars-Chiles-Stovall graphic arts company in Dallas on New Year's Day 1963. He undoubtedly used the company's equipment to prepare the photo-print samples he had sent to the Socialist Workers Party and the Gus Hall Committee a few months earlier when he offered to work for them for free. Now he wanted a better job and enrolled in an evening typing class in January. Marina, for her part, continued to seek out Russians or those with an interest in Russia for social reasons. Through these connections she met Ruth Paine in February 1963. Paine was learning Russian, and she thought practicing with a native speaker like Marina would help. The two women struck up a friendship. Paine had recently separated from her husband, and Marina's husband was gone much of the time, so the women were free to talk and let their children play together.[1]

In March 1963 Oswald received two packages he had ordered. One was a Smith & Wesson .38 caliber revolver; the other was a rifle. He used the alias A. J. Hidell in ordering the pistol and A. Hidell for the rifle. He had used variations of these same aliases previously. Alek James Hidell was the name on identification cards that he forged with equipment at the graphic arts company. No one knows why he used these aliases though. He had called himself "Alexsky" Oswald in getting a hunting permit in Russia. The "Hidell" presumably was an allusion to Fidel Castro. Thus the alias A. J. Hidell mixed his old interest in Russia with an intensified interest in Castro. Oswald kept the rifle in a storeroom at his apartment, a room that he warned Marina not to enter. She testified to the Warren Commission that he took the rifle out for practice, although he barely had time to do so.[2]

Even before the weapons arrived, according to Marina, Oswald began planning to shoot retired general Edwin Walker, an outspoken anti-Communist living in the Dallas area. Oswald photographed Walker's house, the alley behind it, and a nearby railroad track. He recorded his plans in a notebook and checked the schedules for buses that would take him to Walker's home. In the meantime things were not going well in Oswald's personal life. Jaggars-Chiles-Stovall fired him on April 6.[3] Two days later Walker returned from an extended speaking tour during which, according to newspaper reports in Dallas, he had advocated dropping the Eighty-Second Airborne Division into Cuba to "liquidate the scourge" there.[4]

Two days after the newspaper report appeared, on the evening of April 10, Oswald went to Walker's house and fired at him with the rifle but missed. Oswald hid the weapon nearby and rode a bus home. He retrieved the weapon later. It was the same rifle that killed the president. Within two weeks of the shooting, Oswald left his wife and daughter in Dallas and went by bus to New Orleans, saying he had a better chance of finding work there. He probably also wanted to get out of Dallas in case the police were looking for him. Oswald sought out an aunt in New Orleans and stayed with her while he searched for a job. On May 9 he found work with a coffee roaster, the William B. Reily Company. Oswald's job was to lubricate the machinery. He also found an apartment for his family. Oswald called Marina with the news, and the next day Ruth Paine drove Marina and the Oswalds' daughter the five hundred miles from Dallas to New Orleans.[5]

Following the move the Oswalds' life seemed to smooth out. Marina was pregnant again. But the marital tranquility would not last long. On July 19 the Reily Company fired Oswald, apparently because he was spending much of his time reading gun magazines and discussing guns during working hours with the owner of a nearby garage.[6]

By this time Oswald had already applied for a new passport, and he told Marina to write the Russian embassy to ask about her returning to the Soviet Union. She did as he wanted and enclosed a letter from him asking for a visa for each of them. She told the Warren Commission that Oswald wasn't serious about going back to the Soviet Union himself: "His basic desire was to get to Cuba by any means, and that all the rest of it was window dressing for that purpose."[7] In other words, according to Marina by early July, while Oswald was still lubricating coffee machinery and talking guns with the guy next door, he was scheming about how to get to Cuba.

...

John Kennedy didn't want to travel to Cuba; he wanted to invade it. When the Special Group met on April 25, McGeorge Bundy told the attendees that he had received a report placing a high priority on "low-level coverage" of Cuba. The latter term was a reference to photoreconnaissance by low-flying jet aircraft. Low-level flights yielded more detailed photographs but could be shot down more easily than the high-altitude U-2s. Only surface- to-air-missiles could shoot down the U-2s, and they were manned by Russians who didn't fire at the spy planes. The minutes of the meeting record that Bundy said there was "high-level" interest. His resort to euphemism in this instance is laughable not only because it causes confusion when talking about low-level flights but also because only one person was higher than Bundy on national security matters.

The State Department representative warned that the Soviets would interpret low-level flights as a hardening of the American position toward Cuba. He also worried that this might slow Soviet withdrawal from Cuba and affect Soviet policy halfway around the world in Laos.

The discussion then turned to a proposed new policy for Cuba. McCone led off by saying that while the policy of isolating Cuba and making Castro a pariah was useful, it wouldn't topple the regime. Neither would sabotage. And while some in the national security establishment had suggested extreme forms of sabotage, such as the complete destruction of crops, McCone said outright invasion was better than this kind of thing.

Therefore, he recommended that the United States aim for a military coup. FitzGerald took over to explain that several high-level Cuban officials were unhappy with Castro. The task was to organize them and assure them of U.S. support. As an apparent sop to the Kennedys, FitzGerald carved out a role for raids by select Cuban exile groups. The attorney general was constantly urging this type of action, presumably because of his friendship with Brigade 2506 leaders.

When Bundy questioned a statement in FitzGerald's supporting paper to the effect that covert action was not a pretext for military intervention, McCone and FitzGerald said the statement was meant to convey only that covert action was not *intended* as a pretext for invasion. This did not preclude the possibility of military intervention at a later date. In other words, while the CIA was not advocating a military invasion of Cuba, it recognized that invasion might be the result.[8]

This long-range plan apparently didn't satisfy the attorney general. According to historian Michael Beschloss, he complained to the Standing Group that the United States had to do something against Castro even if it couldn't bring him down.[9] Of course FitzGerald's plan would do exactly that.

The military began to lean FitzGerald's way. On May 10, 1963, Maxwell Taylor, chairman of the Joint Chiefs of Staff, forwarded to Secretary of the Army Cyrus Vance "a comprehensive study of the courses of action" in the event of a spontaneous revolt in Cuba. The study offered four options in this event: ignore; discourage; encourage; and support. It concluded that the best alternative was for the United States to exploit any revolution that showed a reasonable promise of success.

Even better, the report implied, would be a revolt that the United States initiated by encouraging disaffected leaders in the Cuban government. If that happened and these leaders asked for help, then the United States could apply its full military power to assure the revolution's success. An estimated 17,000 Soviet troops were deployed in Cuba while Castro had a standing army of about 75,000 and another 200,000 in ready reserves and militia, according to the Pentagon's estimate. Castro's forces would not be able to stand up to a large-scale military invasion by the United States. As for the Soviet forces, the report said coldly, they would have to be neutralized or eliminated, although any such confrontation could, obviously, have serious repercussions.[10] The report doesn't say it, but one repercussion of American soldiers killing Russian soldiers might be World War III.

Thus analyzing the situation apparently independently, both the CIA and the Joint Chiefs of Staff had concluded that a U.S.-initiated coup was the best way to get rid of Castro. Of course the joint chiefs were only speaking from a military point of view. A politician like the president might shudder at the thought of American troops shooting up Cuba, where 17,000 Soviet troops were stationed, particularly a president who called small commando raids noisy.

The CIA's Office of National Estimates gave support to FitzGerald by concluding that things in Cuba just might improve in the event of Castro's death. In a draft memorandum of May 13, 1963, the office provided a rather promising estimate: "We believe the odds are that upon Castro's death his brother Raul or some other figure in the regime would, with Soviet backing and help, take over control. However, there is a good chance that a power struggle would ensue. . . . In any case the loyalties of the military commanders, now committed to Fidel but probably divided after his death, would significantly influence the outcome. Anti-Moscow Cuban nationalists would require extensive US help in order to win, and probably US military intervention."[11]

FitzGerald had won a big bureaucratic victory within the agency by getting the prestigious Office of National Estimates on his side. It had not given such support to Robert Kennedy and General Lansdale eighteen months earlier.

At a lower level, a subcommittee of the ICCCA had been working since February on the problem of countering Communist subversion in other Latin American countries. It focused on putting controls on people traveling to Cuba for indoctrination and training, on propaganda, on the movement of funds, and on the export of arms from Cuba to other countries. In addition it wanted to organize the countries of Latin America for exchanges of intelligence, surveillance, and training in countersubversion and for the creation of multinational military forces to help threatened countries.[12]

The Defense Department's representative on this subcommittee of ICCCA and its chairman was marine major general Victor

H. Krulak. In World War II navy lieutenant Jack Kennedy's PT boat helped evacuate Krulak's forces from an island in the Pacific Ocean after the marine's troops carried out a successful operation against the Japanese. Krulak was awarded the Navy Cross with V for Valor and a Bronze Star for leading the marines in the operation. He promised Lieutenant Kennedy a bottle of whiskey for his help. Krulak didn't have a chance to deliver it until he was a general and Kennedy was president.[13] In the last week of Kennedy's presidency, the big picture of a coup and this relatively minor countersubversion program would come to the fore.

The proliferation of special organizations dealing with Cuban matters was apparently so confusing to those involved that Bundy found it necessary to remind everyone of who was responsible for what. In a memo to the Standing Group, he had to explain that the ICCCA was a coordinating committee for day-to-day action on lower-level matters such as reducing free-world shipping to Cuba, refugees, countersubversion, and propaganda. On covert matters it reported to the Special Group of the National Security Council, which was responsible for covert operations against Cuba. Bundy noted that the Special Group was not to be confused with yet another subcommittee of the National Security Council called the Standing Group. The latter was supposed to deal with contingency plans and long-range policy. It was an organization that had been shelved as unneeded until resurrected by Bundy in April 1963.[14] Its rebirth may not have been a good thing.

The distinctions among these three groups weren't clear either in theory or in practice. The minutes of the May 28 Standing Group's meetings show discussions little different from those of the ICCCA or of the Special Group. Someone had the idea of driving down the price of sugar in order to hurt the Cuban economy. There was discussion of a paper on possible actions in the event of Castro's death.

The subjects would be familiar ones to those who had attended Special Group meetings over the years. The minutes noted that all the courses of action were "unpromising." On a separate matter, Bundy asked with apparent despair: "What do we do about Cuba?" He felt that perhaps nothing could be done until the Soviets left. McCone advocated a refinement of the plan FitzGerald had presented to the Special Group. The United States would cause increased economic hardship in Cuba while at the same time upping the noise level through raids and sabotage in the hope that this would persuade Cuban military leaders to join a CIA-sponsored coup.

Robert McNamara doubted the effectiveness of sabotage. Instead, he said the United States should provoke Castro into giving it an excuse to invade. He offered a frightening example of his thinking by suggesting that the United States should provoke the Cubans into attacking the Guantanamo Naval Base, thus justifying direct U.S. military action against Cuba. McNamara didn't point out that Americans would die in such an attack. Another alternative, he said, would be long-range economic warfare. Or, finally, the United States might somehow "buy off Castro."

McCone and McNamara got into a debate with Under Secretary of State Averell Harriman over the state of relations between the Soviets and Cuba. The attorney general joined the meeting late, while Desmond FitzGerald was making a presentation on possible covert operations, to point out once again that the United States had to do something against Castro even though such actions might not change things. When McCone said that economic sanctions were useless because the allies were reluctant to do this, Robert Kennedy fired back asking what, then, did the CIA director think should be done. McCone fell back on what FitzGerald was recommending, sabotage and a military coup.[15]

Thus despite the proliferation of committees and subcommittees and the theoretical distinctions among them, they were all debating the same issues and coming to the same conclusion: no one but the CIA had a workable long-range plan for getting rid of Castro. And even this plan was too long-range for the attorney general, who wanted action, and visible action, immediately.

Nonetheless, Robert Kennedy and FitzGerald seemed to get along well on the personal level. A CIA officer recalled hearing FitzGerald talk to Kennedy by phone and call him "Bobby."[16] It was quite a contrast from the days when Bill Harvey called the Kennedys "fags" and "fuckers." In early June a new alternative emerged when the Special Group agreed that establishing a channel of communication with Castro would be useful.[17] The president had suggested earlier that he was prepared to pursue several different options simultaneously. FitzGerald might work on a coup; the United States might try to drive down the price of sugar; and someone would try to talk to Castro. Whatever its merits it was a less myopic approach than had been followed previously.[18]

Pressured by the Kennedys to develop a sabotage program, FitzGerald proved deft at staying in their favor not only by restarting the program but also by saying that, despite his earlier opposition, sabotage actually had a role to play in his plan for a coup. FitzGerald outlined his idea for a comprehensive and integrated approach in a paper to the Standing Group dated June 8. According to the CIA paper, it was based on the following assumption: "that current U.S. policy does not contemplate outright military intervention in Cuba or a provocation which can be used as a pretext for an invasion of Cuba by United States military forces. It is further assumed that U.S. policy calls for the exertion of maximum pressure by all means available to the U.S. Government, short of military intervention."[19] Notably, although the paper assumes the policy to be that actions against Cuba should be "short of military intervention" and should not be a pretext for invasion of Cuba, McCone and FitzGerald had already told the Special Group at its April 25 meeting that the CIA approach might nevertheless require the use of the U.S. military.

On June 19 FitzGerald presented the proposal to the president, McNamara, Harriman, and Bundy. McCone and Thomas Parrott of the CIA were also there as was a representative of the Joint Chiefs of Staff.

Two records of the meeting are public. One was prepared by FitzGerald for McCone's private files at CIA. The other was prepared by Parrott for distribution to the members of the Special Group. The two memos generally agree except as noted here. FitzGerald's memorandum begins by recording that "Higher Authority" showed particular interest in the sabotage plan and asked when the first sabotage operation would take place. FitzGerald told him it would be at the first dark moon in July. McCone emphasized that these had to be continuous operations. They could not just be episodic. Moreover, they would have a high noise level, and the president should be prepared to accept that.[20]

Parrott's memo reported that Harriman was the one who said that once started, these operations should not be subject to stop-and-go orders. FitzGerald said sabotage would be directed at four major segments of the Cuban economy: electric power; oil refineries and storage tanks; railroads and highways; and manufacturing. When someone raised the question of deniability, FitzGerald said it was not possible. If the saboteurs were captured and questioned, they could reveal American involvement.

At this point Bundy interjected, "The proposed sabotage program interlocks with two other efforts along the same lines. One of these involves an autonomous operation which will be based in Central America and which will not be in operation until October or November, and the other consists of continuing efforts to develop internal resistance elements [inside Cuba] which could carry out sabotage." The fact that Bundy, not FitzGerald, had to tell the Special Group about what he called "autonomous" operations suggests that these did not operate under the CIA's aegis. The one in Central America was most certainly that headed by Robert Kennedy's friend, Manuel Artime.[21]

FitzGerald's memorandum does not mention one matter that Parrott's does. The latter wrote: "A question was asked as to whether the Cubans would retaliate in kind. The answer was that they would certainly have this capability but that they have not retaliated to date, in spite of a number of publicized raids."[22]

This was the first time that the possibility of Cuban retaliation appears in notes of discussions at the National Security Council level, but it would not be the last. Just as in the summer of 1962, before the Cuban Missile Crisis erupted, the U.S. government seemed largely blind to the fact that it was not operating in a vacuum. The Soviets and the Cubans might have their own plans. Just because Castro had not retaliated in the past did not mean he would not do so in the future.

The security of sabotage operations was always dicey. While the memoranda of meetings in which they were discussed were stamped "Top Secret," the operations themselves leaked like a sieve. One problem was that the men going on these raids would call their relatives in Cuba and warn them to take precautions because there was going to be an operation in their neighborhood. Cuban intelligence monitored those calls and had military forces waiting for the intruders.[23]

Indeed, Castro may have known about parts of FitzGerald's plan before the president did. Two weeks before the June 19 meeting at the White House, army intelligence received a report from the CIA that Manuel Artime, leader of one of the so-called autonomous groups the CIA planned to use, had been in Nicaragua and Costa Rica in May to get bases for operations against Cuba. Artime was explaining his plans to anyone who would listen.[24] Cuban intelligence probably picked up the same information.

FitzGerald's plan met resistance. Secretary of State Rusk had not been at the June 19 White House meeting, so McCone and FitzGerald had to do a repeat performance for him in his office a few days later. Questioned by Rusk, McCone and FitzGerald explained that the phrase "autonomous operations" meant Cuban exile groups. They added that this element was open-ended; any and all groups would be welcome. One, presumably Artime's, was about to receive funds. Rusk suggested it might be better if these raids were timed as retaliation for something Castro did.

When the CIA men said there would be two or three raids per month beginning in July, Rusk noted that Averell Harriman, who was at this meeting, was to be in Moscow then for talks with Khrushchev. Harriman disagreed with the entirety of FitzGerald's plan. Rusk said that Soviet prestige was on the line in Cuba and that the Soviet Union would provide whatever economic and military aid Castro needed to offset damage from the economic sanctions and sabotage.

Rusk asked what the prospects were for reconciliation with Castro. Castro had recently been in Moscow, and Rusk thought his statements since then were conciliatory. McCone disagreed. In his opinion Castro had come back even more firmly tied to the Soviet Union, and the Soviets would have a big say in any attempt at reconciliation. Rusk pointed out, as he had during the missile crisis, that the Soviets might retaliate against the attacks on Cuba by doing something in Berlin.

Before leaving McCone tried to pin Rusk down. Did he favor the CIA's program or not? Rusk's answer was diplomatic. He favored the program except for the "hit and run" operations. These, of course, were a central part of the program. More importantly, they were the ones that higher authority was most interested in.[25]

The CIA director prepared his own memorandum of the meeting. Referencing a separate memorandum for the record by Fitz-Gerald, McCone wrote: "I have the impression that Secretary Rusk is not enthusiastically behind the CIA program. He seems to feel that there is some opportunity for a rapprochement with Castro." McCone believed that Rusk's agreement to sabotage was reluctantly given and that he would call for reconsideration at the first occasion of "noise." He noted he had advised Rusk that rapprochement was "dangerous" from a political standpoint. He did not think the American people would accept a thaw in relations with Cuba unless Castro disavowed exporting the revolution, broke with Moscow, and opened up Cuba for on-site inspections of military installations.[26]

Desmond FitzGerald's first six months on the job proved he was the doer that the Kennedys had been looking for. Instead of tucking his chin down and giving long answers to the attorney general's questions, as Harvey had done, FitzGerald listened to what the Kennedys wanted and adapted it to the CIA's techniques and capabilities. His plans seemed to meet with approval from the president and everyone else except Rusk, and even Rusk seemed to accept that Kennedy's no-invasion pledge did not preclude U.S. military action in support of a coup in Cuba. But as yet none of his plans had been translated into action, and the entire national security establishment had, once again, chosen largely to ignore what its adversaries might be doing.

7

Oswald in New Orleans

J ust as the Kennedys' hopes that the CIA would do something
about Castro brightened at the beginning of July 1963, Lee Harvey Oswald's aspirations seemed to brighten too. He had a
cousin in Mobile, Alabama, who was studying to be a Jesuit priest.
The cousin wrote Oswald on July 6 and asked him to come to the
Jesuit House of Studies in Mobile to talk about his experiences
and observations in Russia. Oswald jumped at the chance. He
took Marina, their daughter, and some relatives from New Orleans along with him. In muddled remarks at the event in late July,
Oswald faulted Russian Communism and said a blend of Communism and capitalism might work better.[1]

Oswald probably had Castro's modified form of Communism
in mind. The previous April Oswald had sent a letter to Vincent
Lee, who headed the national Fair Play for Cuba Committee. Lee
wrote back, and Oswald became a member. The FPCC headquarters in New York was three blocks from the Socialist Workers
Party's headquarters that Oswald had long been in contact with.[2]
Personal ties between the leaders of the two groups were equally
close.[3] Using the alias Lee Osborne, Oswald ordered pamphlets
printed at his own expense with large lettering that said "Hands
Off Cuba" as well as applications and membership cards for a non-
existent New Orleans chapter of the Fair Play for Cuba Committee.

Then, soon after getting back from his talk in Alabama, Oswald
moved in two, opposite directions. On August 5 he visited the
store of Carlos Bringuier in New Orleans. Bringuier was a Cuban
exile and staunchly anti-Castro. Oswald said he wanted to join the
fight against Castro. Since Oswald had never been anti-Castro, he
presumably thought he might work his way into an anti-Castro

organization and spy on it. If Marina was right and Oswald was trying to find a way to get to Cuba, maybe he planned to tell the Cubans that he could give them inside information on anti-Castro activities in New Orleans. Or maybe he was in fact working for Cuban intelligence.

Oswald wasn't clever enough to pull off such a simple espionage operation though. A few days later, he was passing out his Fair Play for Cuba leaflets on the street when Bringuier and some companions saw him. Bringuier naturally concluded that Oswald had been trying to spy on him for Castro, and the men got into a scuffle. The police arrested the whole lot. Oswald spent the night in jail.[4] Interviewed by a police officer while in jail, Oswald said he joined the Fair Play for Cuba Committee in 1958 in Los Angeles.[5] He was lying. The FPCC wasn't created until 1960. He may have been alluding to the same contact with Cubans that his fellow marine Nelson Delgado remembered. Marina said that Oswald "cooled off" somewhat from the experience.

If so, it wasn't for long. A week later he was passing out leaflets again. This time television news in New Orleans reported on what he was doing. That led to a story on a radio station and, within a few days, a radio broadcast of a debate between Oswald and Bringuier on Castro and Communism.

There was no ostensible purpose to what Oswald was doing. During the summer of 1963, he wrote the Communist Party U.S.A., and it wrote back. And he continued to write Vincent Lee at the FPCC, informing him what he was doing and even hinting at the altercation with Bringuier. Lee never answered.[6] Oswald wrote similar letters to the Socialist Workers Party, telling it some of the things he was doing.[7]

The Warren Commission had the FBI examine Oswald's letters, which these organizations had kept and turned over to the FBI, to see if they contained secret writing, for instance, invisible ink. The FBI said no. The Warren Commission's concern was that these organizations might be serving as intermediaries, receiving correspondence from Oswald and passing them on to some foreign intelligence service. It would be easy enough for someone at the SWP or the FPCC to copy and forward Oswald's letters to the

Cuban delegation at the United Nations. But the Warren Commission and the FBI seemed to overlook the fact that the plain text of the letters told anyone who read them what Oswald was doing. He didn't need to encode it. Oswald might have been living in a fantasy world, thinking that the SWP and the FPCC were interested in what he was doing, or he could have been living in a real world where a foreign intelligence service was indeed interested.

...

President Kennedy too was thinking along the lines of recruiting agents, but in Cuba not the United States, for the purpose of instigating a revolt. Although this is not reflected in any contemporary record, Richard Helms remembered it in his testimony to the Church Committee: "Activity against Cuba picked up sometime in that subsequent year [1963]. . . . [President Kennedy] mentioned the desire to have the military or some force inside and rise up against Castro, some internal revolt."[8]

As a result the CIA began work on recruiting high-level agents in Cuba. In early July 1963, Desmond FitzGerald contacted the Department of the Army for help. The army had order-of-battle information on the units and commanders it might face in the event it was ordered to invade the island. The CIA wanted biographies of the commanders. The army obliged. In late July it gave the CIA information on eighty-three individuals. One name that stands out in hindsight was Rolando CUBELA Secedes, who was identified only as "unit information chief."[9] Since the convention in Spanish-speaking countries is to put the family name second, American intelligence followed the practice of using all capital letters for that name to indicate it was the surname. The CIA had its own file on Cubela, as will be explained later. Suffice it to say for now that the CIA wanted this information in order to identity men in the Cuban military that might be asked to join a coup.

Meanwhile, the Standing Group (supposedly responsible for long-range planning) held a meeting on July 9, but it was poorly attended. Only the State Department, the CIA, and the U.S. Information Agency (USIA) were there. FitzGerald gave a briefing on developments since the last meeting three weeks earlier. Averell

Harriman represented State. He remained worried that any CIA sabotage operation would disrupt his upcoming visit to Moscow. The State Department and the USIA also discussed how to handle the public relations problems of the sabotage operations. They agreed that plausible denial was the approach to take: "We should flatly deny any U.S. Government involvement."[10]

A week later the Standing Group met again.[11] It had planned for the president to make a statement on Cuba on July 26, which was the anniversary of Castro's first attack on Batista, but with Harriman in Moscow by this time, it decided to postpone Kennedy's statement until perhaps August 17, which was the anniversary of the Alliance for Progress. According to the minutes of the meeting, the attorney general asked what effect Harriman's visit had on the timing and content of what the president said. It was a pointed question and probably phrased more delicately in the minutes than in the meeting. What Robert Kennedy seemed to be asking was why a trip by a mere deputy secretary of state should determine when his brother the president could speak and what he could say.

The Standing Group then took up the subject of negotiations with Castro. It decided to study the matter further, but Bundy said he thought things would have to get much rougher for Castro before he'd be interested in negotiating, yet no one at the meeting, including CIA director McCone, knew what the economic situation in Cuba actually was. Some believed it would get better since the Soviets were sending massive aid. The Standing Group backed off the idea that had been floated at earlier meetings of trying to drive down the price of sugar. It appeared the international market was increasing production and hence forcing the price down without the help of the U.S. government.

Alexis Johnson of the State Department reported that State would soon recommend against making the controls against free-world shipping to Cuba any more restrictive. He said the proposed new restrictions were far too onerous. They would have the effect of banning the luxury liner *Queen Mary* from docking in American ports. This was apparently because, under the proposed regulations, if only one ship from a company carried things to Cuba, then all ships of that company were to be excluded from American ports.

Finally, the Standing Group talked about press reports that the United States was backing exile raids on Cuba from Central America. The Standing Group knew this was true; it had authorized the so-called autonomous raids. Someone showed the attorney general a July 14 article by Hal Hendrix in the *Miami Herald* with the headline "Backstage with Bobby" that referred to his conversations with anti-Castro leaders. He was in regular contact with Manuel Artime for one. Kennedy was on the defensive. He responded by suggesting that the United States could float other, false rumors to confuse the truth. McCone agreed that this could be done.[12] The Standing Group at this time seemed to be spending as much time backstabbing as doing the long-range planning that was its purpose.

The Special Group—as opposed to the Standing Group—met two days later, on July 18. FitzGerald attended only for the discussion of whether the CIA operation planned for later in the month should be postponed because of Harriman's trip to Moscow. Bundy told FitzGerald that higher authority was leaning to a postponement of the operation and that unless FitzGerald heard from him to the contrary the next morning, he should postpone the operation until the next dark moon, which was in the middle of August. Bundy warned that the president might call off that operation if the negotiations in Moscow went well. FitzGerald recorded this in a memorandum for the record.[13]

The next day FitzGerald and Bundy talked by phone. Bundy confirmed that the operation was called off. However, he mentioned that an "*internal*" sabotage operation might take place on July 26. The underscoring was FitzGerald's in his memorandum for the record. This was not a CIA operation. Bundy was talking about the same sabotage operation he had told the Special Group about at the June 19 meeting. Bundy explained to FitzGerald now that the prohibition against sabotage during Harriman's visit only applied to "across water" operations. This sabotage would be accomplished by people already in Cuba. According to FitzGerald's memorandum, Bundy added: "Higher Authority asked him to convey to us the fact that Higher Authority, in reaching the decision to postpone, was well aware of the morale problem that might result among the Agency case officers and therefore had considerable difficulty in reaching the decision. Mr. Bundy authorized the undersigned [FitzGerald] to quote Higher Authority accordingly to any staff personnel concerned and to add that Higher Authority retains his enthusiasm and interest in the program."[14]

Even the State Department was giving thought to encouraging autonomous sabotage operations despite Secretary Rusk's opposition to sabotage. A July 25 memo by the State Department's Intelligence and Research Special Studies Group proposed that reputable exile leaders be organized under the banner "Authentic 26th of July Movement" to foment sabotage, subversion, and guerilla warfare against Castro. Rather than looking for rapprochement with Castro, the memo advised the United States disengage in order to overthrow him.[15]

Yet while Bundy, FitzGerald, and the rest of the national security establishment stamped their memoranda about the autonomous operations Top Secret, the exiles, including Manuel Artime, weren't so secretive. Indeed, Artime wasn't secretive at all; he readily talked to the press. On July 18, for example, the *Washington Post* reported that Artime was shifting operations to Nicaragua.[16] Six days later he was quoted in the paper as saying: "We are leaving the United States to establish a base in Central America." The article named Puerto Cabezas, Nicaragua, as the destination, adding that Artime had help from former Nicaraguan president Luis Somoza.[17] Artime added: "In much less than one year we'll be fighting inside Cuba." The front page of the same issue of the *Post* carried a wire-service article out of Mexico City, saying that Artime was also seeking help from Costa Rica, Panama, Venezuela, and Columbia.[18]

The Department of Defense had also been mulling over Cuba policy. On July 29 Paul Nitze, head of DOD's internal think tank, International Security Affairs, signed off on a four-month study. The essential conclusions were ones that would have been obvious to anyone who followed the Standing and Special Groups' discussions. First, Cuba was not a military threat to the Western Hemisphere. Second, Cuba had been isolated from free-world trade, but the Soviet bloc was making up the difference to some extent. Third, covert action, namely, sabotage, whether by CIA or exile groups, had been "too low to have much of an impact." Fourth, the United States had made no progress in creating opposition groups inside Cuba. Fifth, countersubversion efforts in Latin America were working. Castro was having difficulty exporting Communism. Sixth, diplomatic efforts to eliminate the Soviet military presence in Cuba had not been successful. Seventh, "barring unforeseen breaks," no change in the situation was expected.

The study saw four alternative courses of action, which it called "tracks," for the United States. Track 1 was the then current policy of economic sanctions and diplomacy. Track 2 was track 1 plus contingency planning that would allow a quick response to new developments, opportunistically turning small events into a crisis that might be resolved to the United States' advantage. Track 3 was for the United States to take affirmative action, one of which might be "covertly-assisted rebellion." Track 4 was to reach an accommodation with Castro.[19]

One of FitzGerald's faults, indeed one fault of the CIA generally, was that he was myopic. He focused only on what he was doing, never on what adversaries were doing. Therefore, such things as the Fair Play for Cuba Committee were of little concern to him. His Special Affairs Staff viewed the FPCC as a domestic organization, which made it the responsibility of the FBI.[20] In point of fact, when the FBI surreptitiously entered the FPCC's New York office in October 1963 and secured its foreign mailing list, there were more than twenty subscribers in Cuba, including one "Dr. Fidel Castro, Oficina Del Primer Ministro." Of course, it was the CIA that wanted the mailing list, but it didn't get a copy until December 1963.[21]

Bundy's mention of "internal" operations in Cuba, ones that FitzGerald didn't seem to know about, apparently piqued the CIA man's interest. On August 9 he wrote Bundy about Luis Somoza, the ex-president of Nicaragua, and his dealings with the exile leader Manuel Artime. The CIA had known about Artime's trip to Nicaragua and Costa Rica for some time. He was seeking bases from which to raid Cuba. FitzGerald told Bundy that Somoza believed that if the exile groups fomented an uprising in Cuba, the United States would have to intervene. Alternatively, if Castro decided to retaliate militarily against Nicaragua, the United States would have come to its aid, and this would trigger a military confrontation with Cuba. Somoza claimed he had assurances to this effect from "leading United States Government officials." This may have been FitzGerald's way of referring to Robert Kennedy. In any event FitzGerald recommended that Artime base his operations in Costa Rica rather than Nicaragua and concentrate on building up a resistance movement inside Cuba, as opposed to undertaking raids.[22] He must have assumed Bundy would pass this suggestion on to the attorney general. Or he may have thought that the national security advisor should at least know what Robert Kennedy was doing outside the auspices of the CIA. Nothing in the memorandum suggests that the CIA controlled Artime.

What FitzGerald did over the next few days is a mystery because the records seemingly have been lost. While the government is not supposed to lose records, it has in this case. On August 13 FitzGerald wrote a memo titled "U.S. Courses of Action in the Event of a Military Revolt in Cuba" to Califano at the Pentagon. Although the National Archives has a record that such a document once existed and was declassified, it doesn't have any copies and is unable to explain what happened to it. The Defense Department doesn't have it either because it gave all its copies to the National Archives.[23] Be that as it may, the title suggests that FitzGerald was alerting the Defense Department to begin preparations to react to a military coup in Cuba. If so, this would be further evidence that Kennedy was prepared to support any coup with U.S. military forces despite his no-invasion pledge.

On August 15 FitzGerald went to the White House to meet with the president, Bundy, and others. This was neither a Standing Group nor a Special Group meeting. Also from the CIA were Director McCone, Helms, William Colby, and Bruce Cheever. No other meeting in this period was attended by so many and by such a diverse assembly of CIA men. Colby was supposed to be working on operations in Southeast Asia. The meeting was taped by the White House recording system and is at the John F. Kennedy Presidential Library in Boston. However, the library's listing states: "Eighteen minutes are deleted as secret." The listing says the tape dealt with "British Guiana." It is surprising that something in British Guiana would merit the attendance of so many high-level CIA officials, especially Colby, whose responsibilities were in the Far East, and FitzGerald, who was focused on Cuba; and if the meeting were about British Guiana, it is surprising that it would still be secret fifty-five years later.[24] While the contents of the two missing records are speculative, the lost memo from FitzGerald to Califano raises the possibility that the CIA communicated its coup plan for Cuba to the Defense Department in August 1963. Similarly, although the still-classified White House tape might not have anything to do with Cuba, and indeed there is some reason to believe it may deal with satellite imagery, the meeting took place at a time when the idea for coups in both Cuba and Vietnam were being discussed, and FitzGerald's and Colby's attendance implies the discussion could have been about coups.

At this critical stage in the effort against Castro, another press leak hit. The *Chicago Sun Times* of August 16 reported that Sam Giancana had an arrangement with the CIA, citing Justice Department sources.[25] The article did not mention that Giancana was targeted at Cuba or that he was trying to assassinate Castro, but CIA director McCone asked questions about the article. DDP Helms gave him a memorandum with the details. It was supposedly the first time McCone knew about the Giancana plot.[26] According to his executive officer, McCone thought assassinations were morally reprehensible.[27] Helms himself testified that when he and McCone talked about the Giancana plot, the word "assassination" was never used. McCone testified he nevertheless understood Helms was talking about assassinations. He also thought everyone at the CIA knew he wouldn't allow such operations. This is McCone's testimony, but the fact is Bill Harvey was put in charge of the underworld plots to assassinate Castro six months after McCone became director of the CIA and continued doing that work for another seven or eight months. McCone was never asked to explain how assassination operations could take place on his watch without his knowledge.

The Defense Department, unlike the CIA, did not have a special staff devoted to Cuba. To the military fighting Communism in Latin America was the same as fighting it in Southeast Asia. Therefore, the Defense Department's report to the Special Group on developments in counterinsurgency for the first seven months of the year covered its worldwide effort against "communist-supported 'wars of national liberation.'" The program in South Vietnam was showing good progress. Defense might withdraw one thousand troops before the end of the year. The effort in Latin America was considerably smaller. About half the $75 million of military assistance in this region was devoted to counterinsurgency, for example, opposing Cuban-supported Communist subversion.[28]

Management problems continued to plague the national security establishment, though, with disastrous results. The National Security Council, for example, had separate staffs for Cuba and for Vietnam, yet the NSC as a whole was considering military coups in both countries. On August 24, with both the president and Bundy on vacations, the NSC staff officer responsible for Vietnam sent a cable to the ambassador there, Henry Cabot Lodge. Kennedy had appointed as ambassador to Vietnam the man he defeated for the Senate in 1952 and as vice president candidate in 1960. The cable authorized Lodge to look into a coup to oust President Ngo Dinh Diem, a Catholic who antagonized Buddhists and was generally considered ineffective. Unbeknown to Lodge, neither the president nor Bundy had approved the cable, so he proceeded to act on it.[29]

The Joint Chiefs of Staff seemed to be the only ones worrying about the chaotic national security structure. On August 24 they wrote to Vance, who was Defense's representative to the ICCCA, suggesting reorganization. The confusion and overlap between the Special Group and the Standing Group needed fixing, they said. The Special Group should deal with covert matters, the Standing Group with everything else. Both should interface with the departments through a revamped Inter-Departmental Coordinating Committee, which in turn would operate with subcommittees. The three major executive departments under the inter-departmental committee would be State, Defense, and the CIA. Other affected agencies were the USIA, HEW, Labor, Justice, Treasury, and the Agency for International Development.[30] It might have been a good idea, but the joint chiefs were rearranging the deck chairs on the *Titanic*, tending to minutiae and ignoring the fact that policies for Cuba and Vietnam were spinning out of control.

8

Assassins and Spies

The *Merriam-Webster Dictionary* defines assassination as "murder by sudden or secret attack often for political reasons."[1] The act has been performed throughout history, and all languages probably have a word for it. Julius Caesar was assassinated. So was Philip II of Macedon, Alexander the Great's father. Four American presidents have been assassinated: Lincoln, Garfield, McKinley, and Kennedy. There have been attempts on the lives of many more.

Americans have historically considered assassination immoral. Yet in World War II, American warplanes tracked down the plane carrying Japanese admiral Isoroku Yamamoto and shot it down. He was killed. Yamamoto was targeted because he had masterminded the attack on Pearl Harbor and was Japan's most talented military man. It was an assassination.

In the midst of the public outcry surrounding disclosures of the CIA programs by the Church Committee in 1975, President Gerald Ford issued the first executive order on assassination. Later presidents have refined it so that today it reads: "No person employed by or acting on behalf of the United States Government shall engage in, or conspire to engage in, assassination." The word "assassination" isn't defined, but the prohibition is generally regarded to apply not only to foreign leaders but also to any official of a foreign government and perhaps even to private citizens in certain circumstances.[2] But the line is murky. Killings of terrorist leaders through bombings from warplanes and pilotless drones are not considered assassinations.

Scott Breckenridge, a former deputy inspector general of the CIA, writes about the Church Committee investigation in *The CIA and the U.S. Intelligence System* and says that the committee staff debated whether assassination could ever be justified. According to Breckenridge, "one aspect of the issue . . . was whether any of them would have condoned assassinating Adolf Hitler. The question was that of balancing one man's life against the estimated 40 million who died." Breckenridge believes the senators, except for Barry Goldwater of Arizona, ducked the question. He quotes Goldwater: "Should a President of the United States have the right to aid the destruction of either a Josef Stalin or Adolf Hitler in peacetime?"[3]

Lee Harvey Oswald was interested in the very same question and had an answer. When his wife, Marina, appeared before the Warren Commission, she was asked why Oswald shot at General Walker. She said: "He [Oswald] said that this [Walker] was a very bad man, that he was a fascist, that he was the leader of a fascist organization, and when I said that even though all of that might be true, just the same he had no right to take his life, he [Oswald] said if someone had killed Hitler in time it would have saved many lives. I told him that this is no method to prove your ideas, by means of a rifle."[4]

The common view of assassination has been shaped by novels and movies. In the 1960s movies based on the character James Bond in Ian Fleming novels were popular: *Casino Royale, From Russia with Love,* and *The Spy Who Loved Me* were a few. The assassins in these movies were always clever and highly trained in order to better challenge the skills of hero James Bond.

According to author Philip Shenon in his book *A Cruel and Shocking Act* about the Warren Commission, staff lawyer David Slawson said that he was briefed by the CIA on the KGB's history of assassinations and concluded that Kennedy's murder would have been completely out of character for the KGB. "They gave us background material on how Russian spies killed people . . . and none of them fitted the pattern of Lee Harvey Oswald," Slawson said.[5]

What the CIA told Slawson differs from a briefing the author received when he was on the Church Committee. In response to the author's assertion that Oswald was hardly the kind of man the KGB would use for an assassination, the briefer disagreed and said he was "precisely" the kind of man the Soviets used in World War II.

Public sources support this. The Soviet Union referred to assassination and sabotage by its intelligence agencies as *mokrie dela*, or "wet affairs."[6] Under Joseph Stalin's leadership, Nikolai Yezhov was charged with the liquidation of those associated with Stalin's political adversary Leon Trotsky. In December 1936 Yezhov formed the Administration of Special Tasks to assassinate people on Stalin's orders. It operated mainly in Spain. In 1937 Yezhov ordered the assassination of General Francisco Franco of Spain. It didn't succeed.[7] But in 1940 an agent of the Administration of Special Tasks assassinated Trotsky in Mexico.

After the German invasion of the Soviet Union in 1941, the job of assassination and sabotage behind German lines was given to the Fourth or Partisan Directorate of the NKVD, the predecessor to the KGB. In charge of the Partisan Directorate was General Pavl Anatolevich Sudoplatov. His deputy had run behind-the-lines operations against Franco in the Spanish Civil War and had planned the operation that led to the assassination of Trotsky.[8]

According to Christopher Andrew and Oleg Gordievsky's definitive study of Soviet Intelligence, KGB: *The Inside Story*, Sudoplatov's Partisan Directorate had a "fearsome reputation" and made a significant contribution to the Soviet Army's success against the Germans on the Eastern Front in World War II. The Germans estimated that they knew of 20,000 Soviet agents working within German lines, and the number was growing by about 3,300 per month. Sudoplatov's men were even recruiting teenagers as agents. Although he was running a bloody business, Sudoplatov himself was described as an intelligent and quiet man with polished manners and confident speech.[9]

That the Partisan Directorate was so successful in recruiting agents is even more astonishing given how efficient German security could be in ferreting out agents and how brutal it was in dealing with them. The Soviets were sending agents on suicide missions. Author John Barron writes of a Sudoplatov protégé who remembered his mentor's instructions for how to recruit men and women willing to die in such dangerous undertakings:

Go search for people who are hurt by fate or nature—the ugly, those suffering from an inferiority complex, craving power and influence but defeated by unfavorable circumstances. . . . The sense of belonging to an influential, powerful organization will give them a feeling of superiority over the handsome and prosperous people around them. For the first time in their lives they will experience a sense of importance. . . . It is sad indeed, and humanly shallow— but we are obliged to profit from it.[10]

The NKVD's assassination and sabotage function was later absorbed into the KGB as Department 13.

The Warren Commission devoted a great deal of its investigative attention and its final report to Lee Harvey Oswald's mental state and motivation. Although the Warren Commission never considered that Oswald fit the psychological profile of a Sudoplatov recruit, the commission's conclusions suggest precisely this:

> Many factors were undoubtedly involved in Oswald's motivation for the assassination, and the Commission does not believe that it can ascribe to him any one motive or group of motives. It is apparent, however, that Oswald was moved by an overriding hostility to his environment. He does not appear to have been able to establish meaningful relationships with other people. He was perpetually discontented with the world around him. Long before the assassination he expressed his hatred for American society and acted in protest against it. Oswald's search for what he conceived to be the perfect society was doomed from the start. He sought for himself a place in history—a role as the "great man" who would be recognized as having been in advance of his times. His commitment to Marxism and communism appears to have been another important factor in his motivation.[11]

The KGB's Department 13 wasn't nearly as formidable as James Bond's adversaries were. At times its operations seemed as clownish as the CIA's nutty schemes. In 1955 the KGB sent a veteran agent to assassinate a Russian émigré in Germany. The agent knocked on the victim's apartment door, went inside, and sat down with him. "I've come to you from Moscow," he said. "The Central Committee . . . ordered your liquidation. The murder is entrusted to my group. . . . I can't let this murder happen." He then turned himself in to American authorities in Germany. The KGB tried to assassinate its own agent for his perfidy. It dispatched someone to inject him with a poison, radioactive thallium, and nearly succeeded. A different agent who was sent on an assassination assignment discovered that his conscience bothered him, so he threw his assassination weapon, a poison, into a river. The KGB learned of his cowardice and made him go back again. He fulfilled the assignment the second time.[12]

The ideal assassination, as an intelligence agency might see it, would be one in which no one noticed that it had taken place, that is, the victim would appear to die of natural causes. No one would see the assassin or find an explosive, knife, gun, or hypodermic needle, and there would no trace on the victim's body or in an autopsy.

Later, during the Cold War, poisons became the weapons of choice for Department 13. A CIA paper provided the Warren Commission said: "Many known or suspected executive action cases in the post-war period have involved the use of poison rather than guns or explosives. It is conceivable that the Soviets favored poisons because murders can be accomplished more surreptitiously in this manner and in some instances without leaving easily recognizable traces of foul play."[13]

The CIA favored poisons for the same reason: they were more clandestine. For example, the CIA had in its weapons stockpile a compressed air pistol that fired a dart coated with shellfish toxin, the deadliest substance CIA scientists could find. It killed instantly and left almost no chemicals in the victim's body. It did not leave "easily recognizable traces of foul play." But the pistol was huge. In the Church Committee's public hearings, senators passed it around for the cameras and laughed because it was anything but surreptitious. There was no way a man carrying it could, if detained by the police, give a convincing, innocent-sounding explanation for why he had such a large, strange weapon.[14]

Assassinations are not always surreptitious though. An intelligence service may want its adversary to know who is responsible as a way of sending a message. In the book KGB, John Barron describes the assassination of a journalist in Afghanistan during the Soviet war there: "The assassination was deliberately crude. Its intent was not only to eliminate an effective Soviet adversary but also to terrorize potential adversaries into silence. The assassins also left behind discernible Soviet traces. Witnesses testified that the men arrived in a Soviet jeep."[15]

The CIA's underworld plots against Castro used poisons. They did so because although the CIA thought the underworld gunned down its victims, Giancana said he wouldn't be able to find anyone to kill Castro in what would be a suicide mission. Not even the mob had hit men who would undertake a suicide mission. The CIA generally preferred contracting out its wet operations. It turned to underworld figures to handle the nasty detail of finding someone to kill Castro, and for this reason Harvey's ZRRIFLE program planned to use contract assassins.

However, the AMLASH plot in 1963, which will be discussed in the next chapter, was an exception to this rule. In that operation CIA case officers, and indeed FitzGerald himself, were in direct contact with the would-be assassin.

The KGB was much more than Department 13, of course. Like the CIA its main functions were the gathering of intelligence and covert action. For example, Georgi Bolshakov was a KGB officer operating under the cover of a journalist in Washington DC in the early 1960s. He made friends with Attorney General Robert Kennedy and sometimes provided back-channel communications between John Kennedy and Khrushchev. Robert Kennedy felt Bolshakov was an honest intermediary, but he apparently never realized the Russian was a KGB officer. Bolshakov fell out of favor with the Kennedys during the missile crisis because Khrushchev lied to him, saying the Soviets did not have missiles in Cuba. Unaware that Khrushchev was lying, Bolshakov passed those lies on to the attorney general, who knew the truth was otherwise.[16]

The KGB also advised and trained the intelligence services of its client states. When Fidel Castro was released from imprisonment in Cuba in 1955, he went to Mexico. There he approached a young KGB officer in Mexico City, Nikolai Sergeevich Leonov, and asked for arms for his planned guerilla campaign to oust Batista. Leonov turned down Castro's request for weapons but did lend moral support. In July 1959, after Castro had taken over Cuba, the head of his intelligence service met secretly with the KGB in Mexico City. This led the KGB to send more than one hundred advisors to Cuba to help build a security system. Many were children of refugees who had fled to Russia from Spain after Franco defeated the Communists there.[17] The result was, as Richard Helms explained, that "the Russians had moved into Cuba, into the Cuban security services and had done a rather astonishing job of bringing the Cubans into the twentieth century when it came to security and counterintelligence. And they ran it with a very skilled hand."[18] It was this security system that bedeviled CIA attempts to infiltrate agents into Cuba during the Kennedy years. Still, it wasn't until 1967 that the KGB developed solid ties with the Cuban Dirección General de Inteligencia (DGI).[19]

Eventually, though, the student surpassed its teacher. In *Castro's Secrets: Cuban Intelligence, the CIA, and the Assassination of John F. Kennedy*, Brian Latell, a former CIA officer and later university professor in Cuban American studies, writes of a retired CIA expert on Cuba saying that the Cubans had "the best intelligence service in the world." This is, says Latell, a view shared by many in American intelligence.[20]

According to Latell Castro himself oversaw the DGI's assassination operations. Castro ordered the DGI to assassinate various Bolivians believed responsible for killing Che Guevara in that country. The DGI also targeted for killing defectors, Latin American leaders who crossed Castro, and indeed anyone who got in his way. The assassin of choice for a target with high visibility and security protection was a non-Cuban, but the DGI also used trained teams of Cubans.[21]

Given that intelligence agencies, both foreign and domestic, performed their tasks, including assassination, in a variety of ways, the Warren Commission devoted inordinate attention to investigating Lee Harvey Oswald's background to prove that no intelligence agency would use him for an assassination. However, he was precisely the kind of man that General Sudoplatov would have recruited for an assignment against the Germans in World War II.

9

AMLASH

The heart of Desmond FitzGerald's plan was to recruit selected Cuban military leaders and convince them to work together to throw Castro out in a coup. The CIA and the State and Defense Departments had independently studied the matter, and each had come to the same conclusion: the military leaders in Cuba would not initiate action because Castro was running a police state, and nothing would happen unless the CIA organized the effort. This was the reason FitzGerald had asked the army for biographical information on Cuban military leaders.

It was also the reason that the CIA decided that one of the men on the army's list, a prominent Cuban its agents had first met the previous year, Rolando Cubela, might be useful. He was given the code name AMLASH.[1] The "AM" designator was for Cuban operations. The meaning of "LASH" is self-evident.

The AMLASH operation remained highly classified as it unfolded. Only a handful of individuals at the CIA knew the identity of the agent or the details of the operation. Since then, however, the CIA records have been made public as has the sworn testimony of those at the CIA who were running the operation. In addition, Cubela told his version of the events to the House Assassinations Committee in 1978, and his statements are public. At the time of the House inquiry, Cubela was serving a twelve-year prison sentence in Cuba for his role in a different plan to overthrow Castro. Cuba never charged him for plotting with the CIA in 1963, although proof of his participation in that plot had been made public many years before he was made available in Havana for questioning by the House committee. The CIA's version of what transpired and Cubela's generally agree, but they diverge in several significant ways as will be seen.

Cubela was six years younger than Fidel Castro. He too had opposed Batista from the beginning. In 1956 Cubela assassinated a Batista intelligence officer and fled to the United States. He returned to Cuba to join Castro's fight. Cubela was careful to keep his followers a separate force from Castro's because he didn't want to take orders from Castro's cohort, the Argentinean Che Guevara. When Batista fled Cuba on January 1, 1959, it was Cubela's men who took over the presidential palace, which, for a time, they refused to turn over to Che as a way of asserting their independence. Cubela went on to earn a medical degree from Havana University, where he also served as president of a government-sponsored student group. His disagreements with Che, and later Fidel Castro, continued, and he had a falling out with the regime. Cubela first came to the CIA's attention in 1961, when he traveled to Mexico. There, at the CIA's instigation, Carlos Tepedino, a friend of Cubela and an exile who was a jeweler in Florida and New York, approached him to sound him out about Castro. Cubela expressed displeasure with the Cuban leader. The CIA gave Tepedino the code name AMWHIP.

Cubela traveled to Helsinki in August 1962, and Tepedino met him again and introduced him to a CIA case officer. In spy parlance a case officer is an employee of the spy agency. CIA case officers were Americans. The term "agent" is applied to the person, for example, a foreign national, who gathers the information. Stated more directly the agent does the spying or dirty work at the request of the CIA case officer. In this instance Cubela was the agent.

At their first meeting, the case officer mainly wanted to see if Cubela wished to defect. However, it soon became apparent that it would be better instead for him "to set up an internal dissent group" for Castro's overthrow and for sabotage. In these initial meetings, according to CIA files, "Cubela said he was not interested in any small undertaking, and declared the assassination of Fidel and other leaders would be the most effective way to rescue the revolution from the Communists."[2]

Cubela traveled to Paris later in the month and again met with the CIA over a period of several days with the meetings taking place in bars, restaurants, and hotel rooms.[3] Asked to explain specifically how Castro could be overthrown, Cubela was vague. When he volunteered that he had also thought about blowing up an oil refinery, the CIA took him to a U.S. military base in France for half a day of training in the use of plastic explosives. He was not given any explosives to take with him though. He was trained in secret writing, that is, disappearing ink, in order to communicate with the CIA once he returned home. In the course of these meetings, Cubela reiterated that he wanted to assassinate Castro, although he abjured the word "assassinate" in favor of euphemisms.[4] His feelings seem similar to those of McCone and Helms, who discussed the CIA's assassination plots with organized crime without once using the forbidden word.

A CIA cable from the first two Paris meetings noted Cubela was very sensitive about security and his personal safety and worried about careless talk by his friends. The case officer felt Cubela was honest and sincere in what he was saying. On the other hand, while he told the CIA that he was willing to undertake an intelligence collection assignment, that is, to spy, he would later say such trivial things were beneath him. Cubela reacted badly to the question of whether he would agree to a lie detector test. The case officer dropped the subject and wrote in his cable to headquarters, "[Pursuing the matter would] have destroyed rapport and probably ended our operational association. Under circumstances unable [to] check bona fides [whether Cubela was acting in good faith] at this time." The cable added that because French surveillance picked up the meeting, the CIA had contacted French authorities and explained it was meeting with Cubela because he might want to defect.

The cable about this first meeting concluded in the usual, cryptic CIA style: "He also has ability and courage prepare violent action to eliminate present leadership as well as acts sabotage. Control problems possible due isolation and personal direction once he returns" to Cuba. The cable also noted, "*Have no intention give LASH physical elimination mission as requirement but recognize this something he could or might try carry out on own initiative.*"[5]

Headquarters replied immediately, saying that it "strongly concur[red]" that Cubela should not be given a physical elimination mission, that is, he should not be asked to assassinate Castro.

Headquarters told the case officer to emphasize to Cubela that his "value to cause" was as a CIA source and not as "torch man." Headquarters opined that once Cubela got back to Cuba and saw how difficult sabotage would be, he would change his mind on his own. It suggested that Cubela's energies be channeled toward identifying and recruiting other disaffected high-level Cubans.[6]

Thus, although Cubela's willingness to work with the CIA made him attractive as an agent, the agency realized it might be difficult to get him to devote himself to useful endeavors. Moreover, it wasn't sure he was dealing with the CIA in good faith. And then there was the fact that French security services, and perhaps others, knew he was meeting with the CIA.

The CIA lost contact with Cubela after he returned to Cuba. He did not contribute intelligence during the Cuban Missile Crisis, when his access to top Cuban officials would have been very useful. He had secret writing materials, so he could have written the CIA. He later claimed he sent two messages, but the CIA received only one. The system that had been worked out in Paris was for Cubela to write an innocuous letter to an intermediary in Europe whom he knew. He would write his message to the CIA in invisible ink on the same paper. Upon receiving the letter, the intermediary would turn it over to the CIA, which could then apply a chemical to the paper to reveal the message.[7] The CIA secret-writing technique of having its agents send letters through intermediaries was similar to what the FBI thought Oswald might be doing in writing the Socialist Workers Party and the CPUSA. In the assassination investigation, the FBI tested the letters and other documents for secret writing and found nothing.[8]

Although Cubela had gone back to Cuba, he wasn't forgotten. On June 19, 1963, the same day that FitzGerald outlined his plan for a coup to the president, a CIA cable borrowed a phrase from a popular children's story and reported an "activation effort to reluctant dragon," meaning apparently that the CIA was trying to reestablish contact with Cubela.[9] By August FitzGerald realized that the Cuban fit perfectly into the new coup plan. Nestor Sanchez was FitzGerald's special assistant responsible for organizing Cuban military officers for the coup. He had previously worked under

Seymour Bolten on "the psychological political action part" of Bill Harvey's Task Force W. He was a natural to be Cubela's case officer: he knew what was needed, and although he was born in New Mexico, he was of Hispanic descent and spoke Spanish. The case officer who worked with Cubela previously did not speak Spanish. Cubela could speak English but not well. Thus the old case officer and Cubela had to talk in English or have Tepedino or a Spanish-speaking CIA officer come along to translate.[10]

When Sanchez learned that Cubela would be at the Pan American Games in Porto Alegre, Brazil, in early September 1963 as Fidel Castro's personal representative, he decided to try to meet with him there.[11] Sanchez arranged for Tepedino to fly to Brazil to talk to Cubela first, on September 5. Cubela had trouble getting free for the meeting because Cuban athletes at the games were defecting, and the whole Cuban delegation was on the alert for more defectors. Still, he somehow managed it. He told Tepedino that Raul Castro had offered him a position in the government, but he, a medical doctor, turned it down, saying he would rather work in a hospital.

Once Tepedino established that Cubela was still interested in talking with the CIA, Sanchez flew to Brazil to meet him on September 7. The Cuban explained away his failure to stay in contact with CIA. He had tried, he said, but the Cuban government was intercepting letters into and out of the island, so he was afraid of using secret writing. Besides, he continued, he had nothing important to report. Sanchez's cable about the meeting, which is dated September 9, added the sarcastic parenthetical, "Such as his having been told personally by Fidel of his planned trip to the Soviet Union fifteen days before the latter left."[12] This was the kind of inside information that made the CIA salivate and the kind that might have been extremely important during the missile crisis the previous year.

Sanchez wrote that Cubela was a "cocky totally spoiled brat who will always be [a] control problem." He didn't have the patience to communicate, which of course was crucial if the CIA were to use him. Therefore, Sanchez cabled: "If commo is to be regularly maintained it obvious a second person necessary this capacity.

Convinced AMLASH not type who will take time or have patience prepare or receive constant stream S/W message, let alone OWL." S/W was the abbreviation for secret writing.[13]

The abbreviation "OWL" stood for a one-way-listen radio receiver. These radio receivers could pick up messages from CIA transmitters outside Cuba. Since they only received messages, there was no danger that Castro's security services could determine their location by electronic means. Thus the CIA could send radio messages to its agents in Cuba. If the agents needed to respond, they would use secret writing. The radios themselves would be of a manufacture that would not arouse the suspicion of a customs officer if carried into Cuba or if found in an agent's house.

FitzGerald must have been ecstatic to learn of the results of Sanchez's meeting with Cubela. FitzGerald and Cubela were thinking alike. Cubela thought the only two options were an "inside job" or else an invasion by the U.S. military. He was waiting for the CIA to tell him what it planned to do.[14]

Writing back to Sanchez on September 9, CIA headquarters dismissed the problems of control and communications. Cubela, it said, was best approached as a "chief conspirator" and allowed to choose cohorts whom he trusted. From among this group, the CIA could surely find someone to handle communications. It also said that it didn't want Cubela to be a "one man band." Instead, he should be the center of the effort.[15] Once Cubela had all this in place, he could proceed to sabotage and more serious matters in an orderly progression. The cable closed with the admonition that Cubela was a "bird in the hand," by which it presumably meant he might not be the perfect agent, but he was the one the agency had and should not be let go.[16]

Notably, years later, when asked by Robert Blakely of the House Assassinations Committee if he had met with the CIA on September 7 in Porto Alegre, Cubela avoided the question. He talked instead about meetings in Paris.[17] He may not have wanted to talk to Blakely about Porto Alegre because, once again, Castro seemed several steps ahead of the CIA.

On September 7, the night of Sanchez's meeting with Cubela in Brazil, Fidel Castro attended a reception at the Brazilian embassy in Havana and agreed to a lengthy interview with Associated Press reporter Daniel Harker. The story ran on the AP wire service, and newspapers used whatever parts they wanted. The *New York Times* didn't carry the story at all. The *Washington Post* carried a portion but not the notable part. The *Chicago Tribune* did under the headline, "Castro Warns U.S. Not to Aid His Foes": "Premier Fidel Castro said tonight that 'United States leaders' would be in danger if they helped in any attempt to do away with the leaders of Cuba." Denouncing what he called recent U.S.-prompted raids on Cuban territory, Castro said: "We are prepared to fight them and answer in kind. *United States leaders should be mindful that if they are aiding terrorist plans to eliminate Cuban leaders, they themselves will not be safe.*"[18]

In his congressional testimony in 1976, Sanchez said that he was unaware of Castro's threat when he was handling Cubela. He was, however, aware of it when he testified. He called the chronological tie between his meeting Cubela in Brazil and Castro's warning that night at the Brazilian embassy in Havana a "coincidence" and advanced the argument that Castro would not have made a public threat if he had planned to assassinate Kennedy.

Q. Castro does give a warning about United States leaders aiding terrorist plans to eliminate Cuban leaders, and you were doing that very thing.

A. There is probably a coincidence there. I don't recall that I knew of this at that time. I've certainly heard of it since, but I don't see the point that you are trying to make, because if Castro is behind or was behind AMLASH to involve him in the assassination of an American leader, then are you proposing that he would also publicly in the Brazilian embassy state that this was going to take place? In other words, was he telegraphing this plan that he had?[19]

Be that as it may, it is surprising that the case officer who was meeting with Cubela wasn't told about Castro's threat at the time. A case officer risks his life every time he meets with an agent, even in friendly countries. Sanchez needed to know of Castro's threat since at the very least it suggested that Cuban intelligence was aware of Sanchez's meeting with Cubela.

Although Castro said his remarks were triggered by U.S.-prompted raids on Cuba, there were no CIA-sponsored raids at this time. FitzGerald had planned his first raid for the dark moon of July 20, but the president had called it off. The next opportunity was the dark moon of August 19, about three weeks before Castro's remarks, but CIA files on Cubela indicate that the only operations in Cuba in this time period were the coastal landings of supplies in August.[20] So while Castro said he was talking about CIA-supported sabotage, there is no evidence of such operations. The only hostile action the CIA was taking against Cuba was Sanchez's meeting with Cubela in Brazil on the same day as Harker's interview of Castro at the Brazilian embassy in Cuba.

Surprisingly, no one at the CIA looked into what Castro was talking about. At least, the CIA has never released a document to show it analyzed Castro's remarks. The man who should have done this was Harold Swenson, chief of counterintelligence for FitzGerald's SAS. His job was to worry about the security of the Cuban operations. Perhaps he did and never committed his thoughts to writing. He couldn't have tied Castro's statements to Sanchez's meeting with Cubela, however, because the AMLASH operation was so closely held that Swenson claimed he didn't know about the meeting.[21] In any event there is no evidence that anyone at the CIA analyzed Castro's threat at the time.

But while neither Sanchez nor anyone else at the CIA seemed to care about Castro's threat, the mid-level Interdepartmental Coordinating Committee of Cuban Affairs did. Only two days after Castro made the threat, a memo was circulated to committee members inviting them to a meeting at the State Department on September 11 to "discuss the status of contingency planning to meet possible retaliatory action by Castro induced by increasing pressures against his regime." It must have been a hurriedly called meeting, and hence in response to Castro's remarks on September 7, because the memo said: "A paper for the meeting will be sent to you if it is ready in time for prior distribution."[22] Clearly this was not a subject that had been in the works for any length of time.

The possible retaliatory actions listed in the paper were such things as harassment at the Guantanamo Naval Base, sniping at and killing marine sentries there, kidnapping or assassinating American officials in Latin America, and sabotage or terrorist bombings in the United States. The glaring omission from the list was the precise thing Castro had threatened: the assassination of the president.[23]

While the ICCCA was worrying about retaliation, the CIA had other concerns. Cubela's name popped up in a September 19 cable from its JMWAVE station in Florida that reported Cubela was part of an anti-Communist group of which Castro was aware, and Castro was trying to serve as moderator between it and the Communists. In other words Castro was aware of Cubela's dissatisfaction with the Communists in the Cuban leadership and was watching him.[24] It is a wonder that he was able to get free of surveillance to meet with the CIA in Porto Alegre. Cuban security there had already been on high alert because of Cuban athletes defecting.

Other warnings of security lapses were coming in. Also on September 19, the navy reported that an individual in Cuba had approached the Guantanamo Naval Base, saying he had eighty-three counterrevolutionaries under his command working for the CIA and needed weapons, ammunition, grenades, and shoes. The navy said it had alerted the CIA but wanted guidance from the ICCCA.[25]

The next day the navy reported that an exile group had asked it to provide packages of Cuban cigarettes to a counterrevolutionary group training in Costa Rica. The report said further that this was Manuel Artime's group and that its training was being financed by the U.S. government through a Swiss bank account. The report then sarcastically observed: "In the event that this allegation is correct, it is believed that a security problem exists which should be referred to the appropriate authority [i.e., the CIA] for resolution."[26]

Many in the United States and Cuba knew something was brewing. On September 30, 1963, the Defense Department's International Security Affairs section prepared for the Joint Chiefs of Staff a draft of its "State-Defense Contingency Plan for a Coup in Cuba." Once the joint chiefs gave their comments, a final plan would be put together.[27]

FitzGerald surely felt good about what he had accomplished. He could truthfully say, as he did at the Standing Group meeting on October 1, that "a swing of the pendulum was taking place." But he didn't want to declare victory quite yet. "Because things were becoming so bad for Castro momentarily," he said, according to the minutes, "we should not overreact and conclude the Cuban problem was on the way to being solved." The plan to drive down the price of sugar had been shelved, but FitzGerald wanted the Standing Group to create an economic warfare subcommittee to coordinate that part of his program. And the long-postponed idea of a presidential statement on Cuba, which originally was to have been issued the previous July 26, was resurrected.[28]

In nine short months, FitzGerald had gotten the national security establishment behind his plan for a coup in Cuba. By all indications Cubela was vital because he was someone who could recruit other disaffected Cuban leaders. He thought, and FitzGerald was probably beginning to agree, that assassinating Castro needed to be the first step in the coup. Yet the operation was leaking, and Castro seemed to know not only the general thrust of the plan but also the most important details.

10

Mexico City

arina Oswald's friend from Dallas, Ruth Paine, arrived in New Orleans on September 20 for a visit, during which it was supposedly decided that Marina would go back to Texas with her. Marina was eight months pregnant. The two women, again supposedly, decided that Marina should be with Paine when the baby was born. The women and the Oswalds' daughter left New Orleans three days later. This was the Warren Report's version.

The true situation was more complicated. According to Marina, sometime in August Oswald said he wanted to go to Cuba to live. He had the idea of hijacking an airplane, but she dissuaded him. Oswald's scheming probably began much earlier. Marina told the Warren Commission that she thought he had something like this in mind as early as February 1963, when he had her write the Russian embassy about getting a visa to return to the Soviet Union, perhaps alone. That was a month before Oswald acquired his rifle and pistol and two months before he fired at retired general Walker. Asked the manner in which Oswald brought up the idea of Marina going back to Russia alone, she testified: "Quite simply he said it was very hard for him here. . . . It would be better for me because I could work in Russia. That was all. Now, I think I know why he had in mind to start his foolish activity which could harm me but, of course, at that time he didn't tell me the reason. It is only now that I understand it."[1] In hindsight Marina was dating the beginning of Oswald's nefarious planning to February.

Marina didn't know everything Oswald was doing. Shortly before shooting at General Walker, Oswald had written the Social Workers Party. The SWP wrote back saying it had given Oswald's name to the Young Socialist Alliance, which was headquartered in Green-wich Village and may have shared offices with the Fair Play for Cuba Committee. This could have been how Oswald became aware of the FPCC.[2] It may have initiated the contact.

Then in early June, Oswald wrote the *Worker*, a publication of the Communist Party USA, saying he had formed a Fair Play for Cuba organization in New Orleans and was enclosing a compli-mentary membership card for Gus Hall and Benjamin Davis. Not until late July did a seemingly puzzled Arnold Johnson respond for the *Worker* to point out that it did not have any "organizational ties" to the FPCC.[3]

By August 1963 Oswald's correspondence with the leftist New York organizations became even stranger. He started asking them for advice and telling them he was moving to the Baltimore-Washington area, a plan Marina apparently did not know about. At first he did no more than send Johnson a New Orleans news-paper clipping about his activities.[4] Then in a letter of August 28, Oswald asked Johnson's advice on whether he should con-tinue to openly proclaim his Communism or whether he should go "underground."[5] Three days later he wrote the *Worker*, which was a CPUSA publication, asking for a job. He also said that he and his family would be relocating to "your" area, presumably meaning that he planned to move to the East Coast.[6] The next day Oswald wrote to both the CPUSA and the Socialist Workers Party saying that he was moving to the Baltimore-Washington area.[7] No other evidence of this planned move has turned up. The War-ren Commission apparently chose not to investigate the matter and did not mention it in its report even though relocating to the Baltimore-Washington area would have given Oswald much better access to the president. Judging by Oswald's correspon-dence, he either fantasized that he worked for a foreign intelli-gence agency, or he actually did.

On September 17 Oswald finally took action and got a tour-ist card for Mexico that was good for fifteen days. Years later for-mer Warren Commission staffer David Belin theorized Oswald may have been motivated by reading Castro's threat against U.S. leaders that had appeared in the *Times Picayune* newspaper nine days earlier, but such speculation misses the mark. Castro didn't say he wanted Kennedy killed. His threat was conditional: Kennedy would not be in danger if he stopped the terrorist activities against Castro, whatever those might have been in Castro's eyes.

In any event Oswald, and presumably Marina, knew he was going to Mexico before Ruth Paine came to visit. Marina seemed to think Oswald was going to Mexico City and then to Cuba without coming back to the United States. If he did this, she needed Paine to take her in. On the other hand, Marina's testimony wasn't always consistent.[8]

Paine and Marina left New Orleans for Texas on September 23, and Oswald left for Mexico City two days later. He took two pieces of luggage. In addition to clothing, he packed various documents, which the Warren Commission thought he planned to use to help him get to Cuba.[9] However, another interpretation is that Oswald simply packed the things he would want if he were allowed to go to Cuba, including what he might have considered treasured documents.

Oswald traveled by bus to Texas, where he crossed the border to Mexico at Laredo. He arrived in Mexico City on the morning of September 27. After checking into a hotel, and despite having been on a bus for more than twenty hours, he went straight to the Cuban embassy to get a visa.[10]

What happened next has been the subject of endless controversy and speculation, but the basic version is as follows. Oswald visited the Cuban diplomatic compound twice that day. According to what the Cuban consul, Eusebio Azcue, later told the House Assassinations Committee, Oswald showed up with a paper accrediting him as a member of the Communist Party of America and "as a member of the Fair Play for Cuba, which was an association aiding Cuba at the time." Azcue told him that a visa to Cuba could be expedited if Oswald had friends in Cuba; otherwise an investigation was necessary. Oswald became upset and said his aim was to go to Russia; he merely wanted to stop off in Cuba on the way. Upon hearing this Azcue sent him to the Soviet consulate to get a visa from it. If he had a visa to the Soviet Union, then Oswald could get a short-term, in-transit visa to Cuba immediately.[11]

The Soviet consulate was only a few blocks away. Oswald walked there and talked to either Pavel Antonovich Yatskov or Valery Vladimirovich Kostikov. The Warren Commission was aware of the fact that both were KGB men. If it were Kostikov, though, the contact was more ominous. He was in the KGB's Department 13, which specialized in assassination. Both KGB men operated under the cover of being consular officers.[12] Oswald probably talked to Kostikov: CIA surveillance of the Soviet embassy in Mexico City picked up the voice of an American identifying himself as Oswald telling a guard at the embassy that he had talked to Kostikov on September 28 and asking if there was anything to report. In addition, after he returned to the United States, Oswald wrote a letter to the Soviet embassy in Washington complaining about "Kostin" in the consulate in Mexico City.[13] When interviewed by the House Assassination Committee, Cuban consul Azcue identified the Soviet consul as Pablo Yazco and said he was a "very good friend." However, he thought Oswald had spoken to someone else at the Soviet embassy.[14]

That same day, tired as he must have been, Oswald went back to the Cuban compound and talked with Sylvia Duran, a Mexican national employed at the consulate. He told her that the Russians wouldn't help him. She called the Soviet embassy and learned it would take at least four months for Moscow to make a decision on Oswald's application for a visa there. According to Duran, Oswald was very upset by this news. She asked Azcue to speak to Oswald. The two men argued. Azcue said people like Oswald were giving the Cuban revolution a bad name. If it were up to him, Azcue said, Oswald would not get a visa. Duran felt sorry for him and gave him her name and phone number, which Oswald wrote down and, despite what Azcue said, sent the application on to Cuba. Supposedly, the Cuban government ruled, a few weeks later, that Oswald would need a Russian visa.[15] There is no indication this information was ever communicated to Oswald, who had left Mexico City by then. In fact, Azcue said, he could not have communicated with Oswald because he didn't have his address.[16] Azcue was not asked to explain why Oswald's application was forwarded to Havana if there was no way to reach him if it was approved.

The Warren Commission could not establish what Oswald did between the visits to these embassies on September 27 and when he left Mexico City on October 2, a period of four full days. It found he generally left his hotel before nine in the morning and returned about midnight. The waitress at a restaurant near his hotel thought she had served him lunch but maybe not. No other guest at the hotel remembered seeing him. He supposedly went back to the Soviet and Cuban embassies once more. But the long and short of it is that Oswald essentially dropped out of sight for four days.[17] He appeared no richer when he left than he had been when he arrived.[18] Indeed, he didn't have nearly enough money to travel from Mexico City to Cuba, stay there for a period of days, and go on to the Soviet Union unless those governments paid for his travel.

The CIA told the Warren Commission, in a formerly classified letter, that a defector from Cuban intelligence, the DGI, said its officers would have interviewed Oswald after he showed up at the consulate wanting to go to Cuba. If he were a known agent, they would expedite his getting to Cuba—unless they had other plans. Otherwise, they would tell him to come back in a few days to give them time to ask Havana what to do.[19] The Warren Report chose not to mention that Oswald probably met with Cuban intelligence. Azcue's statement to the House Assassination Committee makes no mention of this either

Oswald left Mexico City by bus on the morning of October 2, but he didn't go back to New Orleans. Instead, he went to Dallas, where he arrived in the afternoon of October 3. He immediately filed an unemployment insurance claim before spending the night at the YMCA. The next day he applied for a job and called Marina. That night he hitchhiked to Ruth Paine's house in Irving, a Dallas suburb, and spent three days there.[20]

It was at this moment, after more than a year of neglecting Oswald's suspicious activities, that the U.S. government finally began to tighten the net that might ensnare him, but it was too little, too late. On October 4 the New York office of the FBI wrote headquarters acknowledging receipt of an earlier directive, which asked the New York office to obtain samples of Fair Play for Cuba stationery and its foreign mailing list because the CIA wanted to use those to counter the activities of the FPCC in foreign countries. The New York office said it should be able to obtain these items by the end of the month. It also volunteered that the president of the FPCC, Vincent Lee, had announced at a meeting in late September that he planned to resign because he was "fed up" and that the Communist Party USA would take over the FPCC's functions.[21]

. . .

Meanwhile, the CIA continued to meet with Cubela, who was still traveling. Sanchez flew to Paris for an October 5 meeting there. According to Sanchez's cable to headquarters, Cubela was much more relaxed than he had been a month earlier in Brazil and was in a "confessional mood." The Cuban did not feel that the CIA recognized or appreciated the value of having someone in his position who was willing to do what he was proposing. Instead, it had asked him to undertake such unimportant things as collecting intelligence and risking exposure by using secret writing. Sanchez assured Cubela that he was wrong to feel this way. His case was receiving consideration at the "highest levels." Sanchez may have been using the term loosely, but ordinarily those words meant the president. The United States wanted to oust Castro and replace him with an anti-Communist regime, Sanchez told him. With these assurances Cubela relaxed and left the meeting. He said he was ready to return to Cuba and undertake "the big job."[22]

In his cable to headquarters, Sanchez pointed out that because of Cubela's "mercurial temperament," he might get fed up again, pack his bags, and go back to Cuba.[23] In later cables Sanchez continued to mention Cubela's unsteady nature. He might talk about assassinating Castro in a fit of pique and then settle down and talk about organizing a regular military coup in the next breath. Sanchez told Cubela that the CIA did not consider him working for it but rather felt that it was rendering support for a common objective.[24] Another agent with the code name AMSPORT told Sanchez that Cubela was the only man who was still close to the top leadership and "capable of doing job." Cubela was a weak organizer, said AMSPORT, and would need help to stabilize the situation afterward. AMSPORT had some good news: "[Cubela and I] agree that only possibility for successful operation in Cuba today is one organized by as few high ranking officers as possible, in order prevent being penetrated, and strike blow with lightning speed at strategic point. [Cubela and his cohorts] also agree this will cause chaos and require strong support within hours."[25] That Cubela planned to strike a lightning blow that would cause chaos shows that the CIA realized he was continuing to consider Castro's assassination the first step in any coup. Indeed, it would be impossible for a handful of Cuban dissidents to overthrow Fidel Castro unless they commanded a large and loyal military force, and the CIA knew that neither Cubela nor any of his plotters did.

Sanchez concluded his cable by saying that Tepedino was flying to Paris where he would meet Cubela and travel with him to Rome and Brussels. Sanchez was going to stay in Paris, rather than fly back to headquarters, and talk to Tepedino.

A few days later, CIA headquarters cabled Sanchez to tell him that Tepedino would arrive in Paris on October 10. Attending to small details, it noted this would be Tepedino's birthday and suggested Sanchez get him a present.[26] Sanchez and Tepedino got together shortly after Tepedino landed. The jeweler appeared pleased with what Sanchez gave him as a birthday gift. Unfortunately for minutiae lovers, there is no mention of what it was.

Through AMSPORT Sanchez had learned that Cubela really wanted to meet with a senior government official in Washington. He preferred Robert Kennedy as Cubela understood he was responsible for Cuban affairs. (For a mere medical doctor, Cubela had remarkably good intelligence about who controlled Cuban policy in the U.S. government.) If Cubela was going to go through with the plan, he needed to know that the United States would support him, but he also claimed he had the people and equipment to do this without American help. Sanchez's cable warned CIA headquarters that Cubela might insist on meeting with Robert Kennedy. Cubela was temperamental, worried that his case wasn't receiving consideration at the "highest level." Meeting the request could be crucial to keeping him:

Any reasons given [to] discourage such meet will certainly not satisfy AMLASH [Cubela]. While fully realize implications, risks, and problems arranging such meet, recommend SKU [the request] be given highest and profound consideration as feeling drawn by all who in contact AMLASH is that he determined attempt op against AMTHUG [Fidel Castro] with or without . . . [U.S.] support. Lacking full knowledge his plans and our timely support may be element difference between abortion or success. Also feel most difficult period will be immediately following action planned by AMLASH. Do not feel AMLASH has or will give necessary consideration post action problems without our help and support.[27]

Sanchez ended by assuring headquarters that he would do everything possible to discourage a high-level meeting.

FitzGerald called Robert Kennedy after he received this message. The message was received at CIA headquarters around 1:30 in the afternoon and would have been given to FitzGerald immediately.[28] Robert Kennedy's telephone logs show he took a call from FitzGerald within the hour.[29] Kennedy received 477 calls in the period from September 1 to November 21, 1963, but this is the only one from FitzGerald. Though circumstantial it is strong evidence that FitzGerald called to ask if Kennedy would meet with Cubela if necessary. This would not be the last time that a cable about Cubela's plans led to hasty contact between the CIA and the attorney general.

On October 13 Sanchez met with Cubela and Tepedino. Cubela said he wanted to defect, but if the CIA wanted him to go back to Cuba and organize a coup, then a meeting with Robert Kennedy was necessary.[30] It was implicitly understood, Sanchez testified later, that Cubela assumed Robert Kennedy spoke for the president, and the Cuban wanted to be sure that John Kennedy knew Cubela was taking a huge risk.[31]

In his cable to headquarters, Sanchez reported that Cubela felt if he did not get a meeting with Robert Kennedy at this time, it would be almost impossible for him to get out of Cuba again. If this happened, Sanchez wrote, the United States would be in the same position it was the previous year with no decision being made. Just how powerful Cubela's position was can be seen in the following paragraphs from Sanchez's cable, where code names have been replaced and other edits made for ease of reading.

> [Cubela] [a]lso finds it difficult believe why [Robert Kennedy] who receives many [Cubans] would refuse see a major [Cubela] who comes from and is returning to [Cuba] and is willing to risk his life [to] try to solve [Cuban] problem. As [Cubela] adamant his desire have this meet [Sanchez] informed him his request would be sent to Washington for decision.
>
> Risking the obvious feel this case deserves the following consideration. Because of [Cubela's] unique position, decision return [Cuba], and importance he gives meeting with [Robert Kennedy], recommend [Cubela] be flown back by military aircraft to U.S. for two or three days. *Attempt arrange short meeting with [Robert Kennedy]* or if this not possible with other high [U.S.] official responsible for [Cuban] affairs. The rest of the time [Cubela] spends in U.S. can be used to either encourage his operation if such is decision or discourage it as case may be, if decision is to discourage operation feel only place this can be done hoping for success is in Washington where [Cubela] will be convinced he is getting high level treatment. . . .
>
> With full consideration given to handling problem [Cubela] represents facts remain *he does have excellent entrée to highest target level* which believe we cannot afford overlook. If at this time we inform [Cubela] we unable arrange meet it will prove to [Cubela's] own mind what he has always thought that he dealing with low level bureaucratic elements.[32]

FitzGerald cabled back almost immediately. "HQs desires [Sanchez] return HQs soonest for discussions all phases ref case."[33]

The discussions began as soon as Sanchez arrived at CIA headquarters. In later testimony he characterized Cubela as wanting three things: an indication of policy support from the highest level, namely, the Kennedys; material support in the way of weapons and explosives; and a means of protecting himself in a close confrontation with Castro or security forces.[34]

Thus the CIA found itself in a decision crisis connected to Cuba. In some ways it was similar to the Cuban Missile Crisis just a year before. Did it want Cubela to lead a coup, which both he and others thought involved the assassination of Castro? If so what about Cubela's wanting to see Robert Kennedy? Would the CIA fly him back? Would Kennedy agree? What were the risks of doing that? Or would Cubela be satisfied by the CIA's providing something less?

11

Hubris

As soon as Sanchez returned from Paris to CIA headquarters, the discussions on what to do about Cubela began. It was thought that Cubela's main concern might be that Sanchez, a mere case officer, was too low on the national security totem pole. Cubela had said as much when remarking that he wanted to be sure he wasn't dealing with low-level bureaucrats, which he was. Cubela may have had additional reasons for wanting to talk to someone above Sanchez. Many years later, in interviews by Brian Latell for his book *Castro's Secrets*, Tepedino and Cubela said they didn't like Sanchez.[1]

FitzGerald decided he would meet with Cubela himself. While Sanchez was in Washington, another case officer met with both Cubela and Tepedino in Paris on October 17. The case officer reported his talks with them and added that having FitzGerald meet with Cubela might satisfy his desire to talk to a high-level U.S. official.[2]

Not everyone at the CIA supported FitzGerald's decision. Ted Shackley, station chief of the CIA's Florida operation, JMWAVE, and FitzGerald's subordinate, testified: "My advice to [FitzGerald] was that it would probably not be a good idea for [him] to meet with [Cubela]. . . . The only thing I could see coming out of the contact would be that . . . FitzGerald would get a feel for what makes some of these people tick. . . . And that probably was too high a price to pay for the prospect if anything went wrong, an individual as prominent in Washington, both within the Agency and the social world in Washington [as FitzGerald] would be exposed in the press. That would create a flap that I thought was not worth what would be gained from the meeting."[3]

Shackley expressed it somewhat differently to author Evan Thomas, saying: "I told Des that it was something he shouldn't do. If AMLASH [Cubela] does do something [i.e., assassinate Castro], I told him, 'it's quite likely they'll track you down. You have a high profile. What are you going to say. . . . Des shrugged and went on his merry way.'"[4]

FitzGerald's security chief, Harold Swenson, also opposed it. His opposition was in part based on the fact that he considered it an assassination and did not approve of assassination. But he also opposed it purely for security reasons. He testified to the Church Committee: "I didn't trust the people, I didn't consider it a good operation on security grounds or any grounds. . . . I didn't think it was a sensible operation. I felt first that we were dealing with people whose bona fides were subject to question, whose professionalism was subject to question, and I felt that if they had succeeded in killing Castro, that he might have been succeeded by his brother, for example, who would be worse. So I thought it was a pointless operation. I thought it was a lot of nonsense."[5]

Another CIA official, Sam Halpern, told author Evan Thomas that he had walked into a shouting match between Swenson and Fitz-Gerald. According to Thomas Halpern recalled, "The CI [counter-intelligence] man was telling Des not to go to Paris. He felt Cubela was a dangle [bait the Cubans were holding out to hook the CIA], or that he'd talk to his friends. It was a real collision."[6]

Swenson's concerns were well founded. Although only a handful of people at the CIA knew of the meetings with Cubela, people outside the CIA knew. On October 10, 1963, the FBI's field office in Miami reported to headquarters that one of its informants, conceivably Tepedino, said that the CIA was meeting with Cubela for unstated reasons.[7] Indeed, when the CIA polygraphed Tepedino two years later and asked him to identify the people he had told about his connection with the CIA, Tepedino said that "it would be almost impossible, because so many people in New York, in Cuba, in Europe, etc." knew. Tepedino said that while Cubela was not working for Cuban intelligence, he was close to many who were. He also said that Cubela never had a group or a plan for the overthrow of Castro. Even worse from a security standpoint, the polygraph operator could not conclude that Tepedino was answering truthfully.[8] Thus regardless of whether Cubela was working for Cuban intelligence, everyone seemed to know what he was doing, including perhaps Cuban intelligence and Fidel Castro.

Richard Helms told author Evan Thomas that he shared Swenson's qualms, but he didn't veto FitzGerald's plan to meet with Cubela because he was under pressure from Robert Kennedy to do something: "I was also getting my ass beaten. You should have enjoyed the experience of Bobby Kennedy rampant on your back."[9]

Thomas summed up FitzGerald's mental state by saying: "FitzGerald was suffering from hubris, the belief . . . that the normal rules of gravity somehow didn't apply." He would do what no one else had been able to do.[10]

Lest Cubela lose interest while his case was being debated in Washington, Sanchez cabled the Rome and Paris stations to pass a message to Tepedino to tell him, "You [and] our friend's case receiving highest attention and consideration."[11] Sanchez had a bird in the hand, and he wasn't going to let it escape just because FitzGerald was preoccupied with getting the needed approval.

By October 21 the decision had been made. FitzGerald would go to Paris and meet Cubela himself. He would use a false name, but he would pose as a high government official and personal representative of Robert Kennedy. He was in truth both of those things. Although there is no direct evidence that the attorney general specifically approved the meeting with Cubela, all indications are that he did. Indeed, it is preposterous to think that a senior CIA official like FitzGerald, who was a personal friend of Robert Kennedy, would pose as his personal representative without clearing it directly. Not knowing precisely where Tepedino and Cubela were, Sanchez cabled both Rome and Paris, asking the CIA stations there to tell the men to return to Paris by October 27.[12]

A second cable followed to the Paris station. "Great minds think alike," it began. This seems an indication that everyone at CIA headquarters was in agreement, although Swenson and Shackley certainly were not. The Paris station was to arrange a three-hour meeting with Cubela on October 29 at 5:00 p.m. Paris time. It was to provide an impressive safe house for the meeting. It was also to have a Cadillac limousine with a CIA officer at the wheel to chauffer FitzGerald to the meeting. The safe house should be set up so that Cubela would see FitzGerald pull up in the black, chauffeur-driven limo. Paris would also provide a countersurveillance team to make sure no foreign intelligence agents were following Cubela or FitzGerald or observing the meeting. "[Paris should take] any additional measures station feels are necessary to increase security of meet and make it as impressive as possible."[13] In point of fact, the impressive plans would prove beyond the CIA's ability to implement. Fitzgerald was chauffeured to the meeting not in a black Cadillac limousine but in a "beat-up old Peugeot" belonging to the CIA officer driving.[14]

The same day, possibly by coincidence but maybe not, General Wheeler, the chief of staff of the army, sent Defense Secretary Robert McNamara an updated draft of the "State-Defense Contingency Plan for a Coup in Cuba." Wheeler's cover letter said that the joint chiefs still didn't think a coup was likely. However, it noted, a coup initiated by dissident leaders who had prior U.S. approval was another possibility. While the joint chiefs had reservations about how quickly they could put sizable forces into Cuba, the draft plan was feasible from a military standpoint. The most dangerous contingency was the Soviet troops in Cuba. An invasion could lead to a major military confrontation with the Russians. The draft dealt with this possibility by saying, irresponsibly, that whether this led to war would be up to the Russians: "The US should conduct operations so as to leave to the Soviet Union the choice of whether to become directly involved with our armed forces." Moreover, while the joint chiefs thought Soviet forces in Cuba were not strong enough to pose a threat to invading American troops, they warned that the Soviets might move on Berlin or elsewhere.[15] Whether or not Wheeler knew about FitzGerald's plan, he was saying implicitly that a U.S.-supported coup in Cuba could lead to a military confrontation with the Soviet Union that might extend beyond Cuba, depending on what the Soviets did.

The bottom line was that FitzGerald's hubris might lead to World War III. Assuming Wheeler, McNamara, Helms, and McCone were as responsible and prudent as their positions in government required, one or more of them should have cautioned the president about the direction in which FitzGerald was taking the country. There is no evidence they did.

...

On Monday, October 7, Lee Harvey Oswald returned to Dallas after spending a weekend with his wife at Ruth Paine's house in Irving. He began looking for a job and rented a room in a boardinghouse. However, the landlady didn't like him and kicked him out after five days, so he spent the weekend of October 12–13 at Ruth Paine's. She gave him a driving lesson. Although Oswald didn't own and couldn't afford a car, he had taken a sudden interest in being able to drive after returning from Mexico City.

The next Monday he went back into Dallas and found another rooming house, this one at 1026 North Beckley Avenue. It would be his last voluntary move. The room was small, but Oswald could use the kitchen and watch television in another room. He apparently only had with him the things he had taken in two suitcases to Mexico City. These would be the same possessions that Dallas police seized when they went to his room the afternoon of the assassination.[16] The day Oswald got the room, Ruth Paine learned through a friend about a job opening at the Texas School Book Depository. After interviewing Oswald the superintendent told him to start work Wednesday, October 16. It would be his last job.

Oswald struck up an acquaintance with Buell Wesley Frazier, who worked at the book depository and who was the brother of one of Paine's friends. Frazier lived in Irving only a block from Paine, so that weekend Oswald got a ride to her house with Frazier and spent time with his family. It was Oswald's birthday, and they celebrated. On Sunday, October 20, Marina gave birth to their second child, a girl. He visited them in the hospital. Marina said he was happy to have a second child "and even wept a little."[17]

Oswald went back to work at the book depository the next Monday morning and stayed at the rooming house for the rest of the week. One evening he went to a meeting where right-wing general Edwin Walker, the man he had allegedly attempted to shoot the previous April, spoke. He went to Irving again on Friday to spend the weekend with Marina and the children at Paine's house. One of the nights he was there, he went with Paine's estranged husband to an American Civil Liberties Union meeting.[18]

...

If Oswald's actions appeared contradictory, going to a right-wing meeting one night and a left-wing meeting a few nights later, so were the Kennedys'. While they were insisting on increased sabotage in Cuba, a coup, and apparently Castro's assassination, they also gave indications that they were prepared to reach an accommodation with him. Foreign policy mavens would say the Kennedys were taking a "two-track" approach, covert action on the one hand and diplomacy on the other, and waiting to see which was the more promising. The president had indicated on previous occasions that he was willing to explore diametrically opposed alternatives simultaneously.

The diplomatic track was being developed by the deputy ambassador to the United Nations, William Attwood, a former journalist who had once worked as a speechwriter for Adlai Stevenson. The Kennedy administration made him ambassador to Guinea before moving him to the United Nations as deputy to Stevenson, Kennedy's UN ambassador.[19]

In late August Attwood had a conversation with an old friend from Guinea who had become the Guinean ambassador to Cuba. The Guinean said that although the Communists in the Cuban government tried to prevent ambassadors from neutral countries, like his, from talking to Castro, he found a chance to talk to the Cuban leader alone. Castro told the Guinean that he was receptive to changing course and "getting Cuba on the road to non-alignment," but the exile raids were an obstacle because they played into the hands of the Communists.[20]

A few weeks later, Attwood talked with Lisa Howard, a correspondent for ABC News who had once interviewed Castro. She felt that there was indeed a rift between Castro and the Communists in Cuba. With approval from the president, Attwood sounded out Carlos Lechuga, the Cuban ambassador to the UN, about whether Castro might be interested in talking. According to Attwood, Lechuga hinted that Castro was in a mood to talk. Attwood reported this to Robert Kennedy. The attorney general said that it was worthwhile to maintain contact with Lechuga but Attwood should not go to Cuba. The fact Attwood went to Robert Kennedy with this matter rather than to the State Department illustrates the attorney general's complete control over all aspects of Cuban policy.

Attwood's attempt to discern Castro's intent was producing mixed signals. Over dinner with Attwood, a Greek architect just returned from Cuba told him of a one-on-one conversation with Castro. According to the architect, Castro was amenable to a change in direction, but Che Guevara and the other Communists in Cuba thought Castro was "dangerously unreliable" and would "get rid" of him if they thought they could carry on without him. Ironically, if this was true, Che and the Kennedys were thinking alike.

Attwood also opened another channel to Cuba by arranging for the president to be interviewed by French reporter Jean Daniel. Daniel wanted to talk to Kennedy, then go to Havana and talk to Castro for an article on how the two leaders saw the situation.[21]

Yet the conflicting signals continued. On October 28, the day before FitzGerald's planned meeting with Cubela in Paris, Lechuga ran into Attwood at the delegates' lounge at the UN and said that Havana did not think it would be useful to send a representative to the UN for talks. A few days later, Lisa Howard got a call from a person close to Castro, saying, "Castro would very much like to talk," but he very much wanted to do the talking himself rather than through an emissary.[22] On November 8 the State Department sent Bundy a memo, advising that Attwood should not visit Cuba and that as preconditions for talk, Castro should break ties with the Soviet Union and quit stirring up trouble in Latin America.[23]

Meanwhile, the CIA continued its plotting. FitzGerald pulled out all the stops in preparation for the meeting with Cubela. Someone at the CIA prepared for him an eight-page paper with Cubela's weaknesses and other derogatory information on the Cuban. It is a steamy document. In addition to talking about Cubela's participation in killing one of Batista's men, his limited intellectual abilities, his sexual preferences, and the regular reports that he wanted to defect, it noted that a one-time girlfriend was a suspected Cuban intelligence officer.

The most damaging information in the paper, however, was something FitzGerald surely didn't want to read. In 1960 a Cuban businessman had warned the CIA that Cubela was the head of "a fake anti-Government movement" designed to lure dissidents in Cuba into joining so that Castro could find out who was plotting against him. In other words, just as FitzGerald's security chief had warned, Castro had once used Cubela as a dangle.[24] The thought must surely have occurred to FitzGerald that Castro might be doing it again in this instance, but there is no evidence it bothered him. Perhaps he didn't see any immediate risk, and, in any event, he didn't really have an alternative.

At the same time, a memorandum for the record—sanitized by the CIA before being made public—outlines the scenario for FitzGerald's meeting with Cubela. The Paris station would provide an impressive safe house under CIA control and provide counter-surveillance. Tepedino and Cubela would arrive in Paris the night of October 27. Sanchez would arrive then too and contact them the next day. Sanchez would lay the groundwork for FitzGerald's arrival by telling Cubela that because of his request to meet with Robert Kennedy, a personal emissary had been sent to talk to him and report back to the highest levels. He would warn Cubela that he must be totally discreet and never mention such a meeting as having taken place.[25]

A fallback position was also prepared, again appearing to be a sanitized memorandum for the record by Sanchez. It reads simply: "If the above contact in Paris does not have the necessary impact, consideration, based on a new assessment, will be given to bring AMLASH/1 [Cubela] to the U.S. by military aircraft, given first class treatment, and accommodations and another meet with another high government official."[26] In other words if, after meeting with FitzGerald, Cubela still insisted on meeting with Robert Kennedy, then the CIA would fly him to the United States on a military aircraft, give him royal treatment, and have him meet the attorney general. Sanchez may even have talked to the attorney general about this. Years later he told author Brian Latell that he had met with Robert Kennedy at his Hickory Hill home "on a few occasions" in 1963 but refused to discuss the details.[27]

Little wonder that Harold Swenson got into a shouting match with FitzGerald over the idea that he was even thinking of meeting with a possible dangle and a prospective assassin in Paris and bringing him to Washington to meet Robert Kennedy. There would be no plausible denial. If Swenson was right, FitzGerald might be walking the U.S. government into a trap.

12

Carpe Diem

Cuba wasn't the only country commanding the attention of the national security establishment. Vietnam was too. After getting the cable in late August from a National Security Council officer saying that the United States was willing to see Vietnam's president Ngo Dinh Diem replaced, Ambassador Lodge assumed the president approved, which was not the case. Unlike FitzGerald, Lodge wouldn't need to instigate the coup. Vietnamese generals were eager to do that. They didn't even want American help, like Cubela did. They were prepared to do the job themselves. However, they wanted to be assured that the United States would not interfere.

Therefore, just hours after FitzGerald wrapped up his meeting with Cubela on October 29 at the supposedly impressive safe house in Paris, an equally impressive meeting took place at the White House.[1] The president, the vice president, and the attorney general were there. Vice President Lyndon Johnson's presence is notable because he never attended meetings on Cuba. The State Department had four representatives at this one, including Secretary of State Rusk and Under Secretaries Averell Harriman and Alexis Johnson. Among the Defense Department representatives were McNamara, General Taylor, and General Krulak, whom John Kennedy had rescued in World War II. McGeorge Bundy and two of his aides were there. And from the CIA were McCone, Helms, and William Colby, who ran the Far Eastern desk. What happened at the meeting is well documented. Helms and Colby coauthored a memorandum for the record. There is also an audio recording; John Kennedy had a taping system at the White House, and it was running during this meeting.

The alignment of participants differed from what it usually was on Cuba. The State Department favored the coup. Rusk thought a quick, successful coup would bring better leadership to Vietnam. Harriman said unless the government there was changed, the war would be lost because Diem didn't have the necessary leadership qualities.

Taylor and McCone made the point that a coup would cause at least a temporary setback in the war against the Viet Cong because after a coup, the government would be in confusion for a period of time. When the president suggested the matter needed further study before he would make a decision, McNamara warned against sending conflicting signals to Lodge since the latter had been told that U.S. policy was to replace the Diem government.

Robert Kennedy's position seemed dramatically different from his aggressive approach to Cuba. He said that the United States didn't have enough information. It was "putting the whole future in the hands of relatively unknown generals. . . . He felt that the United States was risking too much based on flimsy evidence."[2] On the other hand, his position on Vietnam and Cuba may have been consistent at least in his mind. He wasn't going to back Cubela until FitzGerald vetted him personally. Of course, even if Cubela passed the vetting, he was one of the few assets the CIA had in Cuba who were vetted.

In the end according to the memorandum for the record, the president decided to tell the coup plotters in Vietnam not to go ahead unless they thought they could succeed. A message to this effect was sent to Lodge.[3]

The CIA also has a memorandum for the record of the meeting with Cubela in Paris. Strangely, it is dated several weeks after the meeting. FitzGerald was introduced under the false name "James Clark" and said to be an "emissary from the policy level of the United States Government." Thus on October 29, the United States was moving forward with plans for coups in both Vietnam and Cuba. FitzGerald told Cubela a variation of what was told the generals in Vietnam: "The United States is prepared to render all necessary assistance to any anti-communist Cuban group which succeeds in neutralizing the present Cuban leadership and assumes sufficient control to invite the United States to render the assistance it is prepared to give." FitzGerald emphasized that the coup had to be successful. This was exactly the same policy the president wanted communicated to Lodge in Vietnam.[4]

FitzGerald and Cubela weren't thinking quite the same though. FitzGerald wanted a military coup, like the one that was about to take place in Vietnam, where senior military officers would lead it and could back it up with the troops under their command. Cubela told FitzGerald: "If Castro falls the military will probably break up into four or five groups. Without Fidel Castro the present regime will disintegrate." In other words Cubela didn't have a basic requirement for a coup, control of the military. To him the assassination of Fidel Castro was all that was needed. But FitzGerald wasn't going to quibble over the details. This was his bird in the hand. The meeting concluded by Cubela saying he was satisfied with the policy discussion, but he wanted to know what "technical support" the CIA would give him. In that regard the memorandum says that nothing of an operational nature was discussed.[5]

This begs the question of exactly what the operation was. Testifying years later Sanchez explained that no one used the word "assassinate" around Cubela because he didn't like the term. This was fine as far as the CIA was concerned, said Sanchez, "since we were not willing to discuss specifically [sic, should read "physically"] eliminating Castro, this was never discussed in terms of the operations. We certainly had no doubt that in his mind this was the only way to go about it."[6] At another point in his testimony, Sanchez elaborated: "In general terms, in talking about a military coup and the need to neutralize or eliminate, . . . sometime[s] he would say, get rid of the leadership in order to initiate that coup. . . . In other words, there was going to be—there was no doubt that there was going to be gunfire, and somebody was going to be—well, these were the possibilities of what could happen in a case of that nature."[7]

Parsing Sanchez's circumlocution, a principal reason the CIA was dealing with Cubela was because it thought he could kill Castro if need be. Cubela was not the CIA's candidate to be the next ruler of Cuba, Sanchez said. "He was only evaluated in [the CIA's] dealings with him on the basis of what he and his group could contribute to a coup."[8] His contribution was to be the triggerman.

Cubela's recollection of the meeting when he talked to the House

Assassinations Committee differs from Sanchez's testimony to the Senate committee. Cubela said that at the meeting FitzGerald offered political support: "That in case of being able to carry out either the plot attempt against the Prime Minister of Cuba or any other activity that will put in danger the stability of the regime, they [the United States] would support us." When asked if the support included weapons, Cubela answered, "Yes. . . . Anything I want." Cubela pointed out that although FitzGerald never discussed assassination with him, other CIA officers did. "We discussed different possibilities . . . invasions, upheavals and among these plans also the possibility of having an [sic] plot attempt against the Prime Minister's life."[9]

During Cubela's interview the questioner for the House Committee drove home the point that while lower-level CIA officers approved Cubela's plan to assassinate Castro, he really couldn't know if FitzGerald had approved. Cubela's answer was telling. He admitted that FitzGerald may have wanted plausible denial but argued that he surely knew what Cubela was planning: "Well I think he was well informed of everything. He was the Chief of SAS. Of course he had to know about it—that is elementary—if he is the head of SAS all the rest of officers depend on him. I talk to the officers, the officers have to report to him so it obvious that he is supposed to know, but now, the fact that he did not want to go specifically into the discussion of specific plans maybe in order not to get committed he himself personally because anyway he was a high representative so it is very likely. But I am certain he knew about it. I have no doubt in the least."[10]

Events in Vietnam played out differently. The day before the White House meeting, Ambassador Lodge sent an accurate warning: "It would appear that a coup attempt by the Generals' group is imminent; that whether this coup fails or succeeds, the USG [U.S. government] must be prepared to accept the fact that we will be blamed, however unjustifiably."[11] The morning after the White House meeting, Bundy cabled Lodge: "We do not accept as a basis for U.S. policy that we have no power to delay or discourage a coup."[12] It was an impotent assertion of power. Events were out of Bundy's control. Besides, Bundy had already told Lodge, once a coup began in Saigon, it was in America's interest that it succeed.[13]

At 1:00 a.m. on November 1, Washington time, the White House got word of the coup in Vietnam. Bundy waited until 3:00 a.m. before waking the president to tell him. In Vietnam President Diem refused to accept the fact that the military was trying to overthrow him. His too was an assertion of power that he did not have. Later in the day, Vietnamese soldiers seized him and his brother. They took the two men to the outskirts of Saigon and shot them to death. The White House learned just after midnight on November 2.[14] As Lodge had predicted, the world thought the United States was responsible.

...

In Dallas on Friday, November 1, Oswald rented a post office box and listed it for mail not only in his name but also for the Fair Play for Cuba Committee and the American Civil Liberties Union.[15]

Yet the government's net continued to close around him. While Oswald was at work at the book depository that day, FBI agent James Hosty visited Ruth Paine and spoke briefly with her. That night Oswald came to spend the weekend with Marina at Paine's house in Irving. Paine told him an FBI agent had been there. Hosty returned the next Tuesday, November 5. Marina apparently told Oswald about that in a later phone conversation.

Oswald was outraged. He wrote the Soviet embassy in Washington to complain. It is obviously odd to write the Soviets to complain about the FBI, but that's what he did. After the assassination the Soviets gave the Warren Commission a copy of the letter.[16] Documents turned over to the United States in 1999 indicate that the Soviets saw no harm in giving the Warren Commission a copy of Oswald's letter to the embassy because "the competent U.S. authorities [were] undoubtedly aware of this letter, since the embassy's correspondence [was] under constant surveillance."[17] In other words the Soviets assumed the United States opened and read all mail to the Soviet embassy in Washington.

What the Warren Commission didn't know, because the FBI's Dallas field office didn't tell anyone until 1975, was that a week or so later, Oswald visited the FBI office in Dallas and asked for agent Hosty. When the receptionist told him Hosty wasn't available, Oswald left an unsealed note for the agent. The receptionist said the note threatened to blow up the FBI office if anyone talked to his wife again. Hosty recalled the note differently. He remembered it as saying that if the FBI wanted to talk to Oswald, it should do so directly and that he would take some unspecified action if the FBI bothered Marina. Hosty showed the note to his supervisor, who told him to write a memorandum for the record about it. That the FBI agents in Dallas would be so casual about a threat says a great deal about how poorly prepared the bureau was for terrorism in those days. Things changed dramatically a few weeks later of course. Within hours of Oswald being killed, the supervisor told Hosty to destroy the note and the memorandum, and he did.[18]

...

In Washington the Special Group convened on Tuesday, November 5, for a special meeting on Cuba. The first two items for discussion were a failed sabotage operation in Cuba and two future operations. The conversation then turned to "peace feelers" from Cuba. According to Bundy "Castro would like to have a talk designed to bring about some kind of 'arrangement' with the U.S." William Attwood had been in touch with the Cuban ambassador at the UN, Carlos Lechuga, who wanted Attwood to go to Cuba to talk. Since it was deemed inappropriate for Attwood to go to Cuba in his official capacity, someone suggested he resign and then go to Cuba. Publicly, he could say he planned to write an article for *Look* magazine. An alternate suggestion was that Castro should send his personal physician, Rene Vallejo, to Mexico City for discussion with the American ambassador there.

The CIA's Richard Helms said the idea required more thought before anything was done. Robert Kennedy "emphasized that as a prelude to all this the U.S. must require some fundamental steps such as the end of subversion in Latin America and removing the Soviet troops in Cuba before any serious discussion can take place about a détente." These conditions would presumably be unacceptable to Castro. It isn't clear if the attorney general realized this and intended them to be a bar to even preliminary discussions. In any event the Special Group agreed to postpone any decision and consider the matter again in a few days.[19]

Robert Kennedy gave an oral history in 1964 that confirms the Kennedys were taking a two-track approach:

> Ultimately, I think, the president gave [Attwood] the go-ahead. And he was to go to Havana—I don't know, in December last year [1963] or January of this year—and perhaps see Castro and see what could be done. We had certain things that were required which was the end of the military presence of the Russians and the Communists, and the cut off of ties with the Communists by Cuba, and the end of the exportation of revolution, and, in return for that—those basic points and perhaps more—there would be normalization of relationship. But we discussed that as a possibility. In addition to, we were also making more of an effort through espionage and sabatoge [sic] in the last—-August, September, October.[20]

Thus regardless of whether the Kennedys were serious about negotiating with Castro, Robert Kennedy clearly wanted preconditions that Castro probably would not, and possibly could not, agree to, and it would be surprising if both Kennedys didn't realize this.

• • •

In Dallas on Friday, November 8, Oswald again obtained a ride from Frazier to go from work to the Paine residence for the weekend. Since the next Monday was the Veterans Day holiday, Oswald could spend three days with his family. Paine gave Oswald a driving lesson and took him to get a learner's permit on Saturday, but the licensing office was closed because that was an election day in Texas.[21]

• • •

On Monday, November 11, President Kennedy went to Arlington National Cemetery for a ceremony to commemorate Veterans Day. Secretary of Defense Robert McNamara was there too. Kennedy turned to McNamara and said, "This really is one of the most beautiful places on earth. I think, maybe, some day this is where I'd like to be. "[22] Kennedy didn't finish the thought.

13

The Plot Accelerates

The morning after his visit to Arlington Cemetery, John Kennedy turned his attention back to Cuba and met at the White House with his top national security team. McNamara, Rusk, Robert Kennedy, Secretary of the Army Vance, General Maxwell Taylor, and McGeorge Bundy were all there with their aides. The CIA was represented in abundance by Director McCone, DDP Helms, Desmond FitzGerald, Bruce Cheever, Paul Eckels, and Ted Shackley, the chief of the CIA's station in Miami. Three of the CIA attendees prepared memoranda for the record. This is fortunate because, unlike the White House meeting on the coup in Vietnam, there is no audio tape for this November 12 meeting on Cuba or indeed any meetings on Cuba in the fall of 1963.

McCone began with a review of the situation. Cuba still belonged to Castro, he reported, but his grip was weakening. He continued to control the military although the CIA was beginning to exploit dissension there. Cuba's already tight internal security was getting tighter. The economy was in bad shape because of the economic sanctions and a recent hurricane. Soviet troops had largely been withdrawn; there were no longer any organized military units on the island. However, most of the Soviet equipment was still there including the surface-to-air missiles that could shoot down U-2s.[1]

Then it was FitzGerald's turn. He felt he had made considerable progress since the October 1 meeting, at which he had said the pendulum had turned. (This was a far cry from the days when Bill Harvey spent meetings irritating the attorney general.) McCone spoke up to point out that FitzGerald had developed an "integrated and interdependent" approach. The program to get better intelligence collection in Cuba was impressive, FitzGerald continued. The CIA had seventy-four solo agents operating on the island and another seventy-nine subagents who were parts of intelligence networks. It had one "Black" (infiltrated) team that controlled fifty-five sub-agents. But Castro's security was good. Several Black teams had been lost and others withdrawn rather than risk their capture. The CIA might abandon this approach altogether.

The program to use propaganda to stimulate sabotage was producing results. The CIA was mailing thirty thousand to forty thousand pieces of propaganda into Cuba each month and broadcasting thirty-two hours of radio programming per day over seven different stations. (FitzGerald didn't say whether the Cuban postal system was delivering the mailed propaganda or whether Cubans were listening to the CIA radio broadcasts.) There had been 109 sabotage incidents mentioned in intelligence reports in the last seven months. These included derailing locomotives, burning trucks and factories, and destroying electric lines. FitzGerald implied that these were the result of the propaganda. Of course, he admitted, most effective were the economic sanctions, which the State Department had arranged.

The CIA was supporting two autonomous groups, Manuel Artime's and Manolo Ray's. Artime was developing bases in Costa Rica and Nicaragua. He had ships, and the CIA would supply him with arms in such a way that, as Fitzgerald said, "Even Artime will not know that it comes from the United States." Artime would mount his first harassment action in December. FitzGerald felt that raids by these groups might slow the Cuban roundup of the Black teams.

FitzGerald then turned to the heart of the effort, the coup. Working with the Defense Department's biographical information on the Cuban military, the CIA had identified 150 key military personnel, of which 45 were of interest, meaning that they might be amenable to recruitment. Yet the CIA was in direct contact with only three, whom Cheever's memorandum said had been "Heroes of the Revolution," men who had been in leadership positions in the overthrow of Batista. The memorandum said these three were either in Cuba or about to return. The last was surely a reference to Cubela, who was still traveling in Europe. But while individual military leaders were willing to meet with the CIA, they were afraid to work together because of the tight Cuban security. In addition, said one memorandum of the meeting: "The leaders with whom we are in touch have emphasized the need to be reassured that, should they overthrow Castro, they will not be considered in the same light as Castro himself."

At the conclusion of FitzGerald's presentation Rusk spoke at length about the sabotage operations launched from outside Cuba. He opposed them, arguing that they might cause the Soviets to return their forces to Cuba. He thought that new Soviet pressure in Germany was in response to the raids in Cuba. McNamara disagreed. He saw no connection between what was happening in Germany and the raids. Moreover, he thought the sabotage was having an effect.

There was a question about the autonomous groups, such as Artime's, which were not directly controlled by the CIA. FitzGerald warned, "[Since the CIA doesn't have control,] once Artime was in business, we might expect some events to take place which were not exactly to our liking." The president asked what decisions were necessary. Except for the disagreement by Rusk over the raids, the consensus was that the overall program should continue. This same day Bundy phoned Attwood at the United Nations and told him, as the State Department had advised earlier, to tell the Cubans that the preconditions for talks required them to break with the Soviets and quit exporting the revolution to Latin America.[2]

Thus on November 12, 1963, ten days before the president's trip to Dallas, the CIA briefed John Kennedy, Robert Kennedy, Dean Rusk, Robert McNamara, and General Maxwell Taylor on its plot for a coup in Cuba. It might not seem that FitzGerald had accomplished much on this front since the CIA was in contact with only three of the estimated forty-five military leaders whom it hoped to recruit. But FitzGerald and the CIA officials at the meeting knew that Cubela alone might be enough.[3]

The meeting then turned to a different matter almost as an afterthought. FitzGerald's memorandum for the record states that Bundy raised the subject of an arms cache recently discovered in Venezuela that seemed to come from Cuba. It might be a few months before the full facts could be determined.

The memorandum for the record prepared by the CIA's Paul Eckels was more detailed:

> The view was expressed that CIA, in connection with the Department of Defense, should concentrate on attempting to catch Castro red-handed delivering arms to Communist groups in Latin American countries. It was determined that during the next 90 days from this date an attempt would be made by means of air patrols and surface ships to identify ships carrying arms for Castro to Latin American countries. It was hoped that a ship with Cuban arms could be picked up. Conversations are to be initiated by the Secretary of the Navy with CIA to map out a three-moth operation against Cuban shipping. It was also determined that the Colombian and Venezuelan governments should be asked to join with the U.S. in developing a joint patrol designed to identify ships carrying weapons from Cuba destined for revolutionary groups in Latin American countries.[4]

The Venezuelan arms cache is important because, as will be detailed later, Richard Helms was back in the White House a week later for a hastily arranged meeting that was allegedly for the purpose of showing the president a weapon from the arms cache.

The day after the White House meeting, Nestor Sanchez, the case officer handling Cubela, finally got around to writing up his contact report on FitzGerald's October 29 meeting in Paris with Cubela. It is a notable coincidence that the contact report came two weeks after the contact but only a day after the high-level White House meeting. In later testimony Sanchez said, as an excuse for the delay, that he might have been traveling.

The same day, November 13, the CIA called Cubela's friend Carlos Tepedino to arrange a meeting in New York for November 14. Sanchez later testified that he didn't recall such a meeting and that someone else must have gone. Few people were cleared for the operation. FitzGerald and/or Halpern may have attended; a memorandum of the meeting uses the word "we," suggesting that more than one CIA officer was present. They talked to Tepedino at length about whom Cubela could recruit to help him. The CIA offered some names, and Tepedino offered others. Only about twenty men in all were discussed, with Tepedino rejecting a number of them. This part of the meeting was more or less a brainstorming session. But it seems clear that while Cubela had enough conspirators for an assassination, neither he nor the CIA had nearly enough for a coup.

The principal purpose of the meeting, however, was to determine what Cubela had said to Tepedino after the meeting on October 29 with FitzGerald. According to Tepedino Cubela was satisfied with the policy discussion, that is, he was dealing with high-level officials in the U.S. government, and the United States would intervene if Cubela could start a legitimate coup. However, he was "not at all happy with the fact that he still was not given the technical assistance for the operational plan as he saw it." He felt he was being denied "certain small pieces of equipment which promised a final solution to the problem."[5] Of course, in earlier meetings with the CIA, Cubela had boasted he didn't need its help because he had such weapons.

Whoever wrote the memorandum was careful in phrasing things for the written record. The small pieces of equipment Cubela wanted were assassination weapons. Specifically, they were sniper rifles with telescopic sights, explosives, and some kind of small, easily concealed, specially made device. In his testimony to the Senate, Sanchez used the term "dart pen." He called it a "pellet pen" elsewhere. He said Cubela was worried that he might be caught in a situation where he was not allowed to have a conventional weapon and would need a small, secret weapon for self-defense.[6]

Cubela's statement to the House Assassinations Committee about what he wanted was somewhat different. He said he wanted "a pen that could shoot a bullet," not a "dart pen."[7] According to later CIA investigations, the weapon the CIA made and offered Cubela was neither of these devices. It was ballpoint pen with a hypodermic needle inside.

Meanwhile, the CIA was attending to minor details. It had on October 28 asked the FBI for information on Artime. On November 14 the FBI gave the evasive response that it had not conducted an investigation of him and that all pertinent information about him had previously been provided to the CIA.[8] On the same day, despite the high-level swirl of activity on Cuba, the Department of the Army's general counsel, Joseph Califano, was attending to the mundane task of writing the Defense Intelligence Agency to thank it for loaning two men to the CIA to compile the biographical information the CIA needed to identify potential coup plotters.[9] Califano might not have been told that the purpose of the effort was to organize a coup, but it would have been a reasonable guess.

On November 16 Sanchez sent a cable to the Paris station, saying that it should contact Cubela and ask him if he still wanted communication training and to tell him he needed to get secret writing materials to take back to Cuba before he returned.[10]

Then, as if something new had developed after Sanchez's cable, FitzGerald cabled the Paris station, telling it to contact Cubela and persuade him to delay leaving Paris for five days in order permit one more meeting that he had requested.[11] FitzGerald had something more important than secret writing to discuss with Cubela.

14

The Last Weekend

John Kennedy left Washington on November 16 for a relaxing weekend in Palm Beach, Florida, before a busy week that would see him campaigning in Florida and Texas. It was the final weekend of his life.

...

In Texas Lee Harvey Oswald's weekend was unusual. He did not go to Ruth Paine's house in Irving to spend time with his family. Instead, he stayed home alone at his rooming house in Dallas. The Warren Commission didn't attribute any significance to this, nor did it consider if Oswald had an ulterior motive in spending the weekend alone.

According to the Warren Report, Marina talked by phone with Oswald earlier in the week and told him not to come to Paine's house this weekend because Paine's estranged husband, Michael, was going to be there for his daughter's birthday and Michael was someone "with whom Oswald did not get along."[1] To support this conclusion, the commission cited Marina's testimony.

But this wasn't what Marina said in her testimony. She said Oswald didn't like Michael but did not say that it was the reason he didn't come.[2] He, not Marina, made the decision. He simply said he wasn't coming. Ruth Paine's testimony was different. She said Marina was talking to Oswald on the phone and Paine heard her tell him not to come because she didn't want him to "wear out his welcome" at Paine's house since he had been there the previous, three-day weekend.[3] The Warren Commission didn't try to resolve the significant inconsistencies between the two women's stories. Indeed, what the report says is not supported by anyone's testimony. Since Marina was on the phone with Oswald, and Paine was not, her version seems more trustworthy. Moreover, Marina and Oswald talked to each other in Russian. Ruth spoke Russian but not well, so she might have misunderstood what she overheard. One of Paine's stated reasons for taking Marina under her wing was to improve her Russian by having a native speaker around. Thus it was Oswald's choice to hang around his rooming house the last weekend. For some reason he wanted to remain there, rather than go to Irving to be with his wife and daughters.

A third person testified about why Oswald didn't go to Paine's. This was Oswald's coworker at the book depository, Buell Wesley Frazier, who gave Oswald rides to Paine's house. Frazier said Oswald told him he wouldn't need a ride this weekend because he was going to stay in Dallas and take a driving test.[4] According to Frazier's testimony, Michael Paine's impending visit to Ruth's house had nothing whatsoever to do with Oswald's decision.

Oswald lived at a rooming house operated by Arthur and Gladys Johnson. His room was claustrophobically small, five feet by fourteen feet, barely wide enough for a single bed. Oswald could watch television in the living room of the house and eat in the kitchen. The Johnsons testified that Oswald spent the weekend in his room, going out only briefly to a nearby self-service laundry. They weren't home all the time, though, because they also ran a restaurant a few miles away. Still, their testimony suggests that Oswald did not even go to take a driver's test on Saturday.[5] He may have been lying when he told Frazier that this was his plan.

Oswald is known to have been at the rooming house Saturday afternoon, November 16, because he called Marina on the phone then. After they finished, Marina handed the receiver to Paine. Oswald explained to her that he had gone to get the driver's license earlier in the day but left without a license—Paine said it was going to be a learner's permit—because the line was too long.[6] That he actually did this is suspect because his landlords said that he didn't leave the house the whole weekend except to do his laundry. Granted they weren't at home the whole time, but it presumably would have taken Oswald several hours Saturday morning to go to the license bureau, wait a while, and then return. The

Johnsons didn't indicate they were gone that long. Besides, since Oswald had given up the chance to see his family that weekend for the sole purpose of getting the license, why would a line discourage him? The Warren Commission wasn't curious enough to pursue the matter.

On Sunday Marina asked Ruth Paine to place a call to Oswald at the rooming house in Dallas for her. Only Marina had the number. Someone answered the phone, but when Paine asked for Oswald, she was told that no one by that name lived there. Oswald had rented the room under the name O. H. Lee, not Lee Harvey Oswald.[7]

. . .

In Washington DC that weekend, Attorney General Robert Kennedy was meeting with veterans of Brigade 2506. Earlier in the year, the Kennedys had established a program under ICCCA auspices for brigade returnees to enter the U.S. Army, and about 108 of them did. Thus army intelligence reported to the secretary of the army that the attorney general was meeting some of these men this same weekend:

> Information received from Ft. Holabird, Md. [the army intelligence school in Baltimore], that a former Cuban Brigade member, 2nd Lt. Jose Raul VARONA Gonzales . . . had been invited by 2nd Lt. Erneido OLIVA [former second in command at the Bay of Pigs] to visit Washington, D. C. on 18 Nov 63 to meet with Mr. Robert Kennedy, the Attorney General. VARONA is a student at Ft. Holabird and reportedly was the G-2 [intelligence officer] of Brigade 2506 in the Cuban invasion. When VARONA returned from Washington he did not mention seeing Mr. Kennedy, but did say that he had met with Lt. OLIVA. The actual purpose of the meeting is not known. . . . Mr. Robert Kennedy did confer on 17 Nov 63 with Manuel ARTIME Buesa, Roberto SAN ROMAN aka [also known as] Roberto Perez San Roman, Jose SAN ROMAN, aka Jose Perez SAN ROMAN, and Enrique Jose RUIZ William Alfert. They were also scheduled to meet with Mr. Robert Kennedy on either 21 or 22 November 1963. There is no indication that Ft. Holabird student VARONA was present.[8]

Whether Robert Kennedy in fact met with the Cubans on November 21 or 22 is unknown. His telephone logs show a call from Oliva at 4:45 p.m. on Monday, November 18, and a call at an unspecified time that day from a San Román. He talked by phone to Roberto San Román the next day, Tuesday, November 19.[9] And Enrique Ruiz-Williams was at Hickory Hill for Kennedy's birthday party on November 20.[10]

It was dangerous for the attorney general to be so close to the exile community because he knew what the CIA was doing, and the exiles were penetrated by Cuban intelligence. Anything he told them might be reported to Castro. Cubela told the CIA as early as 1962 that Cuban exile groups in the United States "were completely penetrated by Castro informants and that for them to know of his [Cubela's] cooperation with [the CIA] would be the same as telling Castro, and thus his future would end against the Wall!"[11] In 1966 a CIA informant reported that the CIA's Cuban operations had been penetrated at a high level through a Cuban exile who was knowledgeable of a number of the most important ones.[12] In 1975 CIA director John McCone testified to the Rockefeller Commission that the exile community had been penetrated at the highest level.[13] The euphemism "highest level" would fit the men Robert Kennedy was talking to the week before the assassination.

On this same weekend, the president's speechwriters in Washington were thinking about Cuba too. They were finishing a speech on Cuban policy that the president was to deliver before the Inter-American Press Association in Miami on Monday, November 18.

Kennedy would have a busy schedule on Monday. He would travel to MacDill Air Force Base in Tampa, where he would tour the headquarters of the U.S. Strike Command on the base. The Strike Command was designed to be a quick reaction force the president could deploy at a moment's notice to any place in the world—such as Havana in the event of a coup. After lunch at the officer's club, Kennedy would helicopter to Al Lopez Field, a baseball stadium in Tampa named for a Cuban American baseball player who went on to coach the Chicago White Sox. Kennedy would speak to a crowd there. Next he would be driven a few miles to the Fort Homer Hesterly Armory, where he would speak to the

Florida Chamber of Commerce and then to the International Inn to speak to the United Steelworkers Union in the Crystal Room. For ground travel Kennedy would use the presidential limousine, the very same, open Lincoln convertible in which he was killed in Dallas on Friday.

From Tampa Kennedy would fly to Miami and be greeted at an airport rally by local Democrats before motoring to the Americana Hotel for the speech to the Inter-American Press Association in the evening. The last was to be a major policy address.[14]

At the CIA Desmond FitzGerald was drafting paragraphs to be included in the Miami speech. Having met with Cubela less than a month earlier, he hoped to have John Kennedy himself say publicly what Cubela wanted to hear, which was that the United States would give its support to any non-Communist government that emerged from a coup in Cuba. The CIA might not have arranged a face-to-face meeting between Cubela and John or Robert Kennedy, but it was able to arrange for the president to deliver what was in effect a message to Cubela through the media. The draft CIA language was delivered to the Executive Office Building next to the White House around six o'clock Sunday evening, November 17.[15]

Meanwhile, the CIA warned the White House that Kennedy might run into trouble on the Florida trip. According to the CIA, Cuban exiles planned to demonstrate in Miami because they thought Kennedy was too weak on Castro. They would demand he return the Brigade 2506 flag that he was given at the Orange Bowl in December 1962.[16]

15

A Barrier Once Removed

O swald called Marina on Monday, November 18, and found her upset. Why didn't the person who answered the phone know who Lee Harvey Oswald was when Ruth Paine had called the day before, she asked immediately. Oswald became angry. He told her that he was renting under a fictitious name and that she shouldn't call him there.[1] The Warren Commission did not establish what else Oswald did on Monday, Tuesday, and Wednesday of this final week. Establishing such a chronology is routine police work in major criminal cases, and not doing so is an inexplicable lapse in the investigation of the murder of the president.

...

In Washington this Monday, the Joint Chiefs of Staff met to talk about the order that the President had given McNamara, Vance, and General Taylor at the White House a week earlier to catch Castro red-handed shipping arms to Latin American countries. According to a Defense Department memorandum, two things had occurred since the White House meeting. First, Desmond FitzGerald and Alexis Johnson of the State Department sent instructions on handling the matter to the U.S. ambassador in Venezuela. Second, the ambassador responded with additional details about the cache of arms, including the fact that it had been discovered at Paraguana, Venezuela, earlier in the month. Castro had been caught red-handed exporting the revolution. The Joint Chiefs, unaware of the significance the CIA would later claim for this development, began to implement the president's orders to stop future Cuban intrusions into the hemisphere, focusing on how to interdict Cuban arms shipments along the entire coast of Latin America.[2]

At the White House, Bundy read an ominous warning from the CIA. An expected one thousand anti-Castro exiles would demonstrate against Kennedy in Tampa, and more were expected in Miami. One CIA source feared Castro might "create an incident." The Secret Service was copied.[3]

In Florida on this Monday morning, the president was starting his appearances. He flew into MacDill Air Force Base, went to Strike Command headquarters, and then returned to MacDill for lunch. From there he flew by helicopter to Al Lopez Field to address the gathering in the baseball stadium. His remarks were supposed to commemorate the fiftieth anniversary of scheduled airline service in Tampa—an obviously contrived event—but he veered off to talk about Cuba. The president said that he was committed to bringing the balance of power in the world to the side of freedom and to halt the Communist advance. He noted that the Communist world had suffered setbacks even on the island of Cuba, which had experienced a decline in its standard of living under Castro.[4]

From Lopez Field the president traveled to the armory, the International Inn, and back to MacDill by car. Photographs show him leaving the stadium, passing through crowd-lined streets, and standing straight up in the open convertible waving. In his remarks to the Florida Chamber of Commerce in Tampa, he said his administration was not antibusiness and had achieved "the longest and strongest economic expansion in peacetime in the nation's entire history" before again turning to the subject of Cuba: "We have not been successful in removing Mr. Castro. He still remains a major danger to the United States." Yet, the president added optimistically, Castro was being "isolated."[5] FitzGerald had used this word in briefing the president at the White House a week earlier.

The big event of the day was the evening speech to the Inter-American-Press Association in Miami. According to historian Michael Beschloss, Kennedy had asked speechwriter Ted Sorensen for a speech "that would open a door to the Cuban leader."[6] The text hardly reads that way, however. Rather it opens a door to the Cuban people and to coup plotters like Cubela. In fact, since

FitzGerald drafted key passages, it gave Cubela precisely the assurance of support he had been requesting from high-level government officials, and he couldn't ask for anyone higher than the president himself. Kennedy referred to Castro as a barrier to be removed:

> It is important to restate what now divides Cuba from my country and from the other countries of this Hemisphere. It is the fact that a small band of conspirators has stripped the Cuban people of their freedom and handed over the independence and sovereignty of the Cuban Nation to forces beyond the Hemisphere. They have made Cuba a victim of foreign imperialism, an instrument of the policy of others, a weapon in an effort dictated by external powers to subvert the other American republics. This, and this alone, divides us. As long as this is true, nothing is possible. Without it, everything is possible. *Once this barrier is removed*, we will be ready and anxious to work with the Cuban people in pursuit of those progressive goals which a few short years ago stirred their hopes and the sympathy of many people throughout the Hemisphere.
>
> No Cuban need feel trapped between dependence on the broken promises of foreign communism and the hostility of the rest of the Hemisphere, for once Cuban sovereignty has been restored, we will extend the hand of friendship and assistance to a Cuba whose political and economic institutions have been shaped by the will of the Cuban people.[7]

In context the barrier to be removed was the "small band of conspirators" that had taken over Cuba such as Fidel and Raul Castro and Che Guevara.

The president flew back to Washington that night and arrived at the White House at 11:35 p.m. It had been a long day.[8]

When the Church Committee was trying to determine whether President Kennedy ordered the CIA to assassinate Castro, Senator Charles Mathias (R-MD) questioned the CIA's Richard Helms: "Let me draw an example from history. When Thomas Beckett was proving to be an annoyance, as Castro [was], the King [Henry II] said 'Who will rid me of this man?' He didn't say, go out and murder him. He said who will rid me of this man, and let it go at that."[9] In Miami four days before his own assassination, John Kennedy publicly called Fidel Castro a barrier to be removed.

...

In Mexico City on November 18, Eusebio Azcue, the Cuban consular officer who had met with Oswald in September, had been replaced by Alfredo Mirabal and finally left this day for Havana.[10] Azcue was in Cuba when Oswald killed the president.

16

John Kennedy and the Rogue Elephant

On Tuesday, November 19, the CIA finally, and suddenly, decided to give Cubela the assassination weapons he had long been requesting. The CIA's Richard Helms met with both Robert and John Kennedy this day. The question is whether Helms made the decision on his own or obtained the president's authorization. That is, was the CIA a rogue elephant in making such an important decision only three days before the president himself was assassinated, or did Kennedy order this to be done?

The day started on a pedestrian note. The president arrived at his office at 9:25 a.m. to have the Poultry and National Egg Board present him with the so-called Thanksgiving Turkey. Kennedy pardoned it. His schedule for the rest of the day looked light. It didn't stay that way.

In early afternoon FitzGerald received a cable from Paris, saying that Cubela planned to spend a week in Prague and then return to Cuba before the end of the month. He did not want to carry the OWL radio back to Cuba and wasn't interested in taking secret writing materials either. If the CIA wanted him to use secret writing, it could arrange delivery in Cuba. If his travel plans changed, he would communicate through another agent, whom the CIA codenamed UNSNAFU 5. The cable indicated that UNSNAFU 5 was aware of Cubela's opposition to Castro.

The cable's "slotted" time at headquarters was 1900 universal time. As explained earlier in connection with the cable of October 10 reporting that Cubela wanted to meet with Robert Kennedy, the slotted time was when it was distributed around CIA headquarters, which would be 4:00 p.m. eastern time. However, it would have been given to FitzGerald immediately, which would have been an hour and a half earlier, or around 2:30 p.m.[1] The cable reported this information had come from a meeting with Cubela the night of November 19. Since Paris is six hours ahead of Washington, the cable must have been sent right after the meeting.[2]

This was alarming news. While FitzGerald's meeting with Cubela in late October had convinced the Cuban that he had the Kennedys' support, he was "not at all happy with the fact that he still was not given the technical assistance for the operational plan as he saw it."[3] The CIA had not yet responded to his request for assassination weapons, and now it was going to lose contact with him. If that happened, all FitzGerald's efforts to orchestrate a coup in Cuba were for naught.

Therefore, the coincidence that the CIA's Helms had meetings with Robert and John Kennedy right after this cable arrived merits scrutiny.

Helms's version of the events is contained in his posthumously published memoir, *A Look over My Shoulder*. Helms makes no mention of Cubela or the collapsing coup plan. Instead, he writes that his meetings were in response to the Kennedys' interest in what they called "hard evidence" that Castro was exporting the revolution. The president had always said that his no-invasion pledge was conditioned on Castro behaving himself. If Castro were caught red-handed exporting the revolution, then Kennedy felt the United States was free from the no-invasion pledge.

The arms cache found in Venezuela was precisely what Kennedy meant by Castro exporting the revolution, Helms continues. Earlier in the month, a Cuban agent of the CIA had reported that Castro was about to land three tons of weapons and ammunition in Venezuela with the intent of disrupting the national election there, which was scheduled for December 1. The Communists planned to blow up a tunnel in Caracas and shoot off a few mortar rounds to begin their overthrow of Venezuelan president Romulo Betancourt, who was friendly to the United States. It was a grandiose plan that Helms thought unworkable. Nonetheless, following presidential orders, the CIA investigated it.

Helms was accompanied to the meetings by Hershel Peak, a CIA officer stationed in Venezuela. Peak apparently had flown to

Washington with a weapon from the arms cache. According to Helms this was a "Belgian-made submachine gun" (the same type of rifle, an FAL, that Castro favored).[4] Helms writes that someone had tried to obliterate a Cuban insignia that the Belgium manufacturer had imprinted on the rifles, but CIA technicians applied a chemical that brought out the marking.

Thus Helms and Peak with FAL in hand went to see the attorney general. Helms continues: "And I said, here's the evidence you are looking for." Robert Kennedy listened and "after rather reluctantly surrendering the gun" phoned the White House.[5] A short time later, Helms, Peak, and rifle were in the Oval Office as Helms briefed the president. The White House log confirms that Richard Helms and a Hershel "Peake" arrived at 6:00 p.m.[6] In his memoir Helms states: "When the meeting ended, the President arose from his rocking chair and stood beside the coffee table looking toward the Rose Garden. I leaned over and took the submachine gun from the coffee table and slipped it back into the canvas airline travel bag in which we carried it—unchallenged—from the parking lot to the President's office. As the President turned to shake hands, I said, 'I'm sure glad the Secret Service didn't catch us bring this gun in here.' The President's expression brightened. He grinned, shook his head slightly, and said, 'Yes, it gives me a feeling of confidence.'"[7]

Helms's account is the only available version of his conversations with the attorney general and the president. Although there was a taping system in the Oval Office, no tape of the meeting exists. Indeed, there are no tapes of any White House meetings after early November. Hours after his brother died, Robert Kennedy ordered that all the tapes be secured. He later took possession of them and donated some to the Kennedy library. No one knows if he turned over all the tapes.

Helms's claim that his purpose in meeting with the Kennedys was to show them a Belgian-made FAL from the arms cache is at odds with a later report by army investigators about what was in the cache. Their report says that most of the weapons were American made and had been supplied to the old Batista regime in Cuba. The report makes no mention of Belgian-made FALS. Conceivably, the CIA removed the FAL it showed Kennedy before army investigators did their work.

Helms's story gains weak support from a conversation Secretary of State Rusk had with Soviet ambassador Dobrynin after the assassination, although Rusk did not say the numbers on the rifles had to be restored by a chemical process. According to Dobrynin, Rusk told him:

> It had been precisely determined that the three tons of weapons seized the other day in Venezuela had come from Cuba. (Rusk said: "We checked out in particular the numbers of the rifles purchased by Castro some time ago in Belgium and seized now in Venezuela.")
>
> "I am saying this," Rusk noted, "not as any representation or comment. Nor can this be the subject of an official talk between us, since Castro's government exercises authority in its own country and it is unlikely that it consults with anyone when it decides to send weapons to one Latin American country or another, although the Chinese (Rusk added parenthetically, as it were) might be mixed up in this." Rusk said in conclusion: "I by no means wish to exaggerate the significance of this incident in Venezuela, it's not that great, but I would simply like to bring this last example to the attention of Mr. Gromyko [Rusk's counterpart in the Soviet hierarchy], with whom I spoke about this matter before. Of course, I do not expect any answer in this matter and please don't mention in official conversations and talks what I said today."[8]

Rusk's request that Dobrynin not disseminate his remarks was obviously ignored. But more importantly, whereas he told the Russians that the arms cache wasn't that significant, Helms seemed to feel differently, hurriedly setting up late-afternoon meetings with the Kennedys to show them a weapon from the cache.

Was Helms's tale a cover story? Was his purpose in going to see the attorney general to get a decision on whether the CIA should arrange a meeting with Cubela before he returned to Cuba and promise him assassination weapons? Helms must have indeed talked about the arms cache since the White House logs confirm that Peak was with him, but Peak would definitely not have been allowed to witness conversations with the attorney general and the president about assassination. He would have been asked to step out of the room. The meeting with John Kennedy was extraordinary. Helms rarely if ever met one-on-one with the president, and in the grand scheme of things, one FAL rifle wasn't very important.

This same day William Attwood called Bundy's assistant Gordon Chase to report that, as directed, he had conveyed to the Cubans that he would not visit Cuba and that there were two preconditions to talks, break with the Soviets and stop exporting the revolution.[9]

Back at CIA headquarters, Nestor Sanchez wrote a memorandum for the record this same November 19 on his plan for one last meeting with Cubela. Whether he wrote it before or after the meetings with the Kennedys isn't known, but it expressly says FitzGerald had given his approval, presumably this very day. It consists of four numbered paragraphs.

> Desmond FitzGerald approved telling Cubela he would be given a cache inside Cuba. Cache could, if he requested it, include sabotage materiel, c-4 [an explosive] and assorted equipment, sniper [scratched out and replaced with handwritten "high powered"] rifles w/scopes, hand grenades, pistols, etc., (equipment equivalent to that presently being cached).
>
> Confirm arrangements for deliver of S/W [secret writing] material. Check commo.
>
> Reassure Cubela re policy talks with Mr. Clark, (alias used by FitzGerald during meeting with Cubela in Paris 29 October 1963). "The U.S. Government is prepared to give full support to Cubela and his group if they are successful in real coup against the Castro regime." Show Cubela copy of President's Miami speech. (Remark to Cubela that Mr. Clark helped with speech).
>
> FitzGerald requested written reports on AMLASH operation be kept to a minimum.[10]

The sequence of events this day is strikingly similar to what happened a month earlier when FitzGerald got the cable saying Cubela wanted to meet with Robert Kennedy. That day within an hour, FitzGerald was on the phone with the attorney general.

There seem to be only two possibilities for what happened. On November 19 either the president approved promising Cubela assassination weapons, or the CIA made that decision without consulting the president even though Helms talked to him for half an hour that afternoon. To paraphrase Senator Church, either Kennedy approved, or the CIA was a rogue elephant. In his biography of John Kennedy, author Richard Reeves provides a telling footnote: "Asked in a 1989 interview about the plans for killing Castro, Richard Helms at first told the author, 'I just want to leave that subject where it is, with what I have said before.' But then he added: 'Robert Kennedy ran with it, ran those operations, and I dealt with him almost every day. . . .' Helms described the CIA, 'then and now,' as 'a service organization for the President of the United States.'"[11]

It had been a busy day in Washington for all concerned. The CIA had learned that Cubela was returning to Cuba and that it would thus lose contact with him. Richard Helms met with Robert Kennedy and John Kennedy about the arms cache in Venezuela. He showed both of them a captured Belgium-made FAL rifle. The president joked about his own security. FitzGerald gave Sanchez the green light to meet with Cubela one last time and promise that sniper rifles and explosives would be delivered to him in Cuba. FitzGerald surely had Helms's approval. Sanchez would take a copy of the president's speech before the Inter-American Press Association, give it to Cubela, and tell him that FitzGerald helped write it, which was true. And Castro had been given seemingly unacceptable preconditions for talks.

. . .

In Dallas this day, the morning paper, the *Morning News*, and the afternoon paper, the *Times-Herald*, gave the details of the route the president's motorcade would follow. It would pass right under the windows of the Texas School Book Depository.[12]

. . .

In Havana this day, the French reporter Jean Daniel, who interviewed Kennedy in October for the purpose of writing an article on him and Castro, was cooling his heels waiting for an interview with the Cuban leader. So far he had not been successful, but suddenly on this same November 19, he was summoned for a session with Castro at ten o'clock in the evening. The two men talked until four o'clock the next morning. Castro, according to Daniel, "delivered himself of a relentless indictment of U.S. policy." He said the CIA was trying to foment a coup to overthrow him (which of course is an accurate description of what FitzGerald was trying to do with Cubela). But by the end of the six-hour meeting, Castro held out an olive branch, saying that Kennedy might change and the two leaders might reach an accommodation. Castro joked that Kennedy's likely opponent in the next year's presidential election, the conservative Republican Senator Barry Goldwater, would be worse than Kennedy, and Castro would be willing to endorse Goldwater if doing so would help Kennedy.[13]

17

Washington, Paris, and Dallas

A t CIA headquarters the next morning, November 20, Nestor Sanchez and Sam Halpern, FitzGerald's executive officer, called on Edward Gunn of the Technical Services Division. They had talked to him on a previous occasion about Cubela's supposed desire for a poison dart device. The men had settled on what poison to use, a common pesticide like Black Leaf 40, which is a 40 percent solution of nicotine sulfate. Injected into a man, it can stop his heart. It was readily available in Cuba as a farm pesticide. However, the men had not settled on what the device itself should be. Now with Cubela going back to Cuba and with the authorization from FitzGerald to give Cubela such a device, Gunn needed to come up with the weapon.[1]

Gunn devised a hypodermic needle tucked inside a Paper Mate ballpoint pen. Paper Mates were popular then because they were one of the first pens with a ballpoint that could be retracted by clicking on the top. After seven or eight failed attempts, Gunn finally got the pen right. There is no record of how it worked. Perhaps if you clicked the top of the pen, a needle came out, and you jammed it into the victim to inject poison. Gunn stayed up most of the night and fashioned three pens, two of which he kept in his safe. He gave the third to Sanchez the next morning. Gunn said the needle was so fine that the victim might not feel it. He compared it to the scratch from a starched shirt.[2] Richard Helms wrote in his book years later that he approved giving the device to Cubela, but he denied laying eyes on it and disparaged the object he claimed never to see: "(Had it been shown to me, I would have refused to offer it to AMLASH [Cubela]). At no time and by no one involved, was this clumsy device intended to be an assassination weapon."[3]

Helms omits mention of the fact that rifles with telescopic sights are better assassination weapons, as Oswald was about to prove, and these were promised Cubela at the meeting.

Curiously, none of the CIA witnesses or documents, including the 1967 CIA Inspector General Report, mentions what Cubela says the CIA offered him on November 22: a pen that could shoot bullets in addition to the hypodermic needle hidden inside the Paper Mate.[4] Although the Church Committee spent months looking into the CIA's plots in 1975, it was never told that the CIA proffered two different, surreptitious, assassination weapons to Cubela. It's impossible to know whether he or the CIA was correct. Sanchez told the Rockefeller Commission and the Church Committee that Cubela wanted a "dart pen" or "pellet gun."

In any event, while Gunn worked on the poison pen, Sanchez cabled the CIA station in Paris this same day, Wednesday, November 20, telling it to contact Cubela and ask him to delay returning to Cuba for five days "in order to permit one more meeting which AMLASH/1 requested." Sanchez would fly to Paris for the meeting if Cubela agreed.[5]

The Paris station answered by cable to say it had called Cubela and he agreed to postpone his trip to see Sanchez "if it something interesting." According to the cable, the CIA officer in Paris told Cubela that "he could not assure it interesting but that it was to be a meeting which AMLASH requested." The cable noted that someone was in the room with Cubela during the telephone call, thus limiting what Cubela could say.[6] Sanchez later testified that Cubela would have understood this phone call to mean that the CIA was going to give him the weapons he had been asking for and that the scheduled meeting was to work out the arrangements for delivery in Cuba.[7]

Thus in the evening of November 20, Paris time—afternoon in Havana and Washington DC—the CIA signaled Cubela that it would give him the assassination weapons he had long been requesting, a rifle with a telescopic sight as well as some exotic device.

Years later in responses to the Church Committee's report on the president's assassination, the CIA argued that Cubela would not have known until November 22 that the CIA had approved his plan to kill Castro. The CIA asserted that Cubela "had no grounds prior to . . . [the November 22 meeting] for believing that he had CIA support for his vaguely defined course of action. He knew nothing that, had it leaked, would have served to motivate a Cuban retaliatory strike against President Kennedy."[8]

The CIA's rebuttal is wishful argument. The president himself had said in his speech in Miami on November 18, in passages written by FitzGerald, that the Castro regime was a barrier to be removed. Cubela had been telling the CIA that dissident elements in Cuba needed to hear such things from the United States if he was to organize a coup. Castro told French reporter Daniel in his interview in the wee hours of the morning of November 20 that the CIA was planning to overthrow him in a coup. And in the evening of November 20—not November 22 as the CIA argued—Cubela knew the CIA had decided to give him assassination weapons and would work out the details at a meeting on Friday. Case officer Nestor Sanchez admitted in his testimony before the Church Committee that Cubela would assume from the November 20 phone call that he had the green light. The CIA rebuttal is myopic, viewing things only from its vantage point, or argumentative as was often the case. Besides, unless the CIA had access to the transcript of Sanchez's testimony, which it theoretically should not have had, it could not have known what he told the committee in secret testimony.

...

In Dallas, Texas, Lee Harvey Oswald was leading his lonely life. Marina testified that he typically called her twice a day, once during his lunch break at work and once in the evening. He told her he spent evenings reading and watching television, but his landlady, Gladys Johnson, said he spent evenings in his room.[9] This fit nicely with the Warren Commission's profile of Oswald as an isolated loner and is in the *Warren Report*.

But a reporter for the *Dallas Morning News*, Hugh Aynesworth, discovered something different. The day after the assassination, he went to the rooming house and asked both Gladys and her husband, Arthur, what Oswald did when he came home from work. Mr. Johnson said, "Oswald would retire early and listen to his small radio." Aynesworth added that he couldn't see the room as it looked when

Oswald lived there because "FBI and Secret Service men grabbed up his few belongings" before the press got there.[10] Surprisingly, the radio, a Russian-made portable, wasn't mentioned in *Warren Report*. (The significance of the radio is discussed in appendix A.)

Thus after work at the book depository on Wednesday, November 20, Oswald probably retreated to his room and listened to the radio. The next morning, November 21, he went to work and quickly sought out coworker Frazier to ask for a ride to Ruth Paine's house in Irving after work to get some "curtain rods" for his room. In hindsight the reason Oswald wanted to go to Paine's house was obviously that his rifle was there. He had surely decided to shoot Kennedy the night before and wanted to retrieve his rifle, which was wrapped up in a blanket in the garage of Paine's house along with other possessions of the Oswalds. Since the rifle was crucial to the assassination, Oswald would not likely have delayed getting it until the day of the assassination if he had made the decision to shoot Kennedy prior to November 20.[11]

Oswald's arrival at Ruth Paine's the evening of November 21 caught Marina by surprise. He had not called beforehand to tell her he was coming. He just showed up and lied by telling her he was lonely. He played with his older daughter on the lawn before dinner.[12] Marina said that she was mad at him and that he spent part of the evening trying to placate her. He finally gave up, watched television for a while, and went to bed.[13] Sometime that evening he slipped into the garage, took his rifle out of the blanket, wrapped it in brown paper, and left the package there until morning.[14]

...

In Washington on November 21, Helms informed McCone that exile demonstrations during the president's visit to Florida had been forestalled by CIA efforts. The president's speech and its theme "Fidelismo sin Fidel," the revolution without Fidel, was well received by militant exile groups and was being disseminated in Cuba. Robert Kennedy was copied on the memorandum.[15]

Fig 1. Kennedy leaving stadium in Tampa on Monday, November 18, 1963. FBI agent Moses Aleman was providing security for Kennedy's speech at the stadium and took this picture. Aleman was later assigned to investigate Gilberto Lopez but was not told of allegations that Lopez was involved in Kennedy's assassination. Moses Aleman.

Fig 2. The Kennedys in Dallas, minutes before the assassination on Friday, November 22, 1963. Associated Press.

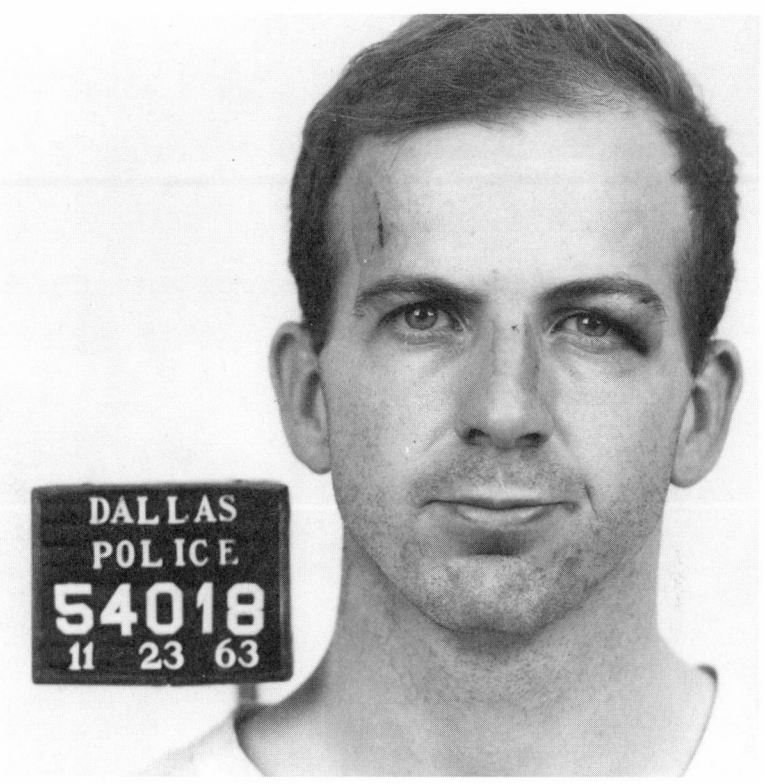

Fig 3. (*opposite top*) Richard M. Helms, deputy
director of the CIA in 1963 and later director of the
CIA. Yoichi Okamoto, Lyndon Johnson Library.

Fig 4. (*opposite bottom*) Rolando Cubela a
hero of the Cuban Revolution against Batista.
Associated Press.

Fig 5. (*above*) Dallas police mug shot of Lee
Harvey Oswald on November 22, 1963. Dallas
Police, Dallas Municipal Archives.

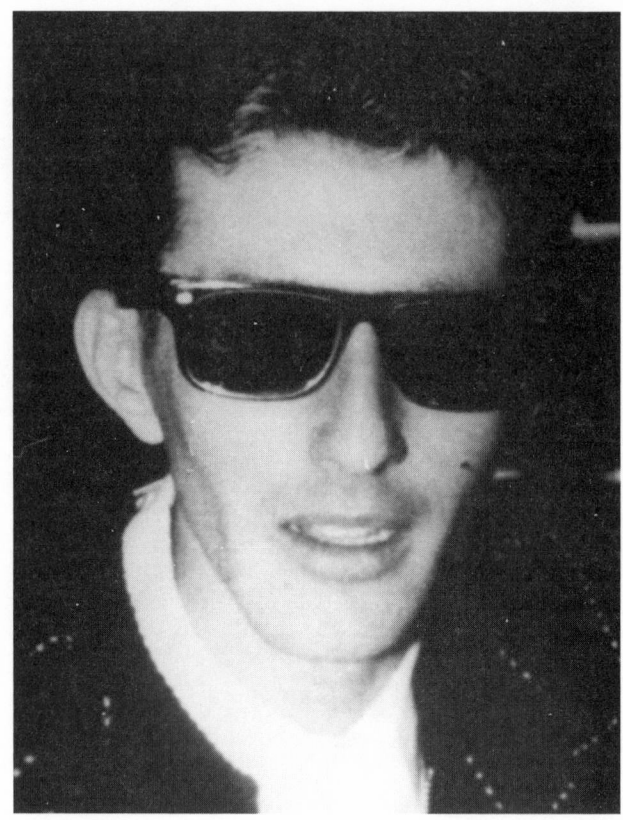

Fig 6. Gilberto Policarpo Lopez was in Tampa on November 18, 1963, waiting for the "go ahead" to return to Cuba. Photograph was taken at night at airport in Mexico City nine days later. He was the only passenger on the regularly scheduled flight to Cuba. CIA sources alleged that he was "involved" in the assassination. National Archives and CIA.

Fig 7. (*opposite top*) Front of Oswald's Turist PMP 56 radio. National Archives.

Fig 8. (*opposite bottom*) Inside of the radio. On the upper left the ferrite antenna has broken off. The copper coil is moved to the right. Although Oswald listened to this radio, it was not working when the FBI received it, and it may never have been tested. National Archives.

Fig 9. Desmond FitzGerald entering the White House Cabinet Room for the meeting on December 19, 1963. The meeting started before everyone arrived, and the White House photographer was taking pictures. Yoichi Okamoto, Lyndon Johnson Library.

Fig 10. The December 19, 1963, "Murder, Inc." meeting. President Johnson told FitzGerald that someday he and others would face the "grand jury" of "public opinion." Yoichi Okamoto, Lyndon Johnson Library.

18

November 22, 1963, in Dallas

L ee Harvey Oswald got up on the morning of November 22, left his wedding ring and wallet with $170 on the dresser, said goodbye to Marina, who was still in bed, and walked out of Ruth Paine's house. He did not eat breakfast, but then he never did. Since he had wrapped the rifle in paper the night before, he merely had to retrieve it from the garage and be on his way. He walked from Paine's house the half block to where Wesley Frazier lived. He stopped by Frazier's car and put the package with the rifle in the back seat. Oswald showed up earlier than usual and peered in the window of Frazier's house. When Frazier saw this, he walked out to meet Oswald at the car. He asked Oswald what was in the package. Oswald told him it was curtain rods for his apartment. Frazier remembered Oswald had told him this the night before. Once they arrived at the book depository, Oswald retrieved the package from the back seat and walked into the building.[1]

John Kennedy had landed in Texas on the afternoon of Thursday, November 21, with his wife, Jackie, and had spent the night in Fort Worth. The first thing he did on the morning of November 22 was to talk to a small rally across the street from his hotel. After that he addressed a chamber of commerce breakfast. His schedule for the rest of the day was similar to one he had followed on Monday in Tampa with several events.

When he returned to his hotel room, Jackie showed him a full-page advertisement in the paper highly critical of him. He remarked that they were in "nut country" and noted someone could have assassinated him with a pistol the previous dark, rainy night. Soon he and Jackie left the hotel for the flight to Dallas. On Air Force One, the president read his morning Intelligence Checklist from the CIA. These checklists were comparatively bland documents. They were not as super-secret as one might suppose. The one for this particular day that has been declassified is comparatively bland with three brief items about Cuba. Nothing as sensitive as the AMLASH operation would be mentioned in the checklist, although one of the Cuban items is redacted.[2] But John Kennedy was thinking about assassination this morning. It may have been coincidence, although Kennedy had a tendency to talk about assassination whenever the CIA was doing something to get rid of Castro. This time, though, he commented on his own assassination, remarking to his wife and aide Kenneth O'Donnell: "If anybody wanted to shoot the President of the United States, it was not really a difficult job—all one had to do was get a high building someday with a telescopic rifle, and there was nothing anybody could do to defend against such an attempt."[3]

Although Oswald rarely ate breakfast, he normally packed a lunch for work. Marina testified that he took his lunch this morning, but then she wasn't up when he left. Frazier testified he asked Oswald where his lunch was. Oswald said he would buy it from a food truck that stopped by the book depository.[4] The Warren Commission did not try to establish whether Oswald ate lunch. It is a small detail, but it illustrates the failure to resolve inconsistent testimony that normally doesn't happen in a major murder case.

Oswald fired from the sixth-floor window on the southeast corner of the book depository. From this location he could watch the presidential limousine turn right off Main Street a block away onto Houston Street and drive straight toward him. Once at the book depository, the motorcade turned left underneath Oswald's window onto Elm Street, which ran in front of the building. The car was so close that Oswald could have lobbed a flowerpot out the window and landed it on the president's head. Just past the book depository, a distance of less than a block, Elm Street bends and begins angling away from the building. The motorcade route here was more or less V-shaped with Oswald being at the bottom of the V. From his perspective the limousine first moved toward him and then almost directly away from him. This made Oswald's task of aiming comparatively easy since he didn't have to adjust for much left-to-right movement, which would make the shot more difficult. The president, sitting in the back seat of the limousine as it drove away from Oswald, would appear to be moving upward in the rifle's telescopic sight.[5] While this made it easier for Oswald to hit his target, it is not necessarily an obvious way to shoot at a moving car. Neither Oswald's military training nor his hunting experience prepared him to assassinate someone in a moving car. However, he had hunted birds in Russia, so he did have experience in shooting at moving targets.

Oswald had the sixth floor to himself since it was lunch hour, and everyone else in the building was either standing outside to see the president go by or looking out a window, like Oswald was. By happenstance no one else chose to use the sixth floor, although Oswald anticipated the possibility by stacking boxes to block anyone on the floor from seeing him in his sniper's lair.[6]

Oswald fired three shots at the president. The first is timed to 12:30 p.m. central standard time and missed. The second came four to five seconds later and hit the president in the back and exited his neck. It then struck Texas governor John Connally, who was riding in a jump seat in front of the president. Warren Commission critics have labeled this the "magic bullet" because it went through two men and followed an arguably odd trajectory.[7] The third shot came four or five seconds later and hit the president in the head. It was a gruesome and fatal wound. The motorcade with the dying president raced to Parkland Hospital in Dallas.[8] Men on the floor below Oswald's location heard what sounded like shell casings hitting the floor above them three times.

Dallas reporter Hugh Aynesworth was in Dealey Plaza when the president was hit. He remembered people pointing to the book depository as the source of the shots. He heard one witness, Howard Brennan, tell police that he saw a man with a rifle lean out one of the windows on an upper floor of the book depository.[9]

Oswald left the rifle behind some book boxes and coolly left the building. He boarded a bus bound for his rooming house, but it became stuck in the traffic snarl caused by the shooting. He got off the bus and hailed a cab. He had the taxi drop him off a block from his rooming house, presumably so the cab driver wouldn't know where he lived. The cleaning woman was there when he got to the rooming house, but Oswald ignored her. He went to his room, where he put on a jacket. His pistol was in a holster in his room. He removed the pistol from the holster and stuck it in the pocket of the jacket along with extra bullets. The cleaning woman estimated he was in his room for four or five minutes before he rushed out the door, zipping up his jacket.

Oswald set off on foot to the south, away from downtown Dallas. He only made it a few blocks before police officer J. D. Tippit stopped him. Tippit got out of his car and walked toward the suspect. Oswald pulled out his gun and fired several shots, felling the officer. He started to walk away, then turned back, and fired one more shot into Tippit's head to make sure he was dead. There were witnesses, but Oswald ignored them, walked away, emptied the spent shells from his revolver, and reloaded. He discarded his jacket in an apparent attempt to change his appearance slightly.[10] Presumably, he did this in case the witnesses described him to police as a man in a light-colored jacket.

Oswald could hear police sirens closing in on him. He ducked into a movie theater. Bystanders told the officers where their suspect was, and the police went in. Oswald was trapped. The theater manager stopped the film and ordered the house lights turned on. Oswald stood up as the police came in, then sat down. He threw a punch at the nearest officer, who punched back and grabbed Oswald. More officers joined in a melee. Oswald pulled out his revolver during the fight. He squeezed the trigger, but the hammer fell on the flesh between an officer's thumb and forefinger instead of the firing pin. The police disarmed and handcuffed the suspect. Only an hour and a half had elapsed since the assassination.[11]

Oswald was taken to police headquarters, where he was questioned on and off for the rest of the day. Eventually, he asked for a lawyer, naming John Abt of New York. Abt had a reputation for representing people charged with being Communists. Oswald was given the opportunity to call Abt, but he didn't. In fact Oswald never had an attorney although the Dallas Bar Association offered to help him get one.[12] Oswald was suspected of the murder of both Officer Tippit and the president, but he was initially charged only with

Tippit's murder because at the time the evidence for this crime was stronger. The arraignment took place at 7:10 p.m.[13]

Jack Rubenstein, better known as Jack Ruby, had been sitting in the advertisement department of the *Dallas Morning News*, composing a weekend ad for the night club he ran, when the president was shot five blocks away. Ruby would have had a view of Dealey Plaza if he had been looking. The Warren Commission didn't ask him if he was. The visit to the newspaper office was supposedly a weekly ritual for Ruby. While he was there, he wandered off to the news department in search of a reporter friend, but the man was out of town, so Ruby went back to the advertisement department. Those around Ruby said he turned ashen when news of the assassination reached the paper's offices.[14] He seemed deeply shaken. He closed his night club for three days and called friends, employees, and relatives. Ruby was Jewish and went to synagogue that night to pray for Kennedy. When a friend said the assassination was "terrible," Ruby replied, "It's worse than that."[15]

After leaving the synagogue, Ruby dropped by a delicatessen and bought ten corned beef sandwiches and soft drinks. He intended them for the police, who, he assumed, were working overtime. He knew many of the officers and called one. Ruby was told food wasn't needed. He later claimed that he attempted to deliver the sandwiches to a local radio station, but no one was there. So Ruby drove to police headquarters. Since he ran a night club and since he often carried cash, he kept a pistol in his car. He parked outside the police station. He left the sandwiches in the car but slipped the gun in his pocket and went into police headquarters where Oswald was being held.

Ruby wandered around, pausing to talk to officers he knew. To one he held up a notebook and said he was working as a "translator for newspapers." It was past ten o'clock in the evening, but the halls of police headquarters were still filled with reporters. Ruby walked among them chatting. The reporters congregated outside the office of Dallas police captain John Fritz, head of homicide, where Oswald was being questioned.

Ruby put his hand on the doorknob to enter the room where Oswald was, but two officers stopped him. One knew him and said, "You can't go in there, Jack." Since Ruby had his pistol in his pocket, he probably intended to shoot Oswald then.

So many reporters were still at the station wanting some sort of news that Dallas police officials decided to parade Oswald in front of them before letting him go to bed. Therefore, at 12:10 a.m. the police took him into a large assembly room for a photo opportunity. Oswald was allowed to answer a few questions from reporters before being ushered out.[16]

A number of the newsmen furnished affidavits to Dallas police about meeting Ruby on this and other occasions after the assassination at police headquarters. UPI photographer Pete Fisher saw Ruby standing near the entrance to the assembly room when Oswald was brought in. Fisher said Ruby was not more than three feet away from Oswald and could have shot him then, but no one else said Ruby got that close.[17] Dallas radio reporter Ronald Jenkins placed Ruby at the police headquarters late in the afternoon of the assassination and again in the assembly room that night. He said Ruby had a notebook in his hand and was standing on a table with some cameramen.[18] Ferdinand Kaufman, an AP photographer, recalled meeting Ruby at the police station between 4:00 and 4:30 on the afternoon of the assassination. Ruby gave him a business card.[19] Jerry Lee Kunkel, a radio announcer for a Dallas station, had met Ruby once at Ruby's nightclub. He saw Ruby in the assembly room standing on a chair when Oswald was brought in. Afterward Ruby was in the hallway of the police station handing out business cards. He also said Ruby talked to a reporter for the radio station to which he intended to deliver the sandwiches and asked him for the station's phone number so he could deliver the sandwiches.[20] Samuel Mack Pate was a reporter for the same station as Kunkel. He was with Kunkel and agreed with what he said about talking to Ruby. He added that Ruby didn't seem particularly upset.[21] David Flint "Mike" Smith, an AP photographer, thought he remembered seeing Ruby in the assembly room the night of the assassination.[22] Ruby later denied to his rabbi that his being at the police station this night was evidence that he was in a conspiracy. It was just the opposite, he argued: "Had I intended to kill him [Oswald], I could have pulled my trigger on the spot, because the gun was in my pocket."[23] Of course, he might not have been close enough.

Thus at the end of that day in Dallas, the president was dead as was officer Tippit. Oswald was in police custody, charged with murdering Tippit. And Jack Ruby, who some said was distraught but who seemed calm to others, was hanging out with a gun in his pocket at police headquarters where Oswald was being held, pretending at times to be a reporter, and had tried to get into the room where Oswald was being questioned.

19

November 22, 1963, in Other Cities

In Washington DC, within thirteen minutes of the shooting in Dallas, FBI director Hoover called Robert Kennedy, who was home at Hickory Hill for lunch, and said bluntly: "I have news for you. The president's been shot. It's believed to be fatal."[1] Twenty minutes later John Kennedy's naval aide phoned the attorney general from Parkland Hospital to report that the president was dead.[2]

Yet in the midst of this chaos and his own crushing grief, Robert Kennedy's thoughts turned to legalities and his brother's legacy. He called McGeorge Bundy to ask who owned John Kennedy's personal papers. After checking with the State Department, Bundy told him that the Kennedy family did, so the attorney general ordered the combinations changed on all the safes in the White House with Kennedy's papers in them.[3] The audio tapes of the president's Oval Office meetings were similarly secured that afternoon by John Kennedy's personal secretary and later given to Robert Kennedy.

The attorney general also began trying to learn who was responsible for his brother's murder. Kennedy's friend Brigade 2506 veteran Enrique Ruiz-Williams was still in town and having lunch at the Old Ebbitt Hotel in Washington with reporter Haynes Johnson. Kennedy called there and talked to Ruiz-Williams. Relying on news reports that Oswald was anti-Castro, Kennedy told the Cuban, "One of your guys did it." The Cuban naturally denied it.[4]

A short distance from Hickory Hill at the CIA, Director John McCone and DDP Richard Helms were having lunch with several other CIA officers in a small room next to McCone's office, which McCone had named the "French Room." The name seems ironic given that on this particular day Nestor Sanchez was meeting with Cubela in Paris, but there was no connection. One of McCone's aides rushed in to say that the president had been shot. Some-one turned on a television in the room. McCone watched for a moment and then said he needed to get over to Hickory Hill and see Robert Kennedy. Once there Kennedy continued his personal inquisition by asking the CIA director if the agency had killed the president. McCone said no.[5]

Helms remembered, "We all went to battle stations over the possibility that this might be a plot—and who was pulling the strings."[6] Given the events of recent weeks, the principal suspect for puppeteer would be Fidel Castro, but Helms never said so. He mentioned only the Russians and the Chinese. According to Helms the CIA couldn't determine where Khrushchev was. There was speculation that maybe the Chinese had decided to assassi-nate the leaders of both major powers at once or that the Russians had done it and Khrushchev had gone into hiding.[7]

Desmond FitzGerald and his aides Sam Halpern and Bruce Cheever weren't eating with McCone and Helms in the French Room. Instead, they were in Georgetown having lunch together at City Tavern.[8] Upon hearing that the president had been assas-sinated and Oswald arrested, Halpern remarked, "I sure hope that guy isn't involved in Cuba some way."[9] Only two days earlier, Halpern had met with Nestor Sanchez and the CIA's technical chief, Edward Gunn, about making the poison device for Cubela.

Paris is six hours ahead of Washington, so at the very moment the CIA men were having lunch, it was evening in Paris and San-chez was telling Cubela that the CIA would give him assassination weapons, including a sniper rifle with telescopic sight (much like, but better than, the one Oswald used to kill the president) and was offering him the poison pen that had concerned FitzGerald and Halpern two days earlier. The CIA men at City Tavern surely won-dered what was happening between Sanchez and Cubela when they heard of Kennedy's assassination.

Sanchez had landed in Paris about 8:30 a.m. Paris time, giv-ing him time to rest before the meeting with Cubela that night. He carried with him a copy of the president's speech to the Inter-American Press Association on Monday as published in the *New York Times* and, of course, the poison pen. He didn't much like having such an ominous device on him though. How could he explain it if customs officials or French police noticed it?[10] (But for that matter, how was Cubela going to get it back into Cuba?)

Sanchez and Cubela met at a safe house. A CIA officer sat in another room while Sanchez and Cubela talked. The meeting must have started before 7:30 because that is when the assassination happened, Paris time, and Sanchez didn't know about the assassination when the meeting began. The meeting ended around 10:00 p.m.[11]

Sanchez didn't get around to writing up his contact report of the meeting until three days later. According to the report, Cubela said he was fully determined to pursue his plans to initiate a coup against Castro. He was pleased to read Kennedy's Miami speech and even more pleased to learn that FitzGerald, whom he knew as "Mr. Clark," helped prepare it.[12]

Sanchez later testified that Cubela was satisfied with the tone of the president's speech: "The extracts that you [the questioner at the Senate hearing] have made here set the tone for the full speech and specifically the one in which once the barrier is removed, we will be ready and anxious to work with the Cuban." When asked if his intent in making reference to the speech was to show Cubela that higher authority was behind him, Sanchez answered: "Yes, precisely."[13] Sanchez reiterated FitzGerald's promise at the October 29 meeting of full U.S. support for a successful coup.

Sanchez reviewed with Cubela the names of Cubans he could count on for support. Cubela named only four men whom he would use in the initial stage of the operation. Once Castro was "removed," there were ten more Cuban officials whom Cubela thought he could count on for support. Sanchez must have been disappointed, although he did not say so. Cubela didn't have enough for a coup.

Cubela also itemized what he wanted the CIA to drop for him in Cuba: twenty hand grenades; two high-powered rifles with telescopic sights; and approximately twenty pounds of C-4 explosive and related equipment. Cubela did not want to carry any incriminating material back to Cuba with him, so he would not carry secret writing pills. Sanchez noted that Cubela's operational thinking seemed much less foggy than in previous meetings and he finally recognized the need to take over the radio station in order to issue a call for support. Sanchez concluded his report of the meeting by saying that when it was over, they learned of the president's assassination. Cubela was visibly moved and asked, "Why do such things happen to good people?"[14]

Omitted from the contact report was any mention of the poison pen. Sanchez said he did this purposefully because of the sensitivity of offering Cubela such a weapon.[15] By the time he testified before the Church Committee, Sanchez couldn't recall what happened to the poison pen. He showed it to Cubela, but Cubela indicated it was not what he had in mind. However, Sanchez couldn't remember whether he took the pen back or whether Cubela left the meeting with it in hand.[16]

The CIA inspector general interviewed Sanchez in 1967 and asked him what happened after the meeting. Sanchez told of receiving a high-priority cable that night or the next morning, "telling him that everything was off." The cable had disappeared from CIA files by the time of the 1967 inspector general report. Nevertheless, Sanchez was asked about its contents by the Church Committee in 1975 and testified: "When we came out of that meeting, we heard the news of President Kennedy's assassination, and I received a cable after that which I thought that this was probably the reason that the whole operation was being reassessed. After all, I had no reason at the time to try to interpret why it was all off. I mean, that's the only thing I could connect it to because nothing else happened other than the assassination."[17]

Cubela's recollection of how the meeting ended was different from Sanchez's version. According to author Brian Latell, Cubela said the meeting with Sanchez "ended abruptly with a phone call" from Desmond FitzGerald, who said that the president had just been shot in Dallas.[18]

Although almost all Americans who were alive on November 22, 1963, could remember exactly what they were doing when they heard of President Kennedy's assassination, Sanchez was different. He had just offered a poison pen to a man who was going back to Cuba with plans to assassinate Fidel Castro, but his memory of that moment was fuzzy. Asked what happened to the pen, for example, did Cubela refuse it or did Sanchez take it back, he testified: "Since I recollect his reaction to it that, you know, it's no good, I just can't logically believe that he would have kept the pen. This is the point. But I don't specifically recall what was done with it except that it was probably destroyed."[19]

That Sanchez, or indeed anyone else at CIA, had such a cavalier attitude at the time about the poison pen is hard to believe. The pen was tremendously compromising. It was clearly American, exotic, and might as well had "Made by the CIA" engraved on it. When Francis Gary Powers's U-2 plane was shot down over Russia, Nikita Khrushchev had the wreckage displayed to the world press in Moscow and called attention to the poisoned needle that the CIA had given Powers to commit suicide rather than be captured.

Khrushchev wasn't the only one to engage in such theatrics. Castro did too. In October 1963 he had gone on Cuban television to denounce the CIA's nefarious schemes against Cuba. On a table in front of him were explosives that had been concealed in cans of fruit packed by an American company in Miami. They had been brought into Cuba as commercial products, but the unusually heavy cans made airport security suspicious. It had opened the cans to discover the explosives, giving Castro the opportunity to use them for propaganda purposes.[20] Castro would have had a field day with the poison pen that was given to Cubela if he needed to accuse the CIA publicly of planning to assassinate him. That Sanchez and the CIA were cavalier about what happened to the pen is not believable.

Helms said he was worried because Khrushchev was out of sight at the moment Kennedy was assassinated. Fidel Castro wasn't out of sight. In fact he was doing just the opposite.

Castro had scheduled a second meeting with the French reporter Jean Daniel for November 22 at Castro's summer residence at Varadero Beach. Cubela owned a house nearby, one of the many reasons he was attractive to the CIA. Like the CIA men in Washington, Daniel, Castro, and his physician, Rene Vallejo, who had been offered as Castro's representative in talks with William Attwood, were having lunch when they got the news of the assassination. It was 1:30 p.m. local time, an hour later than Dallas. A guard interrupted their conversation to tell Castro that the president of Cuba, Osvaldo Dorticos, urgently needed to talk to him on the phone. Then, according to the reporter, Castro spoke into the phone, "'Como? Un atentado?' ('What's that? An attempted assassination?')." The reporter noted, "He then turned to us to say that Kennedy had just been struck down in Dallas. Then he went back to the telephone and exclaimed in a loud voice 'Herido? Muy gravemente?' ('Wounded? Very seriously?')."[21] While they waited for further news, Castro speculated that the shooter might be a madman, a Ku Klux Klan member, or a terrorist, perhaps a Vietnamese. He was well aware of what had happened to President Diem of Vietnam. Later in the prolonged conversation, Castro said there might be people in the world who rejoiced over Kennedy's death, citing the Viet Cong and Madame Nhu, the wife of Diem's brother who had died with Diem in the coup in Saigon.

A radio was brought into the room. The two men could hear for themselves the broadcasts about the assassination from a Miami station. Castro said the United States would put the blame on Cuba. He said he was opposed to assassination; it was "repellent" to him. Kennedy had said the same thing to reporter Tad Szulc several years earlier. Cubela had said the same thing to the CIA, although it was just the word that bothered him. He had in fact assassinated one of Batista's officers. But to reporter Daniel on the afternoon of November 22, Castro said that he did not have Batista killed because he would have just been replaced by another military man, who would seek revenge. Many in the U.S. government had made a similar point about Castro, saying that assassinating him would turn Cuba over to the Communists.[22]

Eventually, Castro got around to asking Daniel what he knew about the new president, Lyndon Johnson. Saving Castro's most significant remark for last, Daniel wrote: "Finally and most important of all [Castro asked]: 'What authority does he exercise over the C.I.A.?'"[23] The answer would come soon enough.

20

The Days After

For a short time after the assassination, the United States was, as a practical matter, leaderless. Although Vice President Lyndon Johnson automatically became president by operation of law upon Kennedy's death, the reality was quite different. Johnson had been in an open convertible two cars behind the president. Rufus Youngblood, the Secret Service agent in Johnson's car, had reacted faster than the other agents. After the second shot, he pushed the vice president down and shielded him with his own body as Oswald's third shot cracked over their heads to kill the president. By the time the motorcade with Kennedy and Johnson reached Parkland Hospital, Secret Service agents realized that Kennedy's ghastly head wound was fatal and shifted primary protection to the vice president. Fearing that he might be the next target, they moved him to a secluded room in the hospital to better guard him. Johnson arranged for a federal judge to meet him at the airport so that he could officially take the oath of office. But he was stuck on the long, sad flight back to Washington on Air Force One with Kennedy's widow and with Kennedy's body in a casket in the back of the plane.

In Dallas the hunt for the assassin and the investigation began within seconds of the shooting, but it too was leaderless and chaotic. The Dallas Police Department had primary legal responsibility for the investigation as a homicide. The Secret Service had legal authority to investigate counterfeiting, and little else. Nonetheless, those agents who did not return to Washington with the new president launched an investigation. After all in their minds they had failed to protect the president. The FBI began an investigation of the assassination under the rubric of its jurisdiction over assaults on federal officials and over national security cases, for example, those involving Communists.

The CIA cast a wide net, cabling all its stations to report anything they thought might be relevant. Oswald had already been of minor concern to the agency since CIA surveillance detected him at the Cuban and Soviet diplomatic establishments in Mexico City in September. In early November the CIA had received an FBI report on Oswald's pro- and anti-Castro activities in New Orleans. The report was given to the counterintelligence section of FitzGerald's SAS. On November 22 the report was turned over to James Angleton's Counterintelligence Division.[1]

Upon returning to Washington that night, Lyndon Johnson went to his office in the Executive Office Building and met with his personal staff, including Bill Moyers, Walter Jenkins, and Jack Valenti, to discuss the future of his presidency. They then adjourned to Johnson's house in northwest Washington to continue the discussion over drinks.[2]

The next morning, the day after the assassination, CIA director McCone met with now president Lyndon Johnson alone in Bundy's office. Johnson asked McCone to stay on as CIA director, and McCone agreed. McCone asked Johnson if he was familiar with the President's Checklist, the daily intelligence report the CIA gave the president. Johnson said no, so it was agreed that for the next several days, McCone would personally brief President Johnson in the morning. McCone returned later in the day to brief Johnson and Bundy on what the CIA had learned about Oswald's trip to Mexico City. As he left the meeting, McCone ran into former president Eisenhower, who was there to talk with Johnson. The two men chatted.[3]

At CIA headquarters Helms convened a meeting to lay out the organization for the CIA's contribution to the assassination investigation. At the meeting were Angleton, head of counterintelligence, Thomas Karamessines, Helms's executive officer, John Whitten, and others.[4] Helms announced that Whitten would be the CIA's point man on matters related to the assassination. Whitten's role wasn't specifically to investigate, but rather, as he described it, "No one in the Agency was to have any conversations with anyone outside the Agency, including the Warren Commission and the Federal Bureau of Investigation, concerning the Kennedy assassination without my being present."[5] Unfortunately, Whitten didn't have any expertise on Cuban matters. He was in the Western Hemisphere Division with responsibility for Mexico and Central America. He reported to J. C. King, not to FitzGerald. Both reported to Helms, who was the link between these two branches of the covert action section of the CIA.[6]

According to Whitten he was tapped for several reasons. First, the CIA knew that Oswald had been at the Soviet and Cuban embassies in Mexico City in September. Indeed, it had known this more than a month before the assassination and had informed the FBI. Since Mexico fell under Whitten's normal responsibilities, he seemed a logical choice to look into the significance of Oswald's trip there. Second, Whitten had earlier done several major investigations for Helms. Third, while Angleton would have been an even more logical choice since he headed the CIA's Counterintelligence Division, which was more adapted to investigations, Angleton was too close to the FBI. Whitten felt Helms believed the FBI had been derelict in investigating Oswald's actions before the assassination and was worried that because of Angleton's ties to the sister agency he might shy away from anything that would embarrass it.[7]

In point of fact, however, the lines of authority were not nearly as clear as Whitten described them. Karamessines testified that he didn't remember Whitten being given any such authority.[8] And Angleton's counterintelligence division certainly didn't hesitate to investigate on its own. Moreover, David Slawson, the Warren Commission lawyer assigned to work with the CIA, didn't remember Whitten when interviewed by author Shenon. Slawson worked mainly with Raymond Rocca of Angleton's counterintelligence division.[9]

One of Rocca's concerns was the significance, if any, of Oswald's meeting Valery Kostikov at the Soviet consulate. Since Kostikov was not simply a KGB officer—he was in Department 13 of the KGB specializing in assassination—the question was whether the Soviets were responsible.

When the CIA station in Mexico City notified headquarters that the Mexican police were planning to arrest Silvia Duran, the Mexican national at the Cuban consulate who had talked to Oswald on his visit, Karamessines first called and then cabled the CIA's Mexico station to prevent the arrest, saying it "could jeopardize U.S. freedom of action on the whole question of Cuban responsibility."[10] In later testimony Karamessines dismissed the importance of the cable. He couldn't remember why he sent it but speculated that he was worried Duran would implicate Cuba in the assassination and that the United States needed time to react.[11] The same evening CIA director McCone telephoned Dean Rusk to tell him about the arrest of Duran. Rusk said he hadn't known about these developments until McCone called.[12] It seems strange that Karamessines would try to buy time for the United States to react and yet wouldn't make sure the secretary of state was told. The CIA may also have been worried about an interrogation of Duran because it knew she had had an affair with Carlos Lechuga, the Cuban ambassador to the UN with whom William Attwood was trying to arrange a dialog between Kennedy and Castro.[13]

In the meantime Nestor Sanchez was flying back to Washington from his meeting with Cubela in Paris. Sanchez arrived at 6:10 p.m. on November 23. He went to the office either that evening or the next morning.[14] He was debriefed on one of those days by FitzGerald, but he did not talk to Helms or McCone. He told Fitz-Gerald that Cubela had definitely decided to return to Cuba and had even reserved a flight. Cubela was pleased that the CIA would deliver the weapons to him in Cuba. According to Sanchez, Cubela did not like the poison pen and would not take it back with him. FitzGerald and Sanchez did not discuss a possible link between the Cuban operations and the Kennedy assassination—although the first thought to pop into the head of FitzGerald's executive officer, Sam Halpern, when he learned of the assassination while lunching with FitzGerald, was that he hoped the assassin didn't have ties to Cuba, and Sanchez said he assumed he was recalled so suddenly because of the assassination.[15] If Cubela was right in saying that his November 22 meeting with Sanchez in Paris was interrupted by a phone call from FitzGerald telling them of the assassination, then there was even more reason for FitzGerald to discuss this with Sanchez upon his return.

The significant event of November 24 was Jack Ruby's murder of Lee Harvey Oswald in Dallas that morning. Police headquarters drew Ruby like a magnet. He had been there Friday evening, and perhaps Friday afternoon, and perhaps Saturday afternoon. It was no secret that Oswald was going to be moved Sunday morning from police headquarters to the sheriff's facilities. Ruby was driving by the latter when he saw a crowd and realized the transfer had not occurred. So he drove to police headquarters. Oddly, he stopped by the Western Union office to send a money order, then walked unmolested down the ramp to where a police car was waiting for Oswald to be brought out. Minutes after Ruby arrived, Oswald was led out of the building in handcuffs. Ruby, who had again brought his pistol along, pulled it out of his jacket pocket, stepped from the crowd, and fired once. Oswald died quickly, bleeding to death before the police could get him to the hospital. Still, one police officer thought to put his face close to Oswald's and ask if there was anything he wanted to say. Oswald didn't answer. He had already denied committing any crime.[16]

That Ruby took time to stop by the Western Union office before walking over to police headquarters to shoot Oswald that Sunday morning persuaded the Warren Commission that Ruby's action was spontaneous. Yet the fact of the matter was that Ruby seemed to be stalking Oswald since his arrest on Friday afternoon. With pistol in pocket, he had attempted to enter the room where Oswald was being questioned Friday evening.

21

An Investigation Hobbled from the Start

Within forty-five minutes of Oswald's death, FBI director J. Edgar Hoover called Walter Jenkins, President Johnson's aide, to summarize what the FBI knew. Hoover began laconically: "There is nothing further on the Oswald case except that he is dead." He said the FBI had warned Dallas police that Oswald might be in danger, but to Hoover, that was water under the bridge. He had already decided the direction the investigation would take: It would be aimed at proving Oswald fired the fatal shots. Any public disclosure of the possibility of foreign involvement should be avoided. Hoover was focused on wrapping up the assassination as a simple case of murder and returning to business as usual. He concluded by telling Jenkins, ominously but somewhat inaccurately, that the FBI had intercepted a letter from Oswald to someone in the Soviet embassy who was in charge of assassinations. Hoover warned that "to have that drawn into a public hearing would muddy the waters internationally." Hoover said he had already discussed his view with Deputy Attorney General Nicholas Katzenbach.[1]

Such a bureaucratic attitude is understandable in Hoover's case; a similar attitude at Robert Kennedy's Justice Department is not. Katzenbach wrote President Johnson's assistant Bill Moyers on November 26, the day after the funeral for John Kennedy, to urge the White House to make a public statement to stop the rumors about the assassination. The guiding principles should be the following: "The public must be satisfied that Oswald was the assassin; that he did not have confederates who are still at large; and that the evidence was such that he would have been convicted at trial. Speculation about Oswald's motivation ought to be cut off, and we should have some basis for rebutting thought that this was a Communist conspiracy or (as the Iron Curtain press is saying) a right-wing conspiracy to blame it on the Communists."[2]

In a book written years later, Katzenbach notes that he is criticized for this wording since it seems to imply a cover-up. He calls it a "badly written memo."[3] He did not mean, he argues, to limit the investigation of the assassination. Be that as it may, Katzenbach's views in 1963 seem to square with the advice he was getting from Hoover, namely, wrap up the investigation quickly. Regardless of what he intended or what he thought in hindsight, his memo surely colored the White House's views and underscored the political pitfalls of the slightest hint of a foreign conspiracy.

That Katzenbach's memo reflected government policy at the time is reinforced by what U.S. ambassador-at-large Llewellyn Thompson, who had formerly been ambassador to the Soviet Union, apparently told the Soviet ambassador, Anatoly Dobrynin. In a top-secret cable of November 26, the Russian wrote the Presidium in Moscow:

> The question also arises as to whether there is any connection now between the wait-and-see attitude of the U.S. authorities and the ideas conveyed by Thompson (though he himself may not be aware of this connection) on the desirability of some restraint on the part of the Soviet press and gradually hushing up the entire matter of Kennedy's assassination. Perhaps that is exactly what the federal authorities were inclined to do when they learned all the facts and realized the danger of serious international complications if the interested U.S. groups, including the local authorities in Dallas, continued to fan the hysteria over the "leftist" affiliations of Kennedy's assassin and the exposés we would have to issue in this case.[4]

The document does not explain what Dobrynin meant by "exposés." It is not inconceivable that the Soviets knew about the AMLASH operation since Castro seemed to know.

National security officials may also have remembered that a study by the Joint Chiefs of Staff had concluded that if the United States sent troops into Cuba to support a coup and if Soviet troops there resisted, the Soviets might retaliate in Berlin and other places around the world. If the public thought Cuba was behind Kennedy's assassination, the political pressure for invasion would be irresistible.

The laboring oar in the investigation went to the FBI's General Investigative Division, which handled criminal investigations. The Domestic Intelligence Division, which handled security cases and dealt with Oswald before the assassination, would have a supporting role.[5] The notion was that even though the suspect, Oswald, was dead, the FBI would build a case for criminal trial. This was in line with what Katzenbach had written.

When the Church Committee looked at the FBI's work thirteen years later, it concluded that the agency did not attempt a wide-ranging investigation into foreign complicity in the assassination.[6] Although the FBI cabled its field offices on November 22 to leave no stone unturned and to investigate anyone who might be suspected of involvement, the very next morning the FBI ordered everyone to return to normal. Oswald was the suspect, and the field offices should investigate only allegations directly related to him or the assassination. They should not try to develop new investigatory leads.[7]

Hoover was not the only one to weigh in on the question of who should investigate. Both the House of Representatives and the Senate were planning to hold hearings. A proposed investigation by the House Un-American Activities Committee, which notoriously looked for Communists under every rock in America, was an example of how bad the "Red-baiting" might get. Hoover told President Johnson that multiple investigations would be "a three-ring circus."[8] That would be an understatement if the House committee were involved. The Democrats certainly didn't want the investigation to turn into a McCarthy-like witch hunt for Communists.[9]

Johnson personally preferred a Texas State Court of Inquiry.[10] He didn't grasp the magnitude of the worldwide concern over how the glamorous president of the United States could be gunned down on the streets of a major American city by someone as inept as Oswald and how the alleged assassin could then be killed while in police custody by a man whose only explanation for the deed was that he was overcome by grief. Nor did Johnson appreciate that after all of this, no one had faith in the authorities in his beloved Texas.

Johnson came around soon enough, however. On November 29 he signed Executive Order No. 11130 creating a seven-member commission, headed by Chief Justice Earl Warren, two private citizens, and two members each from the House and the Senate, to investigate and report on the assassination. Johnson didn't want any surprises coming out of the commission though. He appointed Richard Russell, his old friend from the Senate, as his inside man.[11] CIA director McCone's inside man was his predecessor, Allen Dulles, who reported the Warren Commission's activities to James Angleton of the CIA. He in turn passed the information to Hoover through Sam Papich. Hoover seemed to have his own source on the Warren Commission in congressman and future president Gerald Ford.[12] Johnson made two phone calls to Russell this day. In the second he told Russell that he had appointed the senator to the Warren Commission. Russell objected, but it was too late because the White House had already announced it. Then the two men discussed the possibility of a foreign conspiracy. Johnson said there were things he couldn't talk about over the phone. Neither man thought the Russians were responsible. Russell volunteered, "I wouldn't be surprised if Castro had," but did not finish the sentence.[13]

Six days later, on December 5, Hoover delivered the FBI report on the assassination to the White House.[14] As far as Hoover was concerned, the case was closed. The FBI had to stay involved, however, because although the Warren Commission had a staff of lawyers and researchers, it needed the FBI to be its investigator.

Today, it is hard to imagine a world without personal computers, without the internet and search engines, and without massive computerized databases of information, but that was the way things worked in 1963, including J. Edgar Hoover's FBI. His vaunted files, which struck fear in the hearts of politicians in Washington who thought secrets from their past and present might be housed there, were all paper records kept in heavy steel file cabinets. To manage the massive paper database, the FBI used a cross-reference system keyed to the subject matter and, more importantly, individuals' names. For example, if an FBI report on the Fair Play for Cuba Committee in New Orleans mentioned Sam Smith and Joe Jones, the FBI would keep one copy of the report in a file for New Orleans Fair Play for Cuba, one copy in Smith's file, and one copy in Jones's file. If Smith were later suspected of spying, the FBI could review his file to find the names of all his known associates. It could then go to its files on each of those individuals and see whom they knew. The process is known as a "name trace" and creates a daisy chain of associations, for example, Smith knows Jones, Jones knows John Doe, John Doe knows Smith. Perhaps they are a spy network. It would depend on how they knew each other, but a name trace is a useful investigatory tool. There might also be various forms of paper indexes, but the FBI had so many files that keeping a paper index up-to-date and alphabetized was impossible.

The CIA was different. It loved technology. Like the FBI it still kept paper records. Those on individuals were called "201-files." But unlike the FBI, it had developed a computerized index that cross-referenced the files. Therefore, while an FBI agent had to go through each individual's file to determine who his or her associates were, a CIA officer could turn to the computerized index. If he entered Smith's name, the officer would instantly get a print out of all of Smith's known associates and all associates of those associates. Computerization eliminated the time and effort of doing a name trace the FBI way.[15]

The system wasn't as convenient as today's World Wide Web technology. After getting a print out of the name trace, a CIA officer still needed to retrieve each paper file and review it; he couldn't click on a link to read the file on his computer.[16] But the CIA system was a significant improvement over the FBI's system. Chief Justice Earl Warren was so impressed that, when the CIA demonstrated it to him in the course of the Warren Commission's investigation, he recommended that the Secret Service use the technology to build watch lists of individuals who might pose a threat to the president.[17]

Nonetheless, the technology didn't override the CIA's rigid security discipline known as "compartmentation." Compartmentation means that only people with a need to know should have access to information. Thus just because a CIA officer investigating Smith could use a computer name trace to discover that Smith's name appeared in Jones's file, the investigator was not allowed to read Jones's file unless he needed to know, a need he would have to justify to those who handled Jones.

This compartmentation created an opportunity to conceal the AMLASH operation from the CIA's own assassination investigators. On the morning of November 23, an internal memorandum to Richard Helms's deputy noted that according to an intercepted telephone call, Oswald had met with Valery Kostikov when he visited the Soviet compound in late September. It continued: "Kostikov . . . was a case officer in an operation which is evidently sponsored by the KGB's 13th Department (responsible for sabotage and assassination). This operation, which is controlled by the FBI under the cryptonym TUMBLEWEED, involved a German-national resident of Oklahoma who was recruited in Europe, and met this year with Kostikov in Mexico City and shortly thereafter with a known 13th Department officer, Oleg Brykin, in New York."[18]

The memo went on to make the point that KGB doctrine only allowed case officers to meet "very important agents" inside a diplomatic compound and only if they could use some sort of "open business" as "cover for their presence" in the compound.[19] In other words, although Oswald ostensibly met with Kostikov for the purpose of getting a visa, it was possible that the two men were plotting Kennedy's assassination.

That same day, according to a later CIA document, "the Mexican Secret Service initiated heavy surveillance" of the Soviet embassy and "started close obvious surveillance of Kostikov" and another KGB officer.[20] The Mexican Secret Service was tailing Kostikov wherever he went.

On November 24 CIA headquarters asked the Mexico City station to provide the names of all known contacts of the Russians with whom Oswald met at the Soviet embassy. In addition to Kostikov, it asked for Ivan Gavrilovich Alferiev's contacts. The Mexico City station answered saying that Alferiev and a cultural attaché in the Cuban embassy had arranged a press conference for Rolando Cubela two years earlier.[21] In other words a name trace on Oswald linked him to Alferiev and Alferiev was linked to Cubela. Producing leads like this is the very purpose of a name trace. It proves nothing in and of itself; it is just an investigatory tool.

It could have significantly affected the assassination investigation though. If only two days after the assassination, investigators had known that at the moment of the assassination, the CIA was meeting Cubela, who wanted to assassinate Castro, attention might have been paid to the chronological connection of the AMLASH plot to Kennedy's assassination.

But the investigators didn't get the information. Sam Halpern, FitzGerald's executive officer, testified that the CIA's 201 files contained only biographic information on individuals. They did not include "operational contacts." Even if an investigator at the CIA did a name trace on Cubela and read his 201-file, he would not learn that the CIA was using Cubela to trigger a coup in Cuba. To get that information, the investigator would be referred to the responsible case officer.[22]

Thus the CIA officer performing the name trace on Alferiev should have learned that the CIA had an operational interest in Cubela and been referred to his case officer, Nestor Sanchez. Halpern testified that at this point in the CIA's name-trace process, "it wouldn't be handled routinely." Sanchez would have talked to Fitz-Gerald before letting anyone see the file on Cubela.

For this reason the top document in Sanchez's file on Cubela at the time is significant because it was written by hand in red and read, "Not to leave this office per Sanchez" and dated December 1963.[23] When asked about the note by the Church Committee, Sanchez testified that he probably directed his secretary to put the notation in the file because FitzGerald had ordered Sanchez "to minimize the knowledgeability of this particular operation because of its sensitivity." No one could see Cubela's file except FitzGerald, Helms, and McCone without Sanchez's approval.[24] FitzGerald had already told Sanchez to keep written records about the operation to a minimum.

So although there is no record of what happened with the name trace on Alferiev, investigators should have discovered that the SAS section of the CIA had an operational interest in Cubela and asked for his file. Sanchez could not remember such a request but admitted that he did not want anyone to access the file at this time without his explicit permission. That's why he put the note in the file. In short the documentary record coupled with standard procedures suggest that someone at the CIA must have taken affirmative steps to prevent investigators from learning about the AMLASH operation only two days after the president's death. The name-trace system was working until someone blocked it. Only Helms and McCone had that authority.

McCone didn't like compartmentation and criticized it in his testimony to the Rockefeller Commission in 1975: "I thought that the compartmentation in the CIA was too rigid and was incorrect. To show you just how far that went, the assembly and training of the brigade and the abortive attempt of the invasion of the Bay of Pigs was so compartmented that only a few people knew anything about it in the Agency, and this was unfortunate because of the probability of success or failure being determined by those who were in charge, and they were also the advocates of the program. There was no objective, outside analysis, and had there been one, it never would have taken place."[25]

While all this internal intrigue was going on at the CIA, two of its stations added fuel to the fire by cabling headquarters with reminders of Castro's September 7 interview with the AP reporter Daniel Harker threatening retaliation. First was the JMWAVE station in Florida. On November 24 it told headquarters that a day earlier, November 23, the local FBI office had asked if JMWAVE knew anything about a threat Castro made in September at the Brazilian embassy in Havana. In its cable to CIA headquarters, JMWAVE observed that the threat had been reported in the *Miami Herald* newspaper.[26]

Second was a Mexico City station cable to headquarters on November 25 with a reminder of Castro's threat.[27] John Whitten, the point man for the investigation at the CIA, testified that he thought he knew about Castro's threat. However, he did not know that the CIA had made contact with Cubela in Brazil on the same day that Castro made the threat at the Brazilian embassy in Havana. Whitten added: "Helms was knowledgeable of all of this, and undoubtedly Helms, with whom I kept in very close touch throughout this investigation—it was pretty much a one-way street it seems now—probably was analyzing this 24 hours a day."[28] Whitten put more trust in Helms's capabilities than was justified. As deputy director for plans, Helms didn't have time to be a counterintelligence analyst.

But the AMLASH operation kept cropping up in the assassination investigation. On the same November 25, Helms sent a cable to CIA stations in Canada and Europe directing them to check material from a specific, reliable source "because of obvious significance of any scrap of information bearing on [the Kennedy] assassination."[29] Two days later the Paris station responded, referencing the headquarters' message, and saying Cubela was overheard complaining about Castro. Thus someone in Paris saw a linkage between the AMLASH operation and the president's assassination. Paris's source said that she wished she had had a tape recorder to capture what Cubela was saying.[30] Although the Paris cable was in response to a headquarters cable on the Kennedy assassination, it was not routed to those investigators but rather put in Cubela's file. When asked about Cubela's loose tongue, case officer Sanchez responded: "He stayed at the Cuban embassy. He was a Cuban official at the time. So he had friends who were of like mind that he was. They were not happy with the way the revolution was moving. . . . This was fairly well known [in the Cuban embassy in Paris]."[31] Little wonder that others at the CIA, such as FitzGerald's counterintelligence chief Swenson, worried about the security of the entire AMLASH operation. This is another instance of the CIA taking affirmative action to prevent assassination investigators from learning about the AMLASH operation.

Some in government seemed largely unfazed by events or at least by the details. On November 25 McGeorge Bundy's aide, Gordon Chase, sent him a memorandum asking whether the overture to Castro through William Attwood should be renewed.[32] Later on the same day, Chase forwarded a chronology that Attwood had prepared and sent to the White House. Chase didn't know what should be done in light of the assassination and asked Bundy: "You once mentioned to me that you wanted the written tracks of this operation kept to a minimum, do you want me to tell Bill that he needn't send us any more chronologies? Or did you mean that you wanted no written tracks between Bill and the Cubans?"[33]

Nothing in these documents suggests that Chase, an assistant to the national security advisor, was aware of the fact that Carlos Lechuga, with whom Attwood was dealing, had had an affair with Silvia Duran, who was of intense interest in the investigation of the Kennedy assassination because of the assistance she had given Oswald at the Cuban consulate in Mexico City. The agency knew though.

Indeed, the CIA was growing increasingly alarmed about Cuban involvement as it analyzed the facts that were pouring in. An unsigned and undated CIA document, which seems to have been written shortly after Ruby murdered Oswald on November 24, recited the facts as known at the time, particularly Oswald's visit to the Cuban and Soviet diplomatic establishments in Mexico City, and posed three questions that were never answered explicitly: Was the assassination planned by Fidel Castro and the details worked out in the Cuban Embassy? Who were Oswald's contacts in Mexico? If Castro planned that Oswald assassinate President Kennedy, did the Soviets have any knowledge of these plans, or, were the Soviets merely being asked to give Oswald a visa?[34] The questions are excellent, but there is no written record of them ever being answered.

The man who wrote those questions, possibly Rocca, would have been even more alarmed if he had known about the AMLASH operation, especially that it was nearing a climax at the very moment Kennedy was killed. John Whitten, who was deeply involved in the initial CIA investigation, testified to the Church Committee that he looked into the possibility of Cuban involvement but rejected it at the time. However, he added, he had conducted his investigation without knowing many of the details that the FBI had. He mentioned as an example that he didn't know that Oswald had attempted to shoot General Walker until Whitten finished his investigation and read the FBI's report. More importantly Whitten felt the AMLASH operation would have been a "very significant factor" to have considered. He certainly would have interviewed Sanchez to get his recollections about the meeting with Cubela while they were still fresh in his mind, especially the question of what happened to the poison pen. Whitten, a lie detector specialist, said he would have polygraphed Cubela if he had a chance.[35] None of this was done of course.

In sum within days after the assassination, Hoover was satisfied that the investigation was complete and that the remaining task was to convince the public that Oswald was the assassin. If he had had his way, there would have been no Warren Commission. Deputy Attorney General Katzenbach adopted the same view and advised the White House that speculation about conspiracies should be cut off. The CIA was more opened-minded except when the assassination investigation threatened to expose the AMLASH operation. In most instances compartmentation made it easy to suppress information about the operation. Those running the AMLASH operation simply had to stay silent. However, on occasion it required affirmative action on their part to prevent assassination investigators from learning that at the moment Kennedy was shot, a CIA case officer was having a last meeting with Cubela before the latter returned to Cuba to do "the big job."

22

The Investigation Sputters On

S purious allegations about the assassination poured into the FBI and the CIA. Some were blown completely out of proportion and proved major distractions, consuming precious resources and time to check out. They also diverted attention from more serious leads. A prime example of the spurious ones was made by a man named Gilberto Alvarado a few days after the assassination. He claimed to have seen Oswald in the Cuban consulate in Mexico City on September 18 being given $6,500 to kill Kennedy. The allegation was false on its face; Oswald was known to have been in New Orleans on September 18. Moreover, the CIA knew, or should have known, that Cuban intelligence was not so inept. No experienced intelligence agent would meet with an assassin in his own consulate and talk about something like assassination with others present. Nonetheless, rather than nipping the story in the bud, the CIA relayed it to the White House, adding to the confusion there.[1]

The allegation also provoked a spat between the FBI and the CIA that escalated and commanded the attention of Hoover, McCone, and President Johnson for days. Relations between the two agencies were never easy even in normal times. FBI agents viewed themselves as sophisticated street cops who protected the citizenry from bad guys, whereas they considered their counterparts at the CIA to be wealthy Ivy League snobs who hobnobbed with the rich and famous. The comparison wasn't inaccurate at least with respect to higher-level officials like Helms and FitzGerald. There were also significant legal distinctions between the jurisdictions of the two agencies. The FBI was a law enforcement agency with power to arrest and get court orders; the CIA did not have such power.

The CIA was also prohibited from taking action within the United

States with the major exception of its JMWAVE station in Florida. This meant, for example, that while the CIA was responsible for keeping tabs on a defector like Oswald while he was overseas, the FBI was responsible when he returned.

Effective coordination in national security cases required close cooperation between the two agencies, but Hoover would have none of this. To protect the FBI's independence, he insisted that all coordination with the CIA be effected through one man, Sam Papich.[2] The result was like connecting two great oceans through a drinking straw and expecting their waters to mix.

The spat started innocently enough on the morning of November 28, when Papich was talking to Birch O'Neal at the CIA and told him he had heard from the FBI office in Mexico City that the CIA was turning Alvarado over to Mexican authorities. After checking with Helms, O'Neal told Papich that the CIA was not going to do this without a formal request from the FBI.[3] Papich went back to his office and checked with his superiors. He then called O'Neal and said that the CIA should make the decision because Alvarado was a CIA source. O'Neal assured Papich this was not true. A short time later, Papich called again to make an official request that the CIA turn Alvarado over to Mexican authorities. The CIA quickly complied. This didn't end the squabble between the two agencies on the matter though. A week later they were arguing about which one would give Alvarado a lie detector test.[4]

Lyndon Johnson anticipated that the FBI and the CIA would have trouble getting along. According to a Hoover memorandum, McCone called him early in the week to say that he wanted to be sure the FBI was satisfied with the help it was getting from the CIA. McCone told Hoover that President Johnson "had asked him personally whether CIA [was] giving the FBI full support; he [McCone] said yes but just wanted to be sure."[5] The squabble was hardly the way to start an investigation of a presidential assassination, and the jealousy and lack of cooperation continued.

Worse, the CIA confused the White House in this period by providing it with raw information rather than refined intelligence. It gave blow-by-blow accounts of the investigation rather than waiting until leads were checked out. This was not the way to help

Lyndon Johnson, who had just assumed the presidency. He had literally been under the gun himself days earlier. Besides, he had not regularly participated in foreign policy discussions on Cuba as vice president. On November 28 McCone sent a memorandum to Bundy about the specious Alvarado allegations.[6] He planned to repeat everything the next day in a morning meeting with the president, McNamara, and Bundy according to a talking paper prepared for the meeting.[7] Whether he did isn't known.

The Alvarado fiasco seemed to prompt the CIA to intensify its investigation. On this same November 28, it cabled the Mexico City station: "We wish to stress there should be no let down in your effort to follow all leads and investigate all facts which bear on this case. We have by no means excluded the possibility that other as yet unknown persons may have been involved or even that other powers may have played a role. Please continue all your coverage of Soviet and Cuban installations and your liaison with Mexicans."[8]

FitzGerald's SAS division at the CIA was proceeding as if nothing had changed. On December 2 it ordered the JMWAVE station in Florida to begin preparing to get Cubela the weapons and secret writing materials he had been promised at the November 22 meeting in Paris. It also relayed to the Florida station the names of the men Cubela thought would assist him in the first stage of a coup against Castro and those who would lend support once Castro was "removed."[9] Forwarding the names was apparently designed to get JMWAVE's views on Cubela's associates.

Almost at the same time, the SAS sent another cable to JMWAVE. This one explained that JMWAVE should plan to deliver the material to Cubela in Cuba but that final approval depended on policy talks FitzGerald needed to have in Washington.[10]

Fidel Castro for his part was again putting out peace feelers. On December 2 William Attwood reported to Gordon Chase on the National Security Council that the Cuban delegate to the UN, Lechuga, had received a letter from Castro authorizing Lechuga to proceed with discussions with Attwood. This overture represented a change in position by Castro. In October he had let it be known that any conversations would have to take place in Cuba. Attwood didn't know whether Castro wrote the letter before or after the assassination. Chase conveyed the information to Bundy, adding, "But things are different now, particularly with this Oswald business."[11]

The confusion that abounded from the top to the bottom of the U.S. government still doesn't explain why significant leads were never pursued. One of the more ominous emerged on December 3 and was cavalierly ignored. The CIA station in Mexico City sent a priority cable to headquarters about Gilberto Policarpo Lopez with the cryptonym "GPFLOOR," which the CIA used for cables on the president's assassination. The Mexico City station said it had picked up information on Lopez from Mexican government authorities. Lopez was an American citizen. He had crossed the border from Texas into Mexico shortly after midnight of November 22 on a fifteen-day Mexican visa. He then flew from Mexico City to Havana on November 27. Mexican authorities wanted a name trace on him.[12] Later in the day, the Mexico City station sent a second message to headquarters that was routed to Whitten. According to this cable, Mexican authorities told the FBI office in Mexico City that Lopez had entered Mexico at Nuevo Laredo, the same place where Oswald crossed when he had gone to Mexico in September.[13] The border was closed after the assassination on November 22, so Lopez was stuck in the state of Texas the day of the assassination, waiting to get into Mexico. The obvious significance was that Lopez might be fleeing from Dallas to Havana.

On December 5 Mexico City sent more details to headquarters. Lopez had stayed in the Roosevelt Hotel in Mexico City. On November 27 he left the hotel for the airport at 7:00 p.m. and departed as the only passenger on a Cubana Airlines flight to Havana. Mexican authorities had a photograph of him.[14] Whitten cabled back, informing the Mexico City station that Lopez was a U.S. citizen and pointing out that he was traveling on an expired passport.[15]

That same day the Mexico City station pouched a dispatch to headquarters with the photograph taken of Lopez at the airport as he was about to board a flight to Havana. Lopez had left his hotel at 7:00 that night and the flight was at 9:00 p.m. In the photograph he is wearing sunglasses, presumably to hinder identification. The dispatch contained the additional information that Lopez was the only passenger on the flight, which had a crew of nine. His visa to Mexico had been issued in Tampa on November 20, and he traveled to Cuba on a "Cuban 'Courtesy' visa." Finally, the dispatch noted that Mexican authorities regarded Lopez's travel through Mexico and departure for Havana as suspicious. Mexican authorities urgently requested all available data on Lopez.[16]

Willard C. Curtis handled the matter for the Mexico City station. He wrote a memorandum for the record on December 5, indicating that Mexican authorities at the border at Nuevo Laredo thought Lopez "looked suspicious" when he crossed into Mexico. They became even more worried when they thought they had lost him and couldn't locate him until he left on the flight to Cuba.[17]

This ended the CIA investigation of Lopez in Mexico City. The FBI would follow up in due course as detailed in appendix A. However, the FBI would investigate Lopez as an "internal security case" and not as part of the assassination investigation. No one at either agency connected Lopez's strange travel from Tampa to Texas to Mexico to Havana with the fact that Kennedy had been in Tampa on November 18, standing up in an open-top car, and in Texas on November 22, when he was killed sitting in the same car.

23

Regime Change

W hether you were a cabinet secretary like Robert McNamara, a national security advisor like McGeorge Bundy, a senior CIA officer like Desmond FitzGerald, or a young case officer like Nestor Sanchez, you felt the change, a sea change, in U.S. policy toward Cuba that came within weeks of John Kennedy's death. The major beneficiary was Fidel Castro.

On November 28, the day before creation of the Warren Commission, CIA director McCone met alone with the president. Lyndon Johnson was letting Jackie Kennedy stay in the White House as long as she wanted, which proved to be about two weeks, so McCone went to Johnson's residence to talk. Johnson lived in a brick house called The Elms, tucked into a heavily wooded section of northwest Washington. The house is big, loose, and rangy like its owner and a few miles from CIA headquarters in Virginia via the Chain Bridge. According to McCone's cryptic memorandum of the meeting—only part of which has been made public—the president raised the subject of Cuba. He wanted to know how effective the economic sanctions were and how the CIA was going to get rid of Castro.[1] Although the memo makes no mention of the AMLASH operation, McCone should have answered Johnson's question honestly and told him about it. Of course, since McCone claimed that he did not permit assassination operations, he arguably didn't know about that aspect of the operation. The private meeting fit the way the CIA did business. FitzGerald's deputy, Sam Halpern, did not know if Johnson was briefed, but he explained to the Church Committee how it might be done.

[HALPERN]. If anything like that was told to the President, it would have been told to the President directly and not through the uses of pieces of paper which go through innumerable hands. . . .

[QUESTION]. Would Mr. Bundy have been privy to that information?

[HALPERN]. Not necessarily.[2]

One can imagine the impact on Johnson if McCone told him about the AMLASH operation: that Sanchez was meeting with Cubela at the very moment the third and fatal shot flew over the vice president's head while Secret Service agent Youngblood had him on the floor of the limousine covered by Youngblood's body. But one can only imagine because there is no record of such a conversation taking place, at least none that has been made public. In later years when talking to former Texas governor John Connally about the possibility that Castro had retaliated, as will be detailed later, Johnson said Castro's involvement was consistent with something he was told when he first took office, but he never explained what he meant. Still, the remark lends support to the view that McCone told Johnson about the AMLASH operation and the November 22 meeting with Cubela.

Meanwhile, at the State Department Dean Rusk was being asked to sign off on a joint Defense Department—State Department contingency plan for the invasion of Cuba. This was a revised plan that had been in the works since the end of the Cuban Missile Crisis and finalized in late October. It had been revised because, during the crisis, President Kennedy was chagrined to learn that his only military option was to order a massive assault on Cuba. The Joint Chiefs of Staff and the State Department had spent the past year trying to develop the kind of flexible response Kennedy preferred. But now the Joint Chiefs didn't want to put any more effort into the project without President Johnson's approval. The State Department officer working on the project didn't think Johnson should be asked to approve a mere contingency plan and persuaded the Joint Chiefs that approval by Rusk and McNamara should suffice. The timing suggests that Kennedy's assassination prompted the

State and Defense Departments to ensure that they had an up-to-date plan in the event Castro was found responsible.[3]

The next day McCone met with the president again. This time Bundy was present. The meeting lasted for an hour and a half. The president returned to the question of what to do about Cuba. McCone talked about the Venezuelan arms cache, which had captured Kennedy's attention on November 19, but said that any action against Cuba must be supported by the Organization of American States or risk a confrontation with the Soviets. McCone referenced speeches Kennedy had made in 1962 warning Castro not to export Communism to the rest of Latin America. Notably, McCone did not, according to his memorandum of the meeting, mention Kennedy's far more recent speech to the Inter-American Press Association on November 18, which the CIA had a hand in writing and which said Castro was a barrier to be removed. Bundy said that he was calling a meeting on Cuba the next week, and the president could return to the subject then.[4]

The announcement of an upcoming meeting on Cuban policy rattled the national security establishment. After the State Department convinced the Defense Department that the Cuban invasion contingency plan should not be submitted to the president, Lieutenant Colonel Alexander Haig rushed to get Secretary of the Army Cyrus Vance to approve it and pass it up to McNamara for approval.[5]

Before concluding his testimony to the Rockefeller Commission in 1975, John McCone talked about the atmosphere of an impending war over Cuba if Oswald were found to have acted at Castro's urging: "[Castro] would have granted him [Oswald] that escape hatch because he would have known that if Oswald was apprehended [he] would have sung, he would have laid the blame on Castro, the indignation of this country would have been so great that the Marines would have taken over Cuba, which is probably what would have been the result."[6] McCone's concern that the United States would invade Cuba if that country were deemed responsible for the assassination is curious. A possible invasion to support a coup, triggered by an assassination, was precisely what John Kennedy and the CIA had been aiming for during the fall of 1963 with the AMLASH operation.

The State Department prepared a talking paper for Secretary Rusk to use at the upcoming Cuban policy meeting with the president. It summarized the Kennedy administration policy on Cuba. The ultimate aim, it said, was the "replacement of the present government by one fully compatible with the goals of the United States." Maximum pressure, "short of military force," would be used to achieve this, including sowing discontent in the Cuban military and encouraging it to overthrow Castro.[7]

The phrase "short of military force" was a mischaracterization of Kennedy's policy toward Cuba. But was this an intended change or the result of a diplomatic blunder by Lyndon Johnson? As McCone and FitzGerald had previously told national security officials, including President Kennedy, CIA plans did not contemplate military invasion of Cuba, but the military might have to be sent there to support any coup that developed. The CIA had promised the same thing to Cubela. Moreover, only two weeks earlier, John Kennedy thought that with the discovery of the Venezuelan arms cache, he had hard evidence that Castro was exporting the revolution to Latin America. If so Kennedy would be free of the no-invasion pledge he had made at the end of the Cuban Missile Crisis since it had been conditioned on Castro behaving himself.

Johnson's possible blunder had come when Deputy Soviet Premier Anastas Mikoyan was in Washington for Kennedy's funeral. Johnson met with him on November 26. It was Johnson's first meeting as president with a top Soviet official. Perhaps Johnson thought he could resolve the whole Cuban problem in this first meeting. If so he approached Mikoyan in the wrong way. Or perhaps Johnson was following suggestions from the State Department. According to a memorandum of the meeting, the president opened by saying that the United States did not plan to invade Cuba. Mikoyan pounced. "Mr. Mikoyan said he was happy to hear these words uttered by the new President of the United States," the memo records. "The President's desire to live in peace and friendship with the USSR and with other nations was in full accord with the views of the Soviet Union." Johnson had been president for four days and had made a major change in Kennedy's policy. He may not have realized what he had done because, according to the memorandum, a few minutes later, "the President stated that there would be no change in the Kennedy policy."[8]

In the early evening of December 2, the president met with Rusk, McNamara, McCone, Bundy, Donald Wilson of the U.S. Information Agency, and Edwin Martin of the State Department. Gordon Chase, Bundy's aide, drafted a paper for Johnson with the "main threads and problems" of U.S. policy toward Cuba. That paper has allegedly disappeared. Only Chase's routing note to Bundy survives. He wrote: "I do not yet have a real feel as to how much the President knows about Cuba." Also missing are any minutes of the meeting. Chase was supposed to take notes, but he dropped out because he had heard the president tended to "abhor a crowd."[9] Given the presence of relatively low-level officials like Wilson at the meeting, it is unlikely that anything as sensitive as the AMLASH operation would have been discussed. On the other hand, as Lyndon Johnson would show a few weeks later in a meeting with FitzGerald, he was bothered neither by crowds at meetings nor by discussing the most sensitive information in the presence of uncleared individuals. Chase's remark that he didn't have a feel for how much Johnson knew about Cuba supports the view that the president's promise to Mikoyan not to invade Cuba was a blunder and not a calculated policy change.

Two days later, on December 4, Chase wrote Bundy outlining plans for a Special Group meeting without the president the next week. Chase's plans followed the theme of the Rusk talking paper in that the agenda would include what could be done about getting rid of Castro, short of invasion, and about the "arms cache issue" by which he meant Castro's exporting the revolution to Latin America. Chase said the advantage of calling a Special Group meeting was that it would allow the attorney general to be invited.[10] Of course if Robert and John Kennedy had given Helms the green light to promise Cubela assassination weapons at the November 19 meeting on the arms cache, revisiting the matter by attending this meeting was the last thing the attorney general would want to do.

It was probably clear that Robert Kennedy's presence at a foreign policy meeting with the new president was not welcome. The two men did not like each other. Nicholas Katzenbach, deputy attorney general under Kennedy, writes about the atmosphere: "Everything Bobby said about President Johnson was negative and often bitter. He saw a big turn to the right. . . . [On civil rights matters] Bobby simply did not trust him. He saw everything [Johnson did] as political, not as based on conviction. . . . President Johnson understood this, and while he had never liked Bobby, he made an effort, never really reciprocated by Bobby, to try to help."[11]

The agencies thought President Johnson was going to take an even harder line toward Castro than Kennedy had if that was possible. At the Defense Department, Alexander Haig wrote his superior, Joseph Califano, on December 4 saying he understood that a meeting the next week of the Standing Group was designed to develop "stronger policy tracks" and that president Johnson was anxious to initiate "more positive action" toward Cuba. Haig identified three examples: organizing the Organization of American States to deal with the arms cache issue; increasing political and economic pressure on Cuba; and stepping up covert action, for example, sabotage.[12]

However, at the CIA FitzGerald was having problems getting Johnson's approval for continuing Kennedy's plans, especially with regard to the AMLASH operation. On December 6 Sanchez cabled JMWAVE that the plan to deliver weapons to Cubela might be delayed: "HQS procedure is to present infil ops plans to Higher Authority even though there is a reasonable chance operation may be postponed or delayed." He went on to say that CIA headquarters would have detailed talks with the Florida station once Fitz-Gerald resolved the policy issues.[13] JMWAVE assured headquarters that it could deliver the cache for Cubela in January. It asked headquarters to confirm that the cache should include two sawed-off shotguns, two machine pistols, two pistols with silencers, two .357 magnums, fragmentation and white phosphorous grenades, ten pounds of explosives, and two rifles with telescopic sights.[14]

The next day Sanchez sent another cable to JMWAVE, but this one said, among other things, that one of the Cubans involved in the infiltration operation might be under suspicion by Cuban security forces. If so this would put Cubela in jeopardy.[15]

JMWAVE was perplexed and frustrated by what seemed to be

conflicting orders from headquarters, which probably stemmed from conflicting orders from higher authority. There were "handling problems" with the infiltration team and management problems, JMWAVE wrote. In remarkably strong language, the Florida station chastised headquarters: "Believe we must improve on this situation if we are to make maximum ops impact on . . . [Cuba] and avoid dissipation of our manpower." Finally, JMWAVE pointed out that using this particular infiltration avenue into Cuba was becoming high risk.[16]

FitzGerald was busy. On December 9 he coauthored a memorandum for McCone that was his contribution to the review of Cuban policy. Like the December 2 State Department talking paper for Rusk, FitzGerald's said Castro was a threat to stability throughout Latin American, so the most immediate aim was to orchestrate a coup in Cuba. FitzGerald seemed to echo the Defense Department reading of the new president, saying there was now an opportunity for "a more openly aggressive retaliation approach against the Castro regime."[17]

The direct and simplest solution, FitzGerald wrote, was a military invasion. That had been shunned in the past because of fears of an escalation into global war, but FitzGerald thought the question might be reexamined. Involving the Organization of American States, hence making it a multilateral military operation, could lessen the chances of escalation. But there was the problem of Lyndon Johnson's telling Mikoyan that he wouldn't invade. By this time even FitzGerald knew about it, writing: "A US invasion in the face of the President's remarks might reflect on the good faith of the President and the credibility of future US discussions with high Soviet officials."[18]

Naturally, FitzGerald concluded his analysis by finding that what he called the "CIA's Integrated Covert Action Program" of sabotage, propaganda, economic sanctions, and military coup was the most promising option. "The objective," he wrote, "is to stimulate an internal coup which would dislodge Castro and his entourage. *We currently are in direct contact with several individuals inside Cuba who may be of significance for this program.*"[19]

FitzGerald appended to the memorandum his suggestions for

what the Johnson administration might say to stimulate the dissidents, noting that the CIA had attempted "in a general and very limited manner to provide these assurances," but the president himself needed to say something. He quoted from Kennedy's November 18 speech to the Inter-American Press Association, including the parts that he wrote. He did not, however, mention that he had personally met with a leading Cuban dissident, nor did he quote the part of Kennedy's speech that referred to Castro as a barrier to be removed.[20] Johnson had been president for less than three weeks, and changes in Cuban policy were already being felt throughout the national security establishment.

The next day FitzGerald's Special Affairs Staff followed up with a shorter, punchier "Summary of Principal Actions" that was even more bellicose: "Unless we resign ourselves to a Castro-is-here-to-stay attitude, a much bolder US policy toward Cuba is necessary." It was cosigned by FitzGerald's deputy, Seymour Bolten, and by Chester Cooper. It continued the emphasis on an "integrated program," meaning that all the recommended programs should be implemented simultaneously. It called for intensified sabotage, including unleashing any and all exile groups, air strikes, strong policy statements from the president, discussions with the Soviets to abandon Castro, intensified economic sanctions, feints by the military to wear down Cuban forces responding to alerts, low-level reconnaissance flights, throwing a naval cordon around Cuba to prevent it from exporting arms, and bringing Latin American countries into the effort.[21]

A Standing Group meeting was scheduled for December 10 to discuss possible Organization of American States actions against Cuba. The Standing Group, unlike the Special Group, did not include Attorney General Robert Kennedy. He was, it seems, being eased out of Cuban policy matters by the choice of which group handled matters.

A memorandum prepared for the Defense Department's representative, Secretary of the Army Vance, said that the State Department was pushing adoption of "a more positive OAS program." This was not accurate. The program that was being recommended was the navy's interdiction of Cuba ships bound for Latin American countries in order to cut off arms shipments. According to the memorandum, this approach was within the military's capabilities.[22] No OAS force would be involved.

The State Department went into the Standing Group meeting with a paper that listed the advantages and disadvantages of the CIA's proposals for unilateral action, that is, the United States acting alone. For example, while there were advantages to air strikes, mainly psychological, the paper found seven disadvantages, including the possibility that the Soviets would stop their troop withdrawal from Cuba. The same was true for military feints with three advantages, including psychological, but four disadvantages, including, again, stopping Soviet troop withdrawals. The State Department did not itemize advantages and disadvantages for bilateral action, that is, in concert with other nations, and the proposals it did itemize were, not surprisingly, all diplomatic. One that would stand out in later decisions was what was called "Free-World Shipping in Cuban Trade." The phrase was a high-sounding reference to efforts to get the British ship owner Mavroleon to stop serving Cuban ports.[23] And of course the CIA had its own paper for the meeting that compared the advantages and disadvantages of its covert-action program as a counter to the State Department document.[24]

The Standing Group met on December 13 but wasn't able to get through its agenda because participants were "more concerned with the unsatisfactory results of a November 14–18 surveillance and intercept operation against suspected arms smuggling into Columbia." Nonetheless, it approved the CIA's proposal for air strikes and for unleashing the exiles and the State Department's proposal on free-world shipping. It would consider the other matters at a December 19 meeting with the president.[25]

As vice president, Lyndon Johnson had not been involved in Cuban policy. He did not attend meetings of the Special Group or the Standing Group and did not sit in on any of the meetings on Cuba with President Kennedy, as he did on Vietnam. The December 19 meeting would be his first exposure to the full complement of national security agencies and personalities on Cuban policy. To set the stage, Bundy drafted a twenty-two-page memorandum on what the policy had been and on what was under consideration. The somewhat rambling document is an amalgam of the programs and proposals from Defense, State, and the CIA. It suggests a unified national security establishment and belies the strong differences among the agencies, particularly State and the CIA, on what should be done.

The document draws a distinction between "defensive" measures against Cuba, meaning measures to prevent or detect the Soviets returning nuclear missiles to Cuba, and "offensive operations" designed to oust Castro. Crucial to defense was the CIA's ability to send U-2 aircraft over Cuba to ensure no new missiles were brought in. Since Russian surface-to-air-missiles could shoot down a U-2, the CIA always worried that the Soviets might react to CIA offensive operations by shooting down the U-2s and thus blind the CIA to the reintroduction of nuclear weapons.

Significantly, the paper made no mention of what FitzGerald had been arguing for months: that the CIA's program of raids, sabotage, economic sanctions, propaganda, and recruitment of dissidents was an integrated one. The CIA's covert-action program was not like a Chinese menu from which the president might pick and choose. Rather, it was all or nothing. But Johnson may not have read the long memorandum anyway.[26]

. . .

The showdown between John Kennedy's Cuban policy and Lyndon Johnson's came on December 19, 1963, when the CIA explained its program to the new president. The meeting began at 11:00 a.m. in the Cabinet Room of the White House. Exactly who attended is uncertain as will be explained because although there are four written lists of attendees and six photographs of the meeting, they differ in one important respect: whether Attorney General Robert Kennedy or Ted Sorensen, John Kennedy's speechwriter, was there. Otherwise, the attendees were the expected ones for a meeting on Cuba, but no one of cabinet rank was there, including CIA director McCone, except, oddly, Treasury Secretary Douglas Dillon.

The president arrived five minutes early, before several attendees including national security advisor Bundy. This was

Desmond FitzGerald's meeting though, and the president told him to begin even though the White House photographer was still in the room snapping pictures. FitzGerald's memorandum of the meeting implies he was uncomfortable discussing top-secret covert operations with someone who had no business being at such a meeting. He may also have been uncomfortable having his picture taken with the president. Subordinates had warned him not to meet with Cubela precisely because the United States could not plausibly deny that FitzGerald was a high-ranking government official who could speak for the president. And yet here he was, being photographed in the White House with Lyndon Johnson.

FitzGerald summarized the situation in Cuba and what the CIA had been doing. When FitzGerald got around to explaining the coup plan, the president was both dismissive and highly critical. He said that it did not appear to him that the CIA had gotten very far along this line, charging that, according to FitzGerald's memorandum, "one day those concerned in Cuba matters, including himself [i.e., Johnson], would have to face the 'grand jury' (of domestic public opinion) to account for your progress in our attempts to find a solution to the Cuban situation." FitzGerald responded that the CIA was at its limit in terms of what could be done with covert operations. Johnson may have intended his criticism to be of John and Robert Kennedy, particularly the latter.[27]

Johnson rejected the CIA and Defense Department proposals for large-scale sabotage operations and air strikes. The CIA could proceed with planning smaller operations subject to later authorization from him. When FitzGerald talked about using exile groups, for example, those of Manuel Artime and Manolo Ray, Johnson asked how much these operations cost, what was the cost of all the CIA's Cuban operations, and what was the total CIA budget. FitzGerald said the CIA was spending $5 million on the autonomous operations out of a total of $21–22 million for all Cuban operations. Apparently, not even FitzGerald knew the total CIA budget, or if he did, he wasn't going to divulge it at this meeting, for he doesn't mention it in his memorandum. Perhaps this was Lyndon Johnson's reason for having Treasury Secretary Dillon there. In any event Johnson seemed most interested in the economic sanctions and returned to the subject several times.

After FitzGerald finished, Bundy led a discussion of the points raised in the State Department's proposal to the Standing Group, but there was little comment. Bundy suggested the president might make an even stronger statement than Kennedy's November 18 speech, but Johnson is not recorded as having responded. The CIA's Helms also made a presentation on the Venezuelan arms cache.

The meeting was a major defeat for the CIA. The results were summarized by the CIA's deputy director, General Marshall Carter: "The President, after full discussion, postponed any sizable operations by FitzGerald, primarily to avoid any possible embarrassment to our OAS negotiations on the Venezuelan arms cache. We are authorized to continue to put forward proposals for operations and also to continue preparations for air ops The main thrust was to greatly increase political action with Canada, Spain, Italy, and others in an effort to promote greater economic blockade."[28]

The president's remark about the CIA having to answer to the grand jury of public opinion seems an insult to Kennedy's CIA, so the question of whether it was said in the presence of either Robert Kennedy or Ted Sorensen is important. The White House Daily Diary lists Attorney General Robert Kennedy as being present. The memorandum of the CIA's General Carter does not list him, but it does list Sorensen. Gordon Chase's and Desmond Fitz-Gerald's memoranda list neither.[29] And while there are six photographs of the meeting, neither Kennedy nor Sorensen is in them. Of course the photographer might have left before they arrived.[30]

The differences between this meeting and the one with President Kennedy on November 12, just over a month earlier, are dramatic. Although in his first meeting with Deputy Soviet Prime Minister Mikoyan, Johnson said that he was continuing Kennedy's policies on Cuba, he clearly was not. He dismissed the CIA's coup plot and indeed the whole idea of an integrated covert-action program to get rid of Castro. His focus was on diplomatic efforts and economic sanctions, yet as he would soon discover, those were doomed to fail. Johnson's question about the CIA's budget may be an example of how uninformed he was on intelligence issues even though he had been vice president for nearly three years. And whereas John Kennedy almost invariably favored the CIA over the State Department because he thought that was where the "brains were," Johnson seemed more comfortable with State. Perhaps this was because it operated in a political way that was more familiar to him than through dark, mysterious, covert actions. He would express a variation of this feeling to McCone a week later. Or it may have been because he thought the CIA still owed allegiance to John and Robert Kennedy. In any event Johnson never displayed the interest in Cuba the Kennedys had. The situation in Vietnam was demanding far more of his attention, or at least that is how he may have seen it. As vice president, he had attended meetings on Vietnam. He had attended none on Cuba.

Following the meeting Bundy issued a national security action memorandum, directing the CIA and the Departments of State and Commerce to report on the extent of free-world shipping with Cuba including what goods were being shipped, the companies involved, and the measures taken to stop the shipping.[31]

As the year came to an end, the loose ends of Kennedy's Cuban policy were being wrapped up. Sanchez cabled JMWAVE to go ahead with delivery of arms in Cuba for Cubela. However, the contents had changed. No longer would he be given rifles with telescopic sights, explosives, and grenades. Instead, the cache would have two Belgian FAL rifles, the kind that Castro carried and that were common in Cuba, and two submachine guns.[32] The Florida station replied, saying that it could get the weapons cache there in February. It wanted to hide the cache for Cubela to recover rather than deliver it to an agent inside Cuba. That way there would be "no latent security hazard to any inside asset." JMWAVE did not seem sure that Cubela could be trusted.[33]

As for the Venezuelan arms cache, an army team investigated it in early December. In an interim report of December 23, the team said that "many of the items found were in fact of US origin." They had been shipped to the Batista government in 1956 and 1957 to help fight Castro. The report makes no mention of Belgian-made weapons. Helms may have taken a Belgian-made FAL rifle to show the attorney general and the president on November 19, but the only weapons the army report mentions were antiquated American-made ones.[34] If the CIA made a separate inventory of the arms cache, it has not been made public in the National Archives collection.

Finally, two days after Christmas, CIA director McCone flew down to Texas for a meeting with the president at his ranch. Johnson said that he wanted "to change the image of the DCI [director of Central Intelligence, which was another of McCone's titles] from a cloak and dagger role to the role of the adviser to the President." This seems consistent with Johnson's hostile reaction to FitzGerald's covert-action presentation a few days earlier. McCone said he liked that idea. Then he shifted the conversation to intelligence matters and told Johnson that the Soviets were turning over the operation of the surface-to-air missiles to Cuban troops. The CIA was worried that Cuban troops might use the SAMs to shoot down the U-2s, which the CIA relied on to make sure that Russia was not reinserting nuclear weapons in Cuba. McCone continued by saying that the United States could use its "new development," perhaps a reference to the SR-71, which was then a new, top-secret reconnaissance aircraft that could not be shot down by a SAM.[35]

A month after Kennedy's death, U.S. policy toward Cuba had changed completely. CIA attempts to assassinate Castro and stage a coup were no longer in the cards. At worst the Cuban people, not Castro, would suffer from economic sanctions and even this approach would soon fail. On November 22, when Castro learned that Kennedy was dead and Johnson was the president, he asked reporter Jean Daniel what control Johnson exercised over the CIA. By the end of the year, he had his answer: complete control. Lee Harvey Oswald had done for Castro what Cubela had proposed to do for Kennedy: bring about regime change in his native land.

24

The Warren Report

For Earl Warren heading the investigation into the president's assassination was a demanding, and probably unwelcome, task. He already had a rewarding, full-time job as chief justice of the Supreme Court. He could ill-afford devoting large amounts of time to directing an investigation that required taking testimony, especially since the only point was to calm a nervous public. Moreover, while Warren had once been a prosecutor and attorney general for the State of California, he had never been a trial judge, which was essentially what his role as chairman of the Warren Commission called for. Nonetheless, he dutifully discharged his responsibilities, patiently presiding over commission meetings and hearing witnesses. The same could not be said for other commission members such as Senator Richard Russell and Congressman Hale Boggs, who rarely attended testimonial sessions. All told ninety-four witnesses testified personally before the commission or staff.[1]

The commission's staff consisted of lawyers, researchers, and secretaries, but Hoover's FBI furnished the investigators. It provided the commission with thousands of reports. The FBI had already wrapped up its investigation and given its findings to the president within weeks of the assassination. Still, as Howard Willens, who was on the commission staff, writes in his book *History Will Prove Us Right*, the commission found mistakes in the FBI's initial reports. For example, he notes the FBI did not realize that Governor John Connally was struck by the same bullet that had gone through the president, the so-called magic bullet to Warren Commission critics.[2] Nonetheless, the commission did not have much choice; it could hardly hire a team of investigators and get them security clearances within the time frame the president demanded.

The result was an underlying structural problem with the investigation, which was its independence. This independence was designed to assure the public that the commission wasn't beholden to any government agency, but the downside was that the intelligence agencies held the commission at arms' length. They did what the commission asked them to do, but they didn't volunteer information. The blue-ribbon panel was operating in a vacuum. It didn't know what the agencies were doing, what more they were capable of, or what they were not doing. The latter was the biggest weakness of the structure.

At the CIA, for example, John Whitten, whom Helms arguably had designated point man for the initial investigation, testified to the Church Committee that he did his work without having all the facts. He told of the first time he saw the FBI report on the assassination in late December 1964: "We went to Mr. [deputy attorney general] Katzenbach's office in the Department of Justice and read this very thick report. For the first time, I learned a myriad of vital facts about Oswald's background which apparently the FBI had known throughout the initial phase of the investigation and had not communicated to me. . . . I am certain, although I cannot prove it, that Mr. Angleton [chief of CIA Counterintelligence] throughout the entire period discussed the Kennedy assassination regularly with FBI representatives, never notified me of any of these meetings, and never passed on to me any of the information that he gained in these meetings."[3]

Moreover, the CIA's experts on Cuba were never involved. Whitten had responsibility for Central America from Mexico to Panama but not for Cuba, and he reported to J. C. King of the Western Hemisphere Division. The CIA's expertise on Cuba was concentrated in the Special Affairs Staff of Desmond FitzGerald. The SAS was a CIA in miniature, with its own counterintelligence staff of about thirty, and it was not subordinate to Angleton.

The SAS was never brought into the investigation. Its chief counterintelligence at the time was Harold Swenson. He described himself to the Church Committee: "Probably I was better informed than any other one individual [at the CIA] about Cuban intelligence activities." Swenson testified that he had never worked on the assassination investigation and never discussed it with Fitz-Gerald "because it never appeared pertinent." On the other hand, he did play a passive role by staying alert to any indication of Cuban involvement with Oswald, saying, "I did talk to many people, Cubans, who were knowledgeable about intelligence activities, Cuban intelligence officers, defectors, and I got never a single bit of information indicating there was any association whatsoever."[4] His role seems akin to that of a homicide detective who waits for someone to come in and tell him who committed the murder rather than run an active investigation.

Swenson described a highly compartmentalized CIA, a place where information wasn't casually shared.[5] He was never asked if any of Oswald's contacts in Mexico City were connected with Cuban intelligence, but with the CIA computerized indexing system, anyone with clearance could do a name search on them. Swenson had an uncertain recollection that he, FitzGerald, Sam Halpern, Seymour Bolten, Nestor Sanchez, and others may have discussed the possible connection between the assassination and the AMLASH operation. But if they did, nothing came of it. Swenson would have taken action if something had come up, but he never affirmatively looked for leads.[6] Still, it is surprising that the expert on the Cuban intelligence service would have no contact with the Warren Commission. There is no evidence that the commission or its staff realized this or understood what the SAS was.[7]

James Angleton, who was overall chief of CIA Counterintelligence from 1954 to 1974, described the chaotic CIA investigation to the Church Committee: "Following the assassination, and immediately following the assassination there was no organized approach to the problem. . . . So you had the following elements: You had the Western Hemisphere Division, the Soviet Division, and the Counter-Intelligence staff, who—the Counter-Intelligence staff was the channel of liaison to the FBI, and this material was poured over to them. . . . Everything was dug out of the files that was relevant. And then there was a snowstorm of other requests and other names, many of them very far out."[8]

The CIA's compartmentation, which was a program Angleton oversaw, barred even him from accessing information. When he testified to the Church Committee in 1976, albeit when he was advanced in age and in obvious, declining health, the phrase "Special Affairs Staff" did not register with him. He confused Desmond FitzGerald's headquarters group with the JMWAVE station in Florida and thought J. C. King, who headed the Western Hemisphere Division, not the SAS, controlled JMWAVE. Nonetheless, he had eventually designated his chief research analyst, Raymond Rocca, to investigate the Kennedy assassination, and Rocca followed it for years. Angleton said Rocca normally would not have access to the materials on Cuban operations. He thought Rocca did have such access in his work on the Kennedy assassination but added, "The activities of WAVE were fairly compartmented."[9] In fact neither Angleton nor Rocca was knowledgeable about covert operations against Cuba in the 1960s.

Likewise, the FBI steered the Warren Commission clear of its Cuban experts. In his book on the commission's work, Philip Shenon writes that the FBI's "Cuba experts were effectively cut out of the investigation." The Bureau's expert on Cuba told Shenon he had never attended a single meeting on the assassination and did not know that Castro had threatened American leaders in September 1963.[10]

Thus the Warren Commission's independence from the intelligence agencies meant that it didn't know how rickety the whole national intelligence structure was. The FBI was investigating whatever the Warren Commission asked it to do, but as far as the FBI's Hoover was concerned, the investigation had been over for months. Then there was the fact that all coordination between the FBI and the CIA had to go through one man, Sam Papich, who shuttled between the agencies on a daily basis. At the CIA responsibility was parceled out to the Soviet Division on matters that related to Oswald's life in Russia, to the Counterintelligence Division for questions about the KGB, and to the Western Hemisphere Division as far as Oswald's trip to Mexico City was concerned. FitzGerald's SAS, with its expertise on Cuban intelligence, was excluded.

Angleton realized the structural problem and assigned Raymond Rocca not only to coordinate the CIA's investigation but also to get everything the FBI and the Warren Commission learned. No other agency of government was doing this. Rocca was the only analyst in the entire U.S. government asking for information from other agencies and trying to put all the pieces together as a counterintelligence investigation. Not even the Warren Commission was doing this. But Rocca did not have access to information about FitzGerald's operations. He did not know about the AMLASH operation, about FitzGerald's integrated covert operation to overthrow Castro, about Cubela, about the CIA's hand in writing Kennedy's November 18 speech, about the phone call to Cubela on November 20, or about the November 22 meeting in Paris, where Sanchez offered Cubela a poison pen and promised rifles with telescopic sights, the very kind of weapon used to kill the president.

Only Richard Helms and his deputy Karamessines had access to everything, and Karamessines claimed that he did not know about the AMLASH operation. Helms was not an investigator; he was a manager, a "clean desk" bureaucrat. He had his hands full briefing Director McCone and the president, attending interagency meetings, running covert operations from Havana to Moscow to Saigon, and managing thousands of people. He was not an analyst and did not have the time to be, yet he was the only person who had access to everything about the assassination, not just the only person at the CIA but the only person in the U.S. government, including Earl Warren.[11]

Despite the chaotic bureaucratic structure, the assassination investigation and FitzGerald's integrated covert-operation plan against Cuba stumbled on. On January 9, 1964, Bundy wrote President Johnson about three small sabotage operations that the Special Group had approved and advised:

All of these operations would have been approved three months ago. . . .

I therefore recommend a Cabinet-level review of the whole principle of covert sabotage against Cuba. I know that Rusk had never liked it and that McNamara thinks it does very little good. McCone and the CIA are for it, and so are most of the middle-level officers dealing with the Castro problem. I myself consider the matter extremely evenly balanced, but before hearing full argument, my guess is that in your position I would stop sabotage attacks on the ground that they are illegal, ineffective, and damaging to our broader policy. I might then wish to make a little capital from this decision with the Soviet Union.[12]

Brigade 2506 veteran Erneido Oliva later claimed that this same week he was called to the White House, where President Johnson told him personally that operations against Cuba were over.[13]

A few days later, Lyndon Johnson met with Rusk; McNamara; General Carter, who was the CIA's representative; White House aides Bill Moyers and Jack Valenti; General Maxwell Taylor of the Joint Chiefs; Dr. Glenn Seaborg, chairman of the Atomic Energy Commission; and Adrian Fisher. The meeting was supposed to be about disarmament, hence the presence of Seaborg and Fisher, who was an arms negotiator, but the president veered off to talk about Cuba. General Carter's memorandum for the record of the meeting indicates that Johnson said he thought the CIA's sabotage operations were hypocritical and ineffective. While Johnson's penchant for veering off topic at meetings is in evidence, the remarkable thing about the meeting is how clearly Johnson had eviscerated the Kennedys' Cuban policy.

> While he [Johnson] understood the need for some of them [sabotage operations] to maintain the morale of internal dissidents to the Castro regime and to maintain the morale of Cuban exiles, he thought probably these considerations were outweighed by the hypocrisy of our seeking peace and talking peace and conducting this sort of activity on the side. Rusk said that he had never been in favor of this program and had the same doubts the President did. McNamara said that he too had never been in favor of this program and questioned our participation. I stated that while this program was conducted by the CIA, every action taken had the full approval of the Special Group on which the Secretary of State and the Secretary of Defense were adequately represented and that the program was designed in part for the specific purpose of generating internal sabotage and dissidents with a view to creating as many problems as possible for Castro and with a view to getting an escalation of anti-Castro activities in Cuba, that over the long run any type of

effort such as this was an irritant to Castro and that such action had some effect, even though slight, on the Cuban economy. I said that over the long run you could not expect the Castro regime to fall from these actions alone but that every little bit helped, and that we had noticed over the past four months a considerable increase in sabotage actions generated from internal Cuban elements over which we exercised no control. I said that I could not take exception to the fact that this policy was a hypocritical one in the light of a peace offensive although I did not feel we were trying to make peace with Castro. I also pointed out that sabotage activities in North Vietnam likewise had hypocritical aspects. At this point Mr. McNamara demurred and said North Vietnam was an entirely different matter but he gave no reasons therefor and this point was not developed further. General Taylor noted that in connection with sabotage operations they kept Castro constantly on the alert and kept his forces heavily occupied running hither and yon. The President noted that this was probably true but so little gain in it and generally seemed disaffected with sabotage efforts. Rusk pointed out that there was some value in maintaining some pressure of this type since to completely desist would eventually lead Castro to believe that he was immune from retaliation. The President then directed that he wanted a complete review of our Cuban policy and some new, imaginative thinking developed. . . . In connection with Cuba the President noted that he continued to desire the most drastic pressures on our Allies to insist upon their cooperation and assistance and compliance in our economic denial program against Cuba.[14]

McNamara's saying that he agreed with Rusk and had never favored the CIA's sabotage operations is the complete opposite of his position less than two months early at the November 12 meeting with President Kennedy. At that meeting he had disagreed with Rusk, who worried that the sabotage raids would result in a Soviet move against Berlin, and had gone on to say that he thought the raids were effective. And whereas John Kennedy often found it useful to follow two opposing paths simultaneously, such as opening talks with Castro while trying to overthrow him, Lyndon Johnson labeled this hypocritical.

The AMLASH operation was faring no better. On February 4 John King of the SAS intelligence section sent a memorandum to Nestor Sanchez as a follow-up to a conversation they had that morning. King had specific intelligence collection questions for Cubela. He hoped Cubela would not be insulted. The questions related to Castro's exporting the revolution, which King called "the hottest items in town." For example, he wanted to know how many Latin Americans were training in Cuba, whether Africans were being trained, and the name of the commanding officer of each school.[15] Cubela had told Sanchez the previous fall that he had no interest in performing routine intelligence assignments such as this. His focus was on "the big job." When Sanchez was asked by the Church Committee how he could ask Cubela to revert to collecting intelligence in light of his comments, Sanchez equivocated before finally saying he had ignored King's request: "Receiving a memo from King at that time doesn't necessarily mean that we are going to levy the requirements on AMLASH."[16]

Fidel Castro may have noticed the sabotage was easing up and thought it was a sign of a more sympathetic attitude on Lyndon Johnson's part. On February 12 he told ABC reporter Lisa Howard, who had been a messenger the previous summer for Castro, to tell President Johnson: "That I earnestly desire his election to the Presidency in November . . . though that appears assured. But if there is anything I can do to add to his majority (aside from retiring from politics), I shall be happy to cooperate. Seriously, I observe how the Republicans use Cuba as a weapon against the Democrats. So tell President Johnson to let me know what I can do, if anything."[17]

If Lyndon Johnson read what Castro said and felt flattered, he should not have been. Right after Kennedy's bellicose speech on November 18, Castro said the same thing about Kennedy to the reporter Jean Daniel: "Then Fidel had added with a broad and boyish grin: 'If you see him [Kennedy] again, you can tell him that I'm willing to declare Goldwater my friend if that will guarantee Kennedy's re-election!'"[18] Castro was reusing a line that he had used before.

On February 28 at McCone's request, FitzGerald took the unusual step of meeting alone with Attorney General Robert Kennedy. The attorney general's role in Cuban policy had seemed to stop with his brother's death, so the purpose of this meeting is hard to fathom. According to FitzGerald's memorandum, he handed Kennedy a document he called the "Spectrum Paper" with respect to Cuba and an annex titled "Scenario for Action."

The "Spectrum Paper" is an astonishing document. It outlines, on the one hand, the possible courses of action and their advantages and disadvantages if the United States should decide to "live with Castro." On the other hand, it looks at the possible courses of action if the opposite decision were made, if the United States couldn't live with Castro. Eleven possible ways of bringing Castro down were itemized in ascending order of violence. For example, item 8, called the "Rostow Doctrine," would have the United States prohibit Castro from engaging in certain actions and then destroying "a major installation inside Cuba" each time Castro violated the prohibition. It doesn't say what a prohibited action might be, but probably exporting the revolution would be one. Item 9 was to warn the Soviet Union that the Castro regime was intolerable and that unless it changed its ways, the United States would no longer be constrained by Kennedy's promise to Khrushchev that the United States wouldn't invade Cuba. Item 10 called for a total blockade of Cuba. And item 11 was invasion. One of the disadvantages of an invasion, the paper noted, was "probably heavy casualties on both sides."[19]

The "Scenario for Action" outlined a renewed hard line with respect to Cuba. The Organization of American States was about to meet to decide on what the response should be to the arms cache in Venezuela. The CIA wanted the OAS to pass a "blank check" resolution. This presumably meant that OAS would authorize the United States to take whatever action it felt was necessary against Cuba, including military action. If the OAS failed to pass such a resolution, the scenario argued that the United States should unilaterally declare it was prepared to act alone in the event Cuba made any further attempt to export the revolution. The "Scenario" also recommended that the Soviet Union be informed that the United States would find it intolerable if Castro tried to do so again. It suggested a rule of thumb that Castro's sending twenty trained men and four tons of arms to northeast Brazil might not trigger reprisal by the United States but sending the same small force to a Central American country might.

FitzGerald recorded that Robert Kennedy read the "Spectrum Paper" and "Scenario" carefully. He asked if the Board of National Estimates, which provided long-range intelligence analysis, had ever opined on whether the United States could live with Castro. When FitzGerald said no, Kennedy suggested that it would be a good idea to have the board take up the matter. He then asked what the status of Cuban policy discussions were. FitzGerald indicated that the OAS meeting was about the only thing going on. FitzGerald concluded his memorandum for the record by writing: "The Attorney General said that he was grateful for being given the Spectrum Paper and that he thought it to be useful."[20]

Why FitzGerald met with Robert Kennedy at McCone's request and showed him these documents is hard to understand. Lyndon Johnson had already rejected most of the proposals in the "Spectrum Paper." The president, not the attorney general, had been setting Cuban policy since November 22, 1963. Robert Kennedy no longer had a role in advising on that subject. Conceivably, McCone wanted the attorney general's advice or wanted to get his friend more engaged as a way of helping him get past his brother's death. However, McCone would be taking a political risk in doing this without Lyndon Johnson's approval since Johnson was dismantling Kennedy's Cuban policy. Conceivably, McCone was so unhappy with what Johnson was doing with respect to Cuba that he was trying to goad the attorney general into running against him in the presidential primaries that spring. McCone and FitzGerald were risking their jobs and careers unless Johnson had approved their talking with the attorney general about these things, but there is no evidence that he had. And of course conceivably, the CIA had investigated the president's assassination, concluded that Fidel Castro was responsible, and was trying to get Robert Kennedy's approval for retaliation. In the event nothing came of the meeting.

Castro continued with his penchant for sending out contradictory messages simultaneously. Whereas a month earlier, he had said flattering things about Johnson to Lisa Howard, Richard Helms wrote Bundy in early March to report that Cuban foreign minister Raul Roa told a CIA source that Kennedy had been trying to establish contacts with Cuba before he was assassinated. Roa worried that President Johnson might not be aware of this. But then, said the source, Castro himself had referred to Johnson "in harsh terms in source's presence."[21] Of course Castro's version of what Kennedy had been doing wasn't accurate. Castro had been the one to initiate the overture to Kennedy first through Lisa Howard and later through Carlos Lechuga at the United Nations. Kennedy was following a two-track policy of either overthrowing Castro or negotiating with him, whichever worked. Johnson considered this way of conducting following policy hypocritical. Yet Castro seemed to be doing a variation of the same thing with Johnson, talking nice one minute and tough the next.

Two days later, on March 6, Helms and FitzGerald met with Bundy to discuss the entire CIA Cuban program. FitzGerald summarized the meeting in a follow-up letter. He began by politely reminding Bundy that the CIA's covert-action program was developed in response to a policy established and agreed to by the Special Group the previous June. The aim was to get rid of Castro through a coup. Now that the sabotage raids had been called off, FitzGerald asked if the capability should be dismantled, and whether the CIA should also withdraw its support from Artime and Ray.

FitzGerald wrote that the economic sanctions, which three months earlier Lyndon Johnson had said were the key to getting rid of Castro, had virtually collapsed. The only thing left was the effort to organize a coup, but interest in that among Cuban dissidents rose and fell with their perception of Castro's strength and American commitment. FitzGerald concluded that without an integrated program using all covert resources, the best that could be expected was a slowing of Castro's progress.[22] It was not an optimistic assessment. The CIA was going on record with the White House to say that unless the CIA was allowed to use all its covert-action weapons, Castro would stay in power. By this time Lyndon Johnson may not have cared.

The wind had gone out of the sails of the AMLASH operation and the assassination investigation as well. The CIA continued to stay in touch with Cubela, but the effort was half-hearted. The day after Helms and FitzGerald talked to Bundy, Nestor Sanchez called Tepedino to talk about Cubela.[23] The CIA still hadn't delivered the rifles to Cubela that it had promised at the November 22 meeting. Now that it was March, the CIA finally got around to doing so—albeit Belgian-made FALS instead of rifles with telescopic sights—but the rifles wouldn't fit into the container it planned to leave for Cubela in Cuba. Instead, the CIA decided that the infiltration team would carry FALS, and if Cubela's comrades showed up, the CIA team would simply hand one to them.[24]

While this was going on, the change in policy toward Cuba was set in concrete at a high-level White House meeting on April 7. All the top policy makers and their aides attended: the president and McGeorge Bundy; Dean Rusk and Alexis Johnson; Robert McNamara and Cyrus Vance; General Maxwell Taylor; and McCone, Helms, and FitzGerald for the CIA. The CIA-supported raids continued to be the sticking point. McCone made one last plea for the CIA's integrated approach. Only five raids had been conducted in the fall of 1963, and they had produced a surge of anti-Castro sentiment. If the group felt the CIA should give up its integrated approach, then it was abandoning the effort to eliminate the Communist presence in Cuba. McNamara and Rusk opposed the sabotage raids as they had at previous meetings. The president sided with them. The raids would not resume, but the CIA was directed to retain the capability to launch such raids for two more months.[25] Johnson was continuing to rely on economic sanctions.

Once again the CIA apparently thought it was not getting the message through to Lyndon Johnson. Helms and FitzGerald went back to the White House two days later to talk with Bundy. The problem, they pointed out, was that although CIA-run raids were stopped, Manuel Artime's and Manolo Ray's separate operations would continue. Neither Castro nor the world was likely to make the distinction between the two. The United States would be blamed regardless of whether it was responsible. Yet if the government tried to stop raids by the two exile groups, there would "considerable fallout" among the Cuban exiles in the United States. Bundy said he wanted to be sure the president understood what was at stake and would check with him.[26]

The final nail in the coffin of Lyndon Johnson's idea of how to oust Castro was delivered by the British government. In March Under Secretary of State George Ball gave a speech to the North Atlantic Council in which he said that Castro was trying to extend Communism throughout Latin America but could be stopped by economic sanctions. A month later, in April 1964, just as President Johnson was making his final decisions on Cuba, the British representative to the council responded. Britain, he said, was "opposed in principle to economic warfare. . . . [The] British are a trading people and trade is essence of their survival."[27] Without British participation, economic sanctions against Cuba were useless.

• • •

The independence of the Warren Commission allowed it to do one thing that the intelligence agencies could not: interview Fidel Castro. Staff lawyer William Coleman, who had once met Castro when he visited New York, interviewed him on his yacht off the coast of Cuba. The meeting lasted three hours. Castro denied any involvement in Kennedy's assassination. He said that he "admired" Jack Kennedy and "didn't think ill of him." Coleman conveyed the Cuban president's remarks to the commission but had no opinion about his truthfulness. According to author Philip Shenon, Coleman reported: "I'm not saying he didn't do it. But I came back and I said that I hadn't found out anything that would cause me to think there's proof that he *did* do it."[28]

• • •

As late as June 1964, a few stalwarts in the national security establishment were still discussing the Cuban situation. However, at a meeting with Bundy, McCone, Vance, and Alexis Johnson and Thomas Mann of the State Department, FitzGerald reported the grim news that the entire CIA spy network in the westernmost province of Pinar del Río had been "rolled up" by Castro's security forces and the key man executed.[29] And on July 2, the CIA reported to the White House that the opportunity to overthrow

Castro was gone: "Unless he dies or is otherwise removed from the scene, however, we think the chances of an overthrow of the regime or a major uprising against it . . . [in the next year or two] will remain slim."[30]

To add insult to injury, Carlos Tepedino, who had originally recruited Cubela for the CIA, told an FBI informant on July 29 that he had been acting as the contact man between the CIA and Cubela and that Cubela had constantly complained that the CIA "refused to furnish him with certain necessary equipment with which he could take effective action in Cuba." Tepedino warned the informant not to say anything that would permit the information to reach the CIA or become public because it might result in the death of people in Cuba as well as Tepedino.[31] But of course the informant told the FBI. There is no record that the FBI warned the CIA that one of its principal Cuban agents was talking. Indeed, as previously recounted, although the CIA polygraphed Tepedino a year after this FBI report, he apparently made no mention of what he told the bureau. Worse, Tepedino's saying that he and people in Cuba might be killed if the FBI told the CIA implies he thought either that the CIA might kill him, which is farfetched, or that the CIA was penetrated by Cuban intelligence, which seems quite possible. In any event, whether or not Lyndon Johnson fully understood the decisions he had been making on Cuba after he became president, the Kennedys' three-year attempt to oust Castro, and FitzGerald's yearlong covert-action plan to achieve that, ended in Dallas on November 22.

25

The Never-Ending Investigations

At a White House ceremony on September 24, 1964, Chief Justice Earl Warren handed his commission's 888-page report on John Kennedy's assassination to President Lyndon Johnson. Twenty-six volumes of transcripts, affidavits, and exhibits would follow. The Warren Report concluded that Lee Harvey Oswald acted alone in killing John Kennedy but for undetermined reasons. According to the report, Jack Ruby also acted alone in killing Oswald in a fit of grief and anger. With the imprimatur of the chief justice and the other distinguished commission members, the report was supposed to put an end to the rampant rumors and speculations that there was a conspiracy and that Oswald didn't fire the shots. In this regard the report failed miserably. Neither Lyndon Johnson nor Robert Kennedy believed it. Robert Kennedy's biographer, Evan Thomas, writes: "Possibly, RFK did not want to learn where the trail led."[1]

Issuance of the report did not end the investigation of John Kennedy's death though. While Hoover at the FBI had long wanted to close the book, Angleton at the CIA did not. He had followed the Warren Commission's work and knew that it had not excluded the possibility of a foreign intelligence service being responsible. To him the assassination would always be an open case, and he assigned analyst Raymond Rocca to continue to investigate.

Since Angleton's main adversary was the KGB, he focused on the Soviets. He admitted that the DGI might be responsible, but if so, the KGB would know.[2] On the other hand, Rocca wrote that the KGB didn't develop solid ties with the DGI until 1967.[3] Angleton's preoccupation with the KGB, and perhaps his inherently suspicious personality, also led him to suspect that those challenging the Warren Commission's findings might be part of a "disinformation" campaign. Disinformation means putting out false information to confuse. Thus after the Kennedy assassination, Angleton wondered if the KGB was responsible for the idea that Oswald was not the shooter. He worried about this in 1964 and then again in 1966–67, during the investigation by New Orleans district attorney Jim Garrison, who tried to prove there were other shooters who were employees of the CIA. To Angleton shifting attention from Oswald to the CIA was the kind of thing the KGB did. It isn't an unreasonable opinion. And to the end of his tenure with the CIA, Angleton held fast to the belief that if the Cubans were responsible for Kennedy's assassination, the KGB would know.[4]

Two CIA summaries of its dealings with Cubela underscore the dramatic change in attitudes about assassination after Kennedy's death. The first is based on Nestor Sanchez's meeting with him in later 1964. Sanchez apparently didn't even ask Cubela if he knew anything about the Kennedy assassination.[5] The second summary reports that although Cubela had been promised everything he needed, including silencers and rifles with telescopic sights at the November 22, 1963, meeting, the situation changed as a result of Kennedy's assassination: "Because of this fact, plans with subject changed and it was decided that this Agency could have no part in the assassination of a government leader (including Castro) and it would not aid subject in his attempt. This included the following. 'We would not furnish the silencer, nor scope nor any money for direct assassination: furthermore, we would not lift a finger to help subject escape from Cuba should he assassinate Castro.'"[6] Sanchez quibbled with the details of this document in his Church Committee testimony but not with the overall thrust.[7]

. . .

The next occasion when the CIA might have reconsidered the Warren Commission's findings came in 1965, when the CIA realized that the AMLASH operation was insecure. By then it already knew that Rolando Cubela, the asset it had inside Cuba, and Manuel Artime, whom it was funding for attacks on Cuba, had met. One meeting took place in a park with the two men talking about their strong contacts within the U.S. government, meaning the CIA. The meeting was completely insecure since each man had two companions with him, yet they schemed openly.[8] A short time later, the CIA began to question the security of the whole AMLASH network, which had grown to include a number of Cubans. In May 1965 CIA headquarters cabled its serious concerns to several stations, saying, among other things, that it was worried about the network and wasn't satisfied even with Cubela's good faith. On the copy of the cable that has been made public, someone has underscored the part about doubting Cubela's good faith and written in hand "this is nonsense."[9]

Be that as it may, less than a month later, CIA headquarters sent a dramatic cable to seven of its overseas stations, warning "that entire AMLASH group insecure and that further contact with key members of group constitutes menace" to CIA operations against Cuba as well as to the security of the CIA's staff in Western Europe. Contact with key members of the group was to be terminated as rapidly as possible, and no newly assigned CIA officers and no newly recruited agents were to be exposed to the group. In other words everyone should immediately disengage from any Cuban connected to the AMLASH operation. Carlos Tepedino, who had first introduced the CIA to Cubela, was undergoing "intensive interrogation."[10] A few days later, in an apparent attempt to calm a nervous overseas station chief, headquarters cabled: "No definite evidence AMLASH complex part of doubled op but certainly an insecure one."[11] The AMLASH operation was at an end.

Nine months later, in March 1966, Cuban security forces arrested Cubela and charged him with plotting with Manuel Artime to assassinate Fidel Castro.[12] The trial was quick, and Cubela was convicted. A CIA analysis of whether Cubela told Cuban intelligence about his long dealings with the CIA concluded that he had not. None of those with whom he had been dealing in those days had been arrested. The same analysis dismissed claims by friends of Cubela who said he never really intended to assassinate Castro.[13] Cubela was eventually released from prison and settled in Spain.[14]

...

The CIA claims it did not connect its plots against Castro to Kennedy's death until 1967, when *Washington Post* columnist Drew Pearson broke several stories to this effect. His diary notes, which he donated to the Lyndon Baines Johnson Library and Museum in Texas, shed light on what happened. Like many others Pearson had a continuing interest in the assassination. His diary mentions a lunch with Chief Justice Earl Warren in October 1966 at which the subject came up. The previous day Pearson had been on a radio program where he was questioned about Mark Lane, a prominent critic of the Warren Report. Pearson told the chief justice that Lane said the Warren Report was "all wet." Pearson suggested to Warren that someone should write a rebuttal to Lane, but Warren dismissed the suggestion: "I can't be in the position of answering these books. I haven't read any of them. And I'm not going to. The report is going to stand or fall on what's in it. We did an accurate job. . . . While we were writing our report, Mark Lane was touring Europe making these extravagant representations so we called him back here to give him the benefit of a hearing and give us any information he could help us with. He refused to divulge anything."[15]

Pearson, though, remained open to new theories, and one literally showed up at his door a few months later, in January 1967. Washington lawyer Edward P. Morgan, who knew Pearson, went to his house in Georgetown and said that he had an important tale to tell about the assassination. Pearson ushered him to the seclusion of a back room in the house to hear him out. Morgan said clients of his had worked with the CIA to kill Fidel Castro while Kennedy was president; Castro learned of this; and, he retaliated.[16] Morgan testified later that the information came from conversations with Robert Maheu and Johnny Roselli.[17]

Pearson relayed Morgan's story to the chief justice and later reported Warren's reaction to Morgan: "The Chief Justice had gotten up and walked around his office for fully five minutes. And he was very distressed apparently by it."[18] Pearson asked Warren to talk to Morgan, but the chief justice didn't want to do this. He wanted to tell the FBI and let it handle the matter. Pearson said he preferred that Warren tell the Secret Service.[19]

On January 31, 1967, the chief justice passed the story to James Rowley, who was director of the Secret Service. Rowley supposedly asked Morgan to see him, but when Morgan failed to respond, Rowley informed FBI director Hoover of the allegations on February 13. The FBI refused to investigate.[20]

Pearson also told the story to President Johnson. The president called acting attorney general Ramsey Clark on February 20. Johnson recorded the conversation.

JOHNSON: You know this story going around about the CIA and uh their trying to get, sending in folks to get Castro.

CLARK: To assassinate Castro?

JOHNSON: Have you got the whole story laid out in front of you? Do you know what it is? Has anybody ever told you all the story?

CLARK: No.

JOHNSON: I think you ought to have that. It is incredible. I don't believe there is a thing in the world to it. I don't think we ought to seriously consider it, but I think you ought to know it.

CLARK: Who would I ask?

JOHNSON: I have heard it from three or four. I've forgotten who has come in. I'll have to check.

CLARK: Does the Bureau have it?

JOHNSON: No. I don't think so. You might ask them. Pearson, Drew Pearson, came and gave it to me. Said Morgan told him, Hoffa's lawyer. He says that they have a man that was involved that was brought in to the CIA with a number of others and instructed by the CIA and the Attorney General [Robert Kennedy] to assassinate Castro after the Bay of Pigs.

CLARK: I've heard that uh I've heard that much, I just haven't heard names and places.

JOHNSON: Well let's see who it is. Let's see. I think it would look very bad on us if we had it reported a number of times and we just didn't pay any, just laughed, if this is true. . . .

JOHNSON: But, anyway. That following this Castro said they had these pills and they was supposed to take them when they caught them and they didn't get to take their pills so he tortured them. And they told him all about it, who was present, and why they did it. So he said okay we'll just take care of that. So then he called Oswald and a group in and told them about this meeting and go set it up and get the job done.[21]

A few weeks later, on March 2, 1967, Texas governor John Connally, who had been riding in the same car as President Kennedy in Dallas and who was wounded by the same bullet that had passed through Kennedy's neck, called Johnson. Connally wanted to alert him to developments in the investigation by Jim Garrison in New Orleans. Connally also summarized information he had picked up from reporters.

> After the Missile Crisis, President Kennedy and Khrushchev had made a deal to leave Castro in power. But about six months after the Missile Crisis was over, the CIA was instructed to assassinate Castro and sent people into Cuba. Some of them were captured and tortured. And Castro and his people and I assume Che Guevara heard the whole story. The information they [the reporters] have here, which they're not going to run, is that President Kennedy did not give the order to the CIA but that some other person extremely close to President Kennedy did. They did not name names but the inference was very clear and the inference was that it was his brother who ordered the CIA to send people into Cuba to assassinate Castro. That then one of Castro's lieutenants as a reprisal measure sent in four teams to the United States to assassinate President Kennedy. That Lee Harvey Oswald was one of the members of a team operating out of New Orleans.[22]

Johnson heard Connally out before responding, "We've had that story on about three occasions." He explained his information was coming from Morgan. Johnson felt the allegations were serious. "Now with this CIA thing breaking and the thing turning as it did and *reconstructing the requests that were made of me back there right after I became president* I have talked some more about it and I've got the AG [Attorney General Ramsey Clark] coming down to see me tomorrow night to spend the weekend with me. I thought I'd go over it again with him so that Hoover and them could watch it very carefully." Johnson dismissed the Garrison investigation as groundless: "They say there is not anything to the Garrison story. At least Hoover says so, as near as he can tell."[23]

Johnson seems to be saying that he was told something shortly after becoming president that he connected with the Morgan story. Perhaps when John McCone spent more than an hour alone with the president on November 28 at Johnson's house in northwest Washington, he briefed the new president on the AMLASH operation. In addition Johnson said "requests" were made of him then, but he didn't explain what those might be. He may have been asked to approve steering the Warren Commission clear of the AMLASH plot.

Robert Kennedy apparently heard the story too. By this time he was a senator. On March 4 his secretary called Richard Helms, who had risen to be CIA director, and asked for a copy of the memorandum about the underworld assassination plots that Kennedy had been shown in 1962. In response Helms had lunch with Kennedy and let him read the 1962 report. He did and handed it back to Helms.[24]

Three days later, on March 7, Drew Pearson published the information he had in his column in the *Washington Post*: "The publicity over New Orleans District Attorney Jim Garrison's investigation of a 'Kennedy assassination plot' has focused attention in Washington on a reported CIA plan in 1963 to assassinate Cuba's Fidel Castro, which according to some sources, may have resulted in a counterplot by Castro to assassinate President Kennedy."[25]

A week later, on March 13, Lyndon Johnson entertained Chief Justice Warren and Drew Pearson at the White House. Pearson's diary records that they talked about Kennedy's assassination, but it provides no details. A few words in the diary have been deleted, seemingly for privacy reasons, but nothing suggests that the men discussed Morgan's allegations.[26] They may have, but if so Pearson did not confide the conversation to his diary.

Nonetheless, a few days later, on March 17, presidential assistant Marvin Watson called the FBI and ordered it to interview Morgan. Two FBI agents did so and reported what he told them. According to the FBI reports, Morgan said clients "on the fringe of the underworld" told him they had worked with a governmental agency to assassinate Castro. Castro captured some of those involved, tortured them, and learned what was going on. Castro decided "if that was the way President Kennedy wanted it, he too could engage in the same tactics." According to the FBI report, Morgan said Castro dispatched "teams" to the United States to kill Kennedy and this information had come from sources close to Castro "who had been initially placed there to carry out the original project [Castro's assassination]."[27]

When the White House received the FBI report, it immediately asked the CIA to investigate. CIA director Helms referred the matter to the CIA inspector general, J. S. Earman. He and three other senior CIA officers spent a month interviewing those involved in the plots against Castro and reviewing the documents. The resulting report was 133 pages long. After Helms read it, he ordered Earman to destroy all the notes and keep only the original, ribbon copy. About one-quarter of what is known as the Inspector General Report, or IG Report, dealt with the AMLASH operation.

The only mention of President Kennedy's assassination was the following: "*It is very likely that at the very moment President Kennedy was shot a CIA officer was meeting with a Cuban agent in Paris and giving him an assassination device for use against Castro.* Sanchez states that he received an OPIM [immediate] cable from FitzGerald that night or early the next morning telling him that everything was off. We do not find such a cable in the AMLASH file."[28]

That Kennedy's assassination should be given such small, passing mention is bizarre. The inspector general's investigation was prompted by allegations that Castro had Kennedy killed in retaliation for the CIA plots against him and by President Johnson's order that the CIA investigate.[29] Helms himself told the Church Committee that the Pearson column led directly to his ordering the IG Report: "I believe that there not only had been at that time a column by Drew Pearson but I belive [sic] that Drew Pearson had spoken privately to the President about the subject matter of that column and the President asked me about the facts and I said, well, I would have to try to ascertain them, and it was a result of that that I asked the Inspector General to get into this matter."[30] Yet apparently no one at the CIA or the White House was bothered by the fact that the CIA report was not responsive to the president's request, which stemmed from allegations that Castro had retaliated for the assassination plots against him.

On May 10, 1967, Richard Helms traveled to the White House to brief the president. Helms, when asked by the Rockefeller Commission if he ever had a conversation with anybody about Castro's retaliation, testified: "No. I don't recall discussing that with anybody. I don't recall the thought ever having occurred to me at the time. The first time I ever heard such a theory as that enunciated was in a very peculiar way by President Johnson. I don't even remember what time it was. I heard him say in my presence . . . that because President Kennedy had been responsible for the death of the President Diem of Vietnam that this was why President Kennedy had been shot himself, and I couldn't see how the two things were even remotely connected. . . . But I never heard of retaliation by attempts on Castro's life." Helms's claim that Johnson was the first to mention this can't be taken literally since when the White House ordered him to investigate, it surely explained that there were allegations that Castro had retaliated.

The Rockefeller Commission questioner, bothered by Helms's evasive answer, pressed him: "I'm not asking you about a story Ambassador [Helms was ambassador to Iran at the time]. . . . Did the connection [with Cuba] ever enter your mind?" "I don't recall its having done so," Helms replied.[31]

Presumably, the conversation with Johnson that Helms was referring to took place on May 10, when he briefed the president on the CIA report. George Christian, Johnson's press secretary, was there too. The author once talked to him and asked what had transpired at the meeting. He couldn't recall. However, he added, the president was "a conspiracy buff himself" and once wondered about South Vietnamese involvement in Kennedy's death. Christian said Johnson "always showed displeasure" at what had been going on under Kennedy. He didn't like the overthrow of Diem in Vietnam either.[32]

Helms and Christian seemed to be remembering the same meeting. Thus despite the fact that the 1967 inquiry was prompted by allegations from underworld figures that Castro had killed Kennedy in retaliation for attempts against his life and despite the fact that Helms was at the White House to report the results of the CIA investigation into those allegations, President Johnson's thoughts had shifted to whether Kennedy's death was somehow related to Diem's death in the coup in Vietnam.[33] Johnson let the matter drop and did not order further investigation.

Shortly before his own death, however, Johnson returned to thinking Castro may have retaliated. In an interview with the reporter Leo Janos, the former president said he had ordered Attorney General Ramsey Clark to look into the possibility that Castro had Kennedy killed in retaliation for the CIA plots. Johnson added, with seeming disgust, that Clark reported back after only two weeks of work to say he didn't find anything. Johnson told the reporter that Kennedy was running "a damned Murder, Inc. in the Caribbean," and Johnson still suspected Castro had retaliated.[34] Johnson's phrase, "Murder, Inc.," shows that he was well aware of the CIA's plots against Castro under Kennedy. The former president said much the same thing to Howard K. Smith of ABC New and Walter Cronkite of CBS.[35]

...

The IG Report was far from the last word on the subject. In 1975 the U.S. Senate began looking into CIA misdeeds that had been discovered in the course of Senate hearings on the Watergate affair, which ended Richard Nixon's presidency. To forestall Senate action, then president Gerald Ford created a special commission chaired by and named for Vice President Nelson Rockefeller to investigate. The gambit failed. The Senate proceeded with its own investigation under Idaho senator Frank Church. The Rockefeller Commission and the Church Committee conducted separate investigations seriatim.

The staff director of the Rockefeller Commission was attorney David Belin. He had been on the staff of the Warren Commission and was naturally concerned when he learned that the CIA had withheld from the commission information about the assassination operations against Castro. Belin interviewed the CIA expert on the Kennedy assassination, Raymond Rocca, about a possible connection between the CIA plots and Kennedy's death. Rocca wrote a memorandum for the record of their conversation. According to the memorandum, Belin alluded generally to plots against Castro but apparently did not tell Rocca the specifics of the AMLASH operation. Rocca responded by saying such information would have been relevant, but he still felt the KGB might have been involved.[36]

The Church Committee, for its part, conducted a broad investigation into CIA plots against foreign leaders, including but not limited to Castro. Senators Gary Hart of Colorado and Richard Schweiker of Pennsylvania were on a subcommittee that looked specifically at the Kennedy assassination and for evidence that Castro had retaliated. The committee as a whole issued a report on the CIA assassination plots and concluded that there was no evidence any president had approved them.[37] That is, according to the Senate Committee, the CIA was a rogue elephant. The Hart-Schweiker subcommittee report faulted both the FBI and the CIA in their work for the Warren Commission in 1964. It concluded that the FBI investigation was too narrowly focused and the CIA did not use its full capabilities. It went further though, stating, "Why senior officials of the FBI and CIA permitted the investigation to go forward, in light of these deficiencies, and why they permitted the Warren Commission to reach its conclusion without all relevant information is still unclear." The Senate report speculated that it was possible that these failures were the result of conscious decisions by senior agency officials.[38] It could not prove retaliation but said further investigation was in order.

Two of the men involved in the underworld plots against Castro, Sam Giancana and Johnny Roselli, were murdered at the time of the Church Committee revelations. Giancana was killed before he could testify. He was shot multiple times around the mouth.[39] Roselli was killed a few months after the Church Committee's investigation ended and its reports were issued. His body was found stuffed in a fifty-five-gallon barrel floating in the ocean off the Florida coast. The cause of death was suffocation, and his legs had been broken.[40] The murders were never solved.

Shortly after Roselli's death, the permanent Senate Intelligence

Committee interviewed Santos Trafficante, whom Roselli had brought into his plot. His statements were not under oath. Trafficante said that when he had dinner with Roselli a few months before his murder, Roselli didn't seem concerned for his life. Trafficante didn't know why Giancana and Roselli were killed, but according to the interview notes, he "does fear" for his own life and "keeps their deaths in the back of his mind." He further said that he "accept[ed] the fact Lee Harvey Oswald killed President Kennedy; however, there [was] the possibility that Castro was involved because he would [have] benefit[ted] more than anyone else." He added that Roselli believed Castro's people were behind President Kennedy's assassination as retaliation for the "Bay of Pigs."[41] Trafficante's characterization of Roselli's state of mind is not accurate though; Roselli believed Castro had retaliated for the assassination plots against him, not for the "Bay of Pigs."

Following release of the two Senate reports, the House of Representatives created a committee to take yet another look at the assassination of President Kennedy. It released its final report in 1979. The committee interviewed Fidel Castro and Rolando Cubela. Castro denied involvement in the Kennedy assassination, while Cubela essentially denied being a double agent. Like the Hart-Schweiker report, the House Committee faulted the CIA's investigation of the Kennedy assassination but said it could find no evidence of Soviet or Cuban involvement with Oswald.[42]

26

John Kennedy and the CIA

Even as a senator, John Kennedy believed that the United States should have flexible response capabilities. It shouldn't have to face the choice of going to nuclear war or doing nothing in international crises. Once he became president, Kennedy seemed to realize that assassination was one form of flexible response. It was on his mind soon after he took office in 1961, when he casually mentioned it to Senator George Smathers. Kennedy said he disapproved. If so he failed to communicate his feelings to others in the White House. Someone there told the CIA to create an assassination capability. So Bill Harvey, America's James Bond, was charged with developing ZRRIFLE, an executive action program that would use trained assassins. At the same time, CIA scientist Sidney Gottlieb gave a batch of cigars coated with botulinum toxin to James O'Connell for the purpose of killing Castro. Those believing in this form of flexible response felt it was better to assassinate an opposing leader than to go to war against his army.[1]

Although the confluence of Kennedy's words and the CIA's actions could be dismissed as coincidences, a pattern developed of Kennedy talking about assassination and the CIA doing something about it. In November 1961 Kennedy asked Tad Szulc of the *New York Times*, "What would you think if I ordered Castro to be assassinated?" Szulc said it would be morally wrong, and it wouldn't change things in Cuba. Kennedy agreed. But a week later, Bill Harvey was told to take over contact with the underworld figures who were trying to kill Castro. Harvey was also asked if his trained assassins might be able to do the job. Three days before Kennedy's assassination, Richard Helms met separately with Robert and John Kennedy, and on the same day, the CIA approved telling Rolando Cubela it would give him assassination weapons, including rifles with telescopic sights. On the eve of the assassination, John Kennedy talked about how easy it would be for him to be assassinated by a man with a rifle and telescopic sight, and the next day, November 22, 1963, Nestor Sanchez promised Cubela that the CIA would give him such rifles to kill Castro.

Except for CIA director John McCone, who denied any assassination effort took place on his watch, almost every CIA officer questioned in later investigations testified that they assumed the director and the president knew, although none had proof. When asked about McCone's denial of knowledge, Richard Helms responded with a classic double negative: "I honestly didn't recall that Mr. McCone was not informed."[2]

Senator Church's question of whether the CIA was a rogue elephant looms over these events. Did John and Robert Kennedy authorize the CIA to get rid of Castro, or was it charging off on its own?

For the first two years of the Kennedy administration, CIA efforts to kill Castro were channeled through organized crime. There were various reasons for this, but they boiled down to the fact that many at the agency thought assassination was immoral. Still, if murder had to be committed, they felt it was better that someone else should do it. Besides, the CIA reasoned, the mob issued contracts regularly and knew how to do it.

In fact the men the agency chose, Maheu, Giancana, and Roselli, had no resources of their own, and the men they acquired for the project were no match for Cuban security. They dispatched agents, money, and poison to Cuba to no avail. Maheu and Giancana were not contributing to the operation except by providing introductions to others, such as Trafficante, who knew people in Cuba. Roselli was the man meeting with agents and giving them the poisons. It was, as Maheu said, Roselli's contract.

In March 1962 Giancana's participation became a major embarrassment for the Kennedys. Robert Kennedy apparently did not know the details of whom the CIA was using since he was pushing for prosecution of Giancana. And just when the government caught the mobster ordering an illegal wiretap, the CIA intervened to block the investigation. Even worse FBI director Hoover discovered that the president was having a relationship with Giancana's girlfriend and confronted Kennedy with the information.

The sordid details were covered up, but everyone, including the president, the attorney general, and the CIA, had paid a price for doing business with organized crime. Nonetheless, the underworld assassination operation continued. Bill Harvey was running it by this time and doubted it would produce results. He cut Maheu and Giancana out and worked only with Roselli for security reasons, or so he claimed. This rationale may have been a cover story. The real reason for dropping Giancana may have been the attorney general's animosity toward the man or the president's alleged affair with his girlfriend. In any event Harvey passed more poison tablets to Roselli in May 1962.

The nasty subject of assassination continued to plague the national security establishment. In August 1962 Defense Secretary Robert McNamara created a flap by using the word "assassination" at a national security meeting, and General Lansdale foolishly put the word "liquidation" in a memorandum he circulated. The time spent in phone calls, meetings, and memos to correct and cover up the mistakes might have been better spent thinking about what the Soviets were doing. They were sending nuclear-capable missiles to Cuba.

John Kennedy performed well in the Cuban Missile Crisis, but it ended on a possibly ominous note. There may have been an underworld team in Cuba at the end of the crisis with orders to assassinate Fidel Castro. If it tried to carry out its mission, the president's settlement would, to say the least, unravel.

This version of what happened gains support from John Connally's 1967 telephone conversation with President Johnson, saying he had heard that Castro learned of the underworld plans to kill him from agents captured after the missile crisis and that this was contrary to Kennedy's pledge not to invade Cuba. This interpretation is also consistent with Harvey's testimony and with Ed Morgan's statement to the FBI, alleging Castro forces captured and gained confessions from underworld assassins. Harvey's displays of contempt for the attorney general were reason enough for him to be transferred away from Cuban affairs, but having assassins in Cuba at the end of the missile crisis despite the president's no-invasion pledge, if discovered by Robert Kennedy, would have been unpardonable.

In 1963 Desmond FitzGerald took Harvey's place as head of CIA efforts to oust Castro. He had the personality, résumé, and connections to work with Robert Kennedy. He also had a plan. It was to use the whole arsenal of covert-action weapons—economic sanctions, propaganda, and sabotage—to create unrest in Cuba, particularly among the military. When all was in place, he would orchestrate a coup. He just needed the right man in Cuba.

To say Rolando Cubela was that man would be a stretch. He was a bird in the hand. He had a mercurial temperament; he was a control problem; he was moody; he was egotistical; he had no tolerance for the details of spy craft, such as secret writing and communications; he was far too open about his opposition to the Communists in Cuba; he wasn't shy about telling people he disliked Fidel Castro; and, unbeknown to FitzGerald, he had no intention of doing what he bragged he would do. The CIA focused on the two qualities that Cubela did have: access to Fidel and his boast that he would undertake the big job.

Simply assassinating Castro wasn't enough any more, however. CIA analysts predicted that if this happened, someone equally bad or worse would take his place. So the CIA tried to play along with Cubela's bravado about how he would kill Castro while it used him to lay the groundwork for a coup. But as happened often in Cuban affairs, the CIA was viewing its operations only from its own perspective and not thinking about what its adversary was doing.

FitzGerald acknowledged at White House meetings that Cuban intelligence was good. Castro regularly detected and rounded up CIA agents sent into Cuba. Castro had once found Rolando Cubela useful by dangling him before dissidents in Cuba, like a fisherman dangles a lure for the fish, to see who would bite. Cuban intelligence arrested those who did.

But Cuban intelligence was even better than this. It had to be. It thwarted an estimated thirty-two assassination plots against Fidel Castro in the early 1960s, both homegrown and external.[3] Castro seemed to learn almost instantly that the CIA was meeting with Cubela in Porto Alegre, Brazil, on September 7, 1963. At the Brazilian embassy in Havana that night, Castro pulled aside UPI reporter Daniel Harker to say that if the United States continued to meet with terrorists who were out to get him, then its own leaders would not be safe. The message seems unmistakable. Castro knew about Cubela, and his threat was against John Kennedy. Castro wasn't telegraphing his punch though; he was warning the CIA to stop trying to kill him. As explained in appendix A, Cuban intelligence was so good that it acquired a copy of Kennedy's November 18, 1963, speech and gave it to Cuban television, which broadcast a rebuttal before Kennedy even delivered the speech.

In late 1963 Castro seemed to know that the CIA was plotting to kill him and seemed to be trying to decide if John Kennedy approved. Cubela may have been in league with Castro, and so was a double agent, or he may have been unwitting. He talked openly of his unhappiness with Castro around people who shouldn't hear such things. FitzGerald knew this. He heard, on the one hand, that Castro had used Cubela as a dangle and, on the other, that Castro suspected Cubela of being disloyal. Nonetheless, FitzGerald continued the operation.

While the CIA didn't react to Castro's threat, others in the U.S. government did. They spent two months in meetings to consider what Castro might do and how to protect against it. No one thought to tell the FBI or the Secret Service. Nor did anyone consider the very thing Castro had threatened: the assassination of John Kennedy.

If this weren't enough to dissuade FitzGerald, there was opposition within CIA. His own security officer thought that the AMLASH operation was insecure and Cubela was a dangle. He proved to be right at least on the first count. The head of the CIA's JMWAVE station advised FitzGerald not to meet with Cubela. Many in Washington DC knew that FitzGerald was CIA; he and his wife were significant figures in Washington society; her name was associated with the Kennedy family in the *Washington Post*. There would be no plausible denial if anything went wrong.

FitzGerald wouldn't stop though. When Cubela asked for proof that John Kennedy approved what the CIA was doing, FitzGerald obliged. He flew to Paris and met with Cubela as the personal representative of the president's brother. This wasn't a charade; Robert Kennedy was prepared to meet Cubela in Washington to the same end if necessary. FitzGerald certainly wasn't a rogue elephant at this stage of the operation; he had authority from Robert Kennedy. Whatever label one wants to put on Cubela, double agent, dangle, blabbermouth, or watched man, Castro seemed to be using him to answer the question, Was the CIA a rogue elephant, or did it take its orders from John Kennedy.[4]

The assassination of President Diem of Vietnam in a coup on November 1, 1963, just days after FitzGerald's Paris meeting with Cubela, was undoubtedly interpreted by Castro to mean that he was next. But Castro didn't need to look beyond Kennedy's speech in Miami on November 18 if he wanted to know the president's intentions. Kennedy said Castro was a barrier to be removed.

Cubela wanted more than words from the CIA though. He wanted assassination weapons, and this demand gave the agency pause. Cubela complained that while the CIA and he were in agreement on what needed to be done, the CIA would not give him the small tools to do the job. The tools were sniper rifles with telescopic sights and a pen that fired bullets or a poison dart.

The CIA took the request for the pen at face value. Richard Helms testified that the CIA gave it to him not because the agency wanted to assassinate Castro but rather as an attempt to "placate" Cubela.[5] However, another, worrisome way of viewing his request is that he wanted an exotic, nasty weapon that by its very appearance would say "Made by the CIA" if Castro should get his hands on it and display it for propaganda purposes.

Not until November 19, 1963, did the CIA make the decision to meet Cubela's demands. The CIA's Dr. Gunn worked all that night to craft the poison device. Afterward the operatives at the CIA claimed that Gunn didn't understand what Cubela wanted. What he made was a Paper Mate pen with a hypodermic needle inside, not a dart pen. Cubela may have been disappointed with the device because it was crude and not exotic enough. Richard Helms criticized the pen on this ground.

The Paper Mate looked dangerous enough for Sanchez to dislike carrying it on his person to the Paris meeting. He gave it to

Cubela though, or maybe he didn't. He couldn't recall. He had risen to be a senior and trusted CIA case officer, but he couldn't remember if his Cuban agent had walked off with a compromising assassination weapon at the very moment the president was assassinated by a Cuban sympathizer.

This same November 19, Richard Helms met with Robert Kennedy and then the president about the so-called Venezuelan arms cache. Helms said the purpose of the meetings was to show the attorney general and the president the hard evidence they had been looking for to prove that Castro was exporting the revolution to other Latin American countries. This much seems true. However, Helms may also have discussed whether the CIA should give Cubela the assassination weapons he wanted. The coincidence of the decision to give Cubela the weapons on the same day Helms met with the Kennedys about Cuba powerfully suggests something like that happened. Helms subscribed to the doctrine of plausible denial: he would never say, not even when testifying under oath to Congress, that the president had talked to him about assassination. The only other possibility is that he was the consummate rogue elephant: he met with Robert and John Kennedy on the very day he made the decision to give Cubela assassination weapons but did not mention this to the Kennedys or to anyone else, not even Director McCone, President Johnson, or the Warren Commission.

Of course telling Robert Kennedy about Cubela's plans was dangerous because he was meeting with his friends in the Cuban exile community that week, and everyone, except perhaps Robert Kennedy, knew that the exiles had been penetrated at the highest level.

Later that same November 19, Fidel Castro finally granted French reporter Jean Daniel the interview he had been wanting. Earlier in the day, William Attwood had told the Cubans of the preconditions for peace talks, so that overture seemed closed. But Daniel had interviewed Kennedy a month earlier and was in Havana waiting for a chance to interview Castro. His interview with Daniel that night seemed no more a coincidence than the meetings Helms had with the Kennedys earlier in the day. Castro and Daniel talked from ten in the evening until four o'clock the next morning. Castro seemed to be trying to decide which was the real John

Kennedy, the man working with Cubela to kill him, or the man exploring rapprochement through Jean Daniel, the reporter in front of him. And was Kennedy really abandoning peace talks?

On the evening of November 20 in Paris, a CIA officer telephoned Cubela to ask him to delay his return to Cuba to meet with Sanchez. It would be, the case officer said cryptically, the meeting Cubela had requested. That is the CIA was prepared to give Cubela assassination weapons. From Castro's perspective, if he knew, this would have been proof positive. John Kennedy was not just trying to organize a coup among the military in Cuba; he had finally shown his hand and authorized Castro's assassination.

Castro may have turned the tables on John Kennedy. He had caught the president red-handed authorizing assassination. It was easy to prove that FitzGerald was CIA and had met with Cubela and that Kennedy had called Castro a barrier to be removed in a public speech. And there was that nasty device the CIA was going to give Cubela on Friday. John Kennedy would have trouble plausibly denying that he was trying to kill the Cuban leader.

27

Lyndon Johnson and the CIA

L yndon Johnson was ill prepared on foreign affairs when he succeeded to the presidency. He inherited a Cuban policy he knew little about. He had not attended national security meetings on the subject. Robert Kennedy was overseeing Cuban operations, and he was about as fond of Johnson as he was of Bill Harvey. The CIA clearly should have briefed the new president on the assassination aspect of the AMLASH operation regardless of whether John Kennedy had authorized giving Cubela assassination weapons.

There is no public record of such a briefing though. Johnson later characterized Kennedy's Cuban policy as "Murder, Inc.," but this could have been based on Helms's briefing of Johnson in 1967 about the inspector general's report. On the other hand, earlier that year Johnson had talked to Governor Connally about allegations of assassination plots against Castro and retaliation and said that he had been told something like this shortly after taking office. His strong hostility toward FitzGerald's attempt in December 1963 to continue Kennedy's Cuban policy—a policy he called hypocritical because it consisted of both a peace initiative and a coup attempt—suggests that he knew then about the AMLASH operation.

Nonetheless, almost immediately after the assassination, the U.S. government sent out signals that any public investigation of Kennedy's death should steer clear of the matter of foreign involvement. Less than an hour after Oswald's murder on November 24, FBI director Hoover called the White House and advised it to avoid public hearings because they would raise questions about Oswald's connections to a KGB assassination officer and "muddy the waters internationally."[1] Hoover gave the same advice to Deputy Attorney General Katzenbach.

On November 26 Katzenbach said as much to the White House, stressing the need for rebutting thoughts that the assassination was a Communist conspiracy. He surely had cleared the memo with his boss, Robert Kennedy. U.S. ambassador-at-large Llewellyn Thomson gave a similar message to the Soviet ambassador. And Lyndon Johnson assured Deputy Premier Mikoyan that he would not invade Cuba. In short, while Richard Helms said that the CIA's immediate reaction was to wonder if the Soviets or the Chinese were responsible, upon reflection the U.S. government seemingly decided not to fan a flame that might lead to war.

Within a day of the assassination, the FBI instructed its field offices not to develop new leads. The CIA did not make such a hasty retreat. As late as November 28, 1963, it told its Mexico City station that the assassination may have been the work of a conspiracy, including possible foreign involvement. Yet its own historian has characterized the CIA investigation as "passive, reactive and selective."[2]

Katzenbach's advice to the White House to tamp down notions of foreign involvement is reflected in the introduction to the Warren Report, which seems lifted from his post-assassination memorandum to the White House: "As speculation about the existence of a foreign or domestic conspiracy became widespread, committees in both Houses of Congress weighed the desirability of congressional hearings." President Johnson, it continues, established the Warren Commission to avoid parallel investigations. As for any such foreign conspiracy, the commission found no evidence that Oswald was "employed, persuaded, or encouraged by any foreign government."[3]

While the commission was receptive to evidence of foreign involvement, it didn't go out of the way to look for it. The full commission was never briefed on how foreign intelligence agencies conducted assassinations. It relied solely on a casual CIA briefing of one staff lawyer. And of course, no one connected to the Warren Commission, except Allen Dulles, knew the CIA had no success with professional assassins but instead contracted out the dirty work to the underworld, a fact that might have relevance to Jack Ruby's underworld connections.

The commission knew but did not mention in its report that Oswald met with Valery Kostikov at the Soviet embassy in Mexico City and that Kostikov was in the assassination department of the KGB. There was no reason for the commission to keep this secret from the public other than to avoid inflaming conspiracy theories; the Soviets knew Kostikov was in Department 13. Indeed, they labeled Oswald's letter mentioning him a "provocation," meaning that they thought someone had Oswald do this in order to lay the blame on them.

The commission did not know that a name trace on Kostikov would lead investigators to Cubela, that the CIA worked for three years with the underworld to assassinate Castro, or that the CIA had signaled Cubela only two days before Kennedy was killed that it would give him assassination weapons.

The commission knew about Oswald's contact with Silvia Duran, a Mexican national working for the Cubans in Mexico City. It also knew that she had had an affair with Carlos Lechuga, Cuba's ambassador to the UN. It didn't know that John Kennedy had been taking a two-track approach to Castro, trying to overthrow him with Cubela, on the one hand, and trying to negotiate with him through Lechuga, on the other. No one with the exception of Desmond Fitz-Gerald, Richard Helms, and John McCone could know that Oswald, in his short visit to Mexico City, had stumbled into people connected to both tracks of Kennedy's Cuban policy.

Although the CIA told the commission that Cuban intelligence probably met with Oswald in Mexico City, the commission did not include this in its report. Maybe it did not want to inflame the public, or maybe it did not understand the import. The CIA certainly did.

And then there was Oswald's August 1963 letter to Arnold Johnson of the Communist Party, saying he planned to move to the Baltimore-Washington area. The obvious question was whether Oswald was thinking of moving there to be closer to the president. But the commission conducted only a cursory investigation. It didn't ask Marina Oswald if she knew. It did question Arnold Johnson.

His lawyer, John Abt, wrote later about the interview: "It quickly became obvious that neither the FBI nor the Warren Commission were really interested in digging into the case, to really discover if there was a conspiracy. They certainly weren't interested in trying to show the Communists were a party to the matter."[4]

That so many major agencies of government independently made the decision to avoid an aggressive investigation into the possibility of a foreign conspiracy seems unlikely. More likely the White House may have issued orders not to look into a foreign conspiracy in Kennedy's death, at least not publicly, but there is no direct evidence of this. In sum the rogue elephant possibility—that the CIA promised Cubela assassination weapons without John Kennedy's authorization and withheld this information from the assassination investigation without Lyndon Johnson's authorization—is too incredible and too appalling to accept.

...

Regardless of whether he was told about AMLASH, Lyndon Johnson's thoughts were elsewhere. Within weeks of becoming president, he ended John Kennedy's covert war against Castro, ninety miles away, and focused on his own overt war in Vietnam, nine thousand miles away.[5] Johnson may also have wanted to avoid besmirching the memory of President Kennedy, whom the public had come to view as a martyr. And any suggestion that there was a conspiracy might impeach the legitimacy of Johnson's own presidency. There were good political reasons for Johnson to authorize the CIA to keep the AMLASH operation secret.

Richard Helms had a simple answer to the question of why he didn't tell anyone outside the CIA. When asked by the Church Committee, he replied, "I was not the Director [of the CIA] at that time."[6] He wasn't passing the buck. He was diplomatically reminding his questioner that John McCone was the director, that McCone had been appointed by John Kennedy, and that McCone was a personal friend of Robert Kennedy. If the president or the Warren Commission were to be informed, McCone, not Helms, was the one to do it.

Others, like FitzGerald, seemed to believe that the United States was about to invade Cuba anyway. In that case the Cuban leaders would be captured and interrogated. The Defense Department hurriedly reviewed a contingency plan for invading Cuba at this time. And in early December, FitzGerald put the finishing touches on a memorandum that foresaw an escalation of not only covert action but also overt action, such as air strikes, against Cuba.

Ted Shackley, head of the CIA's JMWAVE station in Florida that was targeted at Cuba, offered the most likely possibility. He said that the CIA officers who knew about the AMLASH operation could have conducted their own investigation separate from the Warren Commission effort. In context Shackley's comment seemed more informed advice than speculation.[7] Yet there is absolutely no evidence of any such investigation in the hundreds of thousands of documents in the National Archives on the Kennedy assassination.

...

The investigation of the Kennedy assassination should be viewed as an intelligence failure, one of the greatest in American history. A litany of small failures spread across the government. The FBI didn't get the hotel registers in Dallas to see who might have been visiting the city at the time of the assassination. It didn't get phone records for calls to and from Oswald's rooming house or from Cuba to the United States in this period.[8]

The FBI didn't pursue questions about the suspicious travels of Gilberto Lopez from Tampa to Texas to Mexico to Havana. The FBI had the names of the drivers and engine numbers of the cars that crossed the border from Texas to Mexico after Kennedy's murder but didn't bother to pursue the matter.[9]

The CIA learned that a Mexican Federal Judicial Police source claimed that Lopez had been "involved in President Kennedy's assassination."[10] The CIA did not investigate. It withheld the report from the Warren Commission. When lawyers from its staff, William Coleman and David Slawson, went to Mexico City a few weeks later, the station chief did not mention Lopez but instead said he had no evidence of a conspiracy. If there had been one, he continued, the CIA would have had some indication of it.[11]

There is also the unexplained the missing report on the assassination from the government of Mexico. The Warren Commission drafted a letter for the U.S. embassy in Mexico to send the government of Mexico, asking for "as detailed a report as is feasible on the investigation conducted in Mexico by national agencies into the activities of Lee Harvey Oswald during the time that he [was] known to have been in Mexico. The embassy would also be most appreciative if the report should include a description of those measures which the government of Mexico may have taken immediately upon hearing of the assassination of President Kennedy, such as special vigilance at points of entry, and other steps related to the aftermath of the assassination."[12] There is no evidence Mexico furnished such a report. Perhaps the State Department vetoed sending the request.

Coordination among the intelligence agencies was piecemeal and episodic. Their representatives never sat down regularly to compare notes. The FBI's Sam Papich was the only human who went between the FBI and the CIA on a daily basis, and the Warren Commission made no attempt to coordinate the effort.

To compound these failings, CIA witnesses seemed at war with the later Church Committee investigation. They never mentioned Cubela requesting a bullet-firing pen as he would claim. Witnesses were not credible in their answers to key questions. Sanchez was too good a case officer not to remember whether Cubela walked out of the November 22 meeting with whatever assassination weapon he was offered. Richard Helms was far too smart not to wonder if Castro retaliated. Almost everyone else has. As Roselli's lawyer Edward Morgan succinctly put it to the Church Committee, "This effort to kill Castro, and then not too long after that Jack Kennedy was killed in Dallas, only an idiot would not put the two together."[13] Richard Helms was not an idiot.

When Helms appeared before the Church Committee, Senator Church asked him, "If we reserve to ourselves the prerogative to assassinate foreign leaders, we may invite reciprocal action from foreign governments . . . wouldn't you agree?" And the CIA man answered, "Yes, sir."[14] Even CIA director John McCone had obviously thought about how Cuban intelligence might have used Oswald when he told the Rockefeller Commission: "[Castro] would have granted him [Oswald] that escape hatch because he would have known that if Oswald was apprehended [he] would have sung, he would have laid the blame on Castro, the indignation of this country would have been so great that the Marines would have taken over Cuba."[15] Thus despite what they said under oath, the CIA men had thought about the possibility that Castro had retaliated, but they avoided talking about their suspicions and conclusions. (A sample of Helms's evasions to both executive branch and congressional questioners appears in appendix B.)

Fidel Castro clearly gained from Kennedy's assassination. Lyndon Johnson reined in the CIA. It never gave Rolando Cubela nor anyone else assassination weapons, and the sabotage raids stopped.

This leads back to the rogue elephant question. Was the CIA a rogue elephant in trying to assassinate Fidel Castro and then hiding this from those investigating the Kennedy assassination? Answering those questions was a Hobson's choice for the Church Committee. Democrats did not want to blame Kennedy and Johnson, two of their party's icons; Republicans did not want the CIA to be blamed. So they split the baby. The committee said that the presidents didn't authorize assassination and ignored answering questions about the CIA's responsibility.

The declassified files tell a different and more complete story. Not only did John and Robert Kennedy know what the CIA was doing; they insisted on it. Lyndon Johnson was appalled and ordered it stopped and yet apparently approved steering the Warren Commission clear of CIA assassination operations and foreign involvement.

Several lessons emerge from all this. One is a simple history lesson. Things happened differently from the way history has recorded them.

Another is that democracy and secret intelligence agencies are strange bedfellows indeed. Although the public wanted answers from the intelligence agencies, they instead bickered among themselves, relied on an old boys' network to do investigatory work, protected political reputations, ultimately failed, and proceeded to hide their failures. Secrecy, compartmentation, and plausible denial prevented the public from learning the truth. The culture of secrecy was so ingrained at the CIA that even when testifying under oath before investigators for both the Rockefeller Commission, which operated under the authority of the president of the United States, and the Church Committee, which was an instrument of Congress, intelligence officers shaded the truth, had memory lapses, turned questions around, and volunteered little.

Last is the danger of letting the spy game compromise fundamental moral principles. The United States could not fully investigate the assassination of John Kennedy for fear the trail would come back to the CIA's Murder, Inc.

ACKNOWLEDGMENTS

Let me begin by thanking those who contributed to my research. Martha Murphy, Britney Crawford, Gene Morris, and Joe Schwarz at the National Archives helped in my research there. Steven Tilley, who has retired from the National Archives, kept me informed of developments years ago when that collection was being put together. Abigail Malangone at the Kennedy Library in Boston provided similar assistance, while Daniel Moorin, a graduate student at the University of Massachusetts Boston, did brief but important research at the library.

I came across FBI agent Moses Aleman in writing this book. The reports he wrote for the FBI in 1964 about Gilberto Lopez are models for what FBI agents could do. In addition, he gave me permission to use the photographs he took of President Kennedy leaving Al Lopez Field in Tampa on November 19, including the one on the cover of this book.

I want to thank my friends Jim Turner and Rob Gunnison. Jim worked with me on the Senate Intelligence Committee, arranged for me to testify twice before Congress on the Assassination Records Review Act, and provided information for this book. Rob, a former journalist, served as sounding board and Internet sleuth par excellence.

Research and writing are only one step in the road to publication. Loch Johnson, Regents Professor of Political Science at the University of Georgia, whom I have known since the Church Committee, consistently provided advice and encouragement while I was working on this book. Douglas Brinkley of Rice University also provided encouragement at a timely phase. Timothy H. Breen, the William Smith Mason Professor of American History Emeritus at Northwestern University, heard the tale and gave me the good advice to take it up a notch. Ronald Chrisman at the University of North Texas Press gave me a very helpful rejection letter. Finally, of course, I must give thanks to editor Tom Swanson with Potomac Books and others at the University of Nebraska Press, including Joeth Zucco, senior project editor; Barbara Wojhoski, my diligent freelance copy editor; and Erin Cuddy, compositor.

APPENDIX A

Where It Might Have Led

The CIA's failure to tell assassination investigators about the AMLASH operation has two important implications. The first relates to motivation. The president was killed by a pro-Castro malcontent just as the CIA plot to kill or overthrow Castro was moving into the final phase. Castro had motivation to commit the crime.

The second is the chronology. Castro's threat to go after U.S. leaders came on the very same day that the CIA renewed contact with Cubela. A few weeks later, Oswald took his trip to Mexico City.

The chronology of the week of the assassination is even more troubling. On Monday Kennedy called for Castro's removal. On Tuesday, after meeting with the president, the CIA decided to give Cubela assassination weapons. The same day Castro sat down with reporter Jean Daniel and asked about Kennedy's intentions. On Wednesday the CIA called Cubela and said it would meet his request for weapons. Later that day Oswald made the decision to assassinate the president.

The chronology, coupled with Roselli's claim that Cuba sent "teams" that were in cities in addition to Dallas, makes Gilberto Policarpo Lopez's actions extremely suspicious. He was in Tampa waiting for a go-ahead call when Kennedy visited there on November 18. He was in Texas on November 22. And he was in Cuba five days after that.

Lopez came to the attention of the CIA on December 3, 1963, by way of a priority cable from the Mexico City station with the cryptonym "GPFLOOR," which was the cryptonym assigned to the president's assassination. The information came from Mexican government authorities. Lopez was an American citizen. He had crossed the border from Texas into Mexico the night of the assas-

255

sination on a fifteen-day Mexican visa and traveled to Mexico City. From there he flew to Havana on November 27. Mexican authorities wanted a name trace on him.[1] Later in the day, the Mexico City station sent a second message: Mexican authorities told the FBI office in Mexico City that Lopez had entered Mexico at Nuevo Laredo.[2] The border was closed immediately after the assassination and not reopened until late in the evening.

Mexico City sent more details two days later. Lopez had stayed in the Roosevelt Hotel in Mexico City. He departed as the only passenger on a Cubana Airlines flight to Havana on November 27, leaving the hotel for the airport at 7:00 p.m. Mexican authorities had a photograph of him.[3] CIA headquarters cabled back, informing the Mexico City station that Lopez was a U.S. citizen and pointing out that he was traveling on an expired passport.[4]

The Mexico City station pouched to headquarters the photograph of Lopez at the airport as he was about to board a flight to Havana. The photograph, taken sometime between 7:00 p.m., when he left the hotel, and 9:00 p.m., when his flight left, shows him wearing sunglasses. Since it was nighttime, the dark glasses were undoubtedly to hinder identification. His visa to Mexico had been issued in Tampa on November 20, and he traveled to Cuba on a "Cuban 'Courtesy' visa." Finally, the dispatch noted that Mexican authorities regarded Lopez's travel through Mexico and departure for Havana as suspicious. Mexican authorities urgently requested all available data on Lopez.[5]

A CIA memorandum for the record on December 5 notes that Mexican authorities at the border said Lopez "looked suspicious" when he crossed. Mexican police became even more worried because they had lost track of him after the crossing. They didn't locate him until he left on the flight to Cuba.[6]

The CIA turned the investigation of Lopez's activities in the United States over to the FBI. Yet although the CIA documents on Lopez bear the GPFLOOR cryptonym, the FBI did not treat it as part of the assassination investigation and never mentioned him to the Warren Commission. The FBI didn't seem to realize that Lopez had been in one and perhaps both cities the president visited the week of the assassination.

The FBI follow-up moved at a leisurely pace over a period of many months as it ordered agents in Florida to investigate. It never told the agents that there were allegations Lopez was involved in the assassination and that he had gone to Cuba a few days after the assassination.

The following narrative emerges from the FBI field reports. Lopez was at the home of a woman named Mary Quist on Sunday night, November 17.[7] According to an FBI informant who was there, Lopez had been at the house for "some time waiting for a telephone call from Cuba which was very important. It was understood that it all depended on his getting the 'go ahead order' for him to leave the United States. He indicated he had been refused travel back to his native Cuba because he was an American citizen."[8]

While this seems plausible, it is at odds with what Azcue, the Cuban consul in Mexico City at this time, told the House Assassinations Committee years later. He said he didn't give Oswald a visa because the Cubans didn't know who he was but that a visa applicant with friends in Cuba would receive expeditious treatment. Lopez had family and friends on the island and had lived there for several years. If Azcue is to be believed, Cuba should not have delayed granting Lopez's visa application.

Quist was hosting the FPCC meeting to show color slides of Cuba, but Lopez was there for the sole purpose of getting the call from Cuba. There is no record of who attended, besides Quist and Lopez, but two of the attendees were FBI informants.[9] The Tampa chapter had been the first one established by FPCC president Vincent T. Lee.[10] In any event Lopez did not get the call from Cuba that night, and Kennedy was in town the next day.[11]

On Wednesday, November 20, Lopez obtained a temporary visa to Mexico from the Mexican consulate in Tampa, so he must have gotten the call from Cuba that day.[12] He headed to Texas. The FBI didn't determine whether he traveled by bus, car, train, or plane.[13]

On March 20, 1964, the Mexico City station sent a startling cable to headquarters. It reported that the Federal Judicial Police in Mexico had a source who alleged Lopez was "involved in Kennedy assassination." The source said Lopez entered Mexico from Laredo, Texas, about noon on the day after the assassination. He was on foot and took a bus to Mexico City. He flew to Havana on November 27 "and was the only passenger allowed on the plane."[14] This cable continued to carry the assassination cryptonym "GPFLOOR." The next day the CIA station in Mexico City cabled headquarters again reminding it that the same information had been provided in early December from a different source. The Mexico City station also asked if the FBI had turned up anything on Lopez.[15]

Moses Aleman was the bilingual FBI agent in Florida who did most of the investigation of Lopez. The FBI furnished copies of his reports to the CIA but not to the Warren Commission. Indeed, some of his work continued after the Warren Report was released because, although the FBI did not consider the matter related to the assassination, the CIA did.[16]

That none of this came to the Warren Commission's attention is unfortunate because its staff went to Mexico City in April 1964 and would surely have looked into the matter while there. The staff does not seem to have been well informed before the trip. In outlining what it would do in Mexico, a staff memo said: "Our evidence so far indicates that Oswald's sole reason for going to Mexico was to travel from there to Cuba by means of an in-transit visa for stopping off in Cuba on the way to Russia." Marina Oswald had already testified to the commission that she didn't think this was what Oswald had in mind. She didn't think he had any intention of going to Russia. The staff memo speculates that Oswald's trip to Mexico might have been designed to lay the groundwork for escape after the assassination. However, it dismisses that possibility as too farfetched because Oswald could not have known that Kennedy would visit Dallas that fall and so could not have been planning the assassination. The memo concludes by saying that while in Mexico, the staff would review what the American and Mexican investigatory agencies had done there.[17] Therefore, it's surprising the staff didn't learn about Lopez while in Mexico since both the CIA station there and Mexican authorities were aware of the recent allegation that Lopez had been involved in the assassination, and the allegation was unresolved. The staff's report of its trip does not mention Lopez; it must not have been told about him while in Mexico.[18]

Tampa FBI agent Aleman was interviewed for this book.[19] The author gave him copies of both his and the CIA's reports that are now declassified. He said no one told him the interest in Lopez was related to the Kennedy assassination. He did not know that Lopez had been in Texas on the day of the assassination or that the CIA had received allegations that he was involved. Aleman said he obviously would have "gone into it a lot deeper" had he known. He noted that if Lopez left Tampa on November 20 and traveled by car to be in Laredo late in the evening of November 22, he could easily have been in Dallas at the time of the assassination.[20]

The AMLASH chronology highlights another investigatory failure: Oswald's communications. Again November 20, the day Oswald must have decided to kill the president, is the focus.

The Warren Commission never looked into Oswald's electronic communications for a possible "go-signal." It never bothered to get telephone company records of calls to or from his rooming house, although it did ask for selected records of Jack Ruby's calls.

If the commission had known about Gilberto Lopez's waiting for a phone call from Cuba about his visa, it might have asked for records of all phone calls from Cuba since Oswald too was waiting to hear about his visa. At the time of the commission's investigation, AT&T had records of every telephone call to or from Cuba in the fall of 1963. Determining whether and when Oswald or anyone else in Dallas was communicating with Cuba and when Lopez was called would have been easy.[21] Not seeking this information is an inexplicable lapse.

Oswald also listened to the radio. While still in the Soviet Union, he purchased a small portable radio, a Turist PMP-56.[22] It could pick up two radio bands, which were used for conventional broadcasts in the Soviet Union. These corresponded to the commercial AM radio band in the United States and a lower band that is used for government and navigation transmission here.

The radio was apparently Oswald's primary means of entertainment in the evening. The Warren Report says that he watched television in the common room of the rooming house, based on what he told Marina. But this second-hand information seems wrong. His landlords told a reporter the day after the assassination that he stayed in his room at night listening to the radio.[23] At the very least, this may have been what he was doing the week of the assassination, which would have been in the landlords' recent memory.

After the assassination Dallas police went to the rooming house, seized the contents of Oswald's room, took them to the police station, and photographed them. In police photos the radio is tuned to approximately 1330 KHZ. A Fort Worth station that broadcast country music was on this frequency in 1963. Oswald could have listened to it, but nothing suggests he enjoyed country music. He liked classical music.[24]

A Cuban station, CMCB, operated on 1330 KHZ and followed a classical-music format.[25] Though far away Oswald might have been able to pick it up. Radio waves travel much farther at night. Indeed, most radio stations in the United States lower their power at night to prevent interference with one another, but Cuban stations don't, at least they didn't in 1963. The nearby Fort Worth station transmitted at a mere ten watts of power at night, but the Cuban station transmitted with one thousand watts of power in 1961 and may have increased power by 1963.[26] In short it is quite possible that Oswald was listening to this Cuban station.[27]

Cuban stations in 1963 commonly broadcast both music and commentary. Transcripts of some commentary exist. The CIA's Foreign Broadcast and Information Service (FBIS) monitored foreign, including Cuban, radio and television and prepared and circulated transcripts to government officials, to give the officials a sense for what was being seen and heard on foreign media. If Oswald was listening to Cuban radio, he may have heard such commentaries.

Cuban television carried a commentary on Kennedy's barrier-once-removed speech in Miami to the Inter-American Press Association on November 18. The commentary was relatively mild, saying Kennedy's remarks were "the same old lies" and were hypocritical and hollow. However, this program was in Spanish, and Oswald supposedly could not speak Spanish.

The broadcast is notable though because it was on the air *before* Kennedy gave the speech. The commentary mistakenly said the president's speech was at noon, whereas it was actually in the evening.[28] Cuban intelligence must have acquired an advance copy early in the day and transmitted it to Havana. Cuban intelligence was so good that it could attack a Kennedy speech before he delivered it.[29]

And if Oswald listened to radio broadcasts from Cuba, he may have gotten secret messages this way. Using conventional broadcasts to send prearranged signals to agents is common in the intelligence business. During World War II, the BBC broadcast coded messages to resistance fighters in Nazi-occupied France. The resistance would be alerted by the announcer saying something like, "Before we begin, please listen to some personal messages," followed by a nonsense phrase such as "there is a fire at the insurance agency," which would have special meaning to the agent in France. As a prearranged signal to alert the resistance to the impending D-Day invasion, the same BBC station broadcast parts of a well-known French poem, thus signaling thousands in the French underground to begin sabotage operations.[30]

Those who are not privy to the prearranged code can't make sense of such a message. A Cuban program on November 20 by the Havana Friendly Voice of Cuba thus stands out. The English language broadcast was a commentary on Raul Castro's proposed new law for compulsory military service. It seems to begin with an alert signal: "To some of our listeners outside of Cuba it may appear on first thought that this is merely an internal matter of interest only to Cubans and that it does not concern anyone else. But if the meaning of the decision to make the term of service three years is fully examined, it will be seen that it is an affair that reaches across the borders of Cuba." The commentary then gives a rambling explanation of the differences between the Cuban army and other armies before switching to talk about the war in Vietnam. Its beginning signal and its pointlessness make it suspicious.[31] Only the sender and the agent might know that this was a coded message. These commentaries were typically broadcast repeatedly for a day or more by the Cuban stations.[32]

A thorough investigation into possible foreign involvement in the president's assassination would have made use of the National Security Agency for the purpose of seeing if Oswald received some kind of go-signal by radio or telephone. NSA capabilities for electronic surveillance and interception of communications in 1963 were light years ahead of the rest of the world. While the CIA's FBIS intercepted and transcribed small samples of transmissions on Cuban radio and television stations, the NSA apparently intercepted everything. Responding to a 1998 request from the Assassination Records Review Board about its capabilities with regard to Cuba, the NSA bragged: "NSA had an excellent capability to meet the SIGINT [signals intelligence] challenges of the 1960s." The NSA letter continues: "A review of the United States Intelligence Board (USIB) records held by NSA shows CIA and NSA top-level Agency cooperation/coordination on intelligence targets via the USIB. However, according to recollections of individuals working at NSA in the mid 1960s, liaison between CIA and NSA for the 1962–1964 timeframe was limited and no record of CIA/NSA cooperation/coordination at the working levels of the agencies was located."[33]

The FBI did ask the NSA for help after the assassination, and the NSA had relevant records. A December 4, 1963, FBI memorandum said that the NSA was going to review recent radio traffic between Cuba and the United States using computer processing for messages containing Oswald's name or aliases as well as other names and contacts the FBI had given it. According to the memorandum, the NSA had already "examined all messages between Cuba and New Orleans and Cuba and Dallas [by computer] and nothing significant was noted. . . . It advised that this project cover[ed] only messages since 10/6/63 as these [were] the only ones which were recorded on tape and [were] thereby susceptible to examination through the computer process (The Cuba-U.S. traffic is too voluminous for personal examination)."[34]

In other words the NSA had relevant intercepts in 1963—and still has them—but no human being has ever listened to them. Rather, the NSA relied on a computer to review the transmissions looking for certain keywords. Given the chronology of the AMLASH operation, the NSA should have had a human review the message traffic for November 20, 1963.

Oswald's radio offers another example of the haphazard investigation. There is no record that anyone has ever thoroughly examined the radio.

The Dallas police seized it and gave it to the FBI. The Warren Commission directed the FBI to give it to the NSA for examination, but the commission did not tell the NSA what to look for. The agency wrote back saying it had found nothing of "cryptological significance." The NSA's internal report said that the radio and its external transformer "were examined and tested by R34 with negative results. The radio (for purposes of the tests the power supply was considered an integral part) conformed closely to one examined by the British in 1959. A copy of R34's findings is attached." This suggests that British intelligence thought these small, portable radios might be used by spies. There is no record that the NSA communicated these suspicions to the Warren Commission, which in any event did nothing more with the radio. Responding to a Freedom of Information Act request by this author, the NSA says that it can't find R34's findings today.[35] In other words no one knows what the NSA inspector looked for or what the British intelligence report said.

The next time anyone looked at the radio was in 1966. Albert Newman, a writer and amateur radio enthusiast, thought Oswald might have been motivated by listening to inflammatory broadcasts on Radio Havana. Newman took a cheap shortwave radio to Dallas and discovered that Radio Havana was the strongest signal on its frequency. A White House aide arranged for Newman to inspect the radio, which was back in FBI possession. Astonishingly, an internal FBI memorandum on the matter states that the bureau "was not aware of any prior allegation that Oswald had used it [the radio] to receive broadcasts from Cuba and this would require further checking."[36] FBI director J. Edgar Hoover then wrote the White House:

The radio is a small, brown, plastic, Russian-made radio commonly known as the "Tourist" and was designed to operate on standard radio broadcast bands. It is similar in this respect to American-made radios commonly found in the American home. When operating properly, the radio, if used in the southeastern section of the United States, would be capable of receiving radio broadcasts from Cuban radio stations, particularly at night. . . . For your added information, the radio was not in operating condition when it was received by the Bureau from the Dallas Police Department. No attempt was made by this Bureau to repair the radio since to have done so would have changed the physical condition of the radio from that in which it was received.[37]

Hoover's letter makes two mistakes. First, his comparison with an American-made radio isn't quite right because the Turist could receive a second frequency band that American radios cannot. Second, while the Turist might be able to pick up Cuban broadcasts in the southeastern United States, it might not be able to do so in Dallas. It needed to be tested.

The statement that the radio was not in operating condition when the FBI got it is strange. If it didn't work, why didn't the NSA tell the Warren Commission that? Its letter to the commission implies that the radio worked and was tested.

As for Newman, he later published a book, *The Assassination of John F. Kennedy*, in which he claims to have examined the radio at the FBI and concluded that Oswald could have used it to listen to Radio Havana on shortwave. Newman too was mistaken. The standard Turist cannot pick up shortwave signals. Perhaps Newman misunderstood the Russian lettering on the dial.

Thus the historical record is that the radio has been examined only three times: once by the NSA; once by the FBI; and once by Albert Newman. If Hoover's 1966 letter is to be believed, it wasn't working on any of these occasions. Yet Oswald's landlords told reporter Aynesworth that Oswald listened to the radio in his room, so it was working when Oswald had it.

The author asked the National Archives, which has possession of the radio, to permit him to inspect it for this book. The archives denied the request, saying that the radio was evidence in a criminal case, so the author asked for it to be photographed inside and out. It has a jack for an external antenna, which might have been a length of wire that would have extended its range, but no such wire was found in Oswald's room. It also has an internal ferrite antenna. Comparing the photographs of Oswald's radio with those of other Turist radios reveals that one end of his radio's antenna had broken off and the copper coil around it moved. Experts advised the author that whether this allowed the radio to pick up short-wave frequencies and whether the radio's electronics were otherwise modified for this purpose can be determined only by testing the radio.

APPENDIX B

Richard Helms's Testimony on the Assassination Investigation

Ambassador Richard Helms (former CIA Director) testimony before
the Rockefeller Commission in 1975. Questions by Executive Director David Belin.[1]

BELIN. Do you recall the fact that poison pills were developed
to be delivered to assets or to people in Cuba for possible insertion in food or drink to be eaten by Castro?

HELMS. Were poison pills taken to Cuba? I never knew anything about this. I don't recall ever having heard anything about
poison pills or any of that. What I want to say in this connection is the fact that I never heard about this doesn't mean that
there weren't many, many ideas discussed in the Agency about
what to do with the Cuban Government but I don't recall anything like poison pills.

BELIN. Do you–

HELMS. Whose idea was this? Do you have the information?

BELIN. Well–

HELMS. I recall somebody discussing me with me one day
an even crazier idea which had to do was some kind of a thing
that might be planted on the beach where Castro walked in
the morning and it would blow up when he put his foot on it,
or something. There were more nutty ideas. It reminded me
of the time of OSS when somebody wanted to get propaganda
into Germany and they discovered there was a herd of cows
that grazed in Germany and were milked in France, so they
devised some suppositories into which there were put a lot of
propaganda leaflets and those were put in the cows on the theory they were being left on the German side of the border when

267

the cows were grazing and nobody would be the wiser. So to say there are nutty ideas cooked up in organizations like this is to tell the truth.

Is there any evidence, may I ask, Mr. Belin, is there any evidence in the record that any Director authorized what I can only refer to by the dictionary definition of assassination of a foreign leader?

BELIN. Well, there is evidence in the record, Ambassador Helms, that there were plans made to try and assassinate Premier Castro of Cuba, that there were several series of plans, and the plans at at [sic] least one or two of the stages included the delivery of poison pills developed in the Agency to be placed in the food or drink–

HELMS. They were delivered in Cuba?

BELIN.   –of Castro, and that the pills were delivered to Mr. Roselli, who in turn delivered them to other people and that the pills eventually found their way to Cuba.

HELMS. How do we know that?

BELIN. There are Agency reports that they were. We do not have any first-hand information that they were, but there are— there are memoranda which indicates that they were through, among others, disaffected Cubans.

HELMS. Who returned to the United States and testified to the fact that they received the pills or something?

BELIN. Who have not testified to anything.

HELMS. I see.

HELMS. That is one–

HELMS. Who authorized this particular operation?

BELIN. This is one of the areas that we are trying to ascertain and I suppose my first question along this line was whether or not you had any knowledge of the existence of such a plan.

HELMS. Not that I recall.

BELIN. And you indicate that you never knew of such a plan?

HELMS. I don't recall any plan.

BELIN. Do you ever recall after you succeeded Richard Bissell that you were approached concerning whether or not you should advise John McCone of the existence of such plans or operations?

HELMS. I was approached to do what?

BELIN. As to whether or not Mr. McCone should be briefed about the existence of such plans or plans?

HELMS. This is after the fact? Or before the fact? Or in the process?

BELIN. During the fact.

HELMS. You mean I had replaced Bissell and somebody in Agency came to me and said we should tell Mr. McCone about a previously authorized plan?

BELIN. Yes. You recall that at all?

HELMS. I don't recall it. I'm sorry.

...

Ambassador Richard Helms (former CIA Director) testimony before the Church Committee in 1975. Questioning by Senator Robert Morgan of North Carolina.[2]

SENATOR MORGAN. Let me—Mr. Helms, you were getting material together for the Warren Commission, you say, and at that time you knew of the assassination plots that had been against Castro, did you not?

MR. HELMS. Yes, sir.

SENATOR MORGAN. And you did not think it important to give that to the Warren Commission?

MR. HELMS. Well, Senator Morgan, I was not the Director at the time.

SENATOR MORGAN. Well you were gathering material.

MR. HELMS. Yes, sir, I was following about orders and requests and I was asked to get together this material but I certainly was not asked to go and testify before the commission.

SENATOR MORGAN. But I'm asking you now if you were gathering the material and you had known for about three years that there were assassination plots and yet you did not think it important to give this material to the Warren Commission. That is correct, isn't it?

MR. HELMS. Well, the way you phrase the question, you say I didn't think it was important, I'm not trying to fence with you, sir, I'm trying to put the circumstances as I understood them at the time. I don't recall that I was ... either instructed or it occurred to me to cover with the Warren Commission the precise details of the Agency's operations not because I made a significant judgment not to do this, but as I said just a moment ago, my recollection at the time was that it was public knowledge that the United States was trying to get rid of Castro.

SENATOR MORGAN. Well, you know, Mr. Ambassador, I don't want to argue with you, but this is what disturbs me about your testimony is that you assume, you thought it was public knowledge, we can never pin anything down. And you were not at that time just an employee of the CIA. You were in the top echelon, the management level, were you not?

MR. HELMS. Yes, I was Senator Morgan.

SENATOR MORGAN. And you'd been part of the assassination plots against Castro?

MR. HELMS. Well, you know—

SENATOR MORGAN. Well this much is true. Is that true, that part? You were—in that regard, you participated?

MR. HELMS. I was aware that there had been efforts made to get rid of him by these means.

SENATOR MORGAN. And you were charged with furnishing the Warren Commission information from the CIA, information you thought was relevant?

MR. HELMS. No, sir. I was instructed to reply to inquiries from the Warren Commission for information from the agency. I was not asked to initiate any particular thing.

SENATOR MORGAN. Well what I understood you to say to give information. In other words, you weren't asked for it you didn't give it?

MR. HELMS. That's right, sir.

APPENDIX C

Sources and Secret Files

The Warren Report was 888 pages long with another 16,000 pages in twenty-six accompanying volumes. The commission also transferred 360 cubic feet of files to the National Archives. Among these were 3,000 pages of nonpublic or classified documents, which became known as the "secret files."

In 1992 to allay public concern that the secret files contradicted the Warren Report, Congress established a review board to oversee declassification and release of all assassination-related records. The review board finished work in 1998. Its work covered not only the 3,000 secret Warren Commission pages but also vastly larger amounts of material from the three later investigations, which had classified everything they did. In 1998 the review board identified 423,000 classified pages from the later investigations and another 560,000 classified pages held by the intelligence agencies. When it went out of business that year, the board was able to release 97 percent of the material.

All these documents are indexed in an online database, which counts documents rather than pages. A search shows that the archives hold 266,339 Kennedy assassination documents. Of these 20,945, almost exclusively from the three later investigations and from government agencies, are restricted in whole or in part. This figure includes 16,085 from the CIA and 3,024 from the FBI. Many are duplicates, and in any event they may not have anything to do with the assassination or Cuba.

In sum it appears that most if not all of the original "secret files" of the Warren Commission are public. Whether the 20,495 still-secret documents from later investigations and from the agencies contain relevant information cannot be determined without examining them.

NOTES

Introduction

1.Leo Janos, "The Last Days of the President: LBJ in Retirement," *Atlantic*, July 1973, https://www.theatlantic.com/past/docs/issues/73jul/janos.htm.

2. Testimony of Richard Helms, April 24, 1975, Rockefeller Commission, 389, National Archives and Record Administration (hereafter NARA) 157-10011-10086.

1. Castro, Oswald, and Kennedy

1. Some claim that Castro was born a year later and that he changed his birth year from 1927 to 1926 in order to enter school a year before he was eligible.

2. Major General V. P. Mock to Joseph A. Califano, "Review of U.S. Policy with Respect to Cuba," March 22, 1963, Attachment, 1–3, 198-10008-10082. The document is a history of relations between the United States and Cuba from 1952 to 1963 and was prepared by Department of the Army staff. Richard Helms also provided, from memory, a similar but less detailed history of Cuban policy in the same period in his testimony to the Church Committee. Testimony of Richard Helms, June 13, 1975, Church Committee, 14–35, NARA 157-10014-10075. Hereafter, testimony before this committee, which was chaired by Senator Frank Church, will be referred to as "Church Committee."

3. Mock to Califano, "Review of U.S. Policy," 3.

4. Mock to Califano, "Review of U.S. Policy," 4.

5. Schoultz, *That Infernal Little Cuban Republic*, 92.

6. Schoultz, *That Infernal Little Cuban Republic*, 95, 99.

7. Mock to Califano, "Review of U.S. Policy," 5.

8. Schoultz, *That Infernal Little Cuban Republic*, 111.

9. Schoultz, *That Infernal Little Cuban Republic*, 114.

10. Schoultz, *That Infernal Little Cuban Republic*, 126.

11. Mock to Califano, "Review of U.S. Policy," 5–8.

12. Schoultz, *That Infernal Little Cuban Republic*, 136.

13. Schoultz, *That Infernal Little Cuban Republic*, 138–39.

14. Mock to Califano, "Review of U.S. Policy," 9–10.

15. *Report of the President's Commission*, 669–77, hereafter cited as *Warren Report*. The *Warren Report* consists of a main volume with a narrative

report and twenty-six additional volumes with transcripts of testimony and exhibits. The additional volumes will be cited as *Warren Report* with the volume number added. The lengthy and meticulously reconstructed biography of Oswald in the narrative attempts to provide a psychological profile of Oswald as a lonely misfit to address the question of why he assassinated the president. In hindsight, however, the commission's attention to details such as how many days Oswald was truant at various schools seems pointless, especially since it never looked into what Oswald was doing during his truancy. He later wrote that he first began to read up on Communism during this period, yet the commission never saw the irony in saying that a truant was interested in learning. In any event, as explained later, the public would have been better served if the commission had put its investigative efforts into determining what Oswald was doing in the last ten days of his life rather than what he was doing in the first twenty years.

16. *Warren Report*, 680–89.

17. Testimony of Nelson Delgado, April 16, 1964, *Warren Report*, 8:240–43.

18. P. Baranov, "Report on the Sojourn of American Tourist L. H. Oswald in Moscow," November 6, 1959, Yeltsin Documents, National Archives at College Park, JFK Assassination Records Collection (Clinton Library). In 1999 Russian President Boris Yeltsin gave U.S. President William Clinton a set of documents the Russians had on Oswald. These were translated by the State Department and turned over to the Clinton library with copies held at the National Archives in College Park. Hereafter cited as "Yeltsin Documents."

19. Mailer, *Oswald's Tale*, 52.

20. *Warren Report*, 694.

21. A. Gromyko and A. Shelepin to CC CPSU, November 27, 1959, Yeltsin Documents.

22. The sum of 5,000 rubles to furnish his apartment and an allowance of 700 rubles per month were authorized. Resolution of the CC CPSU, Yeltsin Documents.

23. *Warren Report*, 705.

24. Barron, KGB, 238.

25. As lawyer for the Senate Intelligence Committee, the author talked with James Angleton, the head of CIA Counterintelligence on a number of occasions. After reading that Oswald was interested in the Patrice Lumumba Friendship University, the author asked Angleton about the university. He said it was called TU at the CIA.

26. *Warren Report*, 705.

27. *Warren Report*, 701.

28. Secretary of the Central Committee, "Regarding the Application of U.S. National Lee Harvey Oswald for Soviet Citizenship," Yeltsin Documents.

29. Testimony of Mrs. Lee Harvey Oswald, February 3, 1964, *Warren Report*, 1:24.

30. Dallek, *Unfinished Life*, 9–20.

31. According to biographer Dallek, Jack Kennedy's IQ score was 119, which would be considered by today's standards "high average." He failed the Latin part of the admission exam to Choate preparatory school but was admitted and graduated sixty-fifth in a class of 110. Dallek, *Unfinished Life*, 33, 41.

32. Dallek, *Unfinished Life*, 42.

33. Dallek, *Unfinished Life*, 42–67.

34. Dallek, *Unfinished Life*, 81–96.

35. Dallek, *Unfinished Life*, 117–33.

36. Dallek, *Unfinished Life*, 159.

37. Dallek, *Unfinished Life*, 160–62.

38. Dallek, *Unfinished Life*, 173–74.

39. Dallek, *Unfinished Life*, 184.

40. Dallek, *Unfinished Life*, 209

41. Sorensen, *Counselor*, 232–33.

42. Sorensen, *Counselor*, 165.

43. Dallek, *Unfinished Life*, 290.

44. John F. Kennedy, Inaugural Address, January 20, 1961, John F. Kennedy Presidential Library (hereafter JFK Library) online, http://www.jfklibrary.org/Asset-Viewer/BqXIEM9F4024ntFl7SVAjA.aspx?gclid=CKb4qafF274CFaVxOgodtlQA3Q.

2. The Bay of Pigs

1. Dallek, *Unfinished Life*, 301.

2. Dallek, *Unfinished Life*, 302–5.

3. Weiner, *Legacy of Ashes*, 167.

4. Reeves, *President Kennedy*, 19.

5. Thomas, *Very Best Men*, 179.

6. Testimony of John McCone before the President's Commission on CIA Activities, May 5, 1975, 100, National Archives and Record Administration, record group 232, record no. 157-100011-10167. The commission was chaired by then vice president Nelson Rockefeller and is commonly called the Rockefeller Commission. That term will be used in citations hereafter.

7. Weiner, *Legacy of Ashes*, 173.

8. Thomas, *Very Best Men*, 87.

9. Thomas, *Very Best Men*, 93–95.

10. Thomas, *Very Best Men*, 165.

11. Dallek, *Unfinished Life*, 341–42.

12. Reeves, *President Kennedy*, 72.

13. Robert F. Kennedy, recorded interview by John Bartlow Martin, February 29, 1964, 81, John F. Kennedy Oral History Program of the John F. Kennedy Presidential Library, hereafter cited as "Robert Kennedy oral history."

14. Testimony of Richard Bissell, June 9, 1975, U.S. Senate Select Committee on Intelligence, 8–16, NARA 157-10011-10020.

15. Weiner, *Legacy of Ashes*, 173–75.

16. Schoultz, *That Infernal Little Cuban Republic*, 152.

17. Bissell testimony, June 9, 1975, Church Committee, 19.

18. Bissell testimony, June 9, 1975, Church Committee, 74. The support chief was not named in the Church Committee report but was later identified as James O'Connell in a House Assassination Committee document that is now public. Deposition with Mr. X: James O'Connell, September 25, 1978. http://www.jfklancer.com/cuba/o-connell.html. He was also identified by name in the CIA Inspector General Report at 16. O'Connell told David Belin of the Rockefeller Commission that Edwards claimed Dulles approved. David Belin, Memorandum to File, Interview with James O'Connell, May 17, 1975, 4, NARA 178-10002-10329.

19. U.S. Senate Select Committee on Intelligence, *Alleged Assassination Plots involving Foreign Leaders: An Interim Report*, November 20, 1975, Eighty-Fourth Congress, First Session, Report No. 94-465, 76. Hereafter cited as *Alleged Assassination Plots*.

20. *Alleged Assassination Plots*, 77, Deposition with Mr. X. In his interview with David Belin, O'Connell said that at the time Roselli had the ice-machine concession at all the casinos in Las Vegas. Roselli was reluctant to take the assignment and refused compensation. "Well, he eventually decided he would try to help us but he made it quite clear, if it was in the interest of national security and so forth, that he would do it." Belin, interview with O'Connell, 5–6.

21. Deposition with Mr. X.

22. *Alleged Assassination Plots*, 79. In 1967 the CIA's inspector general was the first to look into the agency's assassination operations. His report notes that according to Bissell only six people knew of the syndicate operation. However, the authors of the report counted at least thirteen individuals at the CIA who were knowledgeable and another six outside the CIA. J. S. Earman, Inspector General, memorandum for the record, "Report on Plots to Assassinate Fidel Castro," May 23, 1967, 34–35, NARA 104-10213-10101. Hereafter cited as "IG Report."

23. The IG Report said that Giancana thought his girlfriend, Phyllis McGuire of the then famous McGuire sisters, was cheating on him with the comedian Dan Rowan of the Rowan and Martin comedy team. Giancana wanted Maheu to bug the room as a return favor for Giancana's help with the assassination plot against Castro. Maheu hired someone to do it, but the man installed a wiretap on the phone instead of bugging the room. This of course defeated Giancana's purpose. IG Report, 57–59.

24. *Alleged Assassination Plots*, 80. In addition the Church Committee suggested that the wiretap may have been occasioned by concern that Giancana's girlfriend was leaking information about the assassination plot.

25. *Alleged Assassination Plots*, 73; IG Report, 22–25.

26. Thomas, *Very Best Men*, 130.

27. Thomas, *Very Best Men*, 132.

28. This was the gossip among Church Committee staffers when Harvey testified before the committee in 1975.

29. Testimony of William Harvey, morning session, June 25, 1975, Church Committee, 53, NARA 157-10002-10105.

30. Testimony of John Roselli, June 24, 1975, Church Committee, 32–33, NARA 157-10014-10001.

31. Testimony of George Smathers, July 23, 1975, Church Committee, 6–7, 18–19, 25, and Ex. 1, NARA 157-10005-10252; *Alleged Assassination Plots*, 123–24. Smathers couldn't recall exactly when the conversation with the president took place, but the committee's report concludes it was before the Bay of Pigs invasion, which was in April 1961, probably in March.

32. Testimony of William Harvey, afternoon session, June 25, 1975, Church Committee, 75–88, NARA 157-10002-10106.

33. *Alleged Assassination Plots*, 82.

34. That the agent never got the go signal, *Alleged Assassination Plots*, 79–81. That he lost his access, IG Report, 28.

35. Mock, "Review of U.S. Policy," 13.

36. Robert Kennedy oral history, February 29, 1964, 47. In the same interview, Robert Kennedy said the president later learned that the CIA in fact had two Americans on the beach despite the president's saying no Americans would be involved.

37. Schoultz, *That Infernal Little Cuban Republic*, 159.

38. Schoultz, *That Infernal Little Cuban Republic*, 153

39. Mock, "Review of U.S. Policy," 176.

40. Robarge, *John McCone*, 40.

41. Robert Kennedy oral history, February 29, 1964, 49.

42. Reeves, *President Kennedy*, 103.

43. Robert F. Kennedy oral history, February 29, 1964, 57–58. Kennedy ransomed the brigade from imprisonment in Cuba in December 1962 and got to know some of its commanders. He faulted Bissell for believing that once it landed at the Bay of Pigs, the brigade could melt into the countryside if need be and wage a guerrilla war. Perhaps reflecting the sentiment of these commanders, Kennedy said with a laugh: "They never had been told they were to become guerrillas, and there was no guerrilla territory for them to become guerrillas."

44. Mock, "Review of U.S. Policy," 16.

45. Sorensen, *Kennedy*, 306.

46. Reeves, *President Kennedy*, 113.

47. Rusk, *As I Saw It*, 213

48. *Alleged Assassination Plots*, 125.

49. Robarge, *John McCone*, 28.

50. Weiner, *Legacy of Ashes*, 180. Weiner adds that whereas the CIA under Eisenhower had run 170 major covert actions in eight years, the Kennedys ran 163 in fewer than three years.

51. Beschloss, *Crisis Years*, 374–76.

52. IG Report, 4.

53. *Alleged Assassination Plots*, 125.

54. *Alleged Assassination Plots*, 121.

55. Thomas, *Very Best Men*, 239.

56. Robarge, *John McCone*, 31.

57. Bissell testimony, June 9, 1975, Church Committee, 7–8.

58. Beschloss, *Crisis Years*, 416–17.

59. CIA officer comment to author, May 1976. His comments were directed at the committee's report on alleged assassination attempts against foreign leaders, a report that had concluded John Kennedy was unaware of CIA plans to assassinate foreign leaders, and at Senator Church's public statement that the CIA was a rogue elephant.

60. CIA historian David Robarge writes: "Today McCone would be called a 'Type A' executive—dynamic, resolute, and unsentimental. . . . McCone led by power of personality and intellect, amplified by impeccable dress and crisp voice and mannerisms." Robarge, *John McCone*, 34.

61. Weiner, *Legacy of Ashes*, 180.

62. Robarge, *John McCone*, 73.

3. Mongoose

1. Testimony of Richard Bissell, June 9, 1975, Church Committee, 42, NARA 157-10011-10020.

2. Testimony of Richard Helms, July 18, 1975, Church Committee, 49–50, NARA 157-10011-10056.

3. Robarge, *John McCone*, 97.

4. Testimony of John McCone, October 9, 1975, Church Committee, 5, NARA 157-10014-10079.

5. According to CIA historian Robarge, for a period of time, once the Special Group finished its business at meetings, Robert Kennedy "would come in," converting the meeting into the Special Group (Augmented). Robarge, *John McCone*, 85; *Alleged Assassination Plots*, 135.

6. *Alleged Assassination Plots*, 136–37.

7. *Alleged Assassination Plots*, 136n1.

8. Robarge, *John McCone*, 86.

9. Reeves, *President Kennedy*, 46.

10. Reeves, *President Kennedy*, 263–64.

11. *Alleged Assassination Plots*, 137.

12. Goldstein, *Lessons in Disaster*, 65.

13. *Alleged Assassination Plots*, 138, citing testimony of Tad Szulc, June 10, 1975, Church Committee, 25–26.

14. *Alleged Assassination Plots*, 83.

15. Reeves, *President Kennedy*, 267.

16. The "W" was supposedly chosen because a nineteenth-century American adventurer named William Walker engaged in paramilitary operations in Latin America. Robarge, *John McCone*, 85n10.

17. Testimony of Samuel Halpern, April 22, 1976, Church Committee, 5, NARA 157-10014-10008. Halpern served as executive officer for Harvey and his successor, Desmond FitzGerald.

18. Thomas, *Very Best Men*, 287.

19. Thomas, *Very Best Men*, 287. Thomas attributes this quote to Bissell. The Church Committee attributed it to George McManus in a briefing book used for the testimony of Richard Helms. Testimony of Richard Helms testimony, July 17, 1975, Church Committee, 33, Memorandum for the Record, Mongoose Meeting with Robert Kennedy, exhibit, NARA 157-10011-10057. But since the memorandum shown Helms refers to McManus as one of those also present, he is surely not the author.

20. Testimony of William Harvey, July 11, 1975, Church Committee, 106–7, NARA 157-10011-10063.

21. Thomas A. Parrott, Minutes of Special Group (Augmented) on Project Mongoose, March 5, 1962, exhibit to testimony of Richard Helms, July 17, 1975, Church Committee, NARA 157-10011-10057.

22. Thomas, *Very Best Men*, 150–51.

23. Testimony of Walter Elder, August 13, 1975, Church Committee, 37, NARA 157-10002-10046. Elder was McCone's executive officer.

24. *Alleged Assassination Plots*, 77–79.

25. Memorandum from Courtney Evans to Allen Belmont, June 6, 1961, in *Alleged Assassination Plots*, 128. In a footnote, the Church Committee pointed out that Evans was FBI liaison to both the president and the attorney general and that Robert Kennedy had wanted Giancana thoroughly investigated.

26. *Alleged Assassination Plots*, 130.

27. Roselli's case officer, James O'Connell, when asked specifically if there was a connection between the assassination efforts and the Bay of Pigs invasion, said: "There was absolutely none. As a matter of fact, the project handling the Bay of Pigs had absolutely no idea of what was going on as far as we were concerned." David Belin, Memorandum to File, interview with James P. O'Connell, May 17, 1975, 7–8, NARA 178-10002-10329

28. *Alleged Assassination Plots*, 84.

29. Testimony of William Harvey, afternoon session, June 25, 1975, Church Committee, 102, NARA 157-10002-10106. In questioning Harvey Senator Church suggested that Harvey said Roselli had been terminated in order to "falsify the record." Harvey disagreed. He said it was intended to formally end Edwards's involvement with the operation and to show that fact in the records of the Counterintelligence Division. The operation was still shown as active in DDP records. Both men were correct. They just viewed the situation from different perspectives. Compartmentation means that only those with a need to know will be informed. Since Edwards no longer had a need to know what was going on with Roselli, he was cut off by being told the operation was over.

30. *Alleged Assassination Plots*, 128–33.

31. Harvey testimony, afternoon session, June 25, 1975, Church Committee, 91.

32. *Alleged Assassination Plots*, 86.

33. *Alleged Assassination Plots*, 86.

34. Testimony of Richard Helms, Rockefeller Commission, 1975, 161, NARA 157-10005-10376.

35. Robarge, *John McCone*, 89, emphasis in original.

36. Robarge, *John McCone*, 92n31, and 92–93.

37. Robarge, *John McCone*, 92.

38. *Warren Report*, 712–17.

39. Reeves, *Profile of Power*, 342–43.

4. Missile Crisis

1. Beschloss, *Crisis Years*, 385.

2. Reeves, *President Kennedy*, 375.

3. Schoultz, *That Infernal Little Republic*, 184.

4. Beschloss, *Crisis Years*, 385.

5. *Alleged Assassination Plots*, 105.

6. *Alleged Assassination Plots*, 161–63, emphasis added.

7. Robert Kennedy said that McCone's warning never reached the president and that McCone was in any event on a honeymoon in Europe in September 1962 and didn't pursue the warning. Robert Kennedy oral history, April 30, 1964, 224. Richard Helms had a quite different recollection: "[McCone] got himself very much on the other side of the fence from the President and that was over the question . . . of whether the Russians were putting missiles in Cuba. And he stuck to the line that they were putting them in when almost everyone else in the Federal government was saying they were not putting them in and wouldn't be putting them in and he turned out to be right." Testimony of Richard Helms, June 13, 1975, Church Committee, 100–101, NARA 157-10014-10075.

8. *Alleged Assassination Plots*, 2.

9. Weiner, *Legacy of Ashes*, 195.

10. Reeves, *President Kennedy*, 367.

11. Reeves, *President Kennedy*, 373.

12. Beschloss, *Crisis Years*, 428.

13. Reeves, *President Kennedy*, 377.

14. Richard Helms, Memorandum for the Record, "Mongoose Meeting with the Attorney General," October 16, 1962, testimony of Richard Helms, July 17, 1975, Church Committee, exhibit, NARA 157-10011-10057.

15. Reeves, *President Kennedy*, 378–79.

16. Reeves, *President Kennedy*, 378–79.

17. Powers and O'Donnell, *Johnny, We Hardly Knew Ye*, 119–20. Kennedy's speechwriters tweaked the quote a bit. The original used the phrase "Plaza de toros," but the speechwriters, apparently realizing that it didn't make sense for Kennedy to use the Spanish phrase, substituted "plaza full."

18. Reeves, *President Kennedy*, 373.

19. Reeves, *President Kennedy*, 387–88.

20. Reeves, *President Kennedy*, 396.

21. Beschloss, *Crisis Years*, 565.

22. In his testimony before the Church Committee, Richard Helms recalled, "If I remember the temper of those days, there were a lot of lumps in people's throats all over the United States when they realized how close a call we had had on this really extraordinarily daring operation of Khrushchev's to insert those missiles there secretly and have them pointing down the throats of Americans." Richard Helms testimony, June 13, 1975, Church Committee, 23.

23. Thomas, *Very Best Men*, 289–91.

24. Helms, *Look over My Shoulder*, 223.

25. Robarge, *John McCone*, 93.

26. Helms, *Look over My Shoulder*, 223.

27. Thomas, *Very Best Men*, 291.

28. Thomas, *Robert Kennedy*, 235 and footnote at 439. Thomas cites a memorandum by CIA director McCone saying that the attorney general questioned using such valuable assets as infiltrators at a time of tightened security in Cuba, when losses might be high and the benefits questionable. Thomas also cites his own interview with Samuel Halpern, who was Harvey's deputy, and General Charles E. Johnson.

29. Testimony of Walter Elder, August 7, 1975, Church Committee, 38–39, NARA 157-10002-10049.

30. Charles E. Johnson III, interview by J. E. diGenova and Paul Wallach, July 28, 1975, Church Committee, 2, NARA 157-10008-10242.

31. Robert Kennedy oral history, April 30, 1964, 280–81

32. Robarge, *John McCone*, 94.

33. The sabotage operations are listed in a memorandum for Special Group (Augmented), "Operation MONGOOSE/Sabotage Proposals," October 16, 1962, NARA 157-10004-10154. The National Archives' Identification Form indicates that General Marshall S. Carter was the author even though his name does not appear on the document. According to Helms these operations were approved at the October 18 meeting. Helms, Memorandum for the Record, "Mongoose Meeting," October 16, 1962, NARA 157-10011-10057.

34. Robarge, *John McCone*, 120–21.

35. Robarge, *John McCone*, 140.

36. Testimony of John Roselli, June 24, 1975, Church Committee, 43, NARA 157-10014-10001.

37. John Roselli testimony, June 24, 1975, Church Committee, 44.

38. Thomas A. Wadden Jr., in Roselli testimony, June 24, 1975, Church Committee, 42.

39. Memorandum for Special Group (Augmented), "Operation MONGOOSE/Sabotage Proposals," October 16, 1962, NARA 157-10004-10154.

40. Roselli testimony, June 24, 1975, Church Committee, 43.

41. Testimony of William Harvey, June 25, 1975, Church Committee, 72–73, NARA 157-10002-10106.

42. Harvey testimony, June 25, 1975, Church Committee, 73–74.

43. Harvey testimony, morning session, June 25, 1975, Church Committee, 22–23.

44. *Warren Report*, 676–77.

45. Dobbs exhibit 6, *Warren Report*, 19:571.

46. Oswald's notes, *Warren Report*, 16:422–23

47. Tormey exhibit 1, *Warren Report*, 21:674.

48. *Warren Report*, 722.

49. James Tormey to Lee H. Oswald, December 13, 1962, Tormey exhibit 2, *Warren Report*, 21:677.

50. Bob Chester to Lee H. Oswald, December 9, 1962, Dobbs exhibit 12, *Warren Report*, 19:579.

51. Dobbs exhibit 2, *Warren Report*, 19:567.

52. *Warren Report*, 710–23.

5. The Brigade

1. Robert Kennedy oral history, April 30, 1964, 276–77.

2. Thomas, *Robert Kennedy*, 236.

3. Thomas, *Robert Kennedy*, 236.

4. Robarge, *John McCone*, 137.

5. Thomas, *Robert Kennedy*, 237.

6. Photograph, "President and Mrs. Kennedy with leaders of the Cuban Invasion Brigade, 29 December 1962," JFK Library online, https://www.jfklibrary.org/asset-viewer/president-and-mrs-kennedy-with-leaders-of-the-cuban-invasion-brigade-29-december-1962.

7. Thomas, *Robert Kennedy*, 237.

8. Pepe San Román, Wikipedia, accessed April 12, 2018, http://en.wikipedia.org/wiki/Pepe_San_Rom%C3%A1n.

9. Thomas, *Robert Kennedy*, 238.

10. Evan Thomas takes a contrary view in his biography of Robert Kennedy. He writes, "There was little appetite for war among the President's advisors," and "RFK made little progress trying to interest his colleagues in the top echelons of the government in overthrowing Castro." Thomas, *Robert Kennedy*, 238–39. However, the documents this author examined tell the different story detailed here.

11. William Harvey, "Draft Memorandum to the DCI from William Harvey, Operational Plan for Continuing Operations Against Cuba," November 27, 1962, NARA 104-10102-10224.

12. Harvey, "Draft Memorandum to the DCI," November 27, 1962.

13. George McManus, untitled memorandum, November 5, 1962, as exhibit to Richard Helms testimony, Church Committee, July 17, 1975, NARA 157-10011-10057.

14. George McManus, untitled memorandum.

15. Rusk, *As I Saw It*, 241.

16. Rusk, *As I Saw It*, 242.

17. Rusk, *As I Saw It*, 243.

18. Schoultz, *That Infernal Little Cuban Republic*, 185.

19. Rusk, *As I Saw It*, 245.

20. Malcolm Peabody, interview by author, May 29, 2015. FitzGerald's first wife was Peabody's sister.

21. Thomas, *Very Best Men*, 45–54.

22. Thomas, *Very Best Men*, 274–87

23. Thomas, *Very Best Men*, 192.

24. Malcolm Peabody interview.

25. "House Tour Will Preview Turkey Time," *Washington Post*, October 16, 1960, F6.

26. "Georgetown Tables All Set for a Feast," *Washington Post*, November 6, 1960, F10.

27. "Belles of the Ball," *Washington Post*, June 25, 1961, F1.

28. "She Can Show the Experts," *Washington Post*, May 13, 1962, F1.

29. "Three for the Show," *Washington Post*, January 21, 1963, B4.

30. Latell, *Castro's Secrets*, 158.

31. Robert Kennedy oral history, April 30, 1964, 281.

32. Beschloss, *Crisis Years*, 565

33. Beschloss, *Crisis Years*, 566.

34. Executive Committee of the National Security Council, Summary Record of the 31st Meeting, November 29, 1962, in Keefer, Sampson, and Smith, *Foreign Relations, 1961–1963*, 11:216, emphasis added.

35. White House Diary, JFK Library, accessed April 12, 2018, http://whd.jfklibrary.org/Diary/.

36. NSAM no. 213, McGeorge Bundy to Secretary of State, January 10, 1963, NARA 198-10007-10376.

37. Memorandum from Roswell Gilpatric for DOD to McGeorge Bundy, "Interdepartmental Organization for Cuban Affairs," January 10, 1963, NARA 198-10008-10017; memorandum from Cyrus Vance for Mr. Sterling J. Cottrell, NSAM no. 13, January 11, 1963, NARA 198-10008-10024; memorandum from Joseph A. Califano Jr. to Captain E. R. Zumwalt, General Earle Wheeler, Major General C. W. Abrams Jr., Rear Admiral Wendt, Major General J. W. Carpenter III, "Interdepartmental Coordinating Committee of Cuban Affairs," January 12, 1963, NARA 198-10008-10107.

38. Capt. E. R. Zumwalt to Joseph Califano, "Future Policy toward Cuba," undated (but referencing a January 17, 1963, memo), NARA 198-10005-10090.

39. Memorandum from Gordon Chase to McGeorge Bundy, January 19, 1963, in Keefer, Sampson, and Smith, *Foreign Relations*, 11:270.

40. Bromley Smith to Sterling Cottrell, January 21, 1963, with attached Current Intelligence Memorandum, "The Training of Latin Americans in Cuba," OCI no. 0474/63, January 19, 1963, NARA 198-10007-10361.

41. William H. Brubeck to McGeorge Bundy and NSC Executive Committee, Back-up Papers and a Summary of Recommendations of the Coordinator of Cuban Affairs, January 22, 1963, NARA 198-10004-10026.

42. *Alleged Assassination Plots*, 84.

43. "Eliminating Communism," Press Conference, February 7, 1963, from Department of Army Files, NARA 198-10008-10067.

44. White House to Secretary of State, Secretary of Defense, CIA, February 15, 1963, NARA 198-100007-10319.

45. Major Laue OACSI/Collection Division to Secretary of the Army, Fact Sheet, March 13, 1963, NARA 198-10004-10096.

46. H. Johnson, *Bay of Pigs*. Manuel Artime, Pepe San Román, Enrique Ruiz-Williams, and Erneido Oliva contributed to the volume. All of them, together with Ramon Ferrer, are pictured in the book with Robert Kennedy.

47. Robert Kennedy oral history, February 29, 1964, 50.

48. Thomas, *Robert Kennedy*, 238–39.

49. Robert Kennedy oral history, April 30, 1964, 278.

50. "U.S. to Train Members of the Cuban Brigade," *Washington Post*, February 7, 1963, A27.

51. Greg McDonald, "Gen. Erneido Oliva: Second in Command at the Bay of Pigs," *AARP Bulletin*, April 15, 2011, https://www.aarp.org/politics-society /history/info-04-2011/general-erneido-oliva-where-are-they-now.html.

52. List of Participants of the Bay of Pigs Invasion, Cuban Information Archives, accessed March 22, 2018, http://cuban-exile.com/doc_026-050 /doc0035.html. Those men who had photographs taken at Fort Benning's Officer Candidate School are so noted.

53. Memorandum from Joseph Califano to Colonel Francis J. Roberts, "Contingency Planning on Cuba: Meeting of the JCS with the President on Thursday, 28 February 1963," March 4, 1963, with handwritten cover note to Vance dated March 5, NARA 198-10005-10094.

54. From Mr. Bolten to Mr. Rodriguez, Draft Copy, Memorandum to the DCI from Desmond Fitzgerald under Buck Slip Dated March 1963, March 1963, NARA 104-10102-10225.

55. McGeorge Bundy to National Security Council, "Meeting on Wednesday, March 13, at 4:30 p.m.," March 11, 1963, NARA 198-1007-10205. See also Bromley Smith, "Summary Record of NSC Meeting, Latin American Policy," March 13, 1963, NARA 176-10011-10128.

56. Unidentified, Memorandum for the Record, March 22, 1963, in Keefer, Sampson, and Smith, *Foreign Relations, 1961–1963*, 11:297.

57. "Study on Capabilities and Motivation of Cuban Groups relative to Special Operations against Cuba," undated, NARA 198-10005-10106.

58. Briefing by General Fitch, March 9, 1963, NARA 198-10004-10142.

59. Cyrus R. Vance to Deputy Secretary of Defense, "Utilization of Alpha 66 in Operations" undated and marked by hand "Draft not used March 63" but with handwritten cover note from Jim [presumably James Patchell] to Joe [Califano] dated February 28, 1963, NARA 198-10005-10015.

60. Statements by the Departments of State and Justice, March 30, 1963, NARA 198-10008-10037. The NARA cover sheet suggests that the original document included a cover sheet or buck slip from Dick to Joe [Califano] dated April 1, 1963, but it is no longer in the folder.

61. Gordon Chase to McGeorge Bundy, "Cuba Coordinating Committee—Covert Operations in Cuba," April 3, 1963, in Keefer, Sampson, and Smith, *Foreign Relations, 1961–1963*, 11:306. This memo concerns a meeting that took place on April 1, 1963.

62. Quotations and material in this and the following six paragraphs are from Thomas Parrott, Memorandum for the Record, "Meeting on Cuba," April 3, 1963, NARA 178-10003-10097. Desmond FitzGerald, Memorandum for the Record, "Meeting at the White House 3 April 1963 Called to Discuss the Agency Program in Cuba," NARA 104-10310-10245. The memorandum is undated, but NARA's cover sheet gives it a date of April 4, 1963.

63. Gordon Chase to McGeorge Bundy, "Cuban Coordinating Committee—Covert Operations," April 3, 1963, in Keefer, Sampson, and Smith, *Foreign Relations, 1961–1963*, 11:307. This memo concerns a meeting that took place on April 3, 1963.

64. Chase to Bundy, "Cuban Coordinating Committee—Covert Operations," April 3, 1963, in Keefer, Sampson, and Smith, *Foreign Relations, 1961–1963*, 11:307.

65. Memorandum for the Record, April 11, 1963, in Keefer, Sampson, and Smith, *Foreign Relations, 1961–1963*, 11:311. Earlier the same day, FitzGerald had met with the mid-level ICCCA. It had approved sabotage operations only to have the Special Group overrule that decision later in the day. FitzGerald had also made the point that if the United States started using groups inside Cuba for sabotage, it might lose control. The groups might "hit targets we never dreamed of." Memorandum from Gordon Chase to McGeorge Bundy, "Cuba—Covert Actions," April 11, 1963, in Keefer, Sampson, and Smith, *Foreign Relations, 1961–1963*, 11:313.

66. John McCone, "Memorandum of a Conference with President Kennedy on April 15," April 16, 1963, in Keefer, Sampson, and Smith, *Foreign Relations, 1961–1963*, 11:315.

6. Fidel and Hidell

1. *Warren Report*, 723.
2. *Warren Report*, 723–24.
3. *Warren Report*, 724.
4. Newman, *Assassination of John F. Kennedy*, 23.
5. *Warren Report*, 725–26.
6. *Warren Report*, 726–27.
7. *Warren Report*, 727.
8. Thomas Parrott, "Minutes of the Meeting of the Special Group, 25 April 1963," April 25, 1963, in Keefer, Sampson, and Smith, *Foreign Relations, 1961–1963*, 11:323.

9. Beschloss, *Crisis Years*, 595

10. Maxwell Taylor to Cyrus Vance, "Course of Action related to Cuba," May 10, 1963, NARA 198-10004-10206.

11. Office of National Estimates, Draft Memorandum, "Developments in Cuba and Possible US Actions in the Event of Castro's Death," May 13, 1963, NARA 198-10009-10077.

12. Coordinator of Cuban Affairs to Vance, Helms, Ryan, and Katzenbach, "Sub-Committee on Cuba Subversion," May 20, 1963, NARA 198-10007-10391.

13. Victor H. Krulak, Wikipedia, accessed April 12, 2016, http://en.wikipedia.org/wiki/Victor_H._Krulak.

14. Roswell Gilpatric to Cyrus Vance, Cuban Affairs, May 22, 1963, attaching the memo "Bundy to the Standing Group, Committee Responsibilities in Cuban Affairs," May 20, 1963, NARA 198-10008-10020.

15. Bromley Smith, "Summary Record of 7th Meeting of the Standing Group of the National Security Council," May 28, 1963, in Keefer, Sampson, and Smith, *Foreign Relations, 1961–1963*, 11:344.

16. Testimony of AMLASH case officer, July 29, 1975, Church Committee, 54, NARA 157-10011-10125.

17. Sanitized Memorandum for Record, "Minutes of Meeting of the Special Group, 6 Jun 1963," showing only the discussion on item 6, NARA 178-10003-10098.

18. At lower levels, the routine of planning for all contingencies continued. On June 7, 1963, Deputy Assistant Secretary of Defense William Bundy, McGeorge Bundy's brother, wrote the assistant secretary of state for Inter-American affairs asking that the State Department provide guidance with respect to the contingency plan for the civil affairs administration in Cuba in the event of a military invasion. William Bundy to Edwin Martin, June 7, 1963, NARA 198-10004-10126.

19. "Paper Prepared by the Central Intelligence Agency for the Standing Group of the National Security Council," June 8, 1963, in Keefer, Sampson, and Smith, *Foreign Relations, 1961–1963*, 11:346.

20. Desmond FitzGerald, "Meeting at the White House concerning Proposed Covert Policy and Integrated Program of Action towards Cuba," June 19, 1963, in Keefer, Sampson, and Smith, *Foreign Relations, 1961–1963*, 11:348.

21. Thomas A. Parrott to Johnson, Gilpatric, McCone, "Memorandum for the Special Group, Sabotage Program, Cuba," June 19, 1963, NARA 178-10003-10099.

22. Parrott to Johnson, Gilpatric, McCone, "Memorandum for the Special Group, Sabotage Program, Cuba," June 19, 1963.

23. Testimony of Harold Swenson, May 10, 1976, Church Committee, 16–17, NARA 157-10014-10048. Swenson was the chief of counterintelligence for FitzGerald's Special Affairs Staff in the summer of 1963. The SAS was a self-contained microcosm of CIA with a counterintelligence section that operated separately and independently from the Counterintelligence Division, which James Angleton headed and which handled counterintelligence for everything but Cuba.

24. Jim [Patchell] to Joe [Califano], June 18, 1963, handwritten note attaching "Cuban Exile and Refugee Activities," NARA 198-10006-10095. The intelligence report references a CIA document dated June 7.

25. Desmond FitzGerald, Memorandum for the Record, "Meeting in the Office of the Secretary of State re Discussion of Proposed Covert Policy and Integrated Program of Action towards Cuba," June 22, 1963, in Keefer, Sampson, and Smith, *Foreign Relations, 1961–1963*, 11:305.

26. John McCone, Memorandum for the Record, "Meeting with Secretary Rusk—21 June 1963—re Cuba," June 24, 1963, in Keefer, Sampson, and Smith, *Foreign Relations, 1961–1963*, 11:351. FitzGerald's memorandum indicated the meeting with Rusk took place on June 22, whereas McCone's places it a day earlier. Since June 21 was a Friday, McCone's is presumably correct.

7. Oswald in New Orleans

1. *Warren Report*, 728.

2. The FPCC was located at 799 Broadway, and the SWP at 116 University Place.

3. Joe Hansen, who was a student of Leon Trotsky and who was with him when he was assassinated, formed the Fair Play for Cuba Committee after returning from a trip to Cuba with Farrell Dobbs of the SWP in 1960. Gregory Van Wagenen, "Saints of the Fourth International: Remembering Joe and Reba Hansen," *Mormon Worker*, https://www.scribd.com/document/43785389/The-Mormon-Worker-Issue-6-Mar-09.

4. *Warren Report*, 728.

5. Testimony of Francis L. Martello, April 7, 1964, *Warren Report*, 10:54.

6. *Warren Report*, 729. Testimony of Vincent T. Lee, April 17, 1964, *Warren Report*, 10:87.

7. Testimony of Arnold Johnson, April 17, 1964, *Warren Report*, 10:95. For Oswald's letters to Johnson's, see *Warren Report*, 20:257–73. The letters can be read in one of two ways. Either they are the work of a lonely man pretending he is more important than he was by writing these national Communist organizations. Or they are simple, unencrypted communications to Cuban case officers, telling them what Oswald is doing and giving them his address. Several letters contain requests for advice that can be read as coming from a delusional man, but these can also be read as requests for advice by an agent.

8. Testimony of Richard Helms, September 11, 1975, Church Committee, 8–9, 157-10011-10060. In fact Helms said this was how the AMLASH operation originated: "Well, we have just put in the record what has shown President Kennedy authorized in the middle of 1963, and here is a fellow [Cubela] that could work right in our general direction, so that he would almost be kind of an agent that would fit like a hand into a glove" (9–10).

9. Joseph Califano to Desmond FitzGerald, Cuban Military Personalities, July 24, 1963, NARA 198-10007-10010. This letter states it is in response to FitzGerald's memorandum of July 2. Additional letters are filed with the

same number at the NARA. On August 21 John Cheever at the CIA asked for additional information on the individuals and for organizational charts for the Cuban military. He asked this to be expedited for thirteen of the Cuban officers. On August 27 John King of the CIA wrote Lt. Colonel Alexander Haig, who had become Califano's deputy, suggesting the creation of an interagency working group to deal with the biographical information the CIA wanted. Califano forwarded the request to the Defense Intelligence Agency on August 28, saying, "[The work] should provide a valuable ready-reference for our military planning effort." Nothing suggests that Califano knew the CIA was trying to determine who in Cuba could be persuaded to join a coup. On September 14 Califano wrote FitzGerald and designated two analysts to work with the CIA. The army had taken two and a half months to act.

10. Bromley Smith, "Summary Record of the 9th Meeting of the Standing Group of the National Security Council," July 9, 1963, in Keefer, Sampson, and Smith, *Foreign Relations, 1961–1963*, 11:354.

11. On the same day, Joseph Califano, general counsel for the army, wrote the coordinator for Cuban affairs for the lower-level ICCCA noting that the new military junta in Ecuador wanted U.S. recognition. Califano urged that the State Department extract a commitment to anti-Castro measures by the junta as a quid pro quo for recognition. Joseph Califano to Coordinator of Cuban Affairs, Possible U.S. Recognition of Equadorian [*sic*] Junta Regime, July 16, 1963, NARA 198-10004-10035.

12. Bromley Smith, "Summary Record of the 10th Meeting of the Standing Group of the National Security Council," July 16, 1963, in Keefer, Sampson, and Smith, *Foreign Relations, 1961–1963*, 11:356.

13. Desmond FitzGerald, Memorandum for the Record, "Meeting of the Special Group 18 July, 1963," July 19, 1963, NARA 104-10310-10246. Attendees were Bundy, McCone, Gilpatric, Alexis Johnson, and Parrott.

14. FitzGerald, Memorandum for the Record, July 19, 1963.

15. George Denney to John Crimmins, "Cuba: Possible Courses of Action," July 25, 1963, NARA 198-10009-10110. The memorandum was sent to Califano at Defense, who forwarded it to Wheeler and others at the DOD.

16. "Cuban Exiles May Shift Operations to Nicaragua," *Washington Post*, July 18, 1963, A24.

17. Theodore A. Eidger, "Exile Expects Anti-Castro Thrust Soon," *Washington Post*, July 24, 1963, A7.

18. "Cuban Exiles Ask Latin Aid," *Washington Post*, July 24, 1963, A1.

19. Paul Nitze to Secretary of the Army, "Future US Policy toward Cuba," July 29, 1963, NARA 198-10004-10200. The NARA document includes Alexander Haig's memo to Vance and a draft of a thank-you from Vance to Nitze dated September 3, 1963.

20. Testimony of Samuel Halpern, April 22, 1976, Church Committee, 23, NARA 157-10014-10008.

21. Special Agent in Charge New York to Director, FBI, "Fair Play for Cuba Committee," November 27, 1963, NARA 104-10310-10071. The documents suggest that the CIA originated the request for the mailing list and stationery on September 26, 1963. The break-in occurred in October, but the New York office didn't get around to sending it to FBI headquarters until after, and presumably because of, the assassination. It sent a copy to the CIA through liaison Sam Papich on December 5, 1963.

22. Desmond FitzGerald to McGeorge Bundy, "Louis Somoza's Involvement Exile Operations," August 9, 1963, in Keefer, Sampson, and Smith, *Foreign Relations, 1961–1963*, 11:357.

23. Desmond FitzGerald to Joseph Califano, "U.S. Course of Action in the Event of a Military Revolt in Cuba," August 13, 1963, NARA 198-10007-10461. The National Archives only has the identification form. When the author asked the research assistant what happened, she investigated. Although the NARA keeps multiple copies of every document, all copies are missing, suggesting it was never turned over. The author also made a Freedom of Information Act request to the Department of the Army for a copy. It replied that all copies had been transferred to the National Archives. Barbara Garris, U.A. Army Freedom of Information Act Office to author, FOIA 15-0396, January 29, 2015. Since the CIA should have given its copy of the document to the National Archives, it must not have a copy either.

24. Tape 104/A40, JFK Library, accessed April 12, 2018, http://www.jfklibrary .org/Asset-Viewer/Archives/JFKPOF-MTG-104-005.aspx. The author's request to declassify this tape is pending at this writing.

25. *Alleged Assassination Plots*, 107.

26. Testimony of Walter Elder, August 13, 1975, Church Committee, 19, NARA 157-10002-10046.

27. Elder testimony, August 13, 1975, Church Committee, 24–25.

28. George A. Carroll to Members of the Special Group (Counterinsurgency), "Department of Defense Report on Developments in Counterinsurgency," August 21, 1963, NARA 198-10007-10343.

29. Goldstein, *Lessons in Disaster*, 78.

30. Earle Wheeler to Secretary of the Army, "National Level Cuba Planning Relationships," August 24, 1963, NARA 198-10005-10024.

8. Assassins and Spies

1. *Merriam-Webster Dictionary*, s.v. "assassination," accessed December 20, 2018, https://www/merriam-webster.com/dictionary/assassination.

2. Executive Order 12333.

3. Breckenridge, CIA *and the U.S. Intelligence System*, 238–39.

4. Testimony of Marina Oswald, February 3, 1964, *Warren Report*, 1:16.

5. Shenon, *Cruel and Shocking Act*, 119–20. Bill Harvey discussed KGB assassinations with the Church Committee and gave his own views of when CIA assassinations might be justified. Testimony of William Harvey tes-

timony, morning session, June 25, 1975, Church Committee, 11–31, NARA 157-10002-10105.

6. John Barron, *KGB*, 308. Barron catalogs dozens of disappearances and assassinations by Soviet intelligence beginning as early as 1926, including two in New York in the 1930s.

7. Andrew and Gordievsky, *KGB*, 157–58, 221.

8. Andrew and Gordievsky, *KGB*, 309.

9. Andrew and Gordievsky, *KGB*, 309–10.

10. Barron, *KGB*, 309.

11. *Warren Report*, 423.

12. Barron, *KGB*, 311–15.

13. "Soviet Use of Assassination and Kidnaping [*sic*]," accessed April 12, 2018, https://www.cia.gov/library/center-for-the-study-of-intelligence/kent -csi/vol19no3/html/v19i3a01p_0001.htm.

14. CSPAN, "Church Committee 9/16/1975 Hearing on CIA Biological Agents Program, Testimony CIA Director William Colby," https://www.youtube.com /watch?v=Bz4HINzjx4A&list=PLNmHi8s2A7KXM89iiwM39Na2X8g1gYCe1.

15. Barron, *KGB*, 330.

16. Andrew and Gordievsky, *KGB*, 470–73.

17. Andrew and Gordievsky, *KGB*, 468–69.

18. Testimony of Richard Helms, June 13, 1975, Church Committee, 24–25, NARA 157-10014-10075.

19. Raymond G. Rocca, Counter Intelligence Operations CIA, Memorandum for the Record, "Conversation with David W. Belin (1 April 1975)," page 2, NARA 1993.08.11.16:46:36:150059.

20. Latell, *Castro's Secrets*, 1.

21. Latell, *Castro's Secrets*, 119–25.

9. AMLASH

1. Although the CIA has not explained publicly why these code names were chosen, it is publicly known that AM was a designator for Cuba. In the case of individuals, code names are used instead of real names for security purposes. For example, even if someone should get a copy of a CIA report of a meeting where the code name is used, he might not be able to tell who the person really was. Code names also make it harder to break an encoded electronic message. Code names are said to be meaningless although they obviously have a mnemonic value. Despite such dry explanations, the fact remains that Cubela's code name of Lash clearly has a sinister connotation.

2. CIA Biographic Data, Rolando CUBELA Secades, April 13, 1966, with handwritten note: "Sent to RI for classification & filing in Cubela 201," NARA 104-10102-10010. In Cubela's interview by Robert Blakely, chief counsel for the House Assassinations Committee, he did not mention the 1962 meetings with the CIA. Rolando Cubela, interview by G. Robert Blakey and Edwin

Lopez, Riviera Hotel, Havana Cuba, August 28, 1978, House Assassinations Committee, NARA 180-10114-10496.

3. When interviewed by the House Assassinations Committee, Cubela termed some of the locations "special houses" by which he presumably meant "safe houses." Rolando Cubela, interview by G. Robert Blakey and Edwin Lopez, Riviera Hotel, Havana Cuba, August 28, 1978, House Assassinations Committee, 8, NARA 180-10114-10496. A safe house is a facility controlled by an intelligence agency at which secret meetings between case officers and agents can be held.

4. CIA Biographic Data, Rolando CUBELA Secades, April 13, 1966, with handwritten note.

5. CIA cable, Paris to Director, IN 47183, August 17, 1962, NARA 104-10102-10014, emphasis added. Cables received at CIA headquarters have an "in" number as well as the number the sending station assigned the cable. For example, this cable was recorded at CIA headquarters with the in number 47183, but it had a Paris number of 2629.

6. CIA cable, Director to Paris, DIR 30778, August 18, 1962, NARA 104-10102-10016. The DIR prefix to the cable number means that it was outgoing under authority of the director.

7. Background Information on Rolando Cubela Secades, April 13, 1966, 2, NARA 104-10102-10010. Cables in the AMLASH files mention "pills" for S/W," or secret writing; hence, the assumption that he was using some kind of invisible ink.

8. The author examined several of these documents, which are now at the National Archives. All are stained a disquieting blood-red from the chemical the FBI used to test for secret writing.

9. This fact is contained in a memorandum the author wrote in 1976 while on the Church Committee. Jim Johnston to Senator Hart and Senator Schweiker, "Connection between AMLASH Operation and Investigation of JFK Assassination," January 27, 1976, NARA 157-10004-10292. The cable is one of many documents cited in Church Committee reports that are not in the National Archives' JFK collection. In this instance the cable was identified as DIR 48198 to Rome and reported that AMWHIP, Tepedino, had sent a letter as part of the activation effort. The cable itself is not in the National Archives collection.

10. Testimony of AMLASH case officer, July 29, 1975, Church Committee, 40–43, NARA 157-10011-10125; testimony of AMLASH case officer, February 11, 1976, Church Committee, 4, NARA 157-10014-10017. Nestor Sanchez testified to the Church Committee as "AMLASH case officer"; however, he later admitted publicly that he was the case officer. See, for example, Latell, *Castro's Secrets*, 168. Although Sanchez will be identified by name in the text, the citation to his Church Committee testimony will use "AMLASH case officer," which is how the document is labeled. Sanchez's service on Harvey's staff is mentioned in David Belin, "Interview with Mr. Nestor Sanchez," May 19, 1975 2, NARA 178-10002-10335.

11. AMLASH case officer testimony, February 11, 1976, Church Committee, 10–11. The IG Report says that it was the Collegiate Games. IG Report, 86.

12. CIA cable, Porto Alegre to Director, September 7, 1963, IN 15210, NARA 104-10102-10017. Sanchez also wrote that Cubela needed a strong confidant inside to push him and serve as his "chaplain." Sanchez suggested Marcelo Artime. There is no information on Marcelo Artime and nothing to clarify whether Sanchez meant either Manuel Artime, the exile leader who was organizing exile groups for raids on Cuba, or a relative of his. A cable of September 11 from Porto Alegre added that Cubela had reported that all the Soviet IRBMs and bombers had been removed from Cuba. This is another instance of the author's 1976 report referencing a cable, but the cable itself isn't at the National Archives. Johnston to Hart and Schweiker, "Connection between AMLASH Operation and Investigation of JFK Assassination."

13. CIA cable, Porto Alegre to Director, September 7, 1963.

14. CIA cable, Porto Alegre to Director, September 7, 1963.

15. CIA cable, Director to Porto Alegre, September 9, 1963, DIR 67110, NARA 104-10102-10019. Headquarters said Macelo Artime would not work as Cubela's chaplain.

16. AMLASH case officer testimony, February 11, 1976, Church Committee, 8. Unfortunately, the Church Committee report did not append exhibits to many of its transcripts. Therefore, as in this case, the contents of the exhibit can only be gleaned because the questioner read the relevant part of the exhibit to the witness as part of the question. The case officer, Sanchez, also agreed that after the meetings in Brazil, Cubela was not thought of as a collector of intelligence but as a conspirator (9).

17. BLAKELY: And then the next meeting that you had would have been in September the 7th and the indication is that you discussed with them the possibility of a quote "inside job" close quote against Primer [*sic*] Castro and you were awaiting some plan of action from the United States. Did you in fact have a meeting in September of 1963?

CUBELA: It is possible—'62.

BLAKELY: Do you recall who it would have been with?

CUBELA: I don't remember the name.

BLAKELY: Do you recall where it would have been?

CUBELA: It was in France.

Cubela interview, House Assassinations Committee, 9, NARA 180-10114-10496.

18. *Chicago Tribune*, September 9, 1963, 10, emphasis added. The *New Orleans Times Picayune* also carried the story. Some have speculated that Lee Harvey Oswald read it and that this influenced him to assassinate the president. David Belin was one who developed this theory. He had been on the staff of the Warren Commission and didn't focus on Castro's remarks then. However, in 1975 he was executive director of the Rockefeller Commission, which

looked into the CIA assassination plots. In that capacity he interviewed Raymond Rocca, who had been assistant to James Angleton at the CIA in investigating the assassination in 1963–64. Rocca had not known about Castro's remarks when he was working with the Warren Commission. He told Belin he would have looked far more closely at Oswald's connections to Cuba if he had known of Castro's threat. Raymond Rocca, "Conversation with David W. Belin," April 1, 1975, NARA 1993.08.11.16:46:36:150059.

19. AMLASH case officer testimony, February 11, 1976, Church Committee, 90–91.

20. Johnston to Hart and Schweiker, "Connection between AMLASH Operation and Investigation of JFK Assassination."

21. "I cannot recall now whether my knowledge that there were such [assassination] plots was before or after. I would just like to say I heartily disapproved of it, I thought it was a lot of nonsense, and my position on that was very clear, and I don't think people talked to me about it because of the way I felt." Testimony of Harold Swenson, May 10, 1976, Church Committee, 10, NARA 157-10014-10048.

22. Clint E. Smith to Interdepartmental Coordination Committee of Cuban Affairs, "Meeting of September 11," September 9, 1963, NARA 198-10007-10420.

23. Joseph A. Califano to Wheeler, Zumwalt, Alger, Wendt, Carpenter, Elwood, "Interdepartmental Coordinating Committee of Cuban Affairs: Possible Retaliatory Actions by the Castro Government," September 16, 1963, attachment, NARA 198-10007-10421. In his cover letter, Califano asked for comment on the actions on the ICCCA list, but he added that addressees should comment on "other likely actions which might be taken by the Castro government in retaliation for Cuban exile raids." It isn't clear if Califano thought that exile raids had prompted the worry about retaliation.

24. AMLASH case officer testimony, February 11, 1976, Church Committee, 11. Also, according to the author's 1976 memorandum, the CIA's file on Cubela contained a cable from the Paris station reporting the following conversation obtained by covert means. Mary: "I don't want to imagine things but this thing with Amlash [Cubela]." Moreno: "It is either a tremendous secret or a top secret matter [unreadable followed by the word 'treason' or 'reason']" Betty: "I believe it is a top secret matter." Where the conversation took place is not known, but it may have been in the Cuban embassy in Paris. Johnston to Hart and Schweiker, "Connection between AMLASH Operation and Investigation of JFK Assassination."

25. W. F. A. Wendt to Joseph Califano, "Request by Cuban Resistance Elements for Navy Assistance," September 19, 1963, NARA 198-10007-10081.

26. W. F. A. Wendt to Joseph Califano, "Request by Cuban Counterrevolutionaries for Navy Assistance," September 20, 1963, NARA 198-10007-10081.

27. Paul Nitze to Secretary of the Army, "Draft State-Defense Contingency Plan for a Coup in Cuba," September 30, 1963, NARA 198-10004-10002.

28. Bromley Smith, "Summary Record of the 14th Meeting of the Standing Group of the National Security Council," October 1, 1963, in Keefer, Sampson, and Smith, *Foreign Relations, 1961–1963*, 11:368.

10. Mexico City

1. Testimony of Marina Oswald, February 3, 1964, *Warren Report*, 1:12.

2. Joseph Task to Lee H. Oswald, March 27, 1963, Dobbs exhibit 13, *Warren Report*, 19:580. The Young Socialist Alliance mailing address was a post office box at Coopers Station in New York. That post office was located near FPCC headquarters at 799 Broadway. The SWP advertised its publication, the *Militant*, in the Alliance's periodical, *Young Socialist. Young Socialist* 6, no. 9 (November 1963), https://www.marxists.org/history/etol/newspape /youngsocialist/1962-1964/v06n09-w57-nov-1963-TYS.pdf.

3. Arnold Johnson to L. H. Oswald, July 31, 1963, Johnson exhibits 1 and 2, *Warren Report*, 20:257–260.

4. Lee H. Oswald to Arnold Johnson, August 13, 1963, Johnson exhibit 3, *Warren Report*, 20:262

5. Lee H. Oswald to Central Committee CPUSA, August 28, 1963, Johnson exhibit 4, *Warren Report*, 20:262–64.

6. Lee H. Oswald to Mr. Best, August 31, 1963, Johnson exhibit 5, *Warren Report*, 20:266.

7. Lee H. Oswald to Communist Party, September 1, 1963, Johnson exhibit 6, *Warren Report*, 20:270. Lee H. Oswald to Socialist Workers Party, September 1, 1963, *Warren Report*, 19:577.

8. On the one hand, Marina Oswald implied that she knew Oswald hoped to fly to Havana from Mexico City and not return. On the other hand, she asked him to buy her some phonograph records while he was there and bring them back. *Warren Report*, 736.

9. *Warren Report*, 729–30.

10. *Warren Report*, 733–34.

11. Azcue made it seem as though the FPCC, as an "association aiding Cuba," was more closely connected to Castro than the *Warren Report* suggests. Eusebio Azcue, interview by Robert Blakey, House Assassinations Committee, undated but ca. August 28, 1978, 2–7, NARA 180-10114-10495.

12. *Warren Report*, 734. That Kostikov was associated with Department 13 was established by the Church Committee in 1976. U.S. Senate Select Committee on Intelligence, *Investigation of the Assassination*, 92.

13. CIA cable, Mexico City to Headquarters, "Lee Harvey Oswald and Kostikov," October 8, 1963, NARA 157-10004-10245; *Warren Report*, 734.

14. Azcue interview, 9.

15. *Warren Report* 734–35.

16. Azcue interview, 32. Azcue continued, saying that he would not have communicated the approval to Oswald even if he had his address because there would be no point in doing so. Azcue presumably was arguing that

Oswald needed a visa to the Soviet Union and could get an in-transit visa to Cuba once he had the Soviet visa, but this makes little sense. Since the Cubans went to the trouble of sending Oswald's application to Havana, why wouldn't they follow up once it was approved?

17. *Warren Report*, 735.

18. *Warren Report*, 735–36.

19. Richard Helms to J. Lee Rankin, "Role of the Cuban Intelligence Service in Processing Visa Applicants; Reaction of That Service to the Assassination of President Kennedy," May 15, 1963, with attachment, NARA 193.08.11.17:43:51:840059.

20. *Warren Report*, 737.

21. FBI Airtel, SAC New York to Director, "Fair Play for Cuba Committee," October 4, 1963, NARA 104-10310-10070.

22. CIA cable, Paris to Director, no subject, PARI 0934, October 7, 1963, NARA 104-10102-10020. Although the cable itself has no title, the NARA cover sheet assigns the title "Much More Relaxed."

23. CIA cable, Paris to Director, no subject, PARI 0934, October 7, 1963.

24. Testimony of AMLASH case officer, February 11, 1976, Church Committee, 29, NARA 157-10011-10125.

25. CIA cable, Paris to Director, no subject, PARI 0934, October 7, 1963. As will be discussed in a later chapter, the CIA, including both Sanchez, the case officer, and Helms, the DDP, always insisted that the AMLASH operation was a coup and not an assassination. Arguably, that is the way they saw it, although others at the CIA disagreed. But it is certainly clear from the language of this cable that both Cubela and AMSPORT, whoever he was, thought that Castro would be killed. What other kind of "blow with lightning speed" would cause "chaos" and require strong support within hours?

26. CIA cable, Director to Paris, no subject, DIR 74420, October 9, 1963, NARA 104-10215-10242.

27. CIA cable, Paris to Director, no subject, IN 38361, October 10, 1963, NARA 104-10215-10022.

28. The copy of the cable at the National Archives is marked as "slotted at" 1750. Presumably, the CIA message center, which handled messages from around the world, used universal time or Greenwich mean time, meaning that this message was "slotted at" 2:50 in the afternoon of October 11, Washington time. However, according to a CIA memo in 1964, the slotted time on a cable was the time multiple copies had been made and put into internal distribution. The cable would be routed to the action officer, in this case FitzGerald, upon receipt. The CIA memo says the elapsed time between receiving a priority cable, such as this, and slotting it averaged one hour and twenty-six minutes. Thus, although this cable was slotted at 2:50 in the afternoon, it should have been delivered to FitzGerald's office roughly an hour and a half before that, at around 1:30. Memorandum for . . . C/Signal Center, "Processing Time by Cable Secretariat for Immediate and Priority Cables,"

April 12, 1965, https://www.cia.gov/library/readingroom/docs/CIA-RDP84 -00499R000600040139-4.pdf.

29. Phone Call Record, RFK, 2:30, 10/11/63, folder 9/19/63 to 10/30/63, box 257, Papers of Robert F. Kennedy. Attorney General Papers, JFK Library and Museum, Boston MA.

30. Testimony of AMLASH case officer, July 29, 1975, Church Committee, 48–49, NARA 157-10011-10125, emphasis added.

31. AMLASH case officer testimony, July 29, 1975, Church Committee, 16–21.

32. CIA cable, Paris to Director, IN 41028, October 15, 1963, emphasis added, NARA 104-10215-10237.

33. CIA cable, Director to Paris, DIR 75683, October 15, 1963, NARA 104-10215-10240.

34. AMLASH case officer testimony, February 11, 1976, Church Committee, 49–50.

11. Hubris

1. Latell, *Castro's Secrets*, 167.

2. CIA cable, Paris to Director, IN44147, October 21, 1963, NARA 104-10102-10023.

3. U.S. Senate Select Committee on Intelligence, *Investigation of the Assassination*, 17, citing Chief JMWAVE testimony June 19, 1975, at 80 and his testimony on May 6, 1976 at 45–46. Unfortunately, the transcripts of his testimony have not been declassified and transferred to the National Archives. The author read the June 19 testimony when the author was on the Church Committee and led the questioning on May 6. The important parts of his testimony were included in the committee's cited report, and in any event, the author knows of no reason that the JMWAVE chief's testimony should not have been declassified when more significant things have been.

4. Thomas, *Very Best Men*, 300.

5. Testimony of Harold Swenson, May 10, 1976, Church Committee, 23–24, NARA 157-10014-10048.

6. Thomas, *Very Best Men*, 300.

7. U.S. Senate Select Committee on Intelligence, *Investigation of the Assassination*, 71.

8. Interrogation Research Division to WH/C/FI, "Tepedino, Carlos," September 22, 1965, NARA 104-10183-10410. Brian Latell in *Castro's Secrets* at 263n59 references a second polygraph report of Tepedino dated January 19, 1966 (NARA 104-10183-10271).

9. Thomas, *Very Best Men*, 300.

10. Thomas, *Very Best Men*, 300. Thomas also writes that FitzGerald was having financial difficulties. His financial advisor had lost most of the $2 million FitzGerald had entrusted to him (301).

11. CIA cable, Director to Paris and Rome, DIR 76721, October 18, 1963, NARA 104-10215-10236.

12. CIA cable, Director to Paris and Rome, DIR 77176, October 21, 1963, NARA 104-10215-10370.

13. CIA cable, Director to Paris, DIR 7717, October 21, 1963, NARA 104-10102-10024.

14. Lattel, *Castro's Secrets*, 195.

15. Gen. Maxwell Taylor to Secretary of Defense, Draft State-Defense Contingency Plan for a Coup in Cuba, October 21, 1963, NARA 198-10004-10004.

16. The room, on the first floor of the house, was so small that the landlady promised to give Oswald a larger room as soon as one became available. A week later a larger room opened up, and she offered it to Oswald. However, he turned it down because it was on the lower level. He said the room he was renting had more light. This makes little sense since Oswald was never there during the daytime. He worked all day and spent weekends with Marina. On the other hand, he listened to the radio, and the first-floor room would have had better reception.

17. *Warren Report*, 737–38.

18. *Warren Report*, 738–39.

19. William H. Attwood, Wikipedia, accessed April 12, 2018, https://en.wikipedia.org/wiki/William_Attwood.

20. Beschloss, *Crisis Years*, 658.

21. Beschloss, *Crisis Years*, 658.

22. William Attwood to Gordon Chase, Memorandum, November 8, 1963, NARA 178-10003-10062. Gordon Chase was an assistant to McGeorge Bundy.

23. Edwin Martin to McGeorge Bundy, "Cuba," November 8, 1963, NARA 176-10010-10054.

24. "Weaknesses (and Derogatory Information)," October 24, 1963, NARA 104-10215-10235.

25. "Scenario," unsigned, undated, NARA 104-10102-10030.

26. "Fall Back Position," unsigned, undated, NARA 1993.07.19.16:48:01:370270. This document is also filed with the Scenario, NARA 104-10102-10030, referenced in the previous note.

27. Latell, *Castro's Secrets*, 183.

12. Carpe Diem

1. The CIA officer who drove FitzGerald to the meeting told Brian Latell that he drove his own beat-up Peugeot, rather than a limousine, and did not wear a chauffeur's uniform. Latell, *Castro's Secrets*, 195. Also rather than a safe house, the meeting was at the home of the chief of the CIA's Paris station.

2. Richard Helms and William Colby, Memorandum for the Record, "White House Meeting on Vietnam," 4:20 p.m., October 29, 1963, NARA 104-10310-10243. The meeting between FitzGerald and Cubela was planned to last from 5:00 p.m. until 7:00 p.m. Paris time. Paris is six hours ahead of Washington DC, so if the Paris meeting lasted as long as planned, it would have ended about 1:00 p.m. Washington time.

3. Helms and Colby, Memorandum for the Record, October 29, 1963.

4. Sanchez, Memorandum for the Record, AMLASH/1/Dainold, November 13, 1963, NARA 104-10215-10364. "Dainold" was the code name for FitzGerald, whereas "James Clark" was simply the false name he used in Cubela's presence.

5. Nestor Sanchez, Memorandum for the Record, November 13, 1963.

6. Testimony of AMLASH case officer, February 11, 1976, Church Committee, 27–28, NARA 157-10014-10017.

7. AMLASH case officer testimony, February 11, 1976, Church Committee, 64.

8. AMLASH case officer testimony, February 11, 1976, Church Committee, 28.

9. Rolando Cubela, interview by G. Robert Blakey and Edwin Lopez, Riviera Hotel, Havana Cuba, August 28, 1978, House Assassinations Committee, 10–11, NARA 180-10114-10496.

10. Cubela interview, August 28, 1978, House Assassinations Committee, 16.

11. Telegram from the Ambassador in Vietnam (Lodge) to the Department of State, October 29, 1963, in Keefer, *Foreign Relations, 1961–1963,* 4:226.

12. Reeves, *Profile of Power,* 643.

13. Reeves, *Profile of Power,* 642–43.

14. Reeves, *Profile of Power,* 647–48.

15. *Warren Report,* 739.

16. *Warren Report,* 739.

17. A. Dobrynin, cipher telegram, Special no. 2005, November 26, 1963, Yeltsin Documents.

18. U.S. Senate Select Committee on Intelligence, *Investigation of the Assassination,* 96.

19. Minutes of the Special Meeting of the Special Group Meeting, November 5, 1963, in Keefer, Sampson, and Smith, *Foreign Relations, 1961–1963,* 11:373.

20. Robert Kennedy oral history, April 30, 1964, 277.

21. *Warren Report,* 741.

22. Reeves, *Profile of Power,* 654.

13. The Plot Accelerates

1. Unless otherwise noted, account and quotations here and in the following seven paragraphs are from Bruce Cheever, Minutes of the Meeting to Review the Cuban Program, November 14, 1963, in Keefer, Smith, and Sampson, *Foreign Relations, 1961–1963,* microfiche supplement, 718; John McCone, "Meeting on Policy Relating to Cuba—10:30 a.m.—12 Nov 63," in Keefer, Sampson, and Smith, *Foreign Relations, 1961–1963,* 11:375; Paul Eckel, "Cuban Operations," November 12, 1963, in Keefer, Sampson, and Smith, *Foreign Relations, 1961–1963,* 11:376.

2. McGeorge Bundy, Memorandum for the Record, November 12, 1963, NARA 176-10010-10056.

3. Cheever, Minutes of the Meeting to Review the Cuban Program, November 14, 1963; McCone, "Meeting on Policy Relating to Cuba—10:30 a.m.—12 Nov 63," John McCone, "Meeting on Policy Relating to Cuba—10:30 a.m.—

12 Nov 63"; Eckel, "Cuban Operations," November 12, 1963. In his memoir Dean Rusk says: "The Church Committee revelations of 1975 caught me completely by surprise. Had I know about assassination plots, I would have moved to stop them." He also asserts, "Not once did my representatives on the 303 Committee tell me about CIA-hatched assassination plots against Castro and other foreign leaders. I remain convinced that the 303 Committee never discussed them." Rusk, *As I Saw It*, 55. Rusk's denial is curious. For one thing the 303 Committee was the name of the Cuban affairs group under President Johnson; it was called the Special Group or the Special Group (Augmented) under Kennedy. The committee was so named because it met in room 303 of the Executive Office Building. Robarge, *John McCone*, 98. Also the meeting referred to in the text was not a Special Group or 303 Committee meeting; it was a special meeting with both President Kennedy and Rusk himself attending. Granted, according to the various minutes, no one used the word "assassinate." However, it is clear from the minutes the CIA was proposing a military coup in Cuba to get rid of Castro. Just two weeks earlier, at a similar meeting on Vietnam, Rusk had supported letting military leaders there stage a coup against President Diem, who was assassinated by those leaders. Either Rusk was taking cover under the doctrine of "plausible denial" in saying that he had not heard of assassination plots against Castro since the word "assassination" apparently was never used. Or the secretary of state couldn't put two and two together and couldn't see that a coup in Cuba would run the same course as the one in Vietnam had just done.

4. The quoted material appears in the last paragraph of Eckel's memorandum ("Cuban Operations"). The last page of McCone's memorandum is missing from Keefer, Smith, and Sampson, *Foreign Relations, 1961–1963*, microfiche supplement. However, State Department historian Adam Howard obtained it from the CIA and furnished it to the author, saying that it will be added to the supplement. Adam Howard email to author May 27, 2014.

5. Author deleted, Memorandum for the Record, "AMWHIP/1 Meeting, New York City, Thursday, 14 November 1963," NARA 104-10295-10154. Sanchez was not the author. In his testimony to the Church Committee, the questioner refers to the author by name, which is redacted from the transcript, but the questioner is asking Sanchez about a memo written by a named person rather than "you," as he would have if the memo had been written by Sanchez.

6. Testimony of AMLASH case officer, July 29, 1975, 89, Church Committee, NARA 157-10011-10125; David Belin, "Interview with Mr. Nestor Sanchez," May 19, 1975, 9, NARA 178-10002-10335. The 1967 CIA IG Report said that it was a pen with a hypodermic needle full of poison. It did not become clear until 1975 in Sanchez's interview with Belin that Cubela wanted a pen that fired a poisoned dart.

7. Rolando Cubela, interview by G. Robert Blakey and Edwin Lopez, Riviera Hotel, Havana Cuba, August 28, 1978, House Assassinations Committee, 18, NARA 180-10114-10496.

8. Federal Bureau of Investigation, Manuel F. Artime-Buesa, November 14, 1963, NARA record number 0-0-0, series JFK, file number 80T01357A.

9. Joseph A. Califano Jr. to Director, Defense Intelligence Agency, November 14, 1963, NARA 198-10007-10199.

10. Nestor Sanchez to Paris, DIR 83271, November 16, 1963, NARA 104-10215-10361.

11. Desmond FitzGerald to Paris, DIR 83825, undated, NARA 104-10102-10036.

14. The Last Weekend

1. *Warren Report*, 741.

2. Testimony of Marina Oswald, *Warren Report*, 1:54.

3. Testimony of Ruth Paine, March 20, 1964, *Warren Report*, 2:515–16; and March 21, 1964, *Warren Report*, 3:41.

4. Testimony of Buell Wesley Frazier, March 11, 1964, *Warren Report*, 2:210, 217.

5. Testimony of Mrs. Arthur Carl (Gladys J.) and Arthur Carl Johnson, April 1, 1964, *Warren Report*, 10:292, 301.

6. Ruth Paine testimony, March 20, 1964, *Warren Report*, 2:516.

7. *Warren Report*, 740.

8. R. D. Albro to Joseph Califano, Memorandum, "Training of Cuban Refugees in Nicaragua," November 19, 1963, NARA 198-10009-10114. Oliva claimed that he was working for Secretary of the Army Cyrus Vance during this period. Greg McDonald, "Gen. Erneido Oliva: Second in Command at the Bay of Pigs," AARP *Bulletin*, April 15, 2011, https://www.aarp.org/politics-society/history/info-04-2011/general-erneido-oliva-where-are-they-now.html. If so, then this intelligence report was telling Vance what his subordinate was doing.

9. Phone Call Records, RFK, November18, 1963 and November 19, 1963, folder 10/30/63 to 12/13/63, box 257, Papers of Robert F. Kennedy, Attorney General Papers, JFK Library and Museum, Boston MA. Naturally, Robert Kennedy was taking phone calls unrelated to Cuba too. For example the records show calls from John Seigenthaler, who had been a lawyer in the Civil Rights Division of Kennedy's Justice Department but was editor of the *Nashville Tennessean* by this time. Mrs. Rubirosa—Odile Rodin, the beautiful French actress and wife of playboy Porfirio Rubirosa—also called, leaving her number at the St. Regis Hotel in New York. The Rubirosas socialized with the Kennedys, although there might have been a Cuban connection since Mrs. Rubirosa had met Fidel Castro when she lived in Cuba with her husband when he served as ambassador to the Batista government for Rafael Trujillo's Dominican Republic.

10. Biographer Evan Thomas writes of Kennedy's thirty-eighth birthday on November 20. Thomas, *Robert Kennedy*, 275. In Robert Kennedy's oral history, interviewer John Bartlow Martin had this exchange with Kennedy: "Do you, did you have high peop [*sic*]—any Cubans that you used particularly? I remember meeting one at your birthday party who kept in touch with

me." Kennedy answered, "Enrico Williams." Presumably Martin was referencing Kennedy's most recent birthday the previous November. Robert Kennedy oral history, April 30, 1964, 278. Thomas's book cites two documents in the Assassination Records Review Board collection, but this author has been able to find only one in the National Archives JFK Collection.

11. Richard M. Fallucci, "Summary of Contracts with Amwhip/1 and Amlash/1," September 1962, NARA 104-10102-10050.

12. Again, this is based on a now-declassified memo the author wrote for the Church Committee in 1976, but the CIA document itself wasn't found at the National Archives. Jim Johnston to Senator Hart and Senator Schweiker, "Connection between AMLASH Operation and Investigation of JFK Assassination, January 27, 1976, NARA 157-10004-10292.

13. Testimony of John McCone, May 5, 1975, Rockefeller Commission, 103, NARA 157-10011-10167.

14. JFK Diary, JFK Library, http://whd.jfklibrary.org/Diary/.

15. CIA officer conversation with author, May 1976. As stated in an earlier footnote, the CIA officer was discussing the draft committee report on President Kennedy's assassination and talked about what he felt was the larger issue of Senator Church's charge that the CIA was a "rogue elephant," acting on its own without President Kennedy's knowledge. It was in this context that he said FitzGerald drafted paragraphs for the Miami speech and that he personally delivered the draft to the Old Executive Office Building around 6 p.m., Sunday, November 17.

16. CIA to McGeorge Bundy cable, November 14, 1963, NARA 176-10030-10044. The cable notes that Kennedy had already donated the flag to Cuban officers at Fort Benning, Georgia. See also CIA to McGeorge Bundy cable, "Cuban Exiles Plan to Demonstrate during President Kennedy's Visit to Miami on 18 November," November 6, 1963, NARA 176-10030-10046.

15. A Barrier Once Removed

1. *Warren Report*, 740.

2. Commander David H. Bagley, Arms Control Directorate, [Illegible] JCS Meeting, November 18, 1963, NARA 198-10005-10096. The navy didn't have nearly enough ships to execute such an operation. At any given moment, there were an estimated three hundred large civilian ships, those with a displacement of one thousand tons or more, plying these waters and about an equal number of smaller ships. The navy's problem was compounded by the fact that arms could be flown from Cuba to a number of Latin American countries. Venezuela had 154 airfields and Columbia 104. Many were in small, remote locations that could not easily be patrolled. The Joint Chiefs concluded they should concentrate on these two countries first and try to get them to coordinate sea and air patrols. In addition a conference of Latin American ministers of government/interior was scheduled for November 25. The Defense Department would send a representative for the purpose

of exploring the possibility of a joint U.S.-Latin American interdiction program covering additional countries.

3. CIA to McGeorge Bundy cable, "Cuban Exile Plans for Demonstration on 18 November," November 18, 1963, NARA 176-10030-10047.

4. JFK'S Speech at Al Lopez Field in Tampa, Florida, November 18, 1963, https://www.youtube.com/watch?v=azOBZqMJxdM.

5. JFK Diary, JFK Library, http://whd.jfklibrary.org/Diary/.

6. Beschloss, *Crisis Years*, 659.

7. John Fitzgerald Kennedy, Address to Inter-American Press Association, Miami, Florida, November 18, 1963, emphasis added, JFK Library, digital identifier JFKPOF-048-014, pp. 5–6, http://www.jfklibrary.org/Asset-Viewer /Archives/JFKPOF-048-014.aspx.

8. JFK Diary, JFK Library, accessed April 12, 2018, http://whd.jfklibrary .org/Diary/.

9. Senator Charles Mathias quoted in L. Johnson, *Season of Inquiry*, 60.

10. Eusebio Azcue, interview by Robert Blakey, House Assassinations Committee, undated but ca. August 28, 1978, House Assassinations Committee, 8, 31, NARA 180-10114-10495.

16. John Kennedy and the Rogue Elephant

1. As noted earlier, the meaning of slotted time on CIA cables may be found in the Memorandum for . . . C/Signal Center, "Processing Time by Cable Secretariat for Immediate and Priority Cables," April 12, 1965. https://www.cia .gov/library/readingroom/docs/CIA-RDP84-00499R000600040139-4.pdf.

2. Paris to Director, PARI 1546, 19:00 hours, November 19, 1963, NARA 104-10215-10228. The version of the cable at the National Archives is labeled "desensitized." It doesn't show the time the message was sent or arrived, only the time it was slotted to certain individuals in CIA headquarters.

3. Author deleted, Memorandum for the Record, "AMWHIP/1 Meeting, New York City, Thursday, 14 November 1963," NARA 104-10295-10154.

4. Helms, *Look over My Shoulder*, 226.

5. Helms, *Look over My Shoulder*, 226–27.

6. JFK Diary.

7. Helms, *Look over My Shoulder*, 227.

8. A. Dobrynin, cipher telegram Special no. 2054–2056, November 30, 1963, Yeltsin Documents, parentheses in original.

9. Gordon Chase to McGeorge Bundy, untitled, NARA 176-10010-10057.

10. Nestor Sanchez, Memorandum for the Record, "Plans for AMLASH/1 Contact," November 19, 1963, NARA 104-10215-10360. Cryptonyms in the text have been replaced with names for ease of reading. The parentheses are in the original. There are handwritten initials above Sanchez's signature block, presumably his.

11. Reeves, *Profile of Power*, 714n337. Helms also said: "None of that, of course, is in Arthur Schlesinger's book about Robert Kennedy. I have known

Schlesinger since we were in the OSS together in the war, and when he was finishing the Kennedy book I was spending a long weekend at the Harrimans', and Arthur would come over to use the pool every day and I would be there. He had me as a captive for two days and he never asked me about any of that—-because he didn't want to know about any of that."

12. *Warren Report*, 40.

13. Jean Daniel, "When Castro Heard the News," *New Republic*, December 7, 1963. http://www.newrepublic.com/article/115632/castros-reaction-jfk-assassination.

17. Washington, Paris, and Dallas

1. IG Report, 92–93.

2. IG Report, 93.

3. Helms, *Look over My Shoulder*, 231, parentheses in original.

4. Rolando Cubela, interview by G. Robert Blakey and Edwin Lopez, Riviera Hotel, Havana Cuba, August 28, 1978, House Assassinations Committee, 18, NARA 180-10114-10496.

5. Nestor Sanchez to Paris, DIR 83825, November 20, 1963, NARA 104-10215-10358.

6. Paris to Headquarters, IN 64906, November 20, 1963, NARA 104-10215-10357. The incoming cable was slotted at 1500, which would be 3:00 p.m. Washington time.

7. Testimony of AMLASH case officer, February 11, 1976, Church Committee, 30–31, NARA 157-10014-10017.

8. S. D. Breckinridge, Deputy Inspector General, CIA to William G. Miller, Staff Director, Senate Select Committee, June 10, 1976, attachment page 4, NARA 178-10004-10280.

9. Testimony of Mrs. Lee Harvey Oswald, February 4, 1964, *Warren Report*, 1:57–58. The owner of the rooming house said that Oswald spent his evenings in his room. Testimony of Mrs. Arthur Carl (Gladys J.) Johnson testimony, April 1, 1964, *Warren Report*, 10:296.

10. Hugh Aynesworth, "Long Planning? Oswald Rented Room under Alias," *Dallas Morning News*, November 22, 1963, 6. Indeed, a squad of Dallas policemen and a justice of the peace went to the rooming house shortly after Oswald was arrested on November 22. The justice of the peace issued a search warrant, and the police gathered up all of Oswald's belongings. They took them to a police station where they inventoried and photographed everything, including the radio. B. L. Senkel, Detective, Statement, "President's Assassination," CE 2003, *Warren Report*, 24:296. The police photograph of the contents of Oswald's room can be seen online at the Portal to Texas History of the University of North Texas, Dallas, Police Dept. [clothing of Lee Harvey Oswald 2], photograph, ca. November 1963; digital images, http://texashistory.unt.edu/ark:/67531/metapth339422/, University of North Texas Libraries, Portal to Texas History, http://texashistory.unt.edu; crediting Dallas Municipal Archives, Dal-

las, Texas. The radio was photographed separately. Dallas Police Dept. [radio and bag from Oswald residence], photograph, 1963, digital images, accessed April 12, 2018, http://texashistory.unt.edu/ark:/67531/metapth337685/, University of North Texas Libraries, Portal to Texas History, http://texashistory .unt.edu; crediting Dallas Municipal Archives, Dallas, Texas.

11. The rifle was miles away in Irving (*Warren Report*, 15). Oswald had the pistol at the rooming house. He could have stood on the street to shoot at the president with the pistol, but the chances of succeeding would have been small, and Oswald would have had little chance of escape.

12. *Warren Report*, 740.

13. Testimony of Mrs. Lee Harvey Oswald, February 5, 1964, *Warren Report*, 1:65–66.

14. *Warren Report*, 15.

15. Richard Helms to Director of Central Intelligence, "Effects of the President's Miami Visit and of His IAPA Address on the Cuban Exile Community," November 21, 1963, NARA 176-10030-10048.

18. November 22, 1963, in Dallas

1. *Warren Report*, 15; testimony of Mrs. Lee Harvey Oswald, February 5, 1964, *Warren Report*, 1:66.

2. Powers and O'Donnell, *Johnny We Hardly Knew Ye*. In his book *The Crisis Years*, historian Michael Beschloss writes that a CIA analyst had included the Bullfighter's Poem, which Kennedy had recited to the press during the Cuban Missile Crisis, in the November 22 checklist, citing Robert Kennedy's oral history. However, the actual Intelligence Checklist for November 22, with an annotation that it was read by the president in Fort Worth that morning, does not include the poem. The checklist was obtained by a Freedom of Information Act request of the CIA. The CIA's response added that the Bullfighter's Poem was included in a commemorative compilation of the checklist prepared after the assassination. It was a tribute to the dead president, who had started the checklist, and was not in the version read by the president that morning. Michael Lavergne, Information and Privacy Coordinator CIA letter to author, March 25, 2015, FOIA F-2015-00735. This accords with what Robert Kennedy meant in his oral history when he said that the poem was in a checklist "issued" that day. He was referring to the commemorative checklist, not the document John Kennedy read that morning. Putting the Bullfighter's Poem in the real checklist could be interpreted as a coded message to Kennedy that some big development on Cuba, namely, the meeting with Cubela, was taking place that day. This was not the case.

3. *Warren Report*, 42.

4. Testimony of Wesley Buell Frazier, March 11, 1964, *Warren Report*, 2:224–28.

5. The chronology is extracted from Vincent Bugliosi's useful book *Reclaiming History*. Bugliosi did what the Warren Commission did not do by provid-

ing an exhaustive minute-by-minute chronology of the events in Dallas as well as useful maps and diagrams of Dealey Plaza and other places related to the assassination. He did not do an independent investigation though but rather relied on the facts that the Warren Commission collected.

6. Fifteen minutes before the motorcade arrived, a young man named Jerry Boyd Belknap, who had come to Dealey Plaza to see the president, suffered an epileptic seizure almost directly across the street from where Oswald waited at the sixth-floor window. Several police officers left their stations to attend to him. An ambulance from O'Neal's service in Dallas was called to the scene at 12:19 p.m. and took Belknap to Parkland Hospital. Oddly, although the incident obviously was a distraction for police who were in Dealey Plaza for the precise purpose of keeping an eye out for threats to the president and who should have been scanning the windows of the book depository for gunmen, the FBI did not investigate the incident until June 8, 1964, well into the Warren Commission's investigation. Bugliosi, *Reclaiming History*, endnotes, CD-ROM, 23–24. In 1989 this author interviewed the ambulance driver, Aubrey Rike, by telephone to see if Belknap might be Gilberto Policarpo Lopez, using a fictitious name, since Lopez had epilepsy. What is more, Rike had taken the man to Parkland hospital, where he was waiting when the dying John Kennedy was brought in. Rike said Belknap was a "good old boy" from Texas. Within minutes after he got to the hospital with Belknap, the Secret Service stormed into the emergency room waving their guns. Belknap had been transferred to a hospital gurney, and Rike was standing with the one from his ambulance. The Secret Service commandeered this gurney for the president. When Rike called Vernon O'Neal, the owner of the company to ask what he should do, O'Neal told Rike to wait at the hospital. When the doctors declared John Kennedy dead, O'Neal provided a casket. Rike then helped transfer the body to the casket and drove the same ambulance with the casket, Mrs. Kennedy, and a Secret Service agent to Air Force One. As for Belknap he had neglected to take his medicine that morning. He asked a nurse for a cup of water to help down his medicine, felt better, and walked out of the hospital.

7. The so-called magic bullet theory, which argues that someone besides Oswald was firing, has been effectively rebutted by computer simulations. They show that there was no magic to the bullet. A bullet fired by Oswald would indeed have hit the president and Governor Connally and caused the wounds each man suffered.

8. Bugliosi, *Reclaiming History*, 39–41.

9. A short time later, Aynesworth learned of Officer Tippit's shooting and went to that scene as well. Shenon, *Cruel and Shocking Act*, 132–34.

10. Shenon, *Cruel and Shocking Act*, 63–86. The fact that Oswald was fleeing with a light-weight jacket for warmth suggests that he didn't expect to be outdoors very long.

11. Shenon, *Cruel and Shocking Act*, 103–6.

12. Shenon, *Cruel and Shocking Act*, 233.

13. Shenon, *Cruel and Shocking Act*, 153.

14. Shenon, *Cruel and Shocking Act*, 21–23, 172.

15. Shenon, *Cruel and Shocking Act*, 173.

16. Shenon, *Cruel and Shocking Act*, 171–88.

17. Pete Fisher affidavit, December 2, 1963, CE 2253, *Warren Report*, 25:177.

18. Ronald L. Jenkins affidavit, December 10, 1963, CE 2254, *Warren Report*, 25:178.

19. Ferdinand Kaufman affidavit, December 5, 1963, CE 2255, *Warren Report*, 25:180.

20. Jerry Lee Kunkel affidavit, December 6, 1963, CE 2256, *Warren Report*, 25:181.

21. Samuel Mack Pate affidavit, December 4, 1963, CE 2257, *Warren Report*, 25:182.

22. David Flint "Mike" Smith affidavit, December 1, 1963, CE 2258, *Warren Report*, 25:182.

23. Shenon, *Cruel and Shocking Act*, 355.

19. November 22, 1963, in Other Cities

1. Bugliosi, *Reclaiming History*, 60–61.

2. Bugliosi, *Reclaiming History*, 72, citing Manchester, *Death of a President*, 256.

3. Beschloss, *Crisis Years*, 671–72.

4. Thomas, *Robert Kennedy*, 277; Haynes Johnson, "Rendezvous with Ruin at the Bay of Pigs," *Washington Post*, April 17, 1981.

5. Thomas, *Robert Kennedy*, 277. Kennedy's question may be interpreted several ways, and it isn't clear how he meant it. Was he asking if CIA personnel had assassinated his brother? That is an unlikely interpretation since there is no known reason it would have. Or was he asking if the CIA's assassination plot against Castro had backfired?

6. Beschloss, *Crisis Years*, 672.

7. Beschloss, *Crisis Years*, 672.

8. Testimony of Samuel Halpern, April 22, 1976, Church Committee, 15, NARA 157-10014-10087.

9. Halpern testimony, April 22, 1976, Church Committee, 16

10. Testimony of AMLASH case officer, February 11, 1976, Church Committee, 44–45, NARA 157-10014-10017.

11. AMLASH case officer testimony, February 11, 1976, Church Committee, 48.

12. When Sanchez testified before the Church Committee in 1976, the author questioned him about the authenticity of the existing copy of the contact report because the typing on the third page of the four-page report is much fainter than that on the other three pages. He admitted it looked quite different but had no explanation. AMLASH case officer testimony, February 11, 1976, Church Committee, 66–68.

13. AMLASH case officer testimony, February 11, 1976, Church Committee, 71.

14. Contact Report, AMLASH/1, Mathew H. Ontrich (alias Nicholas Sanson), November 22, 1963, Charlie Gray's Apt., Paris, France, November 25, 1963, NARA 104-10215-10227.

15. AMLASH case officer testimony, February 11, 1976, Church Committee, 66.

16. AMLASH case officer testimony, February 11, 1976, Church Committee, 46.

17. IG Report, 94. Testimony of AMLASH case officer, July 29, 1975, Church Committee, 114, NARA 157-10011-10125.

18. Lattel, *Castro's Secrets*, 204.

19. AMLASH case officer testimony, February 11, 1976, Church Committee, 46. Later in his testimony, Sanchez seemed to recall a little bit more of what happened to the pen with this exchange: "It was very simple to just pull the hypodermic needle out of it, and that's probably what was done. But I don't recall specifically that I did it." Question: "Did you do that after the meeting was over?" Sanchez: "No, it was during the meeting, not after" (50).

20. Latell, *Castro's Secrets*, 199.

21. Jean Daniel, "When Castro Heard the News," *New Republic,* December 7, 1963, http://www.newrepublic.com/article/115632/castros-reaction-jfk-assassination.

22. Richard Helms made a similar point to the Church Committee: "Then there is another consideration which comes into this. That if you are going to try by this kind of means to remove a foreign leader, then who is going to take his place running that country, and are you essentially better off as a matter of practice when it is over than you were before? And I can give you I think a very solid example of this which happened in Vietnam when President Diem was eliminated from the scene. We then had a revolving door of prime ministers after that for quite some period of time, during which the Vietnamese Government at a time in its history when it should have been strong was nothing but a caretaker government constantly. In other words, that whole exercise turned out to the disadvantage of the United States." Testimony of Richard Helms, June 13, 1975, Church Committee, 77, NARA 157-10014-10075.

23. Daniel, "When Castro Heard the News." Castro was not wondering if the CIA was a rogue elephant. He knew it was doing the Kennedys' bidding. Rather, he was worried that with John Kennedy dead, the CIA might take its orders from Robert Kennedy instead of Lyndon Johnson.

20. The Days After

1. U.S. Senate Select Committee on Intelligence, *Investigation of the Assassination*, 24. The National Security Agency (NSA) did the same with even less direction or focus than the CIA.

2. Bill Moyers, "An Evening with Bill Moyers," Bennett Forum, Truman Library Institute, Kansas City, Missouri, November 1, 2014.

3. John McCone, Discussion with President Johnson, November 23rd, about 9:15 a.m., November 25, 1963, NARA 1993.08.11.17:33:18:680059. The conversations lasted approximately fifteen minutes.

4. Testimony of John Scelso [John Whitten], May 7, 1976, Church Committee, 7, NARA 157-10014-10083. Whitten testified under the alias John Scelso but has been identified by his real name since then.

5. John Scelso testimony, 56.

6. John Scelso testimony, 4–5.

7. John Scelso testimony, 5, 61.

8. Testimony of Thomas Karamessines, April 18, 1976, Church Committee, 10, cited in U.S. Senate Select Committee on Intelligence, *Investigation of the Assassination*, 25n13. Karamessines testimony was not declassified and transferred to the National Archives. This was presumably an oversight like the failure of the Senate Intelligence Committee to declassify and turn over the transcript of Ted Shackley's testimony to the Church Committee.

9. Shenon, *Cruel and Shocking Act*, 118.

10. U.S. Senate Select Committee on Intelligence, *Investigation of the Assassination*, 25.

11. Karamessines testimony, April 18, 1976, 26–27, cited in U.S. Senate Select Committee on Intelligence, *Investigation of the Assassination*, 25n19.

12. McCone, Discussion with President Johnson, November 23rd, about 9:15 a.m.

13. W. David Slawson, "Trip to Mexico City," April 22, 1964, 22–23, NARA 104-10150-10181. Slawson prepared this lengthy memorandum for the record of the Warren Commission staff trip to Mexico City. While the CIA briefing there told of Duran's relationship with Lechuga, Slawson did not seem to know of the bigger picture that William Attwood was working with Lechuga with the Kennedys' blessing to put out peace feelers to Fidel Castro.

14. Testimony of AMLASH case officer, February 11, 1976, Church Committee, 54, NARA 157-10014-10017.

15. Testimony of Samuel Halpern, April 22, 1976, Church Committee, 18, Church Committee, 5, NARA 157-10014-10008.

16. *Warren Report*, 209–23.

21. An Investigation Hobbled from the Start

1. Mr. J. Edgar Hoover says as follows, November 24, 1963, NARA 178-10003-10068. The memo is initialed WJ. The Church Committee report on the Kennedy assassination quotes from it and indicates that it was written by Walter Jenkins. U.S. Senate Select Committee on Intelligence, *Investigation of the Assassination*, 33:

"There is nothing further on the Oswald case except that he is dead. . . . This morning we called the Chief of Police again warning of the possibility of some effort against Oswald [because the FBI had gotten a threatening phone call] and he again assured us adequate protection would be given.

However, this was not done. . . . Ruby says . . . that he guessed his grief over the killing of the President made him insane. That was a pretty smart move on his part because it might lay the foundation for a plea of insanity later. . . . I dispatched to Dallas one of my top assistants in the hope that he might stop the Chief of Police and his staff from doing so damned much talking on television. They did not really have a case against Oswald until we gave them our information. We traced the weapon, we identified the handwriting, we identified the fingerprints on the brown bag. . . . All the Dallas Police had was three witnesses who tentatively identified him as the man who shot the policeman and boarded a bus to go home shortly after the President was killed. . . . Oswald had been saying he wanted John Abt as his lawyer and Abt, with only that kind of evidence could have turned the case around, I'm afraid. . . . That letter from Oswald [to the Soviet embassy in Washington, which the FBI had intercepted] was addressed to the man in the Soviet Embassy [in Mexico City, Valery Kostikov] who is in charge of assassinations. . . . To have that drawn into a public hearing would muddy the waters internationally. . . . And since this has nothing to do with proof that Oswald committed the murder, I made the suggestion to Mr. Katzenbach [at the Justice Department] that instead of a Presidential Commission, we do it with a Justice Department Report based on an FBI report."

Hoover erred in claiming that Oswald's letter was addressed to Kostikov. The letter merely mentioned that Oswald had talked to a "Kostin" in Mexico City.

2. U.S. Senate Select Committee on Intelligence, *Investigation of the Assassination*, 23, citing the memorandum from Nicholas deB. Katzenbach to Bill Moyers, November 26, 1963.

3. Katzenbach, *Some of It Was Fun*, 133.

4. A. Dobrynin, cipher telegram, Special no. 2005, November 26, 1963, Yeltsin Documents.

5. U.S. Senate Select Committee on Intelligence, *Investigation of the Assassination*, 32.

6. U.S. Senate Select Committee on Intelligence, *Investigation of the Assassination*, 32.

7. U.S. Senate Select Committee on Intelligence, *Investigation of the Assassination*, 39–40.

8. U.S. Senate Select Committee on Intelligence, *Investigation of the Assassination*, 34.

9. However, the questioning of witnesses by the Warren Commission reflects these concerns. Although commission members would occasionally ask whether a person was a Communist, the staff assiduously avoiding questioning along these lines.

10. Caro, *Passage of Power*, 441–42.

11. Caro, *Passage of Power*, 441–42.

12. D. J. Brennan, Jr. to W. C. Sullivan, December 19, 1963, Warren Commission, NARA 104-10310-10057.

13. Telephone Conversation between the President and Senator Russell, November 29, 1963, 8:55 p.m., https://www.maryferrell.org/mffweb/archive/viewer/showDoc.do?docId=912&relPageId=5.

14. U.S. Senate Select Committee on Intelligence, *Investigation of the Assassination*, 34.

15. The descriptions of the FBI and CIA files systems are based on the author's experience when he was on the Church Committee and on his work with the declassified files. There was no formal briefing.

16. Testimony of Harold Swenson, May 10, 1976, 19, Church Committee, NARA 157-10014-10048.

17. Richard Helms to Chief, United States Secret Service, Information Collation by Computer, April 29, 1964, NARA 104-10310-10008.

18. Acting Chief, SR Division to Assistant Deputy Director, Plans, "Contact of Lee Oswald with a Member of Soviet KGB Assassination Department," November 23, 1963, 1, NARA 104-10050-10149.

19. Acting Chief, SR Division to Assistant Deputy Director, Plans, "Contact of Lee Oswald."

20. Mexico City Station to Headquarters, "Surveillance of Soviet Embassy & Kostikov," November 26, 1963, NARA 157-10004-10199.

21. U.S. Select Committee on Intelligence, *Investigation of the Assassination*, 25; testimony of AMLASH case officer, Church Committee, February 11, 1976, 95, NARA 157-10014-10017; Swenson testimony, May 10, 1976, Church Committee, 12. Kostikov was arrested in Mexico in 1968 after pulling a gun on two Mexican oil engineers. Barron, *KGB*, 397.

22. Testimony of Samuel Halpern, April 22, 1976, Church Committee, 35, NARA 157-10014-10008.

23. Halpern testimony, April 22, 1976, Church Committee, 36.

24. Testimony of AMLASH case officer, February 11, 1976, Church Committee, 96–97, NARA 157-10014-10017.

25. Testimony of John McCone, May 5, 1975, Rockefeller Commission, 105–06, NARA 157-10011-10167.

26. JMWAVE to Director, "Threatening US Leaders," November 11, 1963, NARA 157-10004-10201.

27. U.S. Senate Select Committee on Intelligence, *Investigation of the Assassination*, 27.

28. Testimony of John Scelso [John Whitten], May 7, 1976, 37, Church Committee, NARA 157-10014-10083.

29. U.S. Senate Select Committee on Intelligence, *Investigation of the Assassination*, 29.

30. Chris Hopkins, "Identification of Sensitive Source," April 20, 1977, NARA 104-10102-10043. The document appears to be a memorandum for the record by Mr. Hopkins of the CIA to note that the cable was shown to Senators Schweiker and Gary Hart on June 11, 1976.

31. AMLASH case officer testimony, February 11, 1976, Church Committee, 86.

32. Gordon Chase to McGeorge Bundy, Cuba—Item of Presidential Interest, November 25, 1953, NARA 178-10003-10066.

33. Gordon Chase to Mr. Bundy, Cuba—Bill, November 25, 1963, NARA 178-10003-10065.

34. Anonymous, CIA document, Lee Harvey Oswald, NARA 104-10310-10041.

35. John Scelso testimony, May 7, 1976, Church Committee, 38–39. Whitten testified under the alias of John Scelso, a fact that has since been made public.

22. The Investigation Sputters On

1. John A. McCone to the President through McGeorge Bundy, November 28, 1963, NARA 177-10001-10013.

2. During the assassination investigation, Papich usually visited the CIA every day. His contact in the counterintelligence section of FitzGerald's Special Affairs Staff was Austin Horn. Testimony of Harold Swenson, May 10, 1976, Church Committee, NARA 157-10014-10048.

3. Birch D. O'Neal, Memorandum for the Record, "Lee Harvey Oswald," November 29, 1963, NARA 104-10125-10281.

4. Birch D. O'Neal, Memorandum for the Record, "Lee Harvey Oswald," December 3, 1963, NARA 104-10125-10276.

5. John Edgar Hoover to Tolson et al., memorandum, November 26, 1963, NARA 104-10310-10056.

6. John A. McCone, Memorandum for the President, through Mr. McGeorge Bundy, November 28, 1963, NARA 178-10003-10103.

7. John McCone, "Late Developments on the Mexico City Investigation of Oswald's Activities," November 29, 1963, with notation "To be used by DCI in meeting with the President at 10:30 on 29 November 1963 with Secty. McNamara and Bundy," NARA 1993.08.11.17:26:42:780059. The paper said that Mexican authorities had reported that their interrogation of Silvia Duran, who was the employee at the Cuban consulate whom Oswald met, turned up nothing significant. The paper also reported that Alvarado had been turned over to Mexican authorities for questioning at the specific request of the FBI, pointedly noting this was "because FBI [was] in control of the investigation." It added that Alvarado's story was becoming increasingly questionable because the same story had been on a radio broadcast in Mexico before Alvarado came forward. In other words he was just repeating something he heard on the radio.

8. CIA to Mexico Station, "Request to Follow All Leads in Assassination Investigation," November 28, 1963, NARA 157-10004-10185.

9. Director to JMWAVE, DIR 86473, December 2, 1963, NARA 104-10102-10038.

10. Director to JMWAVE, DIR 87800, December 2, 1963, NARA 104-10102-10040.

11. Gordon Chase to McGeorge Bundy, "Bill's Activities," December 2, 1963, NARA 178-10003-10067.

12. Mexico City to Director, MEXI 7216, IN 72615, December 3, 1963, NARA 104-10125-10274.

13. Mexico City to Director, MEXI 7224, IN 72829, December 3, 1963, NARA 104-10103-10218.

14. Mexico City to Director, MEXI 7253, IN 74227, December 5, 1963, NARA 104-10103-10231.

15. Director to Mexico City, DIR 87188, December 5, 1963, NARA 104-10103-10229.

16. Chief of Station, Mexico City to Chief, WH Division, GPFLOOR/Gilberto LOPEZ, December 5, 1963, NARA 104-10103-10226.

17. Willard C. Curtis, Memorandum for the Record, "Gilbert Lopez, U.S. Citizen," December 5, 1963, NARA 104-10422-10130. For Curtis to write a memorandum for the record on the topic seems unnecessary since the same information was in the cable and the dispatch he sent to headquarters. It raises the suspicion that Curtis felt a need to have his own record of what he told headquarters because he had reason to think headquarters might not pursue it.

23. Regime Change

1. John McCone, editorial note from McCone's files of meetings with the president. The meeting was on November 28. McCone's memorandum, from which the note was taken, was dated November 29. Keefer, Sampson, and Smith, *Foreign Relations, 1961–1963*, 11:381.

2. Testimony of Samuel Halpern, April 22, 1976, Church Committee, 39–40, NARA 157-10014-10008. McCone repeatedly testified under oath that he didn't know about any assassination operation that was going on while he was CIA director. But since Helms and others argued that the AMLASH operation was a coup, not an assassination, McCone may have made that distinction too. He wasn't asked. Thus he might have known about the AMLASH operation but rationalized answering the way he did because he did not want to consider it an assassination.

3. U. Alexis Johnson to Dean Rusk, memorandum, "Cuban Contingency Planning," November 29, 1963, in. Keefer, Smith, and Sampson, *Foreign Relations, 1961–1963*, microfiche supplement, 720.

4. Keefer, Sampson, and Smith, *Foreign Relations, 1961–1963*, 11:381, editorial note. The note is based on CIA files of "DCI Meetings with the president, 23 November–31 December 1963." The full documents are not publicly available. An explanatory note to the editorial note dates Kennedy's speeches to 1963 rather than 1962 as stated in the note itself, but it seems clear that McCone was talking about Kennedy's speeches in 1962. He made no speech about Cuba on November 20, 1963, but did in 1962.

5. A. M. Haig to Colonel Lindjord, Note, November 29, 1963, NARA 198-10004-10003.

6. Testimony of John McCone, May 5, 1975, Rockefeller Commission, 109–10, NARA 157-10011-10167.

7. Edwin Martin to Dean Rusk, "Transmits Talking Points for Rusk's December 2 Meeting with President Johnson on Cuba," December 2, 1963, in Keefer, Sampson, and Smith, *Foreign Relations, 1961–1963*, Foreign Relations, 11:721.

8. Memorandum of Conversation, November 26, 1963, in Keefer, Sampson, and Smith, *Foreign Relations, 1961–1963*, 11:380.

9. Keefer, Sampson, and Smith, *Foreign Relations, 1961–1963*, 11:383, editorial note.

10. Gordon Chase to Bundy, "Cuba Meeting (without President) Next Tuesday, December 10, 1963," December 4, 1963, in Keefer, Sampson, and Smith, *Foreign Relations, 1961–1963*, 11:385.

11. Katzenbach, *Some of It Was Fun*, 134.

12. A. M. Haig to Joseph Califano, "Meeting at State, 4 December 1963," December 4, 1963, NARA 198-10004-10045.

13. Director to JMWAVE, DIR 87980, December 6, 1963, NARA 104-10295-10161.

14. JMWAVE to Director, IN 75929, December 7, 1963, NARA 104-10295-10162.

15. Director to JMWAVE, DIR 87618, December 7, 1963, NARA 104-10215-10226.

16. JMWAVE to Director, IN 8702, December 8, 1963, NARA 104-10215-10225.

17. Desmond FitzGerald and Chester L. Cooper to Director of Central Intelligence, "Considerations for US Policy toward Cuba and Latin America," December 9, 1963, NARA 198-10006-10000.

18. FitzGerald and Cooper to Director of Central Intelligence, "Considerations for US Policy."

19. FitzGerald and Cooper to Director of Central Intelligence, "Considerations for US Policy," 5.

20. "Suggestions for Additional Administration Statements on Cuba to Stimulate Anti-Castro Action on the Part of Dissident Elements in the Cuban Armed Forces," December 9, 1963, in Keefer, Smith, and Sampson, *Foreign Relations, 1961–1963*, microfiche supplement, 723. The same document appears as table A to FitzGerald and Cooper's "Considerations for US Policy."

21. Seymour Bolten and Chester L. Cooper to Director of Central Intelligence, "Summary of Principal Actions Proposed in Referenced Memorandum [the FitzGerald/Cooper Memorandum of December 9]," December 10, 1963, NARA 198-10006-10051.

22. Memorandum for the Secretary of the Army, "Standing Group Meeting on Cuba, 1700 Hours, December 10, 1963 at the White House," December 10, 1963, NARA 198-10004-10047. The meeting was postponed to December 13. A. M. Haig to Joseph Califano note, December 12, 1963, NARA 198-10004-10174.

23. "Memorandum from [Benjamin] Read to McGeorge Bundy, December 12. Transmits paper entitled 'Possible Further Unilateral and Bilateral

Actions to Increase Pressure on Cuba (Short of the Use of Force)' for discussion at the NSC Standing Group Meeting December 13," December 12, 1963, in Keefer, Smith, and Sampson, *Foreign Relations, 1961–1963*, microfiche supplement, 727.

24. Memorandum prepared in the CIA, December 12, 1963, "Current U.S. Policy with Respect to Cuba," in Keefer, Smith, and Sampson, *Foreign Relations, 1961–1963*, microfiche supplement, 725.

25. Smith and Patterson, *Foreign Relations, 1964–1968*, 10:386, editorial note.

26. Keefer, Smith, and Sampson, *Foreign Relations, 1961–1963*, microfiche supplement, 727.

27. "Memorandum for the record prepared by General Carter, December 19. Transmits FitzGerald's memorandum for the record of a meeting with President Johnson on Cuba on December 19," December 19, 1963, in Keefer, Smith, and Sampson, *Foreign Relations, 1961–1963*, microfiche supplement, 733. Gordon Chase also prepared a memorandum of the meeting: Gordon Chase, "Memorandum of Meeting with President Johnson," December 19, 1963, in Keefer, Sampson, and Smith, *Foreign Relations, 1961–1963*, 11:388. In addition to the president, Chase's memorandum lists George Ball, Lewellyn Thompson, Alexis Johnson, and Edwin Martin from the State Department; Roswell Gilpatric, Cyrus Vance, and Gen. Edwin Wheeler from Defense; Secretary of the Treasury Douglas Dillon; Marshall Carter, Richard Helms, Desmond FitzGerald, Donald Wilson, and John Crimmins from CIA; and McGeorge Bundy, William Moyers, George Reedy, and Gordon Chase from the White House.

28. "Memorandum for the record prepared by General Carter."

29. Vice President's Daily Diary, December 19, 1963, http://www.lbjlibrary.net/assets/lbj_tools/daily_diary/pdf/1963/19631219.pdf. Apparently, the White House was still using Johnson's old diary from his vice-presidential days.

30. Contact sheets of White House photographer Yoichi Okamoto for December 19, 1963, furnished by link in email from Christopher Banks to author, May 24, 2018. The six photographs are numbered w 207–28 a and b through w 207–33 a and b. Each is in JPEG and TIFF format.

31. National Security Action Memorandum No. 274, December 20, 1963, Keefer, Smith, and Sampson, *Foreign Relations, 1961–1963*, microfiche supplement (for vol. 110), 389.

32. Director to JMWAVE, DIR 90966, December 23, 1963, NARA 104-10215-10219.

33. JMWAVE to Director, December 27, 1963, IN 88419, NARA 104-10215-10218.

34. Lt. Col. Alexander Haig to Gen. Earle Wheeler, "Interdepartmental Coordinating Committee of Cuban Affairs: Interim Report by US Military on Venezuelan Arms Cache," December 23, 1963 NARA 198-10006-10056.

35. December 27, 1963, in Keefer, Smith, and Sampson, *Foreign Relations, 1961–1963*, microfiche supplement (for vol. 11), editorial note.

24. The Warren Report

1. Willens, *History Will Prove Us Right*, 284–85 and 58.

2. Willens, *History Will Prove Us Right*, 42

3. Testimony of John Scelso [John Whitten], May 7, 1976, Church Committee, 6–7, NARA 157-10014-10083.

4. Testimony of Harold Swenson, May 10, 1976, Church Committee, 9 and 12, NARA 157-10014-10048

5. Swenson testimony, May 10, 1976, Church Committee, 14.

6. Swenson testimony, May 10, 1976, Church Committee, 20–37.

7. Swenson testimony, May 10, 1976, Church Committee, 62.

8. Testimony of James Angleton, February 6, 1976, Church Committee, 16, NARA 157-10014-10003.

9. Angleton testimony, February 6, 1976, Church Committee, 19.

10. Shenon, *Cruel and Shocking Act*, 153.

11. Warren Commission defenders typically point out that Allen Dulles was on the commission and that he had been CIA director two years earlier. But a lot had happened in those two years that Dulles would know nothing about. If Karamessines, Helms's deputy, and Angleton didn't know about the AMLASH operation, Dulles most certainly would not have. Besides, Dulles did not have an analyst's mentality. He once advised an underling, "Do you read the society pages? Young man, that's where I get a lot of valuable information." Evan Thomas, *Very Best Men*, 168. Of course, in his Senate testimony, Helms made the point that Dulles knew about the underworld plots to assassinate Castro. Testimony of Richard Helms, June 13, 1975, Church Committee, 67, NARA 157-10014-10075.

12. McGeorge Bundy to President Johnson, "Memorandum from the President's Special Assistant for National Security Affairs (Bundy) to President Johnson," January 9, 1964, in Keefer, Lawler, and Yee, *Foreign Relations of the United States, 1964–1968*, 32:224.

13. Greg McDonald, "Gen. Erneido Oliva: Second in Command at the Bay of Pigs," AARP *Bulletin*, April 15, 2011, https://www.aarp.org/politics-society /history/info-04-2011/general-erneido-oliva-where-are-they-now.html.

14. Gen. Marshall S. Carter, Acting Director of CIA, "Disarmament Meeting on 18 January 1964 at White House," undated, in Keefer, Lawler, and Yee, *Foreign Relations, 1964–1968*, 32:225.

15. John K. King, Chief, SAS/Intel to Nestor Sanchez, "Requirements for AMLASH-1," February 4, 1964, NARA 104-10234-10442.

16. Testimony of AMLASH case officer, Church Committee, February 11, 1976, Church Committee, 99, NARA 157-10014-10017.

17. Verbal message from Cuban prime minister Castro to President Johnson, February 12, 1964, in Keefer, Lawler, and Yee, *Foreign Relations, 1964–1968*, 32:240.

The full message reads:

Havana, February 12, 1964.

1. Please tell President Johnson that I earnestly desire his election to the Presidency in November . . . though that appears assured. But if there is anything I can do to add to his majority (aside from retiring from politics), I shall be happy to cooperate. Seriously, I observe how the Republicans use Cuba as a weapon against the Democrats. So tell President Johnson to let me know what I can do, if anything. Naturally, I know that my offer of assistance would be of immense value to the Republicans—so this would remain our secret. But if the President wishes to pass word to me he can do so through you [Lisa Howard]. He must know that he can trust you; and I know that I can trust you to relay a message accurately.

2. If the President feels it necessary during the campaign to make bellicose statements about Cuba or even to take some hostile action—if he will inform me, unofficially, that a specific action is required because of domestic political considerations, I shall understand and not take any serious retaliatory action.

3. Tell the President that I understand quite well how much political courage it took for President Kennedy to instruct you [Lisa Howard] and Ambassador to phone my aide in Havana for the purpose of commencing a dialogue toward a settlement of our differences. Ambassador suggested that I prepare an agenda for such talks3 and send the agenda to my U.N. Ambassador. That was on November 18th. The agenda was being prepared when word arrived that President Kennedy was assassinated. I hope that we can soon continue where Ambassador 's phone conversation to Havana left off . . . though I'm aware that pre-electoral political considerations may delay this approach until after November.

4. Tell the President (and I cannot stress this too strongly) that I seriously hope that Cuba and the United States can eventually sit down in an atmosphere of good will and of mutual respect and negotiate our differences. I believe that there are no areas of contention between us that cannot be discussed and settled within a climate of mutual understanding. But first, of course, it is necessary to discuss our differences. I now believe that this hostility between Cuba and the United States is both unnatural and unnecessary—and it can be eliminated.

5. Tell the President he should not interpret my conciliatory attitude, my desire for discussions as a sign of weakness. Such an interpretation would be a serious miscalculation. We are not weak . . . the Revolution is strong . . . very strong. Nothing, absolutely nothing that the United States can do will destroy the Revolution. Yes, we are strong. And it is from this position of strength that we wish to resolve our differences with the United States and to live in peace with all the nations of the world.

6. Tell the President I realize fully the need for absolute secrecy, if he should decide to continue the Kennedy approach. I revealed nothing at that time . . . I have revealed nothing since . . . I would reveal nothing now.

Source: Johnson Library, National Security File, Country File, Cuba, Contacts with Cuban Leaders, 5/63–4/65. The message was given to Lisa Howard of ABC News on February 12 in Havana. All brackets are in the source text.

18. Jean Daniel, "When Castro Heard the News," *New Republic*, December 7, 1963. http://www.newrepublic.com/article/115632/castros-reaction-jfk-assassination.

19. "Spectrum of Courses of Action with Respect to Cuba," February 21, 1964, furnished the author by Michael Lavergne, information and privacy coordinator CIA, in response to Freedom of Information Act request, CIA Reference F-2015-00735. The spectrum paper was requested under the act because the National Archives does not have a copy on file with FitzGerald's memorandum of the meeting. The Rostow Doctrine was presumably named for Walt Rostow, Bundy's protégé and successor.

20. Desmond FitzGerald, "Meeting with the Attorney General, 28 February 1964," February 28, 1964, NARA 104-10310-10189.

21. Richard Helms to McGeorge Bundy, "Alleged Contacts between Castro and American Government," March 4, 1964, NARA 178-10003-10123.

22. Desmond FitzGerald to McGeorge Bundy, "Letter from the Chief of the Western Hemisphere Division of the Central Intelligence Agency to the President's Special Assistant for National Security Affairs," March 6, 1964, in Keefer, Lawler, and Yee, *Foreign Relations, 1964–1968*, 32:249.

23. He talked to Tepedino on March 7 and cabled Paris about Tepedino's travel plans and messages from Cubela. Nestor Sanchez, "Telephone Conversation between Nestor Sanchez (alias Nicholas Sanson) and AMWHIP/1," March 7, 1964, NARA 104-10234-10328; DIR to Paris, DIR 06248, March 7, 1964, NARA 104-10234-10327.

24. JMWAVE to Director, WAVE 3454, IN 89084, March 13, 1964, NARA 104-10102-10042.

25. Desmond FitzGerald, "Meeting at the White House 7 April 1964, Review of Covert Program directed against Cuba," April 7, 1964, attachment John McCone, "Washington, April 8, 1964, Dictated by Mr. McCone," in Keefer, Lawler, and Yee, *Foreign Relations, 1964–1968*, 32:259.

26. Peter Jessup, "Memorandum for the Record, Washington, April 9, 1964," April 9, 1964, in Keefer, Lawler, and Yee, *Foreign Relations, 1964–1968*, 32:260.

27. Sir Charles Arthur Evelyn Shuckburgh, Speech, April 15, 1964, in Keefer, Lawler, and Yee, *Foreign Relations, 1964–1968*, 32:255, editorial note.

28. Shenon, *Cruel and Shocking Act*, 391–92.

29. Peter Jessup, "Minutes of the Meeting of the 303 Committee, 18 June 1964," June 22, 1964, NARA 178-10002-10100.

30. Unsigned, "Central Intelligence Agency Memorandum, No. 1601/64," July 2, 1964, in Keefer, Lawler, and Yee, *Foreign Relations, 1964–1968*, 32:275.

31. Testimony of Raymond Wannell, May 11, 1976, Church Committee, 7–8, NARA 157-10014-10010. The original FBI report was an exhibit to Wannell's deposition to the Church Committee and was read into the record. However, the Church Committee testimonial exhibits are not at the National Archives, so the only public record is the question in the transcript.

25. The Never-Ending Investigations

1. Thomas, *Robert Kennedy*, 284.

2. James Angleton, interview by author, 1976. Unlike most of the CIA witnesses before the Church Committee, who viewed the staff as an adversary, Angleton was friendly and talkative. He was confident in his ability to engage in a dialog without giving away too much. Besides, he had a genuine, continuing interest in whether the KGB was somehow responsible for Kennedy's assassination and therefore felt a common purpose with the Hart-Schweiker subcommittee. He readily offered his insights.

3. Raymond Rocca, "Conversation with David W. Belin, 1 April 1975," April 1, 1975, NARA 1993.08.11.16:46:36:150059.

4. Angleton, author interviews.

5. "Background Information on Rolando Cubela Secades," April 13, 1966, NARA 104-10102-10010.

6. Jim Johnston to Senator Hart and Senator Schweiker, "Connection between AMLASH Operation and Investigation of JFK Assassination, January 27, 1976, NARA 157-10004-10292. Testimony of AMLASH case officer, Church Committee, February 11, 1976, 76–84, NARA 157-10014-10017.

7. AMLASH case officer testimony, Church Committee, February 11, 1976, 76–84.

8. Nestor Sanchez, "First Meeting between AMBIDDY-1 and AMLASH-1 in Madrid on 27 December 1964," January 3, 1965, NARA 104-10234-10399.

9. Director to deleted stations, DIR 13256, May 25, 1965, NARA 104-10216-10415. The initials on the handwritten note may be those of CIA Inspector General J. S. Earman, although that seems odd because Earman wouldn't know if challenging Cubela's good faith was nonsense.

10. Director to six deleted stations and JMWAVE, DIR 22113, June 23, 1965, NARA 104-10216-10403.

11. Director to deleted station, DIR 23142, June 26, 1965, NARA 104-10216-10397.

12. "Anti-Castro Plot Laid to 7 Cubans," *New York Times*, March 6, 1966, NARA 104-10517-10099.

13. Unsigned Memorandum for the Record, "The Cubela Trial," April 14, 1966, NARA 104-10102-10008. The memorandum reads like Nestor Sanchez wrote it. In his testimony before the Church Committee, Sanchez argued that Cubela was not a double agent.

14. The Cuban History.com, accessed June 22, 2018, http://www.thecubanhistory.com/2012/07/rolando-cubela-secades-cia-aka-amlash/.

15. Drew Pearson, Diary, October 26, 1966, Warren Earl no. 2, G246, 3 of 3, LBJ Library and Museum, Austin, TX.

16. Testimony of Edward P. Morgan, March 19, 1976, Church Committee, 12, NARA 157-10011-10040.

17. Morgan, testimony, March 19, 1976, Church Committee, 5. Morgan testified that he had gotten this information in various conversations with the two men. However, Morgan said he had not gone to Pearson with the story as part of any legal work for them; he was not doing any work for them at the time. Rather, after thinking it over for several months, he decided that the information should be given to Earl Warren. Morgan didn't know the chief justice, but he knew Pearson and knew that Pearson was a friend of Warren, so he went to him (6–11).

18. Morgan testimony, March 19, 1976, Church Committee, 12–13.

19. U.S. Senate Select Committee on Intelligence, *Investigation of the Assassination*, 80.

20. U.S. Senate Select Committee on Intelligence, *Investigation of the Assassination*, 80. In his testimony to the Church Committee, Morgan did not remember Rowley contacting him.

21. President Lyndon Johnson and Acting Attorney General Ramsey Clark, February 20, 1967, tape WH6702.05, citation 11556, LBJ Library. The tape was originally misdated February 18, 1967.

22. President Lyndon Johnson and Texas governor John Connally, March 2, 1967, tape WH6703.01, citation 11612, LBJ Library.

23. President Lyndon Johnson and Texas governor John Connally, March 2, 1967, emphasis added.

24. IG Report 66.

25. Drew Pearson, "Senate Aide Scouted Deals for Dodd," March 7, 1967, *Washington Post*, C13.

26. Drew Pearson, Diary, March 13, 1967, Warren, Chief Justice Earl, no. 1, G246, 3 of 3, LBJ Library.

27. U.S. Senate Select Committee on Intelligence, *Investigation of the Assassination of President John F. Kennedy*, 84. The Church Committee took testimony from Morgan and Roselli. That testimony is publicly available. Morgan remembered telling Drew Pearson about this but had no recollection of talking to the FBI. Roselli said that he had always held the view that Castro had been responsible for Kennedy's death, but he had no basis for that except what he read in the newspapers. Furthermore, he said that the agents he sent into Cuba to kill Castro did not know he was working with the CIA. If they had been captured, tortured, and talked, they would have said they were working for Wall Street interests. Sam Giancana, who worked for a time with Roselli, was murdered in 1975 while under subpoena from the Church Committee and before he could testify. Roselli was murdered in 1976 after he had testified.

28. IG Report, 84, emphasis in original, NARA 104-10213-10101.

29. Equally odd is that while the report was done in the midst of the Garrison investigation in New Orleans, which Angleton and Rocca were following, Helms never told those two about the IG Report. It was an example of compartmentation at its worst.

30. Testimony of Richard Helms, June 13, 1975, Church Committee, 35–36, NARA 157-10014-10075.

31. Testimony of Richard Helms, April 24, 1975, Rockefeller Commission, 389–91, NARA 157-10011-10086.

32. George Christian, telephone interview with the author, August 10, 1995.

33. Conceivably, Helms might have misreported what Johnson said or misunderstood him. Johnson might have been saying that Diem's death was proof to Castro that he was next.

34. Leo Janos, "The Last Days of the President, LBJ in Retirement," *Atlantic*, July 1973, https://www.theatlantic.com/past/docs/issues/73jul/janos.htm. Johnson said much the same thing to others. Testimony of Walter Rostow, Rockefeller Commission, May 5, 1975, Rockefeller Commission, 175, NARA 157-10011-10167. Califano, *Inside*, 126. The citation of Rostow's testimony refers to excerpts in the Church Committee files at the National Archives. The NARA database indicates it also has the testimony at NARA 178-10002-10117.

35. Shenon, *Cruel and Shocking Act*, 526,

36. Raymond Rocca, "Conversation with David W. Belin, 1 April 1975," April 1, 1975, NARA 1993.08.11.16:46:36:150059.

37. U.S. Senate Select Committee on Intelligence, *Alleged Assassination Plots*.

38. U.S. Senate Select Committee on Intelligence, *Investigation of the Assassination*, 7.

39. Lawrence Meyer and Joel Weisman, "Giancana, Linked to CIA Plot, Slain," *Washington Post*, June 21, 1975, A1.

40. Dan Morgan, "Castro Plot Figure Found Murdered," *Washington Post*, August 9, 1976, A1; Rudy Maxa, "The Calculated Rise and Abrupt Descent of Johnny Roselli," *Washington Post*, September 12, 1976, 157.

41. Santos Trafficante, interview, "Santos Trafficante and His Role in the Assassination Plots against Castro," U.S. Senate Committee on Intelligence, October 1, 1976, 4–5, NARA 157-10014-10066.

42. U.S. House of Representatives Select Committee on Assassinations, *Final Report*, part 2.

26. John Kennedy and the CIA

1. When asked by Senator Church how the CIA could be so seemingly casual about hatching plans to assassinate Castro, Helms explained: "I have to say in all fairness and honesty that in the perceptions of the time people were losing their lives in raids, a lot of people had lost their lives at the Bay of Pigs, agents were being arrested left and right and put before the wall and shot. . . . Frankly, at the time it [the underworld plot] didn't loom

large and that is not because I don't have any moral judgment or because I am a cynical know-nothing, it was simply because in the perceptions of the time and the things we were trying to do this was one human life against many other human lives that were being lost." Testimony of Richard Helms, Church Committee, June 13, 1975, Church Committee, 63–64, NARA 157-10014-10075.

2. Helms testimony, June 13, 1975, Church Committee, 90. Helms repeatedly addressed the rogue elephant charge in his testimony, saying earlier in the same session: "I don't want to leave in anyone's mind in this room that I ever regarded myself as an unguided missile or that I had authorities or powers that were exercised in my own right. And therefore, whatever things may have occurred, or whatever it may seem in 1975 looks poor on the record, I can only say that I felt that I was acting always under orders." (31).

3. Turner, *Burn before Reading*, 98

4. Richard Helms was so dead set on denying that the AMLASH operation was an assassination that he practically made the case that Cubela was a dangle: "The pressures, as I recall it, for guns and things of that kind all came from Cubela himself, they didn't come from the Agency. This wasn't something we were trying to set up. This was something Cubela was trying to set up. He hated Castro and wanted to get rid of him." Helms testimony, June 13, 1975, Church Committee, 39.

5. Helms testimony, June 13, 1975, Church Committee, 135.

27. Lyndon Johnson and the CIA

1. [Walter Jenkins] Mr. J. Edgar Hoover says as follows, November 24, 1963, NARA 178-10003-10068.

2. David Robarge, "Death of a President, DCI John McCone and the Assassination of President John F. Kennedy," 8, accessed April 12, 2018, http://nsarchive.gwu.edu/NSAEBB/NSAEBB493/docs/intell_ebb_026.PDF. This piece was a chapter from Robarge's 2005 book on McCone's tenure at CIA that the agency declassified and made public on the fiftieth anniversary of the assassination.

3. *Warren Report*, 21.

4. Abt and Meyerson, *Advocate and Activist*, 252.

5. Looking back at the change from Kennedy to Johnson and from Cuba to Vietnam, Helms testified: "It was after that [1965], I believe, or around this time that we began to ask for some relief from this responsibility because Vietnam was picking up in those days and there was a need for manpower that understood paramilitary activities and things of this kind, not only in Vietnam, but in Laos, so that the Agency was running short of effective manpower in this field. Therefore the Cuban effort dropped off as interest in Cuba tended to drop off and cool and interest in Vietnam built up." Testimony of Richard Helms, June 13, 1975, Church Committee, 25, NARA 157-10014-10075.

6. Helms testimony, June 13, 1975, Church Committee, 82.

7. The author posed the question that elicited Shackley's answer that appears in the Church Committee report on Kennedy's assassination.

8. Such records were readily available. Because of the economic sanctions imposed on Cuba, AT&T could not pay the Cuban phone company for its end of a phone call between the United States and Cuba. However, the two companies kept their wires connected, but no money could be transferred to Cuba. Therefore, the Cuban company would accept and complete a call from the United States without charge. If the call originated in Cuba, AT&T would accept and complete it only if it were a collect call. AT&T retained these records until roughly 1995, when it destroyed them. Author's telephone conference with Louisa Legalato, regional attorney, AT&T International Caribbean and Latin America Communications Service Group, May 30, 1995.

9. The name of the driver of the seventh car crossing from Texas into Mexico after the border was reopened on the night of November 22 matches a name in the 1963 Tampa telephone directory. Federal Bureau of Investigation, "Gilberto Policarpo Lopez," January 31, 1964, NARA JFK36:F34 1993.07.22.11:12:52:210530.

10. CIA Mexico to Director, Cable on Gilberto Lopez, March 20, 1964, NARA JFK36:F34 1993.07.22.13:44:09:310530.

11. Shenon, *Cruel and Shocking Act*, 295.

12. W. David Slawson, "Trip to Mexico City," April 22, 1964, attachment, NARA 104-10150-10181.

13. Testimony of Edward Morgan, March 19, 1976, Church Committee, 21, NARA 157-10011-10040.

14. Helms testimony, June 13, 1975, Church Committee, 78.

15. Testimony of John McCone, May 5 1975, Rockefeller Commission, 109–10, NARA 157-10011-10167.

Appendix A

1. Mexico City to Director, MEXI 7216, IN 72615, December 3, 1963, NARA 104-10125-10274.

2. Mexico City to Director, MEXI 7224, IN 72829, December 3, 1963, NARA 104-10103-10218.

3. Mexico City to Director, MEXI 7253, IN 74227, December 5, 1963, NARA 104-10103-10231.

4. Director to Mexico City, DIR 87188, December 5, 1963, NARA 104-10103-10229.

5. Chief of Station, Mexico City to Chief, WH Division, GPFLOOR/Gilberto LOPEZ, December 5, 1963, NARA 104-10103-10226.

6. Willard C. Curtis, Gilbert Lopez, U.S. Citizen, December 5, 1963, NARA 104-10422-10130.

7. Quist was a member of the Tampa Chapter of the Fair Play for Cuba Committee. According to an article in a Sarasota newspaper in 1954, she was born in Hungary and, after coming to the United States, had once signed a document saying she was a member of the Communist Party USA. When the

government began trying to deport her for that reason, she claimed she had been forced to sign the document. *Sarasota Herald-Tribune*, March 6, 1954, 8.

8. Gilberto Lopez was not so different from Oswald. They were about the same age. Lopez was twenty-three years old; Oswald was twenty-four. Lopez was an American citizen because his mother had been born in Florida, but he had been born and raised in Cuba. He wanted to come to the United States in 1960, so he applied for citizenship and a U.S. passport. Both applications were approved, but the passport was valid for only three years. It had expired by November 1963 and was invalid. Lopez was married and had been living in Key West, Florida, until approximately June 1963, when he and his wife moved to Tampa. They had marital problems though, and she moved back to Key West. He had worked at bakeries and bottling companies in Key West. He may have worked for the Menendez Construction Company in Tampa. Lopez suffered from grand mal epilepsy and had been receiving treatment for it. FBI SA Moses A. Aleman, Gilberto Policarpo Lopez, Tampa, August 26, 1964, NARA JFK36:F34 1993.07.22.11:27:48:370530. Agent Aleman was interviewed by the author. He said he was completely bilingual in English and Spanish. One of his assignments was the Cuban American community in Tampa, which was centered in Ybor City there. Another agent was responsible for the FPCC, and Aleman got his information about it from that agent, who passed away several years ago.

9. FBI SA Aleman, Gilberto Policarpo Lopez, March 31, 1964, NARA 104-10103-102334.

10. Why Lopez had to be there to take the call in person and how communications were handled were not explained. If the purpose of the call was merely to tell him that he could return to Cuba, Quist could have taken a message. Therefore, Lopez must have needed to talk to the caller directly. Nor is it known how Lopez knew to expect a call. Someone in Cuba may have called Quist on a prior occasion to arrange for her to have Lopez at her house that afternoon. She is known to have talked to people in Cuba on later occasions. That an FPCC chapter was still active in Tampa conflicts with a different and earlier FBI report saying that the president of the FPCC, Vincent Lee, planned to resign at the end of September and fold the FPCC into the Communist Party USA. Thus the national organization was theoretically defunct by November 17. Mary Quist must have been operating the Tampa Chapter on her own.

11. Regarding Lopez not receiving the call, see FBI SA Aleman, Gilberto Policarpo Lopez, March 31, 1964. NARA 104-10103-102334.

12. After the assassination the FBI obtained the visa number. It did not, however, bother to ask when he had applied for the visa. Since the CIA call to Cubela to arrange the meeting was in the afternoon, eastern standard time, Lopez may have already obtained the visa. It would be incriminating if Lopez applied for the visa after the call to Cubela.

13. An FBI source had reported on December 2, 1963, that Lopez had entered Mexico at Nuevo Laredo in a privately owned automobile, one owned by

another person. The FBI also acquired the passenger manifest for Lopez's flight to Cuba, showing him as the only passenger. On December 19 the FBI obtained a list of the engine numbers (but not license plates) of the cars and drivers crossing into Mexico at Nuevo Laredo between 8:00 p.m. on November 22 and 2:00 a.m. on November 24. This list could be used to determine who was driving Lopez. However, there is no indication that anyone followed up to see who owned those cars or if any belonged to someone from Florida. Federal Bureau of Investigation, "Gilberto Policarpo Lopez," January 31, 1964, NARA JFK36:F34 1993.07.22.11:12:52:210530.

14. Mexico City to Director, IN 43193, March 19, 1964. NARA 104-10103-10233.

15. Mexico City to Director, IN 43840, March 20, 1964, NARA 104-10103-10234.

16. The FBI report rehashed much that was already known. According to passport records, Lopez was born in Cuba in 1940 to an American mother. In June 1960 he applied for a United States passport. It was granted, and Lopez moved to the United States. On November 20, 1963, two days before the president's assassination, two different FBI sources reported that the Tampa Chapter of the Fair Play for Cuba Committee had met around 3:00 p.m. on Sunday, November 17, at the home of a Mary Quist. The purpose of the meeting was to show some color slides taken in Cuba. Lopez was there, and indeed had been there for some time, according to the FBI's sources. Lopez was waiting for an important phone call from Cuba that would give him the "go ahead order" for him to leave the United States. He had been refused travel back to Cuba. One of the sources said Lopez had a brother in the Cuban militia. Shown the photograph of Lopez taken at the airport in Mexico City, the source confirmed that it was the same man who had been at the FPCC meeting in November. Another source reported that one of the FPCC members had called a friend in Cuba to verify that Lopez had returned. He reportedly borrowed approximately $190 to make the trip. Special Agent Moses Aleman to FBI Headquarters, "Gilberto Policarpo Lopez," March 31, 1964, forwarded to CIA April 9, 1964, NARA JFK36:F34 1993.07.22.111:32:42:370530:

17. [William] Coleman-[David] Slawson, "Additional Lines of Investigation in Mexico Which May Prove Worthwhile," April, 3, 1964, 1–2, 11, NARA 1993.08.11.18:11:06:810059.

18. W. David Slawson, "Trip to Mexico City," April 22, 1964, NARA 104-10125-10297.

19. In June 1964, Aleman determined that Lopez had no arrest record but did have a number of relatives living in Florida. Two were employed at the Naval Air Station in Key West, although Lopez was not close to them. All his relatives were anti-Castro. A source in Tampa said that as of May 1964, Lopez still had not paid back $125 of the $150 loan that someone gave him to go to Cuba. Lopez "wrote a nasty letter" from Cuba to that person, saying he did not owe anyone anything. The source said Lopez was an "ingrate." Special Agent Moses Aleman, "Gilberto Policarpo Lopez," June 19, 1964. The FBI furnished the report to the CIA on June 26. NARA JFK36:F34 1993.07.22.11:29:55:350530.

Moses Aleman, telephone interview by the author, May 7, 2014. In August the FBI agent reported that Lopez had been under a doctor's care for grand mal epilepsy and took prescription medicine to control convulsions. Lopez had lived for a time with an uncle at 1124 Seminary Street in Key West and there worked for Molina Bakery, which was operated by a cousin and which is still in business. According to another cousin, Lopez originally came to the United States because he was afraid of being drafted into the Cuban army. But the draft board in the United States classified him 4-F due to a language barrier. His physician wrote the draft board that Lopez needed daily medication for epilepsy. This surely disqualified him for medical reasons as well. One of Lopez's brothers was in the militia in Cuba. Another had been sent to study in Russia by the Cuban government. Agent Aleman didn't ask where the brother was studying, but conceivably it was at the Patrice Lumumba Institute. The cousin told Aleman that Lopez had returned to Cuba in November 1963 because he was afraid of being drafted in the United States, but of course that couldn't be true since he was 4-F. Lopez was very pro-Castro. He and the cousin had gotten into a fistfight over some of Lopez's pro-Castro statements just as Oswald had in New Orleans. Still, Lopez was not a member of any pro-Castro organization, whereas Oswald had joined the FPCC. Lopez married Blanche Andrea Leon on August 11, 1962, in Key West. She was eleven years older than the twenty-three-year-old Lopez and had a teenage son from a previous relationship. Lopez took a job with the Pepsi Bottling Company in Key West. He and his wife moved to Tampa in June 1963, but they had marital problems, and she moved back to Key West in August 1963. In Tampa Lopez worked for the Menendez Construction Company. Lopez's wife had gotten a letter from him after he returned to Cuba. He told her he was going to return to Cuba. According to his wife, he wanted to go back because he was close to his mother and father there. But she also said that he wanted to go back so that his mother and father could take care of him. In his letter to her, Lopez wrote that he was working as an elevator operator. His wife said that he did not have enough money to travel to Cuba and had received financial assistance from some organization in Tampa. She was sure he knew that it was illegal for an American to travel to Cuba. According to her Lopez had not been in contact with any Cuban refuge organizations or individuals in Tampa and spent most of his free time with her. The FBI talked to yet another cousin. This one said he had hired Lopez to work at Molina's Bakery in Key West for about six months when he first arrived in the United States. He was a good worker until he went to Cuba for a few weeks. He rehired Lopez when he returned, but Lopez seemed to have changed. He complained of the hours and the work and did not get along with fellow employees. Finally, his cousin fired him. Lopez told the cousin that he had come to the United States because of some kind of trouble with a man in the militia and because the Cuban government was trying to draft him. Nonetheless, Lopez was sympathetic to the Castro regime. Special Agent Moses Aleman,

"Gilberto Policarpo Lopez," August 26, 1964. The FBI sent the report to the CIA on September 2, NARA JFK36:F34 1993.07.22.11:27:48:370530. In October 26, the FBI reported it had tracked down one of Lopez's acquaintances who had moved to Miami. This source said he knew Lopez from meeting him at Cuban recreational parlors in Key West, where they would play dominoes and go to parties together. But even at parties, Lopez would draw away from his friends. The FBI learned the name of the woman who had loaned Lopez the $150 to travel to Cuba. The FBI heard from a source that Lopez was not employed in Cuba and spent much of his time, in the fall of 1964, playing dominoes. Special Agent Moses Aleman, "Gilberto Policarpo Lopez," October 26, 1964. The FBI sent the report the CIA on November 2. NARA JFK36:F334 1993.07.22..11:23:55:810530.

20. Aleman interview, May 7, 2014. Aleman pointed out that it might not have been too far out of the way to drive through Dallas in going from Tampa to Mexico City in 1963. Today the trip from Dallas to Laredo on interstate highways is about 430 miles and would take about six and a half hours.

21. Such records were readily available. Because of the economic sanctions imposed on Cuba, AT&T could not pay the Cuban phone company for its end of a phone call between the United States and Cuba. However, the two companies kept their wires connected but no money could be transferred to Cuba. Therefore, the Cuban company would accept and complete a call from the United States without charge. If the call originated in Cuba, AT&T would accept and complete it only if it were a collect call. AT&T retained these records until roughly 1995, when it destroyed them. Author's telephone conference with Louisa Legalato, regional attorney, AT&T International Caribbean and Latin America Communications Service Group, May 30, 1995.

22. The Radio Museum provides an online resource of radios. The images of the Turist match the radio Oswald owned. www.radiomuseum.org/r/vef _turist_pmp_56.html, accessed April 12, 2018.

23. After seizing Oswald's radio on the afternoon of the assassination, Dallas police took it to a police station and photographed it. In the photograph the radio is tuned approximately to either 820 meters or 225 meters, depending on which of the radio's two bands was selected. These wave lengths convert to 365 KHZ and 1330 KHZ. Assuming no one moved the dial, the last broadcast that Oswald listened to was on one of those frequencies. The lower one is allocated to navigation and would likely be a tone or Morse code. Oswald wouldn't be listening to that unless Cuban intelligence were using it to communicate with him. The Warren Commission arranged for the National Security Agency to examine the radio. The NSA reported it was "a normal receiver and there was no evidence of its use for any other purpose." Testimony of Gordon A. Blake, President's Commission on the Assassination of President Kennedy, July 16, 1964, CE 2768, *Warren Report*, 26:155. Of course, this was somewhat misleading. Oswald's radio was not ordinary since it could pick up the long-wave band, which ordinary radios could not.

Besides, the NSA knew that spy agencies throughout the world used ordinary broadcasts for secret messages.

24. *Warren Report*, 687.

25. Oscar Luis Lopez, "Historia de la Radio en Cuba," accessed September 10, 2014, histroiadelaradioencuba.blogspot.com.

26. *World Radio TV Handbook* (1961) 161. The frequency was also used by several stations in Texas in 1963, but these stations operated at reduced power at night. It is typically easier to pick up a distant AM station than a closer one. And reception is better in winter months, when the air is colder. No record of what power the Cuban radio stations were using in 1963 can be found today.

27. Thinking Oswald might be listening to Radio Havana in his room at night, Albert Newman, an author and amateur radio operator, took a cheap shortwave radio to Dallas in the late 1960s. He discovered that Radio Havana was the strongest signal on its frequency and could be picked up much better in Dallas than in New York. Newman wrote in his 1970 book, *The Assassination of John F. Kennedy*, that Oswald was well versed on the ins and outs of radio. He had a shortwave radio when he was a child. His Marine Corps experience was in radio. He worked in a radio factory in Russia. Newman had a good point. Oswald was by no means a radio engineer, but he certainly knew how to use radios. Unlike the temperamental Rolando Cubela, who was unable or unwilling to use the OWL (one-way listen) radio that the CIA wanted to give him, Oswald, the loner, was comfortable with the technology. He already owned an OWL and used it almost nightly, including probably this night, November 20. Newman was wrong, however, about the radio being a short-wave. The Turist had two frequency bands, which are known as long wave and medium wave, selected by buttons on the top. The medium-wave band is the same as AM radio in the United States. Short waves travel farther than the longer wave bands. That Newman was able to pick up Radio Havana in Dallas on a short-wave frequency isn't surprising, but picking up Cuban stations on the frequencies that Oswald's radio was designed for might be harder. Frequencies used for AM radio travel well over water at night but degrade within a short distance after reaching land. Therefore, while a Cuban station operating on the AM band might be heard at night at water's edge along the Gulf Coast, Oswald might have had difficulty hearing it inland in Dallas. On the other hand, an amateur radio operator in Dallas, contacted for this book, said that he is able to pick up shortwave transmissions from Cuba on a frequency that is just above the AM radio band. Bob Winn, email to author, August 19, 2014.

28. The commentary said, "May President Kennedy therefore enjoy the applause he received at noon today." Louis Gomez Wanguemert, commentary, Havana Domestic Television Service in Spanish, 0100 GMT, November 19, 1963, Foreign Broadcast Information Service. The historical FBIS Daily Reports 1941–1996 is available through subscription to the Readex service at many university libraries. The time of the commentary, 0100 GMT on Novem-

ber 19, converts to 8:00 p.m. EST on November 18. Kennedy began his speech at 8:30 p.m. EST and spoke for twenty-eight minutes whd.jfklibrary.org/diary.

29. A different commentary on Cuban television on November 20, again in Spanish, contained a somewhat stronger attack on the speech. "Mr. Kennedy . . . is engaged in electioneering, seeking votes with an eye to the forthcoming elections. . . . A consummate demagogue, he falls into a thousand contradictions. . . . Naturally, the millionaire president spoke about Cuba. . . . He asserted that the factors dividing Cuba from the United States are due to the fact that the revolution . . . [was betrayed by] a small group of conspirators." Jose Maria Gonzalez Jerez, commentary, Havana Domestic Television Service in Spanish, 1800 GMT, November 20, 1963, Foreign Broadcast Information Service.

30. Radio Londres, Wikipedia, accessed September 10, 2014, en.wikipedia.org/wiki/Radio_Londres.

31. Havana Friendly Voice of Cuba in English, "Comment on Compulsory Military Service, 1730 GMT, November 20, 1963. FBIS. The FBIS only used excerpts. The next paragraph reads: "In some countries the bulk of the army is engaged in nothing more than routine infantry drill. The service concerned with the handling of complicated weapons is confined to a small select group of people who have had the chance to get a better education. Under such conditions two years of training for the majority of the soldiers engaged in unskilled operations is enough. But in Cuba, where there is no privileged class and education is available to all, the majority of the army can learn to master complicated operations connected with rockets and jets, and that is why three years of training is preferable in such a case. Now, why should anyone outside of Cuba be interested in the fact that so many members of the army here are taught to operate [t]echnical weapons? It will help to answer this question if we keep another fact about the Cuban army in mind. Military training here is designed for only one purpose: to defend the country from outside attack and maintain independence. This means that the soldiers are trained for guerrilla warfare. Now to understand why outsiders should be concerned about this, let us shift the scene for a moment to South Vietnam." And the commentary concludes with a paragraph about the fighting in Vietnam.

32. Speculating, one can also imagine that if this station were broadcasting classical music, the musical selection itself might be the message. For example, the go-signal might be something like the 1812 Overture, in which case Oswald would have to hear only a snippet to get the message.

33. Joann H. Grube, Deputy Director of Policy, NSA to Mr. T. Jeremy Gunn, Assassinations Records Review Board, April 1, 1998, https://www.nsa.gove/public_inforfiles/jfk/jfk00281.pdf.

34. D. J. Brennan Jr. to W. C. Sullivan FBI, December 4, 1963, NARA 144-10001-10203.

35. John R. Chapman, Chief, FOIA/PA Office, NSA to James Johnston, September 12, 2016, FOIA Case: 79300A.

36. Sterling B. Donahoe memorandum to Cartha DeLoach, "Lee Harvey Oswald Assassination of President Kennedy," June 22, 1966, NARA 124-10060-10032.

37. J. Edgar Hoover letter to Douglass Cater, untitled, June 24, 1966, NARA 124-10060-10031.

Appendix B

1. Testimony of Richard Helms, April 23, 1975, Rockefeller Commission, 160–63, NARA 157-10011-10086.

2. Testimony of Richard Helms, June 13, 1975, Church Committee, 81–83, NARA 157-10014-10075.

BIBLIOGRAPHY

Abt, John, and Michael Meyerson. *Advocate and Activist: Memoirs of an American Communist Lawyer*. Chicago: University of Illinois Press, 1993.

Andrew, Christopher, and Oleg Gordievsky. KGB: *The Inside Story of Its Foreign Operations from Lenin to Gorbachev*. New York: HarperCollins, 1990.

Barron, John. KGB: *The Secret Work of Soviet Secret Agents*. New York: Reader's Digest Press, 1974.

Beschloss, Michael R. *The Crisis Years: Kennedy and Khrushchev, 1960–1963*. New York: HarperCollins, 1991.

Breckenridge, Scott D. *The CIA and the U.S. Intelligence System*. Boulder CO: Westview Press, 1986.

Bugliosi, Vincent. *Reclaiming History: The Assassination of President John F. Kennedy*. New York: W. W. Norton, 2007.

Califano, Joseph. *Inside: A Public and Private Life*. New York: PublicAffairs, 2011.

Caro, Robert A. *The Passage of Power: The Years of Lyndon Johnson*. New York: Knopf, 2012.

Dallek, Robert. *An Unfinished Life: John F. Kennedy, 1917–1963*. Boston: Little, Brown, 2003.

Gates, Robert M. *From the Shadows: The Ultimate Insider's Story of Five Presidents and How They Won the Cold War*. New York: Simon & Schuster, 1996.

Goldstein, Gordon. *Lessons in Disaster*. New York: Henry Holt, 2008.

Helms, Richard. *A Look over My Shoulder: A Life in the Central Intelligence Agency*. With William Hood. New York: Random House, 2003.

Johnson, Haynes. *The Bay of Pigs: The Leaders' Story of Brigade 2506*. With Manuel Artime, Pepe San Román, Enrique Ruiz-Williams, and Erneido Oliva. New York: W. W. Norton, 1964.

Johnson, Loch. *Season of Inquiry: Congress and Intelligence*. Athens: University of Georgia Press, 1988.

———. *Spywatching: Intelligence Accountability in the United States*. New York: Oxford University Press, 2018.

Katzenbach, Nicholas deB. *Some of It Was Fun: Working with RFK and LBJ*. New York: W. W. Norton, 2008.

Keefer, Edward C., ed. *Foreign Relations of the United States, 1961–1963*. Vol. 4, *Vietnam, August–December 1963*. Washington DC: U.S. Government Printing Office, 1996.

Keefer, Edward C., Daniel Lawler, and Carolyn B. Yee, eds. *Foreign Relations of the United States, 1964–1968*. Vol. 32, *Dominican Republic; Cuba; Haiti; Guyana*. Washington DC: U.S. Government Printing Office, 2005.

Keefer, Edward C., Charles S. Sampson, and Louis J. Smith, eds. *Foreign Relations of the United States, 1961–1963*. Vol. 11, *Cuban Missile Crisis and Aftermath*. Washington DC: U.S. Government Printing Office, 1996.

Keefer, Edward C., Louis J. Smith, and Charles S. Sampson, eds. *Foreign Relations of the United States, 1961–1963*. Vols. 10/11/12, *American Republics; Cuba 1961–1962; Cuban Missile Crisis and Aftermath*. Microfiche supplement. Washington DC: U.S. Government Printing Office, 1998.

Latell, Brian. *Castro's Secrets: Cuban Intelligence, the CIA and the Assassination of John F. Kennedy*. New York: Palgrave Macmillan, 2012.

Mailer, Norman. *Oswald's Tale: An American Mystery*. New York: Random House, 1995.

Manchester, William. *Death of a President*. New York: Harper & Row, 1967.

Morley, Jefferson. *Our Man in Mexico: Winston Scott and the Hidden History of the CIA*. Lawrence: University Press of Kansas, 2011.

Newman, Albert H. *The Assassination of John F. Kennedy: The Reasons Why*. New York: Clarkson N. Potter, 1970.

Patterson, David S., ed. *Foreign Relations of the United States, 1964–1968*. Vol. 10, *National Security Policy*. Washington DC: U.S. Government Printing Office, 2002.

Posner, Gerald. *Case Closed: Lee Harvey Oswald and the Assassination of JFK*. New York: Random House, 1993.

Powers, Dave, and Kenneth O'Donnell, *Johnny, We Hardly Knew Ye*. New York: Little Brown, 1972.

Reeves, Richard. *President Kennedy: Profile of Power*. New York: Simon & Schuster, 1993.

Report of the President's Commission on the Assassination of President Kennedy. Washington DC: U.S. Government Printing Office, 1964.

Robarge, David. *John McCone As Director of Central Intelligence 1961–1965*. Washington DC: Center for the Study of Intelligence, CIA, 2005. https://www.cia.gov/library/readingroom/docs/DOC_0001262720.pdf.

Rusk, Dean. *As I Saw It*. As told to Richard Rusk. Edited by Daniel S. Papp. New York: W. W. Norton, 1990.

Russo, Gus. *Live by the Sword: The Secret War against Castro and the Death of JFK*. Tulsa: Bancroft Press, 1998.

Schoultz, Lars. *That Infernal Little Cuban Republic: The United States and the Cuban Revolution*. Chapel Hill: University of North Carolina Press, 2009.

Shenon, Philip. *A Cruel and Shocking Act: The Secret History of the Kennedy Assassination*. New York: Henry Holt, 2013.

Smith, Louis J., and David S. Patterson, eds. *Foreign Relations of the United States, 1961–1963*. Vol. 10, *Cuba 1961–1962*. Washington DC: U.S. Government Printing Office, 1997.

Sorensen, Ted. *Counselor: A Life at the Edge of History.* New York: Harper Luxe, 2008.

———. *Kennedy: The Classic Biography.* New York: Harper & Row, 1965.

Thomas, Evan. *Robert Kennedy: His Life.* New York: Simon & Schuster, 2000.

———. *The Very Best Men: Four Who Dared; The Early Years of the CIA.* New York: Simon & Schuster, 1995.

Turner, Stansfield. *Burn before Reading: Presidents, CIA Directors, and Secret Intelligence.* New York: Hyperion, 2005.

U.S. House of Representatives. Select Committee on Assassinations. *Final Report.* Ninety-Fifth Congress, Second Session, House Report No. 9501828 (1979).

U.S. Senate Select Committee on Intelligence. *Alleged Assassination Plots involving Foreign Leaders: An Interim Report.* Eighty-Fourth Congress, First Session, Report No. 94-465 (November 20, 1975).

U.S. Senate Select Committee on Intelligence. *The Investigation of the Assassination of President John F. Kennedy: Performance of the Intelligence Agencies.* Eighty-Fourth Congress, First Session, Report No. 94-755 (April 23, 1976).

Weiner, Tim. *Enemies: A History of the FBI.* New York: Random House, 2012.

———. *Legacy of Ashes: The History of the CIA.* New York: Doubleday, 2007.

Willens, Howard P. *History Will Prove Us Right: Inside the Warren Commission Report on the Assassination of John F. Kennedy.* New York: Overlook Press, 2013.

INDEX

Abt, John, 166, 248, 309n2
Acheson, Dean, 42–43, 56
Aleman, Moses, 253, 258–59, 323n78, 324n19, 326n20
Alferiev, Ivan Gavrilovich, 186–87
Alpha 66, 66–67
Alvarado, Gilberto, 192–94, 311n7
Amlash. *See* Cubela, Rolando
Amlash operation: assassination or coup, 295n25, 312n2; end of, 202–4, 218, 221–27; first phase, 101–8, 287n8; after Kennedy's assassination, 179–80; meetings in Europe, 116–25, 127–29, 131–33, 137–42, 152–57, 242–44; on November 22, 171–74; opposition within CIA, 121–23, 127–29; poison pen, 159–61. *See also* Kennedy, John F.: barrier speech
Amthug code name for Fidel Castro, 118
Amwhip. *See* Tependino, Carlos
Angleton, James, 177–78, 184, 212–14, 225–26, 274n25, 286n23, 315n11, 317n2, 320n29
Artime, Manuel, 54, 63–64, 71, 81–82, 88–91, 109, 138–39, 141, 145, 207, 221–22, 226–27, 292n12
assassination: Castro on, 100, 107, 175, 323; CIA on 94–95, 99, 122, 132–33, 141, 152, 190, 226, 238, 248, 278n22, 289n5, 295n25; Cubela on, 102–3, 117, 132–33, 141; definition of, 94–95, 98; DGI, 100, 225; euphemisms for, 17, 20, 39, 239; Helms on, 92, 103, 153–54, 156–57, 159–60, 231, 238, 243, 268–70, 295n25, 307n22, 321n4; John Kennedy on, 20–21, 30, 153–54, 156–57, 164,

237–38, 248; KGB history of, 95–99, 120, 178, 186, 290n6, 309n1; Lyndon Johnson on, ix, 197, 207, 233, 234, 245, 248; McCone on, 92, 103, 197, 238, 268, 312n2; Oswald on, 95; Rusk on, 299n3; Swenson on, 122, 293n21; versus coup in Cuba, 295n25, 301n2, 321n4. *See also* Amlash operation; poisons; underworld
Assassination Records Review Act, xi, 253, 271
assassins: Department 13 of KGB, 96–99, 114, 178, 247, 294n12; hit men, 19, 99; psychology of, 96–77, 273n15
Attwood, William, 126–27, 135–36, 139, 156, 174, 179, 189–90, 194, 243, 308n13
Aynesworth, Hugh, 161, 165, 305n9
Azcue, Eusebio, 113–15, 151, 205n11, 294n16

Ball, George, 48, 56, 59, 223
Batista, Fulgencio, 1–2, 4, 22, 54, 87, 99, 102, 127, 138, 154, 175, 209
Bay of Pigs operation: assassination as part of, 17, 19–21, 229, 236, 279n27, 284n52; operation, ix–x, 14–17, 19–26, 53–54, 63–64, 69–70, 188, 277n43, 320n1; underworld in, 17–19, 33, 236
Belin, David, 112, 234–35, 292n18
Berlin, Germany, 14, 41, 43, 83, 124, 182, 217
Bissell, Richard, 14–17, 19–23, 25, 27–29, 31–32, 40, 276n22, 277n43, 279n19
Blakely, Robert, 106
Bolten, Seymour, 105, 204, 213
Bond, James, 45, 95, 97, 237
Breckenridge, Scott, 94–95

Brigade 2506, 15, 21–23, 36, 53–72, 76, 145, 147, 170, 188, 216. *See also* Bay of Pigs operation

Bringuier, Carlos, 84–85

Bundy, McGeorge, 16, 149; coup, 75, 80–81, 87–91, 137–40, 288n13; in Cuban Missile Crisis, 36–38, 43, 45–46, 53; in early 1963, 60–63, 68–69, 75–76; under Johnson, 177, 189, 197–99, 205–9, 215–16, 221–23, 314n27; as manager, 23, 36–37, 75, 78, 93; rapprochement, 127, 130; sealing Kennedy's files, 170; Vietnam, 93, 130–35

Bundy, William, 286n18

Califano, Joseph, 61, 91, 142, 202, 288n9, 288n11, 293n23

Cardona, Miro, 71

Castro, Fidel, 273n1, 300n9; on assassination, 175; assassination attempts against, 19–20, 35, 51, 118, 150; comments about John Kennedy and his assassination, 175, 223; early life, 1–5, 99–100; FPCC membership, 90; rapprochement with U.S., 82, 126–27, 135–36, 158, 194, 218, 220–21, 308n13, 315n17; relationship with Rolando Cubela, 102, 105, 123, 132, 321n4; retaliation, ix, 100, 106–7, 188, 230, 232, 319n27, 320n33; temperament, 22, 57, 158

Castro, Raul, 1–2, 20, 77, 105, 150, 262

Central Intelligence Agency. *See* CIA

Chase, Gordon, 61–62, 156, 189, 194–95, 201, 208, 314n27

Cheever, Bruce, 91, 137–38, 171, 287n9

Christian, George, 233

Church, Frank, xi, 26, 157, 234, 238, 301n15

Church Committee investigation, xii, 26, 94, 98, 180, 234–35, 250–52, 276n28, 291n9, 292n16, 296n3, 299n3, 318n2, 319n27

CIA: code names, 20, 31, 101–2, 116, 119, 152, 290n1, 298n4; computerization, 184–86, 213; falsifying records, 34, 279n29; investigation of Kennedy assassination, 186–96, 212–15, 232–34, 246, 255–58, 269–70; 1967

Inspector General report, 232–34; pressure from Kennedys, 15, 24, 55, 71, 80, 122–23; relationship with FBI, 192–94, 214, 250, 258, 289n21, 311n2; relationship with Warren Commission, x, 95, 98, 114, 115, 177–78, 184, 185, 213–15, 225–26, 231, 235, 243, 246, 248–51, 258, 269–70, 308n13, 315n11; time stamp on cables, 118, 152, 295n28. *See also* poisons; underworld: CIA assassination plots with

Clark, James. *See* FitzGerald, Desmond

Clark, Ramsey, 229–30, 234

Colby, William, 58, 91–92, 130

Coleman, William, 223, 249

Communist Party of the United States (CPUSA), 51–52, 104, 112, 322n7 (appendix A), 323n10

compartmentation, 185–86, 188, 191, 213, 251, 320n29

Connally, John, 165, 198, 211, 230, 239, 245, 305n7

coup: in Cuba, x–xi, 77, 83, 91–92, 109, 124, 137–39, 147–49, 156, 158, 172, 194, 203, 207–8, 242, 245, 295n25, 298n3; in Vietnam, 92–93, 130–31, 133–34, 175, 234, 242, 298n3. *See also* Amlash operation

CPUSA. *See* Communist Party of the United States

Cronkite, Walter, 234

Cuban exiles, 4–5, 35, 64, 147, 149, 216, 222; friendship with Robert Kennedy, 54, 63–64, 88, 91, 145–46, 170; penetrated by DGI, 146, 243; publicity, 89

Cuban Missile Crisis, 38–45; assassins in Cuba during, 45–51, 230, 232, 304n2

Cubela, Rolando, 86, 102, 140–41, 218; as assassin, x, 102, 132–33, 156, 172, 194, 202, 209, 224, 226–27, 240, 243, 248, 295n25; on assassination, 132, 173; bona fides, 103, 122, 128, 318n9; Brazil meeting with CIA, 105–8; coup plot, 86, 101, 149–51, 156–57, 172, 194, 221, 242, 287n8; in Cuban revolution, 138; later dealings with CIA, 226–27, 261; in name trace, 186–88, 247; and Nestor Sanchez, 119, 121, 133; Paris meetings with CIA, 102–3, 116–24, 127–28, 131–33, 142, 152–53, 156–57, 159–61, 171–74, 179–80, 297n2, 323; personality, 102–3, 116–19, 127–28, 172, 240, 292n12, 327n27; relationship with Castro, 109, 152, 174, 227, 241, 292n17; ties to Cuban intelligence, 117, 122, 189, 242, 293n24. *See also* dangle

Curtis, Willard C., 42, 196, 312n17

dangle, 122, 128–29, 240–42, 315n11, 320n4, 321n4

Daniel, Jean, 127, 157–58, 161, 174–75, 210, 218, 241, 243–44

Department 13 of KGB, 97–99, 114, 178, 247

DGI (Direccion General de Inteligencia), 100, 115, 225

Diem, Ngo Dinh, 93, 130–31, 134, 175, 233–34, 242

Dillon, Douglas, 206–7

Direccion General de Inteligencia. *See* DGI

disinformation, 225–26

Dobrynin, Anatoly, 155, 182

Donovan, James, 53–54, 71

Dulles, Allen, 14–15, 17, 22, 25, 28, 184, 246, 315n11

Duran, Sylvia, 114, 179, 190, 247

economic sanctions: Eisenhower administration, 18; Johnson administration, 197, 203–8, 221–23, 240; Kennedy administration, 62, 79, 82, 90, 137–38

Edwards, Sheffield, 17, 31, 34, 40

Eisenhower, Dwight, ix, 2–4, 11–15, 17, 25, 27, 39–40, 65, 177

executive action, 20–21, 31, 98, 237

exporting the revolution, 32, 83, 139, 148, 153, 156, 200–201, 218–19, 243

Fair Play for Cuba Committee (FPCC), 90, 116, 287n2; and Lopez, 257, 323n8, 323n10, 324n16, 325n19; and Oswald, 84–86, 112, 294n2, 294n11

FBI (Federal Bureau of Investigation): Gilberto Lopez investigation, 195–96, 255–59, 324n13, 323n12, 323n13, 324n16, 324n19; investigation of Kennedy's assassination, 85, 161, 176–77, 181–88, 190–96, 211–14, 235, 245–50, 262–64, 305n6, 308n1; investigation of Oswald before assassination, 36, 90, 115, 134–35; knowledge of underworld and CIA assassination plots, 19, 33, 112, 224, 228–32, 319n27; relationship with CIA, 178, 192–93, 213, 250, 289n31, 311n7

Federal Bureau of Investigation. *See* FBI

FitzGerald, Desmond: after Kennedy's assassination, 171–79, 187, 194, 232; Amlash plot, 68–72, 75–77, 80–83, 86, 88–91, 101, 104–6, 108, 110, 137–40, 152–53, 156–57, 239–42, 288n9, 301n14; background and personal life, x, 57–60, 65–66, 285n65, 296n10; under Lyndon Johnson, 202–4, 206–9, 221–23, 245, 248–49; meeting with Cubela, 121–25, 127–29, 131–33, 140–42, 147, 297n1, 297n2, 298n4; meeting with Robert Kennedy after assassination, 218–20; phone call to Robert Kennedy on Cubela meeting, 118–20

Ford, Gerald, 94, 184, 234

Foreign Broadcast and Information Service (FBIS), 260, 262, 327n28, 328n31

FPCC. *See* Fair Play for Cuba Committee

Frazier, Buell Wesley, 125, 136, 144, 162, 163–64

free-world shipping, 66, 78, 87, 205, 209

Garrison, Jim, 226, 230–31

Giancana, Momo Salvatore "Sam," x; CIA assassination operation: 18–19, 31, 92, 99, 238, 276n24; murder of, 235–36, 319n27; wiretap, ix, 19, 33–34, 238–39, 276n23, 279n25

Goldwater, Barry, 95, 158, 218

Gottlieb, Sidney, 19–21, 237

GPFLOOR, 195, 255–56, 258

Guantanamo, 4, 79, 109

Guevara, Ernesto "Che," 2–3, 20, 100, 102, 127, 150, 230

Gunn, Edward, 159–60, 171, 242

Haig, Alexander, 64, 199, 202, 288n9

Halpern, Samuel, 59, 122, 140, 159, 171, 179, 187, 197–98, 213, 279nn17, 281n28

Harker, Daniel, 107–8, 188, 241

Harriman, Averell, 79–82, 87–88, 130–31, 303n11

Hart, Gary, 27, 235–36, 310n30, 318n2

Harvey, William: on assassination, 39, 50, 99, 289n5; assassination operations, 19–21, 30–31, 34–35, 37, 40, 92, 99, 237; confrontations with Robert Kennedy, 44–51, 54, 59, 63; in Cuban Missile Crisis, 44–51; dislike of Kennedys, 32–33, 45–47, 57, 79; falsifying record, 34, 279n29; opinion of Lansdale, 45; prediction on Kennedy's future policy, 54–56; relationship with Helms and McCone, 45–46, 48; Roselli relationship, 31, 34–35, 40, 48–49, 62, 237; with Special Group, 32, 35, 39, 48, 279n17, 281n28, 291n10

Helms, Richard, 35, 41–42, 67–68, 91, 100, 130, 135, 137, 162, 246; on assassination, 92, 103, 159–60, 242, 250, 267–70, 273n2, 280n7, 281n22, 295n25, 302n11, 307n21, 320n1, 321n1, 321n4, 321n5; background and personal life, 32; investigation of Kennedy assassination, 171, 174, 177–79, 186–91, 201, 215, 247, 270; and Lyndon Johnson, 220–22, 232–34, 245, 314n27, 320n33; on McCone's knowledge of assassination plots, 26, 92, 238, 248, 315n11; meeting with Robert Kennedy about assassination memo, 231; on rogue elephant, 321n2; Venezuelan arms cache, 140, 152–57, 208–9, 243; views on the Kennedys, 27–28, 45, 58, 86, 123, 157, 287n8, 321n2

Hidell, Alek James. See Oswald, Lee Harvey

Hoover, J. Edgar: 14; and CIA assassination plots, 19, 33–34; John Kennedy's affair, x, 33, 238–39; John Kennedy's assassination, 170, 181–84, 191–93, 225, 245–46, 308n1; Oswald's radio, 263–64; relationship with CIA, 193; Roselli allegations, 229, 231; and Warren Commission, 211, 214, 225, 231

Hosty, James, 134–35

House Assassinations Committee, xii, 101, 106, 113, 141

Howard, Lisa, 126–27, 165, 211, 218, 220–21, 234, 316n17

Interdepartmental Coordinating Committee for Cuban Affairs (ICCCA), 60–64, 67, 70–71, 77–78, 93, 109, 145, 285n65, 288n11, 293n23

invasion of Cuba, ix, 23, 32, 38, 41, 42, 48, 67, 75–76, 80, 106, 133, 183, 198–201, 203, 219, 286n18; confrontation with Soviet troops, 124; no-invasion pledge, 55, 59–60, 65, 83, 91, 153, 240

Janos, Leo, 234

Jenkins, Walter, 168, 177, 181, 308n1

Johnson, Alexis, 29, 87, 130, 148, 222–23, 288n13, 312n27

Johnson, Arnold, 112, 247–48, 287n7

Johnson, Arthur and Gladys, 144–45, 161

Johnson, Charles, 46–47, 50–51, 261n28

Johnson, Haynes, 170

Johnson, Lyndon: after Kennedy's assassination, 175–77; cover-up, x, 181, 230–31, 243, 245–46, 248; Cuban policy, 202, 204, 206–9, 215–17, 221–23, 299n3; on hypocrisy of Kennedy's Cuban policy, 206–9, 215–17, 251; meeting alone with McCone, 197–98, 230–31; Murder, Inc., ix, xi, 206–9, 234, 320n34; no-invasion pledge, 200–201, 203, 239; relationship with Earl Warren, 231; on retaliation allegations, 229–34, 320n33; and Robert Kennedy, 202, 218–20, 245, 307n23; as vice president, 12, 60, 130, 205, 209, 245; Vietnam, 205, 248, 321n5; views on CIA and State Department, 192–94, 209–10, 251; Warren Commission, 183–84, 225

Karamessines, Thomas, 177–79, 215, 308n8, 315n11

Katzenbach, Nicolas, 181–83, 191, 201, 212, 246, 309n1

Kennedy, Ethel, 26, 59

Kennedy, Jackie, 59, 163, 197, 305n6

Kennedy, John F: anticommunism, 4, 10–11, 13, 28–29; on assassination,

20–21, 30, 164, 175, 237-38, 278n59; assassination of, 163–65, 173, 305n6; background, 8–13, 78, 275n31; barrier speech, 147, 149–51; Bay of Pigs invasion, 15–17, 21–25, 277n43; Brigade 2506 flag, 53, 147, 301n16; bullfighter poem, 43, 304n2; coup in Cuba, 86, 137–40, 150, 287n8; exile raids, 66–67; on exporting the revolution, 62–63; on Fidel Castro, ix, 23; Florida trip, 146–47, 149–50, 162; Giancana's girlfriend, x, 19, 33–34, 239; knowledge of assassination plots, x, xii, 20–21, 30–31, 157; no-invasion pledge, 44, 59–60, 64–65, 75–76; November 19 meeting with Helms, x, 152–54, 243; rapprochement with Cuba, 126–27, 136–37, 156, 308n13; on sabotage, 68–70, 72, 80–81, 88–89, 137; Vietnam, 30, 130–31, 133–34, 321n5; views on CIA and State Department, 15–16, 157; White House tapes, 91–92, 136, 154, 170. See also Cuban Missile Crisis

Kennedy, Robert F.: closeness to CIA, 24–28, 127, 280n7; and the Cuban exiles, 53–54, 60–61, 63–64, 75–76, 88, 145–46, 170, 281n28, 284n46, 300n9, 300n10, 306n5; February 29, 1964, meeting with FitzGerald, 218–20; and FitzGerald, 59, 79, 241; knowledge of Amlash operation, 118–19, 123, 242; investigation of Kennedy's assassination, 170, 181–82; knowledge of underworld plots, 33–34, 51, 231; and Lyndon Johnson, 202, 218–20, 245, 307n23; management under, 23, 25, 27, 35, 63, 71, 93; November 19, 1963, meeting with Helms, 152–54, 243; pressure on CIA, 29–31, 41–42, 55–56, 69–70, 79, 123; on Warren Report, 225; and underworld, 33–34, 238–39, 279n25. See also Harvey, William: confrontations with Robert Kennedy

KGB, 8, 20, 69, 95–100, 186, 214, 225–26, 235, 245, 289n5, 318n2. See also Department 13 of KGB

Khrushchev, Nikita, 171, 174, 219; Castro's opinion of, 57; in Cuban Missile Crisis, 38–44, 48, 56, 99, 230, 281n23; support of Cuba, 3, 8

King, J. C., 150, 178, 212, 214, 218

Kostikov, Valery Vladimirovich, 114, 178, 186, 247, 294n12, 309n1, 310n21

Krulak, Victor H., 78, 130

Lane, Mark, 228

Lansdale, Edward: Alpha 66 use, 67; on assassination, 39, 239; and Harvey, 45–48, 50, 63; and the Kennedys, 28–31, 55–56, 61; Mongoose, 34–37, 41–42

Lechuga, Carlos, 126–27, 135, 179, 190, 194, 221, 247, 308n13

Lee, Vincent, 84–85, 116, 323n10

Leonov, Nikolai Sergeevich, 99

Lodge, Henry Cabot, 11–12, 93, 130–34

MacDill Air Force Base, 146, 149

Maheu, Robert, 18–21, 31, 33–34, 228, 238–39, 276n23

McCarthy, Joseph, 11, 183

McCone, John, 32, 209; on assassination, 49, 92, 103, 238, 312n2; background, 25–26, 278n60; Bay of Pigs invasion, 15, 22, 25; on compartmentation, 188; during coup plan, 60, 63, 65–66, 71–72, 75, 78–83, 87–88, 124, 137, 287n26, 299n4; Cuban exiles, 146, 162; after Cuban Missile Crisis, 54–55; in Cuban Missile Crisis, 39, 41–50, 280n7, 281n28; knowledge of assassination plots, 28, 92, 238, 268–69, 312n2; Lyndon Johnson's Cuban policy, 201, 222–24, 312n4; Murder, Inc., 197–99, 231; and president's assassination, 170–71, 177, 179, 199, 247, 250–51, 308n3, 312n1; relationship with Robert Kennedy, 26, 218–20; Vietnam, 130–31; and Warren Commission, 184, 187–88, 192–94, 197, 248

McManus, George, 55–56, 279n19

McNamara, Robert: on assassination, 39, 40, 49, 239; Cuba, 29, 55–56, 60, 63, 79, 80, 137–39; invasion of Cuba, 79, 124; on Kennedy hysterical about Cuba, 24; and Lyndon Johnson on Cuba, 201, 216–17, 222; on sabotage, 79, 139, 215; Vietnam, 30, 130–31, 217, 222

Mikoyan, Anastas, 3, 39, 57, 200–201, 203, 208, 246

missile crisis. *See* Cuban Missile Crisis

missing records. *See* National Archives and Records Administration: missing records

mob. *See* underworld

Mongoose operation, xi, 27–31, 34–35, 38, 41–42, 45, 47–48, 51, 55–56

Monroe Doctrine, 3, 5

Morgan, Edward, 228–32, 239, 250

Morgan, Robert, 269–70

Moyers, Bill, 177, 181, 216

murder: of Giancana, 235–36; of officer Tippit, 166–67, 305n9; of Oswald, 180–81; of Roselli, 235–36

Murder, Inc., ix, xi, xiii, 234, 245, 252

Murrow, Edward R., 39

name trace, 185–87, 195, 247

National Archives and Records Administration, xi, 91, 253, 264, 271, 291n8, 302n2, 317n19; missing records, 91, 92, 201, 210, 249, 289n23, 291n9, 292n12, 296n3, 301n10, 301n12, 308n8, 318n31; Yeltsin documents, 274n18

National Board of Estimates, 30

National Security Agency. *See* NSA

Newman, Albert, 263–64, 327n27

Nitze, Paul, 43, 89

Nixon, Richard, 4, 12–13, 234

no-invasion pledge, 55, 59–60, 65, 83, 91, 153, 200

NSA, 261–64, 307n1, 326n23

O'Connell, James, 17–18, 20, 237, 276n18, 276n20, 279n27

Oliva, Erneido, 63–64, 145–46, 216, 284n46, 300n8

O'Neal, Birch, 193

O'Neal's ambulance service, 305n6

Organization of American States (OAS), 4, 199, 202–5, 208, 219–20

organized crime. *See* underworld

Osborne, Lee, 81

Oswald, Lee Harvey: in Alabama, 84; aliases and weapons, 73–75, 145, 148; on assassination, 95; assassination of president, 163–69, 304n11, 305n6, 305n7 305n10; attempt on General Walker, 74, 95, 125; on communism, 5–6, 51–52, 84; connection with Cubela, 186–87, 190; connection with Lechuga, 190, 247, 311n7; in Dallas, 125–26, 134–35, 136, 143–45, 161–62; decision to assassinate president, 161–62, 249, 255, 259–65, 326n23, 327n27, 328n32; driving, 125, 144; early life, 5–8, 13, 35–36, 274n18, 297n16, 303n9, 303n10, 304n11; employment, 36, 74; FPCC, 85–86, 115–16, 125, 134; left-wing organizations, 51–52, 84, 86, 104, 111–12, 287n7; meetings with KGB and Cuban intelligence, x, 113–15, 178–79, 186, 190, 192, 199, 213, 226, 230, 236, 245, 247, 250, 294n18, 308n1; in Mexico City, 112–15, 195, 250, 257–58, 294n8, 294n16; moving to East Coast, 112, 247–48; murder of, 180–81, 245, 308n1; murder of officer Tippit, 166–67, 305n9; in New Orleans, 74, 84–86, 292n18; psychology, 36, 51, 95, 97, 100, 183, 274n15; similarities to Gilberto Lopez, 324n10; threat against FBI, 134–35; Warren Report portrayal, xii, 95, 97, 115, 180–81, 225, 246–47, 274n15. *See also* radio: Oswald's portable

Oswald, Marguerite Claverie, 5–7

Oswald, Marina Presakova: on assassination, 95; contact with Oswald before president's assassination, 143–45, 148, 161–64, 259, 297n16; on Oswald's contacts with leftist organizations, 112, 247; on Oswald's trip to Mexico, 111, 113, 258, 294n8; on Oswald's views on assassination, 95; relationship with Oswald, 8, 36, 51, 73–75, 84, 125–26, 134; and Ruth Paine, 73, 111, 115, 126, 134, 143–45

OWL (one-way listen) radio. *See* radio: OWL

Papich, Samuel, 184, 193, 214, 250, 289n21, 311n2

Parrott, Thomas, 45, 58, 68, 80–81

Patrice Lumumba Friendship University, 7

Peak, Hershel, 153–55

Pearson, Drew, 228–29, 231–32, 319n17, 319n27

plausible denial, 87, 129, 133, 241, 243, 251, 299n2

poisons, 19–22, 24–25, 31, 34, 40, 49, 53, 98–99, 159–60, 171–74, 179, 191, 215, 239, 242, 267, 299n6

Porto Alegre, Brazil, meeting, 105–6, 109, 241, 292n12

Powers, Francis Gary, 53, 174

Praetorian Guard, x–xi

President's Checklist, 177, 309n2

PT-109, 10, 53

Quist, Mary, 257, 322n7, 323n10, 324n16

radio: Oswald's knowledge of, 6, 7; Oswald's portable, 161–62, 259–65, 297n16, 303n10, 326n22; OWL, 106, 138, 152; use in intelligence, 34, 63, 105–6, 138, 240, 261–62

radio broadcasts from Cuba, 48, 259–64

rapprochement: under John Kennedy, 83, 87, 89, 126–27, 135–36, 139, 156, 174, 179, 189, 190, 194, 243–44, 308n13; Lyndon Johnson thought hypocritical, 216–17, 221, 245

Ray, Manolo, 138, 207, 222

regime change, x, 15, 17, 64, 197–210

retaliation, x, 45, 83, 51, 81–82, 109, 188, 198, 228–36, 245, 250–51, 293n23

Rike, Aubrey, 305n6

Roa, Raul, 221

Rocca, Raymond G., 178, 190, 214–15, 225, 235, 293n18, 320n29

Rockefeller Commission, xii, 146, 160, 188, 199, 233–34, 250, 267, 275n6, 276n18, 292n18

rogue elephant, xi, 26, 152, 157, 235, 238, 242–43, 248, 251, 278n59, 301n15, 307n23, 321n2

Roselli, Johnny: in assassination plots, 18, 20–21, 31, 33–34, 40, 45–46, 62, 238–39, 268, 276n20, 279n27, 279n29, 319n27; in Cuban Missile Crisis, 48–49; murder of, 235–36; on retaliation, 51, 228, 250, 255

Rostow, Walter, 16, 219

Rowley, James, 229, 319n20

Ruby (Rubenstein), Jack, 167–69, 180, 190, 225, 247, 309n1

Ruiz-Williams, Enrique, 63–64, 146, 170, 284n46, 301n10

Rusk, Dean: on assassination; 39, 299n3; after president's assassination, 179, 198, 200–201; on Bay of Pigs, 21; on Castro, 57, 82; in Cuban Missile Crisis, 41, 43–44, 53, 56–57; on John Kennedy, 23–24; meeting with Soviets after president's assassination, 155; in Mongoose, 31; in 1963, 60, 63, 82–83, 89, 130–31, 137–39; on sabotage, 83, 89, 139, 215, 216–17, 222; Venezuelan arms cache, 155; on Vietnam, 130–31, 299n3

Russell, Richard, 184, 211

sabotage: Cuban retaliation for, 81, 108–9; and Cubela, 102–4, 106, 156; the Kennedys' interest in, 29, 42, 68–72, 80–83, 126, 135, 138–39; KGB's Department 13's combining with assassination, 96–97, 186; and Lyndon Johnson's rejection of, 202–4, 206–7, 215–18, 221–22, 251; role in coup planning; 61, 67–72, 75, 79–83, 87–90, 138–39, 240, 285n65; role in Mongoose operation, 35, 39, 42, 47–48, 281n33

safe house, 123–24, 128, 130, 171, 291n3, 297n1

Sanchez, Nestor, 291n10; after Kennedy assassination, 189, 190, 198, 202, 209, 213, 218, 222, 226, 232, 317n23, 318n13; Brazil meeting with Cubela, 104–8, 292n12, 292n16; meetings with Cubela in Europe, 116–19, 121, 123, 128, 140–42, 156, 299n5; on name trace, 187–88, 306n12; November 22 Paris meeting, 156–57, 159–61, 170–74, 179–80, 215, 238, 242, 244, 250, 299n6, 302n10, 307n19; on whether Amlash operation was assassination, 132–33, 242, 295n25

San Roman, Jose Perez "Pepe," 54, 63–64, 71, 145–46, 284n46

San Roman, Roberto, 63, 145–46, 284n46

SAS, 58, 90, 133, 187, 194, 204, 212–14, 218, 286n23, 311n2

Schweiker, Richard, 235–36, 310n30, 318n2

Secret Service, 149, 154, 162 176, 185, 198, 228–29, 241, 305n6

secret writing (S/W), 85, 103–6, 116, 142, 152, 156, 172, 194, 240, 291n7, 291n8

Senate Select Committee on Intelligence. *See* Church Committee investigation

Shackley, Ted, 121–23, 137, 249, 296n3, 322n7

Slawson, David, 95, 178, 214, 223, 308n13

slotted time, 152, 295n28, 302n1, 302n2, 303n6

Smathers, George, 20–21, 30, 237, 277n31

Smith, Howard K., 234

Socialist Workers Party (SWP), 6, 51–52, 73, 84–86, 104, 111–12, 287n2, 287n3, 294n2

Sorensen, Theodore, 12–13, 23, 149, 206, 208

Special Affairs Staff. *See* SAS

Special Group (Augmented): after president's assassination, 201, 215–16, 221; confrontation between Robert Kennedy and Harvey at, 46, 48; in coup plot, 61, 63, 69–71, 75, 80–81, 88–89, 92–93, 135, 285n65; difference between and Standing Group, 78–79, 88–89, 93, 204; discussed assassination, 39–40, 299n3; during Mongoose, 24, 26, 28–29, 31–32, 35, 38–39, 278n5, 281n33; rapprochement, 79–80, 135–36

Standing Group, 76, 78, 80, 86–88, 91, 93, 110, 202, 204–5, 208, 313n22. *See* also Special Group (Augmented): difference between and Standing Group

Stevenson, Adlai, 11–12, 126

Sudoplatov, Pavl Anatolevich, 96–97, 100

Swenson, Harold, 108, 122–23, 129, 189, 212–13, 286n23

Szulc, Tad, 1, 30–31, 175, 237

taping system in White House, 91, 130, 137, 154, 170, 289n24, 319n21

Task Force W, 31, 54–56, 58, 105

Taylor, Maxwell, 25, 27, 29–31, 37, 41, 43, 55, 60, 76, 130–31, 137, 139, 148, 216–17, 222

Tepedino, Carlos, 102, 105, 117, 121–23, 128, 140–41, 222, 224, 227, 291n9, 296n8, 317n23

Texas School Book Depository, 125, 134, 144, 157, 162, 163–65

Thompson, Llewellyn, 182, 314n27

Trafficante, Santos, 18–19, 236, 238

Trotsky, Leon, 52, 96, 287n3

underworld: CIA assassination plots with, ix–xi, 18–19, 24, 30–31, 33–34, 40, 45, 48–49, 51, 92, 103, 237–40, 320n1; Earl Warren's knowledge of, 228; hit men, 19, 99, 238; and John Kennedy, x, 33–34, 37; John McCone's knowledge of, 92; Lyndon Johnson's knowledge of, ix, 229–33; murder of underworld figures 235; Robert Kennedy's knowledge of, 33–34, 37, 231; Warren Commission knowledge of, 247, 315n11. *See also* Giancana, Momo Salvatore "Sam"; Roselli, Johnny; Trafficante, Santos

U-2 aircraft, 22, 39–41, 44, 53, 174, 206

Valenti, Jack, 177, 216

Vance, Cyrus, 61, 64, 67–68, 70–71, 76, 93, 137, 148, 199, 204, 222–23, 300n8, 314n27

Varona, Jose Raul Gonzales, 145

Venezuelan arms cache, 139–40, 153–55, 157, 199–202, 208–10, 219, 243

Vietnam, 57–58, 93, 175, 209, 233–34, 307n22, 321n5; and Cuba, 29–30, 130–34, 137, 175, 205, 209, 217, 233, 242, 248, 261, 299n3, 307n22, 321n5, 328n31

Walker, Edwin, 58, 60, 74, 95, 111, 125, 190

Warren, Earl, 184–85, 211, 215, 225, 228–20, 231, 319n17

Warren Commission, ix–xi, 271; challenges to, 225–26; creation of, 191, 197, 246; investigation and failures, 51, 85–86, 112–15, 134–35, 143–45, 148, 161–62, 164, 167, 180, 213–15, 231, 234–35, 248, 250, 256, 258–59, 263–64, 269–70, 292n18, 304n5, 305n6, 308n13, 309n9; knowledge of CIA and foreign

assassination operations; 95, 98, 100–101, 114, 134, 234, 246, 248, 251, 315n11; relationship with intelligence agencies, 137, 178, 184–85, 197–98, 211, 213–15, 223, 225, 249, 258, 263–64, 269–70, 326n23; report, 5, 7–8, 97, 165, 246, 250
Watson, Marvin, 231

Whitten, John, 177–78, 188–91, 195, 212, 308n4, 310n35
Wilson, Donald, 202, 314n27

Yatskov, Pavel Antonovich, 114
Yeltsin documents: defined, 274n18
Youngblood, Rufus, 176, 198

Zrrifle, 20, 31, 99, 237